1988

THE ETHNIC IMAGE IN MODERN AMERICAN LITERATURE: 1900–1950

Volume II

ALSO BY PHILIP BUTCHER

The Minority Presence in
American Literature, 1600–1900, 2 vols.

The William Stanley Braithwaite Reader

George W. Cable

George W. Cable: The Northampton Years

THE ETHNIC IMAGE IN MODERN AMERICAN LITERATURE: 1900–1950

Volume II

Edited by
PHILIP BUTCHER

HOWARD UNIVERSITY PRESS
Washington, D.C.   1984

Printed in the United States of America

Library of Congress Cataloging in Publication Data

Main entry under title:

The Ethnic image in modern American literature, 1900–1950.

  Includes index.
  1. American literature—20th century.   2. Minorities—
United States—Literary collections.   3. United States—
Ethnic relations—Literary collections.   4. American
literature—Minority authors.   I. Butcher, Philip,
1918–
PS509.M5E86   1984   810'.9'3520693   83–8440
ISBN 0–88258–110–4 (set)
ISBN 0–88258–119–8 (v. 1)
ISBN 0–88258–120–1 (v. 2)

*To Jennie
and her generation*

Contents

IDENTITY IN QUESTION
"Passing"

PROTEST AND PROPHECY

POTPOURRI

THE WAR ABROAD
The Battle at Home

"KING PREJUDICE"

ETHNIC ROUNDUP

Preface

THIS ANTHOLOGY is intended to enlighten and entertain the general reader and to instruct the student, for whom it can serve as a text or reference in a variety of academic situations. The selections have been chosen to portray the realities of ethnic participation in American culture as well as the stereotypes that have stigmatized, at one time or another, all Americans of ancestry other than white Anglo-Saxon Protestant (WASP). The collection constitutes a significant survey of our literature and social history over a fifty-year span (1900–1950), a period not treated in my earlier anthology, *The Minority Presence in American Literature, 1600–1900* (2 vols., 1977), and one rich in representations of the multicultural character of our society.

During the first half of the twentieth century many ethnic groups moved toward or achieved assimilation, while new arrivals, refugees or immigrants to the Promised Land, took their place in the lower ranks of the national hierarchy. Others, although hindered by their high visibility, improved their image in literature and their status in the social order. Charles M. Sheldon, whose *In His Steps* (1896) sold twenty million copies, began *Richard Bruce* (1892) with the claim that the hero of the novel was "a typical American" whose grandfather and grandmother were born in the heart of New England "of what we call Anglo-Saxon ancestry." Fifty years later so effective had the Americanization process been and so much had the social order changed, the concept of American identity could not be restricted to so narrow a definition.

In publishing without comment writing that expresses a variety of attitudes toward those Americans who were once placed beyond the pale because they were "different" and, at the same time, were disparaged as being "all alike," an editor may appear to approve of bigotry and chauvinism, stereotyping and gratuitous insults. But I depend on the reader to appraise each selection on the basis of its integrity in depicting ethnic life and character as well as on its merits as literature. An author who does not grant to characters of a race or religion or culture other than his own their full stature and an equal claim to the rights of all human beings will not escape detection.

The readings are assembled under thematic headings and are arranged within these groups in chronological order. In some instances excerpts from a single work may be found in more than one classification. An index is provided, but space limitations and other considerations account for the omission of bibliography, chronology, and author biographies. Mounting interest in the ethnic experience has made available an abundance of reference books and other guides which the reader may consult, along with the standard literary and historical sources, as needed.

Every anthology may be charged with neglecting items that ought to be included, and this work is no exception. Some pieces have been omitted because permission to reprint could not be arranged with copyright owners. It may seem that particular ethnic groups have been overlooked. Why is there nothing about Puerto Ricans, Hungarians, Vietnamese? In general, the explanation for unrepresented and underrepresented groups is either their slight literary impact by the 1950 cutoff date or their recent arrival on the American scene.

Inevitably there will be laments about what is included as well as about what is not. Why reprint the work of authors once popular but no longer accepted as artists of consequence? Their one-time popularity, it may be argued in rebuttal, attests to their value as spokesmen for their time and as recorders of—perhaps even influencers of—the prevailing ethnic image. Why resurrect the work of serious but obscure writers now remembered only by scholars? Neglected pieces that present the realities of the ethnic predicament and ethnic feeling must not be ignored in a survey of the ethnic presence in American writing. Why bother with fragments extracted from works dealing with that presence only in a peripheral way? The casual epithet and incidental attention to groups that are "foreign" or "alien" can be as illuminating as a tract on the democratic ideal or a tome on the status of minorities in the United States.

This collection provides material likely to interest some readers for other than literary reasons, but it is essentially an anthology of American writing of a restricted period. The authors, many concerned about the underdog and some especially interested in their own ethnic group, are among the most important of their time, but the focus of this anthology is on the ethnic image, not on the identity of the writers. American literature began as reports about the New World by transplanted Englishmen. Now it is multi-ethnic writing about a complex multi-cultural society that still is more like a mosaic than a melting pot. Here is a rich sample of our literary heritage—a record of where we have been and a guide, perhaps, to where we are going.

PHILIP BUTCHER

Acknowledgments

The copyrighted selections reprinted in this book are used by permission of and special arrangement with the proprietors of their respective copyrights. Apologies are offered to any copyright holder we were unable to locate.

Grateful acknowledgment is made to the following:

Doubleday & Company, Inc. for permission to reprint "An Afternoon Miracle" and "The Coming-Out of Maggie" from *The Complete Works of O. Henry* and "Black Boy" from *Fifty Stories* by Kay Boyle, first published in *The New Yorker* (Copyright 1945, 1950, © 1955, 1964, 1966, 1980 by Kay Boyle).

Harcourt Brace Jovanovich, Inc. for selections from *Virginia* by Ellen Glasgow (Copyright 1913, 1930, 1938 by Ellen Glasgow; renewed 1941 by Ellen Glasgow; 1958, 1966 by Richmond, Virginia SPCA); *Strange Fruit* by Lillian Smith (Copyright 1944 by Lillian Smith; renewed 1972 by Paula Snelling); *Lost Boundaries* by W. L. White (Copyright 1948 by W. L. White; renewed 1976 by Katherine K. White); "The Shovel Man" and "Fish Crier" from *Chicago Poems* by Carl Sandburg (Copyright 1916 by Holt, Rinehart and Winston, Inc.; Copyright 1944 by Carl Sandburg); *Focus* by Arthur Miller (Copyright 1945, 1973 by Arthur Miller); *Guard of Honor* by James Gould Cozzens (Copyright 1948, 1976 by James Gould Cozzens); "Burbank with a Baedeker: Bleistein with a Cigar" from *Collected Poems 1909–1962* by T. S. Eliot (Copyright 1936 by Harcourt Brace Jovanovich, Inc.; Copyright © 1963, 1964 by T. S. Eliot); *The Autobiography of Lincoln Steffens* (Copyright 1931 by Harcourt Brace Jovanovich, Inc.; renewed 1959 by Peter Steffens); and *The Loon Feather* by Iola Fuller (Copyright 1940 by Iola Fuller Goodspeed; renewed 1968 by Iola Fuller McCoy); all reprinted by permission of Harcourt Brace Jovanovich, Inc.

Ellen C. Masters for permission to reprint "Yee Bow" from *Spoon River Anthology* by Edgar Lee Masters.

Random House, Inc./Alfred A. Knopf, Inc. for selections from "All God's Chillun Got Wings" from *Nine Plays* by Eugene O'Neill (Copyright 1924 and renewed 1952 by Eugene O'Neill); *The Ox-Bow Incident* by Walter Van Tilburg Clark (Copyright 1940 and renewed 1968 by Walter Van Tilburg Clark); "Delta Autumn" by William Faulkner (Copyright 1942 by William Faulkner. Reprinted from *Go Down, Moses* by William Faulkner) and *Light in August* by William Faulkner (Copyright 1932 and renewed 1960 by William Faulkner); *Kingsblood Royal* by Sinclair Lewis (Copyright 1947 by Sinclair Lewis); and *BUTTERFIELD 8* by John O'Hara (Copyright 1935 and renewed 1963 by John O'Hara); all reprinted by permission of Random House, Inc.

Random House, Inc./Alfred A. Knopf, Inc. for selections from *Java Head* by Joseph Hergesheimer (Copyright 1918 and renewed 1946 by Joseph Hergesheimer); "Roland Hayes Beaten" by Langston Hughes (Copyright 1948 by Alfred A. Knopf. Reprinted from *Selected Poems of Langston Hughes* by permission of the publisher); *Serenade* by James M. Cain (Copyright 1937 and renewed 1965 by James M. Cain); and "Mother and the Armenian" by Clarence Day (Copyright 1935 by

Clarence Day and renewed 1962 by Katherine B. Day. Reprinted from *The Best of Clarence Day*; all reprinted by permission of Alfred A. Knopf, Inc.

Harper & Row, Publishers, Inc. for "Incident" from *On These I Stand* by Countee Cullen (Copyright, 1925, by Harper & Row, Publishers, Inc. Renewed, 1953, by Ida M. Cullen) and excerpts from *Kitty Foyle* by Christopher Morley (J. B. Lippincott, Publishers) (Copyright, 1939, by Christopher Morley); *Tomorrow Will Be Better* by Betty Smith (Copyright, 1948, by Betty Smith); *Black Boy: A Record of Childhood and Youth* by Richard Wright (Copyright 1937, 1942, 1944, 1945 by Richard Wright); *The Chosen People* by Sidney L. Nyburg (Copyright, 1917, by J. B. Lippincott Co. Renewed, 1945, by Sidney L. Nyburg); "John-John Chinaman" in *The Woman Who Was Changed and Other Stories* by Pearl S. Buck (Thomas Y. Crowell, Publishers) (Copyright 1942, © 1970 by Pearl S. Buck); "The Booker Washington Incident" from *Dissertations by Mr. Dooley* by Finley Peter Dunne; "The Briar Patch" by Robert Penn Warren from *I'll Take My Stand* by Twelve Southerners (Copyright, 1930, by Harper & Row, Publishers, Inc. Renewed © 1958 by Donald Davidson); and *Their Eyes Were Watching God* by Zora Neale Hurston (Copyright, 1937, by J. B. Lippincott Company. Renewed © 1965 by John C. Hurston and Joel Hurston); all reprinted by permission of Harper & Row, Publishers, Inc.

E. P. Dutton, Inc. for permission to reprint "Quid Pro Quo" and "Red Chant" from *Selected Poems* by Alfred Kreymborg (Copyright, 1945, by Alfred Kreymborg. Renewal, 1973, by Dorothy Kreymborg) and excerpts from "From Africa to America" from *Man and Shadow* by Alfred Kreymborg (Copyright, 1946, by Alfred Kreymborg. Renewal, 1974, by Dorothy Kreymborg); Section IV from "The Mexican" in *The Nightborn and Other Stories* by Jack London (Copyright, 1913, by D. Appleton Co. Renewal, 1941, by Charmain K. London); *The Winning of Barbara Worth* by Harold Bell Wright (Copyright 1911 by Harold Bell Wright, renewed 1938); and *Knock on Any Door* by Willard Motley (Copyright 1947 by Willard Motley. Renewal, 1975, by Frederica Westbrooke), all reprinted by permission of E. P. Dutton, Inc.

John Schaffner Associates, Inc. for permission to reprint "Operation" (first published in *Story*, March, 1934) by Hubert Creekmore.

New Directions Publishing Corporation for permission to reprint "Nice Day for a Lynching" from *Collected Poems* by Kenneth Patchen (Copyright 1939 by New Directions Publishing Corporation).

Howard Fast for permission to reprint the excerpt from *The Last Frontier* by Howard Fast.

Samuel French, Inc. for permission to reprint the selection from *Abie's Irish Rose* by Anne Nichols (Copyright ©, 1924, by Anne Nichols. Copyright ©, 1927 (Novel) by Anne Nichols. Copyright ©, (Acting Edition), 1937, by Anne Nichols. Copyright ©, 1952, (In renewal) by Anne Nichols).

Houghton Mifflin Company for permission to reprint "Papago Wedding" from *One Smoke Stories* by Mary Austin (Copyright 1934 by Mary Austin. Copyright © renewed 1962 by Kenneth M. Chapman and Mary C. Wheelwright) and excerpts from *My Ántonia* by Willa Cather (Copyright 1918, 1926, 1946 by Willa Sibert Cather. Copyright 1954 by Edith Lewis. Copyright © renewed 1977 by Walter Havighurst) and *The Big Sky* by A. B. Guthrie, Jr. (Copyright 1947 and copyright © renewed 1974 by A. B. Guthrie, Jr.).

Liveright Publishing Corporation:
Selection from *Ninth Avenue* by Maxwell Bodenheim is reprinted by permission of Liveright Publishing Corporation. Copyright 1926 by Boni & Liveright. Copyright renewed 1954 by Liveright Publishing Corporation.

Selection from *The Dust of New York* by Konrad Bercovici is reprinted by permission of Bertha Klausner International Literary Agency, Inc. Copyright 1919 by Boni & Liveright. Copyright renewed 1947 by Konrad Bercovici.

Harriet F. Pilpel for permission to reprint the excerpt from *Show Boat* by Edna Ferber (Copyright © 1926 by Edna Ferber. Copyright © renewed 1954 by Edna Ferber. All Rights Reserved.

Charles Scribner's Sons for the selections from "Fathers and Sons" in *The Nick Adams Stories* by Ernest Hemingway (Copyright © 1972 the Ernest Hemingway Foundation); *The Sun Also Rises* by Ernest Hemingway (Copyright 1926 Charles Scribner's Sons; copyright renewed 1954 Ernest Hemingway); *The Great Gatsby* by F. Scott Fitzgerald (Copyright 1925 Charles Scribner's Sons; copyright renewed); "This Is the Man" in *Now With His Love* by John Peale Bishop (Copyright 1933 Charles Scribner's Sons; copyright renewed 1961 Margaret G. H. Bronson); and *Of Time and the River* by Thomas Wolfe (Copyright 1935 Charles Scribner's Sons; copyright renewed

1963 Paul Gitlin, Administrator C.T.A.); all reprinted by permission of Charles Scribner's Sons.

Little, Brown and Company for permission to reprint selections from *Drums Along the Mohawk* by Walter D. Edmonds (Copyright 1936, © renewed 1964 by Walter D. Edmonds) and *So Little Time* by John P. Marquand (Copyright 1943 by John P. Marquand; © renewed 1971 by John P. Marquand, Jr. and Christina M. Welch).

John Fante (by Joyce Fante) for permission to reprint excerpts from "Helen, Thy Beauty Is to Me—" by John Fante (Copyright 1941 by The Curtis Publishing Company) and "The Odyssey of a Wop" from *Dago Red* by John Fante (Copyright © 1940, 1968 by John Fante).

Sophie M. Appel for permission to reprint the selection from *The Dark Stain* by Benjamin Appel.

The Dial Press for permission to reprint the excerpt from *The Foxes of Harrow* by Frank Yerby (Copyright © 1946 by Frank Yerby).

Macmillan Publishing Co., Inc. for permission to reprint the selection from "Our Heroine" in *Tales of the South Pacific* by James Michener (Copyright 1946, 1947 by The Curtis Publishing Company. Copyright 1947, 1974, 1975 by James A. Michener) and "Our Mother Pocahontas" from *Collected Poems* by Vachel Lindsay (Copyright 1917 by Macmillan Publishing Co., Inc., renewed 1945 by Elizabeth C. Lindsay).

McIntosh and Otis, Inc. for permission to reprint the selections from *Blood Brother* by Elliott Arnold (Copyright © 1947 by Elliott Arnold. Copyright renewed © 1975 by Elliott Arnold) and "Country Full of Swedes" from *We Are the Living* by Erskine Caldwell (Copyright © 1932 by Yale University. Renewed effective 1959 by Erskine Caldwell).

Harold Ober Associates Incorporated for permission to reprint "Who's Passing for Who?" from *Laughing to Keep from Crying* (Copyright © 1952 by Langston Hughes. Renewed 1980 by George H. Bass as Executor for the Estate of Langston Hughes); "Let America Be America Again" from *A New Song* by Langston Hughes (Copyright © 1938 by Langston Hughes. Renewed 1965 by Langston Hughes); "A Black Man Talks of Reaping" in *Personals* by Arna Bontemps (Copyright © 1963 by Arna Bontemps); and the excerpt from *Dark Laughter* by Sherwood Anderson (Copyright © 1925 by Boni & Liveright. Renewed 1953 by Eleanor Copenhaver Anderson).

Roslyn Targ Literary Agency, Inc. for permission to reprint the excerpt from *Call It Sleep* by Henry Roth (Copyright 1934, renewed 1962 by Henry Roth).

The Dorese Agency, New York, NY 10024 and the author for permission to reprint the selection from *What Makes Sammy Run?* by Budd Schulberg (Copyright © 1941).

Linda K. Press for permission to reprint the selection from "The Facts of Life" by Paul Goodman (Copyright © 1941, 1979 by Paul Goodman and Sally Goodman and published in *The Facts of Life, Stories 1940–1949: Volume 3* of *The Collected Stories of Paul Goodman* published by Black Sparrow Press), first published in *Partisan Review*.

Saturday Review for permission to reprint the excerpt from "Why I Remain a Negro" by Walter White (Copyright © 1947 by *Saturday Review*. All rights reserved).

W. Montague Cobb, M.D., Vice President, the Crisis Board and President, National Board, NAACP, for permission to reprint "To End All Stories" by Chester Himes, first published in *The Crisis*.

Hill and Wang, a division of Farrar, Straus and Giroux, Inc., for permission to reprint "Simple on Indian Blood" from *The Best of Simple* by Langston Hughes (Copyright © 1961 by Langston Hughes).

Farrar, Straus and Giroux, Inc. for permission to reprint "The Imaginary Jew" from *The Freedom of the Poet* by John Berryman (Copyright 1945 by John Berryman, Copyright renewed © 1973 by Kate Berryman. This story first appeared in *The Kenyon Review*.); "Defeat" from *The Selected Poems* by Witter Bynner (Copyright 1944 by Witter Bynner. Copyright renewed © 1972 by the Estate of Witter Bynner); "After You, My Dear Alphonse" from *The Lottery* by Shirley Jackson (Copyright 1943, 1949 by Shirley Jackson. Copyright renewed © 1971, 1977 by Laurence Hyman, Barry Hyman, Mrs. Sarah Webster, and Mrs. Joanne Schnurer. This story originally appeared in *The New Yorker*); the excerpts from *A Cool Million* by Nathanael West (Copyright © 1949, 1969 by Laura Perelman); and "Navaho Interlude" from *Red, Black, Blond and Olive* by Edmund Wilson (Copyright © 1956 by Edmund Wilson).

Paul R. Reynolds, Inc. for permission to reprint "I Have Seen Black Hands" by Richard Wright (Copyright © 1934 by *New Masses*).

Sterling A. Brown for permission to reprint "Strong Men" from *The Collected Poems of Sterling A. Brown* (Copyright © 1980 by Sterling A. Brown).

William F. Boni, president, Readex Microprint Corp., for permission to reprint portions of *Boston*, by Upton Sinclair, and *Shanty Irish*, by Jim Tully, both published in 1928 by Albert & Charles Boni.

Evelyn Singer Literary Agency for permission to reprint the selection from *Jews without Money* by Michael Gold.

Second Chance Press, Sag Harbor, N.Y. 11963 for permission to reprint the excerpt from *The History of Rome Hanks and Kindred Matters* by Joseph Stanley Pennell, all rights reserved.

Karon Kehoe for permission to reprint the selection from *City in the Sun* by Karon Kehoe.

Irwin Shaw for permission to reprint "Act of Faith" from *Selected Short Stories* by Irwin Shaw.

The author and the author's agents, Scott Meredith Literary Agency, Inc., 845 Third Avenue, New York, New York 10022, for permission to reprint the selection from *The Naked and the Dead* by Norman Mailer.

Harold J. Dies, Trustee, The Dreiser Trust, for permission to reprint the excerpt from *The 'Genius'* by Theodore Dreiser.

Holt, Rinehart and Winston, Publishers, for permission to reprint "The Vanishing Red" from *The Poetry of Robert Frost* edited by Edward Connery Lathem (Copyright 1916, © 1969 by Holt, Rinehart and Winston. Copyright 1944 by Robert Frost) and the excerpt from *The Green Pastures* by Marc Connelly (Copyright 1929, 1930, © 1957, 1958 by Marc Connelly).

Grove Press, Inc. for permission to reprint the selection from *Tropic of Capricorn* by Henry Miller (Copyright © 1961 by Grove Press, Inc.).

Laura Z. Hobson for permission to reprint the excerpt from *Gentleman's Agreement* by Laura Z. Hobson.

Norma Millay (Ellis), Literary Executor, for permission to reprint "Macdougal Street" from *Collected Poems* by Edna St. Vincent Millay (Harper & Row) (Copyright 1922, 1950 by Edna St. Vincent Millay).

Crown Publishers, Inc. for permission to reprint "A Nigger Who Was Hanged" from *Broken Necks* by Ben Hecht and the excerpt from *Born to Be* by Taylor Gordon.

Robert Nathan for permission to reprint the selection from *One More Spring* by Robert Nathan.

Vanguard Press, Inc., the publisher, for permission to reprint the selection from *The Young Manhood of Studs Lonigan* in the trilogy *Studs Lonigan* by James T. Farrell (Copyright © 1932, 1934, 1935, by Vanguard Press, Inc. Copyright © renewed 1960, 1962, 1963 by James T. Farrell).

Viking Penguin Inc. for permission to reprint "Arrangement in Black and White" by Dorothy Parker from *The Portable Dorothy Parker*, Revised and Enlarged Edition, edited by Brendan Gill (Copyright 1927 by Dorothy Parker. Copyright renewed 1955 by Dorothy Parker. Originally published in *The New Yorker*).

The New Yorker for permission to reprint "Ten Years on a Desert Island" by Edward Newhouse (Copyright © 1940, 1968 by The New Yorker Magazine, Inc.).

THE ETHNIC IMAGE IN MODERN AMERICAN LITERATURE: 1900–1950

Volume II

ABUSE
AND
VIOLENCE

Now all the hungry broken men stand here
Beside my bed like ghosts and cry: Why don't
You shout our wrongs aloud? Why are you not
Our voice, our sword? For you are of our
    blood;
You've seen us beaten, lynched, degraded,
    starved;
Men must be taught that other men are not
Mere pawns in some gigantic game in which
The winner takes the gold, the land, the work,
The breath, the heart, and soul of him who
    loses!

> Frank Yerby
> The Fishes and the Poet's
> Hands

ALL *(in unison):* That's it! Damn foreigners!
Damn dagoes! Damn Catholics! Damn sheenies! Damn niggers! Jail 'em! Shoot 'em! Hang
'em! Lynch 'em! Burn 'em!

> Elmer Rice
> *The Adding Machine*

From

AN AFTERNOON MIRACLE
by O. Henry

Alvarita heard a sudden crunching of the gravel below her. Turning her head she saw a big, swarthy Mexican, with a daring and evil expression, contemplating her with an ominous, dull eye.

"What do you want?" she asked as sharply as five hairpins between her lips would permit, continuing to plait her hair, and looking him over with placid contempt. The Mexican continued to gaze at her, and showed his teeth in a white, jagged smile.

"I no hurt-y you, Señorita," he said.

"You bet you won't," answered the Queen, shaking back one finished, massive plait. "But don't you think you'd better move on?"

"Not hurt-y you—no. But maybeso take one *beso*—one li'l kees, you call him."

The man smiled again, and set his foot to ascend the slope. Alvarita leaned swiftly and picked up a stone the size of a cocoanut.

"Vamoose, quick," she ordered peremptorily, "you *coon!*"

The red of insult burned through the Mexican's dark skin.

"*Hidalgo, Yo!*" he shot between his fangs. "I am not neg-r-ro! *Diabla bonita,* for that you shall pay me."

He made two quick upward steps this time, but the stone, hurled by no weak arm, struck him square in the chest. He staggered back to the footway, swerved half around, and met another sight that drove all thoughts of the girl from his head. She turned her eyes to see what had diverted his interest. A man with red-brown, curling hair and a melancholy, sunburned, smooth-shaven face was coming up the path, twenty yards away. Around the Mexican's waist was buckled a pistol belt with two empty holsters. He had laid aside his sixes— possibly in the *jacal* of the fair Pancha—and had forgotten them when the passing of the fairer Alvarita had enticed him to her trail. His hands now flew instinctively to the holsters, but finding the weapons gone, he spread his fingers outward with the eloquent, abjuring, deprecating Latin gesture, and stood like a rock. Seeing his plight, the newcomer unbuckled his own belt containing two revolvers, threw it upon the ground, and continued to advance.

"Splendid!" murmured Alvarita, with flashing eyes.

As Bob Buckley, according to the mad code of bravery that his sensitive conscience imposed upon his cowardly nerves, abandoned his guns and closed in upon his enemy, the old, inevitable nausea of abject fear wrung him. His breath whistled through his constricted air passages. His feet seemed like lumps of lead. His mouth was dry as dust. His heart, congested with blood, hurt his ribs as it thumped against them. The hot June day turned to moist November. And still he advanced, spurred by a mandatory pride that strained its uttermost against his weakling flesh.

The distance between the two men slowly lessened. The Mexican stood, immovable, waiting. When scarce five yards separated them a little shower of loosened gravel rattled down from above to the ranger's feet. He glanced upward with instinctive caution. A pair of dark eyes, brilliantly soft, and fierily tender, encountered and held his own. The most fearful heart and the boldest one in all the Rio Bravo country exchanged a silent and inscrutable communication. Alvarita, still seated within her vine, leaned forward above the breast-high chaparral. One hand was laid across her bosom. One great dark braid curved forward over her shoulder. Her lips were parted; her face was lit with what seemed but wonder—great and absolute wonder. Her eyes lingered upon Buckley's. Let no one ask or presume to tell through what subtle medium the miracle was performed. As by a lightning flash two clouds will accomplish counterpoise and compensation of electric surcharge, so on that eye glance the man received his complement of manhood, and the maid concealed what enriched her womanly grace by its loss.

The Mexican, suddenly stirring, ventilated his attitude of apathetic waiting by conjuring swiftly from his bootleg a long knife. Buckley cast aside his hat, and laughed once aloud, like a happy school-boy at a frolic. Then, empty-handed, he sprang nimbly, and Garcia met him without default.

So soon was the engagement ended that disappointment imposed upon the ranger's war-like ecstasy. Instead of dealing the traditional downward stroke, the Mexican lunged straight with his knife. Buckley took the precarious chance, and caught his wrist, fair and firm. Then he delivered the good Saxon knock-out blow—always so pathetically disastrous to the fistless Latin races—and Garcia was down and out, with his head under a clump of prickly pears.

(1907)

From

VIRGINIA

by Ellen Glasgow

At the end of the next mile, midway between Dinwiddie and Cross's Corner, stood the small log cabin of the former slave who had sent for him, and as he approached the narrow path that led, between oyster shells, from the main road to the single flat brown rock before the doorstep, he noticed with pleasure how tranquil and happy the little rustic home appeared under the windy brightness of the March sky.

"People may say what they please, but there never were happier or more contented creatures than the darkeys," he thought. "I doubt if there's another peasantry in the world that is half so well off or half so picturesque."

A large yellow rooster, pecking crumbs from the threshold, began to scold shrilly, and at the sound, the old servant, a decrepit negress in a blue gingham dress, hobbled out into the path and stood peering at him under her hollowed palm. Her forehead was ridged and furrowed beneath her white turban, and her bleared old eyes looked up at him with a blind and groping effort at recognition.

"I got your message, Aunt Mehitable. Don't you know me?"

"Is dat you, Marse Gabriel? I made sho' you wan' gwineter let nuttin' stop you f'om comin'."

"Don't I always come when you send for me?"

"You sutney do, suh. Dat's de gospel trufe—you sutney do."

As he looked at her standing there in the strong sunlight, with her palsied hand, which was gnarled and roughened until it resembled the shell of a walnut, curving over her eyes, he felt that a quality at once alien and enigmatical separated her not only from himself, but from every other man or woman who was born white instead of black. He had lived beside her all his life—and yet he could never understand her, could never reach her, could never even discern the hidden stuff of which she was made. He could make laws for her, but no child of a white mother could tell whether those laws ever penetrated that surface imitation of the superior race and reached the innate differences of thought, feeling, and memory which constituted her being. Was it development or mimicry that had brought her up out of savagery and clothed her in her blue gingham dress and her white turban, as in the outward covering of civilization?

Her look of crumbling age and the witch-like groping of her glance had cast a momentary spell over him. When it was gone, he said cheerfully:

"You mustn't be having troubles at your time of life, Aunt Mehitable," and in his voice there was the subtle recognition of all that she had meant to his family in the past, of all that his family had meant to her. Her claim upon him was the more authentic because it existed only in his imagination, and in hers. The tie that knit them together was woven of impalpable strands, but it was unbreakable while he and his generation were above the earth.

"Dar ain' no end er trouble, Marse Gabriel, ez long ez dar's yo' chillen en de chillen er yo' chillen ter come atter you. De ole ain' so techy—dey lets de hornet's nes' hang in peace whar de Lawd put hit—but de young dey's diff'rent."

"I suppose the neighbourhood is stirred up about the murder. What in God's name was that boy thinking of?"

The old blood crimes that never ceased where the white and the black races came together! The old savage folly and the new freedom! The old ignorance, the old lack of understanding, and the new restlessness, the new enmity!

"He wan' thinkin' er nuttin', Marse Gabriel. We ole uns kin set down en steddy, but de young dey up en does wid dere brains ez addled ez de inside uv er bad aig. 'T wan' dat ar way in de old days w'en we all hed de say so ez ter w'at wuz en w'at wan't de way ter behave."

Like an institution left from the ruins of the feudal system, which had crumbled as all ancient and decrepit things must crumble when the wheels of progress roll over them, she stood there wrapped in the beliefs and customs of that other century to which she belonged. Her sentiments had clustered about the past, as his had done, until the border-line between the romance and the actuality had vanished. She could not help him because she, also, possessed the retrospective, not the constructive, vision. He was not conscious of these thoughts, and yet, although he was unconscious of them, they coloured his reflections while he stood there in the sunlight, which had begun to fall aslant the blasted pine by the roadside. The wind had lowered until it came like the breath of spring, bud-scented, caressing, provocative. Even Gabriel, whose optimism lay in his blood and bone rather than in his intellect, yielded for a moment to this call of the spring as one might yield to the delicious melancholy of a vagrant mood. The long straight road, without bend or fork, had warmed in the paling sunlight to the colour of old ivory; in a neighbouring field a young maple tree rose in a flame of buds from the ridged earth where the ploughing was over; and against the azure sky in the south a flock of birds drifted up, like blown smoke, from the marshes.

"Tell me your trouble, then," he said, dropping into the cane-seated chair she had brought out of the cabin and placed between the flat stone at the doorstep and the well-brink, on which the yellow rooster stood spreading his wings. But Aunt Mehitable had returned to the cabin, and when she reappeared she was holding out to him a cracked saucer on which there was a piece of preserved watermelon rind and a pewter spoon.

"Dish yer is de ver'y same sort er preserves yo' mouf use'n ter water fur w'en you wuz a chile," she remarked as she handed the sweet to him. Whatever her anxiety or affliction could have been, the importance of his visit had evidently banished it from her mind. She hovered over him as his mother may have done when he was in his cradle, while the cheerful self-effacement in which slavery had trained her lent a pathetic charm to her manner.

"How peaceful it looks," he thought, sitting there, with the saucer in his hand, and his eyes on the purple shadows that slanted over the ploughed fields. "You have a good view of the low-grounds, Aunt Mehitable," he said aloud, and added immediately, "What's that noise in the road? Do you hear it?"

The old woman shook her head.

"I'se got sorter hard er heahin', Marse Gabriel, but dar's al'ays a tur'able lot er fuss gwine on w'en de chillen begin ter come up f'om de fields. 'T wuz becase uv oner dem ar boys dat I sont fur you," she pursued. "He went plum outer his haid yestiddy en fout wid a w'ite man down yonder at Cross's Co'nder, en dar's gwine ter be trouble about'n hit des ez sho' ez you live."

Seated on the flat stone, with her hands hanging over her knees, and her turbaned head swaying gently back and forth as she talked, she waited as tranquilly as the rock waited for the inevitable processes of nature. The patience in her look was the dumb patience of inanimate things; and her half-bared feet, protruding from the broken soles of her shoes, were encrusted with the earth of the fields until one could hardly distinguish them from the ground on which they rested.

"It looks as if there was something like a fight down yonder by the blasted pine," said the rector, rising from his chair. "I reckon I'd better go and see what they're quarrelling about."

The negress rose also, and her dim eyes followed him while he went down the little path between the borders of oyster shells. As he turned into the open stretch of the road, he glanced back at her, and stopping for a moment, waved his hand with a gesture that was careless and reassuring. The fight, or whatever it was that made the noise, was still some distance ahead in the shadow of the pine-tree, and as he walked towards it he was thinking casually of other matters—of the wretched condition of the road after the winter rains, of the need of greater thrift among the farmers, both white and black, of the touch of indigestion which still troubled him. There was nothing to warn him that he was approaching the supreme event in his life, nothing to prepare him for a change beside which all the changes of the past would appear as unsubstantial as shadows. His soul might have been the soul in the grass, so little did its coming or its going affect the forces around him.

"If this shooting pain keeps up, I'll have to get a prescription from Doctor Fraser," he thought, and the next minute he cried out suddenly: "God help us!" and began to run down the road in the direction of the blasted pine. There was hardly a breath between the instant when he had thought of his indigestion and the instant when he had called out sharply on the name of God, yet that flash of time had been long enough to change the ordinary man into the hero. The spark of greatness in his nature flamed up and irradiated all that had been merely dull and common clay a moment before. As he ran on, with his coat tails flapping around him, and his thin legs wobbling from the unaccustomed speed at which he moved, he was so unimposing a figure that only the Diety who judges the motives, not the actions, of men would have been impressed by the spectacle. Even the three hearty brutes—and it took him but a glance to see that two of them were drunk, and that the third, being a sober rascal, was the more dangerous—hardly ceased their merry torment of the young negro in their midst when he came up with them.

"I know that boy," he said. "He is the grandson of Aunt Mehitable. What are you doing with him?"

A drunken laugh answered him, while the sober scoundrel—a lank, hairy ne-er-do-well, with a tendency to epilepsy, whose name he remembered to have heard—pushed him roughly to the roadside.

"You git out of this here mess, parson. We're goin' to teach this damn nigger a lesson, and I reckon when he's learned it in hell, he won't turn his grin on a white woman again in a jiffy."

"Fo' de Lawd, I didn't mean nuttin', Marster!" screamed the boy, livid with terror. "I didn't know de lady was dar—fo' de Lawd Jesus, I didn't! My foot jes slipped on de plank w'en I wuz crossin', en I knocked up agin her."

"He jostled her," observed one of the drunken men judicially, "an' we'll be roasted befo' we'll let a damn nigger jostle a white lady—even if she ain't a lady—in these here parts."

In the rector's bone and fibre, drilled there by the ages that had shaped his character before he began to be, there was all the white man's horror of an insult to his womankind. But deeper even than this lay his personal feeling of responsibility for any creature whose fathers had belonged to him and had toiled in his service.

"I believe the boy is telling the truth," he said, and he added with one of his characteristic bursts of impulsiveness, "but whether he is or not, you are too drunk to judge."

There was going to be a battle, he saw, and in the swiftness with which he discerned this, he made his eternal choice between the preacher and the fighter. Stripping off his coat, he reached down for a stick from the roadside; then spinning round on the three of them he struck out with all his strength, while there floated before him the face of a man he had killed in his first charge at Manassas. The old fury, the old triumph, the old blood-stained splendour returned to him. He smelt the smoke again, he heard the boom of the cannon, the long sobbing rattle of musketry, and the thought stabbed through him, "God forgive me for loving a fight!"

Then the fight stopped. There was a patter of feet in the dust as the young negro fled like a hare up the road in the direction of Dinwiddie. One of the men leaped the fence and disappeared into the tangled thicket beyond; while the other two, sobered suddenly, began walking slowly over the ploughed ground on the right. Ten minutes later Gabriel was lying alone, with the blood oozing from his mouth, on the trodden weeds by the roadside. The shadow of the pine had not moved since he watched it; on the flat rock in front of the cabin the old negress stood, straining her eyes in the faint sunshine; and up the long road the March wind still blew, as soft, as provocative, as bud-scented.

(1913)

YEE BOW
by Edgar Lee Masters

They got me into the Sunday-school
In Spoon River
And tried to get me to drop Confucius for Jesus.
I could have been no worse off
If I had tried to get them to drop Jesus for Confucius.
For, without any warning, as if it were a prank,
And sneaking up behind me, Harry Wiley,
The minister's son, caved my ribs into my lungs,
With a blow of his fist.
Now I shall never sleep with my ancestors in Pekin,
And no children shall worship at my grave.

(1915)

From

ALL GOD'S CHILLUN GOT WINGS
by Eugene O'Neill

ACT ONE

Scene Two

The same corner. Nine years have passed. It is again late Spring at a time in the evening which immediately follows the hour of SCENE ONE. *Nothing has changed much. One street is still all white, the other all black. The fire escapes are laden with drooping human beings. The grocery store is still at the corner. The street noises are now more rhythmically mechanical, electricity having taken the place of horse and steam. People pass, white and black. They laugh as in* SCENE ONE. *From the street of the whites the high-pitched nasal tenor sings: "Gee, I Wish That I Had a Girl," and the Negro replies with "All I Got Was Sympathy." The singing is followed again by laughter from both streets. Then silence. The dusk grows darker. With a spluttering flare the arc-lamp at the corner is lit and sheds a pale glare over the street. Two young roughs slouch up to the corner, as tough in manner as they can make themselves. One is the* SHORTY *of* SCENE ONE; *the other the Negro,* JOE. *They stand loafing. A boy of seventeen or so passes by, escorting a girl of about the same age. Both are dressed in their best, the boy in black with stiff collar, the girl in white.*

SHORTY. *(scornfully)* Hully cripes! Pipe who's here. *(To the girl, sneeringly)* Wha's matter, Liz? Don't yer recernize yer old fr'ens?

GIRL. *(frightenedly)* Hello, Shorty.

SHORTY. Why de glad rags? Goin' to graduation? *(He tries to obstruct their way, but, edging away from him, they turn and run).*

JOE. Har-har! Look at dem scoot, will you! (SHORTY *grins with satisfaction*).

SHORTY. *(looking down other street)* Here comes Mickey.

JOE. He won de semi-final last night easy?

SHORTY. Knocked de bloke out in de thoid.

JOE. Dat boy's suah a-comin'! He'll be de champeen yet.

SHORTY. *(judicially)* Got a good chanct—if he leaves de broads alone. Dat's where he's wide open. (MICKEY *comes in from the left. He is dressed loudly, a straw hat with a gaudy band cocked over one cauliflower ear. He has acquired a typical "pug's" face, with the added viciousness of a natural bully. One of his eyes is puffed, almost closed, as a result of his battle the night before. He swaggers up).*

BOTH. Hello, Mickey.

MICKY. Hello.

JOE. Hear you knocked him col'.

MICKEY. Sure. I knocked his block off. *(Changing the subject).* Say. Seen 'em goin' past to de graduation racket?

SHORTY. *(with a wink)* Why? You int'rested?

JOE. *(chuckling)* Mickey's gwine roun' git a good conduct medal.

MICKEY. Sure. Dey kin pin it on de seat o' me pants. *(They laugh)* Listen. Seen Ella Downey goin'?

SHORTY. Painty Face? No, she ain't been along.

MICKEY. *(with authority)* Can dat name, see! Want a bunch o' fives in yer kisser? Den nix! She's me goil, understan'?

JOE. *(venturing to joke)* Which one? Yo' number ten?

MICKEY. *(flattered)* Sure. De real K. O. one.

SHORTY. *(pointing right—sneeringly)* Gee! Pipe Jim Crow all dolled up for de racket.

JOE. *(with disgusted resentment)* You mean tell me dat nigger's graduatin'?

SHORTY. Ask him. (JIM HARRIS *comes in. He is dressed in black, stiff white collar, etc.— a quiet-mannered Negro boy with a queerly-baffled, sensitive face).*

JIM. *(pleasantly)* Hello, fellows. *(They grunt in reply, looking over him scornfully).*

JOE. *(staring resentfully)* Is you graduatin' tonight?

JIM. Yes.

JOE. *(spitting disgustedly)* Fo' Gawd's sake! You *is* gittin' high-falutin'!

JIM. *(smiling deprecatingly)* This is my second try. I didn't pass last year.

JOE. What de hell does it git you, huh? Whatever is you gwine do wid it now you gits it? Live lazy on yo' ol' woman?

JIM. *(assertively)* I'm going to study and become a lawyer.

JOE. *(with a snort)* Fo' Chris' sake, nigger!

JIM. *(fiercely)* Don't you call me that—not before them!

JOE. *(pugnaciously)* Does you deny you's a nigger? I shows you—

MICKEY. *(gives them both a push—truculently)* Cut it out, see! I'm runnin' dis corner. *(Turning to* JIM *insultingly)* Say you! Painty Face's gitten' her ticket tonight, ain't she?

JIM. You mean Ella—

MICKEY. Painty Face Downey, dat's who I mean! I don't have to be perlite wit' her. She's me goil!

JIM. *(glumly)* Yes, she's graduating.

SHORTY. *(winks at* MICKEY) Smart, huh?

MICKEY. *(winks back—meaningly)* Willin' to loin, take it from me! (JIM *stands tensely as if a struggle were going on in him).*

JIM. *(finally blurts out)* I want to speak to you, Mickey—alone.

MICKEY. *(surprised—insultingly)* Aw, what de hell—!

JIM. *(excitedly)* It's important, I tell you!

MICKEY. Huh? *(Stares at him inquisitively—then motions the others back carelessly and follows* JIM *down front).*

SHORTY. Some noive!

JOE. *(vengefully)* I gits dat Jim alone, you wait!

MICKEY. Well, spill de big news. I ain't got all night. I got a date.

JIM. With—Ella?

MICKEY. What's dat to you?

JIM. *(the words tumbling out)* What—I wanted to say! I know—I've heard—all the stories—what you've been doing around the ward—with other girls— it's none of my business, with them—but she—Ella—it's different—she's not that kind—

MICKEY. *(insultingly)* Who told yuh so, huh?

JIM. *(draws back his fist threateningly)* Don't you dare—! (MICKEY *is so paralyzed by this effrontery that he actually steps back).*

MICKEY. Say, cut de comedy! *(Beginning to feel insulted)* Listen, you Jim Crow! Ain't you wise I could give yuh one poke dat'd knock yuh into next week?

JIM. I'm only asking you to act square, Mickey.

MICKEY. What's it to yuh? Why, yuh lousy goat, she wouldn't spit on yuh even! She hates de sight of a coon.

JIM. *(in agony)* I—I know—but once she didn't mind—we were kids together—

MICKEY. Aw, ferget dat! Dis is *now!*

JIM. And I'm still her friend always—even if she don't like colored people—

MICKEY. *Coons,* why don't yuh say it right! De trouble wit' you is yuh're gittin' stuck up, dat's what! Stay where yeh belong, see! Yer old man made coin at de truckin' game and yuh're tryin' to buy yerself white—graduatin' and law, for Christ sake! Yuh're gittin' yerself in Dutch wit' everyone in de ward—and it ain't cause yer a coon neider. Don't de gang all train wit' Joe dere and lots of others? But yuh're tryin' to buy white and it won't git yuh no place, see!

JIM. *(trembling)* Some day—I'll show you—

MICKEY. *(turning away)* Aw, gwan!

JIM. D'you think I'd change—be you—your dirty white—!

MICKEY. *(whirling about)* What's dat?

JIM. *(with hysterical vehemence)* You act square with her—or I'll show you up—I'll report you—I'll write to the papers—the sporting writers—I'll let them know how white you are!

MICKEY. *(infuriated)* Yuh damn nigger, I'll bust yer jaw in! *(Assuming his ring pose he weaves toward* JIM, *his face set in a cruel scowl.* JIM *waits helplessly but with a certain dignity).*

SHORTY. Cheese it! A couple bulls! And here's de Downey skoit comin', too.

MICKEY. I'll get yuh de next time! *(*ELLA DOWNEY *enters from the right. She is seventeen, still has the same rose and white complexion, is pretty but with a rather repelling bold air about her).*

ELLA. *(smiles with pleasure when she sees* MICKEY*)* Hello, Mick. Am I late? Say, I'm so glad you won last night. *(She glances from one to the other as she feels something in the air)* Hello! What's up?

MICKEY. Dis boob. *(He indicates* JIM *scornfully).*

JIM. *(diffidently)* Hello, Ella.

ELLA. *(shortly, turning away)* Hello. *(Then to* MICKEY*)* Come on, Mick. Walk down with me. I got to hurry.

JIM. *(blurts out)* Wait—just a second. *(Painfully)* Ella, do you hate—colored people?

MICKEY. Aw, shut up!

JIM. Please answer.

ELLA. *(forcing a laugh)* Say! What is this—another exam?

JIM. *(doggedly)* Please answer.

ELLA. *(irritably)* Of course I don't! Haven't I been brought up alongside— Why, some of my oldest—the girls I've been to public school the longest with—

JIM. Do you hate me, Ella?

ELLA. *(confusedly and more irritably)* Say, is he drunk? Why should I? I don't hate anyone.

JIM. Then why haven't you ever hardly spoken to me—for years?

ELLA. *(resentfully)* What would I speak about? You and me've got nothing in common any more.

JIM. *(desperately)* Maybe not any more—but—right on this corner—do you remember once—?

ELLA. I don't remember nothing! *(Angrily)* Say! What's got into you to be butting into my business all of a sudden like this? Because you finally managed to graduate, has it gone to your head?

JIM. No, I—only want to help you, Ella.

ELLA. Of all the nerve! You're certainly forgetting your place! Who's asking you for help, I'd like to know? Shut up and stop bothering me!

JIM. *(insistently)* If you ever need a friend—a true friend—

ELLA. I've got lots of friends among my own—kind, I can tell you. *(Exasperatedly)* You make me sick! Go to the devil! *(She flounces off. The three men laugh. MICKEY follows her. JIM is stricken. He goes and sinks down limply on a box in front of the grocery store).*

SHORTY. I'm going to shoot a drink. Come on Joe, and I'll blow yuh.

JOE. *(who has never ceased to follow every move of JIM's with angry, resentful eyes)* Go long. I'se gwine stay here a secon'. I got a lil' argument. *(He points to JIM).*

SHORTY. Suit yourself. Do a good job. See yuh later. *(He goes, whistling).*

JOE. *(stands for a while glaring at JIM, his fierce little eyes peering out of his black face. Then he spits on his hands aggressively and strides up to the oblivious* JIM. *He stands in front of him, gradually working himself into a fury at the other's seeming indifference to his words)* Listen to me, nigger: I got a heap to whisper in yo' ear! Who is you, anyhow? Who does you think you is? Don't yo' old man and mine work on de docks togidder befo' yo' old man gits his own truckin' business? Yo' ol' man swallers his nickels, my ol' man buys him beer wid dem and swallers dat—dat's the on'y diff'rence. Don't you 'n' me drag up togidder?

JIM. *(dully)* I'm your friend, Joe.

JOE. No, you isn't! I ain't no fren o' yourn! I don't even know who you is! What's all dis schoolin' you doin'? What's all dis dressin' up and graduatin' an' sayin' you gwine study be a lawyer? What's all dis fakin' an' pretendin' and swellin' out grand an' talkin' soft and perlite? What's all dis denyin' you's a nigger—an' wid de white boys listenin' to you say it! Is you aimin' to buy white wid yo' ol' man's dough like Mickey say? What is you? *(In a rage at the other's silence)* You don't talk? Den I takes it out o' yo' hide! *(He grabs JIM by the throat with one hand and draws the other fist back)* Tell me befo' I wrecks yo' face in! Is you a nigger or isn't you? *(Shaking him)* Is you a nigger, Nigger? Nigger, is you a nigger?

JIM. *(looking into his eyes—quietly)* Yes. I'm a nigger. We're both niggers. *(They look at each other for a moment. JOE's rage vanishes. He slumps onto a box beside JIM's. He offers him a cigarette. JIM takes it. JOE scratches a match and lights both their cigarettes).*

JOE. *(after a puff, with full satisfaction)* Man, why didn't you 'splain dat in de fust place?

JIM. We're both niggers. *(The same hand-organ man of SCENE ONE comes to the corner. He plays the chorus of "Bon-bon Buddie The Chocolate Drop." They both stare straight ahead listening. Then the organ man goes away. A silence. JOE gets to his feet).*

JOE. I'll go get me a cold beer. *(He starts to move off—then turns)* Time you was graduatin', ain't it? *(He goes. JIM remains sitting on his box staring straight before him as*

THE CURTAIN FALLS

(1924)

INCIDENT
by Countee Cullen

Once riding in old Baltimore,
    Heart-filled, head-filled with glee,
I saw a Baltimorean
    Keep looking straight at me.

Now I was eight and very small,
    And he was no whit bigger,
And so I smiled, but he poked out
    His tongue and called me, "Nigger."

I saw the whole of Baltimore
    From May until December:
Of all the things that happened there
    That's all that I remember.

                 (1925)

QUID PRO QUO
by Alfred Kreymborg

I've heard the derisive phrase, Jew down, jew down,
Flung at almost any innocent face
That questions the price of goods in my home town
Where saving a sou is laid to the Hebrew race.
I hear it again among these Yankee folk,
A race that gives no more than it receives,
And paying the price they raise until I'm broke,
I'm tempted to say, Go on, yank up, you thieves.
From what I've known of higher things than prices,
From love of self to love or martyrdom,
The Gentiles own at least one half the vices
And yet their virtues give them Kingdom Come.
A Jew gave up his life to give them that,
They say, and pay the Jew this tit-for-tat.

                 (1927)

OPERATION
by Hubert Creekmore

They took him to Crown Point the night he was arrested. The jail there was no better than the one in Cattabena County, but removal to another county was the accepted gesture of protection to criminal Negroes.

He sat backed close to the wall, his hands grasping the edge of the cot under him. He stared alertly ahead, vague wonder and self-condemnation revolving in his head. The bottoms of his jeans and his shoes were caked with mud from the ditch where he was caught. The sleeves had been cut from his shirt for comfort while hoeing cotton. Down his left arm blood was clotted in the scratches the woman had given him. He could not reason now, any more than yesterday morning when he was free and blameless, the apparently inevitable sequence of events. He had planned nothing; he had simply acted on impulse.

She had seemed to faint. Then when he heard noises from the house, she screamed out for her husband. They were behind the smokehouse. He heard the husband calling and he choked her to stop her cries. Frantically he leaped up and ran away through the corn rows. She was dead.

He sat in the corner all night, asleep sometimes, then waking with a shudder as an automobile whirred past. It was a long time before his trembling muscles grew calm again. Once he slid to the middle of the cot and peeped through the bars of the window. He could look down on the roof of the front porch and the bare yard with a line of petunias and zinnias along the brick wall and a big sweetgum tree at one side. The branches of the tree hid the street.

Earlier in the evening he had heard the jailer's wife playing the piano. Perhaps later she had sat on the porch with her husband and talked behind the flower boxes and hanging baskets of vines. In the morning he heard rattling in the kitchen and smelled coffee and bacon.

They gave him breakfast and afterwards the sheriff came. He hadn't said more than two sentences when the deputy, Mr. Cole, entered hurriedly.

"Potter just called from Eltonville and said six cars of 'em had started here. They've got ropes and guns."

The Negro's eyes got wide and soft. The corners of his thick lips jerked. His throat felt a sudden tug. He looked at the sheriff.

"I'll meet 'em at the edge of town," the sheriff said. "Get Tucker and both of you come with me."

He turned down the hall while Cole slammed the iron grating shut and locked it. Cole followed him downstairs.

The Negro took a few steps to the door, almost feeling his way. "Mr. Sheriff," he called in a low plaintive voice.

At the city limits the sheriff, Cole, and Tucker stopped two of the cars and turned them back. The others rushed past not heeding the signals.

They drew up quietly in front of the jail and got out. The Negro heard the brakes and sliding gravel and motors dying. He leaned forward in his corner and looked out the window. Through a long slit he could see the tree leaves and under them the white and blue shirts of men moving toward the porch. He sank back and pressed his hands between his legs. The skin grew very tight over his body.

There were voices below—one, then several at once. A man shouted some profanity and a murmur of agreement rose. The voices quieted. Someone said, "Let her through, men." It was the jailer's wife leaving. The Negro heard her saying, "Excuse me, gentlemen, I have to go see—" It dwindled away.

His moist black chest hardly rose as he breathed. Great recurrent waves of fever burst in his head and were succeeded by chilly calm. He rubbed one muddy ankle against another and listened to the rising argument outside.

"He's got the keys an' he ain't here," the jailer cried.

Finally the sheriff returned and spoke to them.

"I ain't aiming to have no trouble with you men, but you know the law. Two of your cars have done gone back. Now you all get in yours and go back peaceful, too. They ain't no use in doing things like this. He'll get a trial and what's coming to him."

At length the men drove away. The Negro was hot and thirsty but he did not call. About noon the jailer came through the corridor.

"Mr. Jailer," said the Negro. "Can I please have some water?"

When he had it, it tasted peculiar and he found it difficult to swallow. He held the cup in one hand and then the other.

"Is they a-coming back—an' take me away—"

The jailer reassured him in a matter of fact manner and took the cup.

"The sheriff's wired the Governor for militia to protect you. They won't bother you."

In the late afternoon they did come back. Two cars drove up. The men came on the porch pushing a man whose wrists were handcuffed.

"Open up, we got a prisoner," they said.

"Ain't got a key," said the jailer, eyeing the demure prisoner.

"Ain't got a key? Ain't you the jailkeeper? What are you anyway, the housemaid?"

They pushed inside of the downstairs hall. The jailer told them they would have to find the sheriff.

"Can't open without his orders."

The turmoil and vociferation increased. The Negro heard their cries and insults, heard them shaking the iron door at the stairway.

"Where is the sheriff?" someone asked at last.

"He's out at Fenner's Springs," the jailer said.

"Let's go get him," said the prisoner, ripping off the unlocked handcuffs and striding out. The others followed him.

"We'll be back. We'll get that bastard," they called. "We'll get Tim Blalock or the sheriff. I guess he'll come across then. He'll fix it."

The Negro walked about his room slowly, nervously. Even the walls sometimes frightened him. He saw the men leave. The jailer's wife cooked him some supper and then went out carrying a bundle. It was her nightgown which she would wear in some more tranquil bed than hers at the jail. His excitement did not die. Now he was merely waiting. Soon it would begin again.

But not until late night did they return. The sheriff had not been at Fenner's Springs, of course, and the party went home to Eltonville for more supporters and fresh enmity.

The Negro waited. A gentle revelation came to him that he was living his last moments. The laws of humanity and the boasting of civilization could not stop what was coming. Resistance was useless and ridiculous; he was not a hog in the slaughter-pen.

When the men came at eleven-thirty he was sitting again in his corner. They were late because they had to wait for some of their party who were at the movies. The Negro heard them coming. Their headlights shone through the tree and their motors were left running. There were many more than the morning's crowd. There were so many that even without shouting they were unable to be quiet. The yard seemed filled with them. Some had handkerchiefs over their noses and mouths. Others had them knotted around their necks ready to slip up as masks.

The Negro wondered where the militia was. Perhaps they were waiting till morning to come. Anyway, could they fire on their own white folks, even if it meant saving him for the expense of court trial and hanging?

The crowd below surged up on the porch, jostling the mossy hanging baskets. They stood on the petunias and zinnias, looking up at the windows.

"Which one is he in?" they asked each other.

"The middle one."

"No. This one on the end."

"Is that the sheriff at the door?"

"Yeah, that's him. You'd think he was a nigger-lover."

"Well, Jim Blalock talked to him after supper tonight. It's all right now."

The Negro listened to the sounds. He could not control his muscles. The hollow hereafter of his preacher could not compensate for the loss of death. Many tiny pleasures he had known danced in his mind and were routed by images of dying and nothingness.

The noises of commotion came up the stairwell now. The men were in the lower hall. He pressed his back closer into the corner.

There was a burst of sound and a cry in the hall. It was taken up outside in a tumult.

"He turned his back and they knocked him down! They've got the keys! Come on, boys!"

The Negro's face strained into the darkness. He was not moving and yet it seemed that his whole body was rising out of him. Already he felt knives in his throat, his breast, his bowels. As he heard the rattle of keys in the door below, and the thunder of feet rushing up the stairs, and the cries of his masters, a whimper like a dog's broke through his lips. The men poured down the hall like a flood from a burst dam. They looked in all the cells, flashing lights and striking matches.

Several had climbed up the porch posts and were lumbering over the roof. They swarmed to his window when they saw the others unlocking the cell-door.

"They've got him!" they shouted to the ones on the ground.

The Negro did not move when they came toward him. He did not hear their insults or feel their abuse. Terror had nullified all minor pains. They stood him on his feet but he could not straighten up. They tied him with the ropes and dragged him out of the jail. He saw the sheriff in the hall pretending to be held by three men, but he made no appeal for mercy.

In the yard he saw a face he knew. It was Mr. Frank Ashton. He used to keep Mr. Frank's two bird dogs and go hunting with him in the fall. He knew where all the coveys of partridges were. Mr. Frank had been good to him. Now he stood there looking. The Negro noticed the strange expression on his face but could not tell that it was bewildered rebellion and aching helplessness.

When they were in the car, all the others ran to their motors dividing around Mr. Frank like a tide about a pile. The procession rushed down the highway in a long stream of dust.

Several miles out of town they tied him to a tree, stripped off his clothes, castrated him, surrounded him with burning branches, and slashed his skin with knives. Finally everyone who wanted to shot him and they swung the horrible carcass to a limb of the tree.

Then a strange feeling came over most of the men. They did not talk of the Negro or his crime or his death. They turned to the highway as from a religious service, soberly and quietly and shamefully. Whitewashing their memories, they entered their automobiles and drove away.

"I got to get home. My wife and baby's all alone. They'll be scared."

(1934)

NICE DAY FOR A LYNCHING
by Kenneth Patchen

The bloodhounds look like sad old judges
In a strange court. They point their noses
At the Negro jerking in the tight noose;
His feet spread crow-like above these
Honorable men who laugh as he chokes.

I don't know this black man.
I don't know these white men.

But I know that one of my hands
Is black, and one white. I know that
One part of me is being strangled,
While another part horribly laughs.

Until it changes,
I shall be forever killing; and be killed.

(1939)

From

THE OX-BOW INCIDENT
by Walter Von Tilburg Clark

"It's Larry's gun," Farnley said. "Look," he said to the rest of us, and pointed to the butt and gave it to us to look at. Kinkaid's name, all of it, Laurence Liam Kinkaid, was inlaid in tiny letters of gold in the ivory of the butt.

Tetley recovered the gun and took it over and held it for the Mex to see.

"Where did you get this?" he asked. His tone proved he would take only one answer. Sweating from his wound, the Mex grinned at him savagely.

"If somebody will take this bullet out of my leg, I will tell you," he said.

"God, he talks American," Ma said.

"And ten other languages," said the Mex, "but I don't tell anything I don't want to in any of them. My leg, please. I desire I may stand upright when you come to your pleasure."

"What's a slug or two to you now?" Farnley asked.

"If he wants it out, let him have it out," Moore said, "there's time."

The Mex looked around at us all with that angry grin. "If somebody will lend me the knife, I will take it out myself."

"Don't give him no knife," Bartlett said. "He can throw a knife better than most men can shoot."

"Better than these men, it is true," said the Mex. "But if you are afraid, then I solemnly give my promise I will not throw the knife. When I am done, then quietly I will give the knife back to its owner, with the handle first."

Surprisingly, young Tetley volunteered to remove the slug. His face was white, his voice smothered when he said it, but his eyes were bright. In his own mind he was championing his cause still, in the only way left. He felt that doing this, which would be difficult for him, must somehow count in the good score. He crossed to the Mex and knelt beside him, but when he took the knife one of the men offered him, his hand was shaking so he couldn't even start. He put up a hand, as if to clear his eyes, and the Mex took the knife away from him. Farnley quickly turned the carbine on the Mex, but he didn't pay any attention. He made a quick slash through his chaps from the thigh to the boot top. His leg, inside, was muscular and thick and hairless as an Indian's. Just over the knee there was the bullet hole, ragged and dark, but small; dark tendrils of blood had dried down from it, not a great deal of blood. Young Tetley saw it close to his face, and got up drunkenly and moved away, his face bloodless. The Mex grinned after him.

"The little man is polite," he commented, "but without the stomach for the blood, eh?"

Then he said, while he was feeling from the wound along his leg up to the thigh, "Will someone please to make the fire better? The light is not enough."

Tetley ordered them to throw on more wood. He didn't look to see them do it. He was watching Gerald stagger out toward the dark in the edge of the woods to be sick.

When the fire had blazed up the Mex turned to present his thigh to the light, and went to work. Everybody watched him; it's hard not to watch a thing like that, though you don't want to. The Mex opened the mouth of the wound so it began to bleed again, freely, but then again he traced with his fingers up his thigh. He set his jaw, and high on the thigh made a new incision. His grin froze so it looked more like showing his teeth, and the sweat beads popped out on his forehead. He rested a moment when the first cut had been made, and was bleeding worse than the other.

"That is very bad shooting," he said. He panted from the pain.

Nonetheless, when he began to work again he hummed a Mexican dance tune through his teeth. He halted the song only once, when something he did with the point of the knife made his leg straighten involuntarily, and made him grunt in spite of himself. After that his own hand trembled badly, but he took a breath and began to dig and sweat and hum again. It got so I couldn't watch it either. I turned and looked for young Tetley instead, and saw him standing by a tree, leaning on it with one hand, his back to the fire. His father was watching him too.

There was a murmur, and I looked back, and the Mex had the bloody slug out and was holding it up for us to look at. When we had seen it he tossed it to Farnley.

"You should try again with that one," he said.

Sparks brought some hot water to the Mex, and after propping the knife so the blade was in the coals, he began washing out the two wounds with a purple silk handkerchief he'd had around his neck. He took care of himself as carefully as if he still had a lifetime to go. Then, when the knife blade was hot enough, he drew it out of the fire and clapped it right against the wounds, one after the other. Each time his body stiffened, the muscles of his jaw and the veins of his neck protruded, and the sweat broke out over his face, but still he drew the knife away from the thigh wound slowly, as if it pleased him to take his time. He asked for some of the fat from the steaks, rubbed the grease over the burned cuts, and bound them with the purple kerchief and another from his pocket. Then he lit a cigarette and took it easy.

After inhaling twice, long and slow, he picked up the knife he'd used and tossed it over in front of the man who had lent it. He tossed it so it spun in the air and struck the ground point first with a chuck sound, and dug in halfway to the hilt. It struck within an inch of where the man's boot had been, but he'd drawn off quickly when he saw it coming. The Mex grinned at him.

Martin and old Hardwick were bound again. Tetley told them they needn't tie the Mex, he wouldn't go far for awhile. The Mex thanked him, grinning through the smoke of his cigarette.

But when Tetley began to question him about the gun, all he'd say was that he'd found it; that it was lying right beside the road, and he'd brought it along, thinking to meet somebody he could send it back with. When Tetley called him a liar, and repeated the questions, the Mex at first just said the same thing, and then suddenly became angry and stubborn-looking, called Tetley a blind fool, lit another cigarette, and said no sabbey as he had at first.

(1940)

From

THE LAST FRONTIER
by Howard Fast

The riders of the Eagle Bar D ranch, twelve strong, coming in from the range with their chuck wagon, topped a rise of ground and saw the two Indians skinning a buffalo cow. The riders splashed forward, and the two Indians, glancing up, seeing them, ran for their ponies. One Indian reached his saddle with a long, running leap. The other fell with a bullet in his leg. They closed on the wounded Indian who was twisting desperately to reach his gun. Mark Ready, the foreman, kicked the gun away. Axel Green laced his spurred boot into the fallen Indian's face.

The other Indian rode off about three hundred yards before he turned his pony and halted to watch them. The range was too long for any sort of revolver practice and there were only two rifles in the party. Kling and Sanderson, both of whom were good rifle shots, had a few tries at the Indian, but without any success. Green wanted to go after him, but Ready said:

"No, we got one—to hell with the other."

Sanderson agreed. "That's a Dog Soldier," he decided, nodding at the Indian who lay on the ground with a broken leg and a bleeding face. "Maybe the whole herd's hereabouts."

The Indian who had escaped rode off slowly. The other lay on one elbow, motionless, not even looking at the riders, murmuring a strange, minor-key tune.

"What's that?"

"That's a death song," Sanderson said. Marcy, whose grandfather had been killed by Indians, who felt it incumbent upon himself to hate Indians a good deal more than most others hated them, grinned widely.

"What about him?" Green demanded.

"The dirty red bastard," Marcy said good-naturedly.

"Let him be," Ferguson said. Ferguson was the cook. "It's no business of ours."

The Indian kept his eyes on the ground, lying on his side and supporting himself with one elbow. He was a young man, under thirty, clean-featured, with a long, powerful body that swept into a barrel mass of chest and shoulder. If his lacerated face or broken leg gave him pain, he showed no sign of it. He lay perfectly still in his old dirt- and blood-stained buckskins.

"We'll find a tree," Ready decided—"give him a Christian finish."

"Hell, no!"

"Look, Ready," the cook said, "we got no call to lynch him. Maybe he's a Dog Soldier, maybe he ain't. There's nobody here knows that much about Injuns. But we got no call to lynch him."

"The hell he ain't—look at the moccasins!"

The moccasins, worn through at the soles, frayed and tattered, still showed signs of former glory, beaded all over with infinite care and patience.

"Dog Soldier moccasins," Sanderson agreed.

Ferguson glanced from face to face; half of the party were young, under twenty, lithe, brown-faced boys. Ferguson had grouped them and separated them during long nights of gentle ribbing; that was right; every range outfit ribbed the cook. And Ferguson had seen each of those boys in human display, the lonely selflessness of men who live simply.

"Don't lynch him," Ferguson said. "Christ, leave him alone here if you want him to die."

"Shut up, cookie," Marcy said.

No one else offered anything. They stood in a circle, looking at the fallen man but not at the cook. Ferguson went to the chuck wagon, got a dipper of water, and held it out to the Indian.

"Drinkee—you um drinkee?" Ferguson asked.

The Indian raised his eyes, stared at Ferguson a moment, then took the water and drank. He said something in his own tongue.

"Hell, tie him and put him on his horse," Ready snapped, driven by the fact that he had made his decision, that all of him the men knew was in making decisions and carrying them out.

Ferguson shook his head helplessly, turned around, and climbed into the chuck wagon. They tied the Indian onto his own horse and then proceeded stolidly for about two miles before they came to a tree large enough to hang a man on. It was a big, mottled cottonwood dipping over the edge of a creek. They looped a lariat over a branch, stood the Indian up with the noose on his neck, and tied the other end to the bone pommel of his pony's saddle.

Somehow, the Indian managed to stay erect on his one good leg. Dignity was the only thing he strove for; his face was impassive and without fear; his eyes were closed.

"I wish to hell he could say something," Sanderson murmured. "I sure hate to see a man die without saying something."

Then Ready lashed the pony away and the Indian hung in the air.

(1941)

LOVE CONQUERS ALL?

I must not see upon your face
Love's softly glowing spark;
For there's the barrier of race,
You're fair and I am dark.
>> Claude McKay
>> The Barrier

. . . Tom's Uncle Chan, was in New York,
too. . . . It was from one of Uncle Chan's
letters that the people at home learned of the
dramatic marriage of the eldest son Daiko to
an Italian girl named Flora. Tom's father had
not thought the fact even worth mentioning.
>> Lin Yutang
>> *Chinatown Family*

Close was our flesh through the winking hours,
closely and sweetly entwined.
Love did not guess in the tight-packed dark
it was flesh of varying kind.
>> Gwendolyn Brooks
>> In the Mecca

From

JAVA HEAD
by Joseph Hergesheimer

. . . Rhoda saw the barouche draw up before the house. She had a glimpse of a figure at Gerrit Ammidon's side in extravagantly brilliant satins; there was a sibilant whisper of rich materials in the hall, and the master entered the library with a pale set face.

"Father," he said, "Rhoda and William, allow me—my wife, Taou Yuen."

Rhoda Ammidon gave an uncontrollable gasp as the Chinese woman sank in a fluttering prostration of color at Jeremy's feet. He ejaculated, "God bless me," and started back. William's face was inscrutable, unguessed lines appeared about his severe mouth. Her own sensation was one of incredulity touched with mounting anger and feeling of outrage. The woman rose, but only to sink again before William: she was on her knees and, supported by her hands, bent forward and touched her forehead to the floor three times. Gerrit laughed shortly. "She was to shake your hands; we went over and over it on shipboard. But anything less than the *Kû l'on* was too casual for her."

She was now erect with a freer murmur of greeting to Rhoda. The latter was instantly aware of one certainty—Chinese she might be, she was, but no less absolutely aristocratic. Her face, oval and slightly flat, was plastered with paint on paint, but her gesture, the calm scrutiny of enigmatic black eyes under delicately arched brows, exquisite quiet hands, were all under the most admirable instinctive command. Rhoda said:

"I see that I am to welcome you for Gerrit's family." The other, in slow lisping English replied:

"Thank you greatly. I am humbled to the earth before your goodness."

"You will want to go to your room," Rhoda continued mechanically. "It was only prepared for one, but I'll send a servant up at once." She was enraged at the silent stupidity of the three men and flashed a silent command at her husband.

"This is a decided surprise," the latter at last addressed his brother; "nor can I pretend that it is pleasant." Jeremy Ammidon's gaze wandered blankly from Gerrit to the woman, then back to his son.

31

Never before had Rhoda seen such lovely clothes: A long gown with wide sleeves of blue-black satin, embroidered in peach-colored flower petals and innumerable minute sapphire and orange butterflies, a short sleeveless jacket of sage green caught with looped red jade buttons and threaded with silver and indigo high-soled slippers crusted and tasseled with pearls. Her hair rose from the back in a smooth burnished loop. There were long pins of pink jade carved into blossoms, a quivering decoration of paper-thin gold leaves with moonstones in glistening drops, and a band of coral lotus buds. Pierced stone bracelets hung about her delicate wrists, fretted crystal balls swung from the lobes of her ears; and clasped on the ends of several fingers were long pointed filagrees of ivory.

"Taou Yuen," Gerrit repeatedly shortly, with his challenging bright gaze. "That means Peach Garden. My wife is a Manchu," he asserted in a more biting tone; "a Manchu and the daughter of a noble. Thank you, Rhoda, particularly. But I have always counted on you. Will you go up with her? That is if—if my father has a room, a place, for us?"

"This will always be your home, Gerrit," Jeremy said slowly, with the long breath of a diver in deep waters.

IV

In the room that had been his since early maturity Gerrit Ammidon gave an involuntary sigh of relief. Taou Yuen, his wife, was standing in the middle of the floor, gazing about with a faint and polite smile. Her eyes rested on a yellow camphor chest—one of the set brought home by his father—on a severe high range of drawers made of sycamore with six legs, on her brilliant reflection in the eagle-crowned mirror above the mantel, and the sleigh bed with low heavily curved ends.

The situation below, however brief and, on the whole, reasonably conducted, had been surprisingly difficult. At the same time that he had felt no necessity to apologize for his marriage he had known that Taou Yuen must surprise, yes—shock, his family. She was Chinese, to them a heathen: they would be unable to comprehend any mitigating dignity of rank. Where they'd actually suffer, he realized, would be in the attitude of Salem, the stupid gabble, the censure and cold pity caused by his wife.

Personally he regarded these with the contempt he felt for so many of the qualities that on shore bound the interests of everyone into a single common concern. It gave him pleasure to assault the authority and importance of such public prejudice and self-opinion; but, unavoidably implicating his family, at once a part of himself and Salem, he was conscious of the fact that he had laid them all open to disagreeable moments. He was sorry for this, and his regret, principally materialized by his father's hurt confusion, had unexpectedly cast a shadow on a scene to which he had looked forward with a distinct sense of comedy. Where the realities were concerned he had no fear of Taou Yuen's ability to justify herself completely. He possessed a stupendous admiration for her.

He watched her now with the mingled understanding and mystification that gave his life with her such a decided charm. Her gaze had fastened on the mirrorstand above the drawers: she must be wondering if she would have to paint and prepare herself for him here, openly. He knew that she considered it a great impropriety for her face to be seen bare; all the elaborate processes of her morning toilet must be privately conducted. He recognized this, but had no idea what she actually thought of the room, of his family, of the astonishing situation into which her heart had betrayed her.

One and then another early hope he saw at once were vain. It had seemed to him that in America, in Salem, she might become less evidently Chinese; not in the incongruous horror of Western clothes, but in her attitude, in a surrender to superficial customs; he had pictured her as merging distinctively into the local scene. In China he had hoped that in the vicinity of Washington Square and Pleasant Street she would appear less Eastern; but, beyond all doubt, here she was enormously more so. The strange repressed surrounding accentuated every detail of her Manchu pomp and color. The frank splendor of her satins and carved jades and embroidery, her immobile striking face loaded with carmine and glinting headdress, the flawless loveliness of hands with the pointed nail protectors, were, in his room, infinitely dramatized.

The other, less secure possibility that she might essentially change perished silently. In a way his wish had been a presumption—that a member of the oldest and most subtle civilization existing would, if she were able, adopt such comparatively crude habits of life and thought.

She moved slowly up to the bed, examining it curiously; and again he understood her look of doubt—in China beds were called *kang*, or stoves, from the fact that they were more often than not a platform of brick with an opening beneath for hot coals. She fingered the ball fringe of the coverlet, and then turned with amazement to the soft pillow. A hand with the stone bracelet falling back from her smooth wrist rose to the complicated edifice of her headdress.

"Your pillow is coming along from the ship," he told her; "the women here do up their hair every morning."

She considered this with geranium lips slightly parted on flawless teeth, and nodded slowly. The westering sun striking through the window overlooking the Common illuminated her with a flat gold unreality.

"I'll have a day bed brought for you," he continued, realizing that, as the result of fortunate chance, she understood most of what he said without an actual command of the individual words. In reply she sank before him in the deep Manchu gesture with one knee sweeping the floor, the humility of her posture dignified by grace. He touched the crystal globe of an earring, pinched her chin, in the half light manner by which he instinctively expressed his affection for her. She was calm and pleased. "Taou Yuen," he continued, "you miss Shanghai, with the wall of ten gates and the river Woosung stuck full of masts. You'll never think Salem is a paradise like Soochow."

"This is your city," she replied, slowly choosing the words. "Your ancestors are here." There was not a shade of regret in her voice or manner. He tried once more, and as vainly as ever, to penetrate the veil of her perfect serenity. She never, it became apparent, descended from the most inflexible self-control; small emotions—surface gayety of mood, curiosity, the faintest possible indication of contempt, he had learned to distinguish; the fact that she cared enough for him to desert every familiar circumstance was evident; but beyond these he was powerless to reach.

His own emotions were hardly less obscured: the dominating feeling was his admiration for her exquisite worldly wisdom, the perfection of her bodily beauty, and the philosophy which bore her above the countless trivialities that destroyed the dignity of western minds. He realized that her paint and embroidery covered a spirit as cold and tempered as fine metal. She was totally without the social sentiment of his own world; but she was equally innocent of its nauseous hypocrisy, the pretensions of a piety covering commercial dishonesty, obscenity of thought and spreading scandal. The injustice he saw practiced on shore had always turned him with a sense of relief to the cleansing challenge of the sea; always, brought in contact with cunning and self-seeking men and heartless schemes, with women cheapened by a conviction of the indecency of life, he was in a state of hot indignation. From all this Taou Yuen offered a complete escape.

On the purely feminine side she was a constant delight, the last possible refinement, he told himself, of instinct and effect. She was incapable of the least vulgarity; never for an instant did she flag from the necessity of beauty, never had he seen her too weary for an adornment laborious in a hundred difficult conventions. She was, too, a continuous source of entertainment, even as his wife she never ceased to be a spectacle; his consciousness of her as a being outside himself persisted.

*　　*　　*　　*　　*

They turned inside, William was in the library, and Gerrit instinctively followed his father into the room. William surveyed him with a moody discontent. "What I can't understand," he proceeded; "is why you call it a marriage, why you brought your woman here to us, to Rhoda and the children."

"It's simple enough," Gerrit replied; "Taou Yuen is my wife, we are married exactly as Rhoda and you are. She is not my woman in the sense you mean. I won't allow that, William."

"How can it matter what you will or will not allow when everyone'll think the other? Shipmasters have had Chinese mistresses before, yes, and smuggled them into Salem; but this conduct of yours is beyond speech."

Gerrit Ammidon said:

"Don't carry this too far." Anger like a hot cloud oppressed him. "I am married legally and, if anything, by a ceremony less preposterous than your own. Taou Yuen is not open to any man or woman's suspicions. I am overwhelmingly indebted to her."

"But she's not your race," William Ammidon muttered; "she is a Confucian or Taoist, or some such thing."

"You're Unitarian one day a week, and father is Congregational, Hodie's a Methodist, and no one knows what I am," Gerrit cried. "Good God, what does all that matter! Isn't a religion a religion? Do you suppose a Lord worth the name would be anything but entertained by such spiteful little dogmas. A sincere greased nigger with his voodoo must be as good as any of us."

"That is too strong, Gerrit," Jeremy objected. "You'll get nowhere crying down Christianity."

"If I could find it," the younger declared bitterly, "I'd feel differently. It's right enough in the Bible. . . . Well, we'll go on to Boston to-morrow."

"This is your home," his father repeated. "Naturally William, all of us have been disturbed; but nothing beyond that. I trust we are a loyal family. What you've done can't be mended with hard words."

"She may become very fashionable," Gerrit mockingly told his brother. It'll be a blow to Camilla," Jeremy chuckled. "Some rice must be cooked."

"Manchus don't live on rice," Gerrit replied. "They don't bind the feet either nor wear the common Chinese clothes. Rhoda will understand better."

Again in his room he found his wife bending over a gorgeous heap of satins, bright mazarines and ornaments. "We'll go down to supper soon," he told her. Already there were signs of her presence about the room: the chest of drawers was covered with gold and jade and green amber, painted paper fans set on ivory and tortoise shell, and lacquer fan boxes; coral hairpins, sandalwood combs, silver rouge pots and rose quartz perfume bottles with canary silk cords and tassels. On a familiar table was her pipe, wound in gilt wire, and the flowered satin tobacco case. An old coin was hanging at the head of the bed, a charm against evil spirits; and on a stand was the amethyst image of Kuan-Yin *pu tze*, the Goddess of Mercy.

Taou Yuen sank on the floor with a little embarrassed laugh at the confusion in which he had surprised her. "Let your attitude be grave," he quoted from the Book of Rites with a pretended severity. Her amusement rose in a ripple of mirth. He opened his desk, rearranging the disorder brought about by its transportation; and, when he turned, she was prostrate in the last rays of the sun. *"O-me-to-Fuh,"* she breathed; *"O-me-to-Fuh,"* the invocation to Buddha. This at an end she announced, "Now I am grave and respectful for your family."

(1918)

From

ABIE'S IRISH ROSE
by Anne Nichols

ACT ONE

Solomon Levy's apartment, New York.

SCENE: *The home of a New York business man, a prosperous one. The living room is comfortably furnished, without particular effort made to follow any special period, both as to architecture and decoration. The ensemble is rich in appearance and denotes very good taste.*

* * * * *

As the curtain goes up COHEN *is on the davenport. He has the funny part of the evening paper which he is reading with evident enjoyment.* MRS. COHEN *and* RABBI *are seated at table.*

* * * * *

SOLOMON. *[Grabs the telephone, picking it up.]* Thank God! *[He has the receiver off the hook by this time.]* Hello! Who iss it? Yes vot? Me! Yes, it's me! Who am me? Say who am you? What number? I don't know the number! I didn't get the phone to call myself! Oh, Abie wishes to speak vid his fadder? Pud him on! *[To* RABBI.*]* Abie. *[*SOLOMON *laughs at* OTHERS. MRS. COHEN *makes a knowing face at* COHEN, *they are* ALL *interested.* SOLOMON *seems very angry at the telephone.]* Hello! Iss dod you? Oh it iss? Vell you—you—loafer! V-here have you been all tay and vot iss it? I've a good notion to— Vot? Huh? A vod vid you? You vont to bring a lady home to dinner? *[He turns to* COHEN *and winks, belying his bad humor. In a whisper, as though* ABIE *could hear.]* He vonts to bring a lady home to dinner! *[Then back in the telephone again.]*

COHEN. *[To* SOLOMON, *who with his eyes warns* COHEN *of* MRS. COHEN'S *presence.]* Oy, I can't wait! *[Throws one leg excitedly over the other. Turns around, sees* MRS. COHEN—*and is squelched.]*

SOLOMON. Vot, I didn't heard you—say it twice! Oh, she's a very sweet girl? Oh I vill, vill I? *[He turns to them again.]* He says I'll like her! She's a sveet girl. *[Then immediately back into telephone.]* Jewish? *[He smiles and turns to them again.]* He says, vait till I see her! *[Then back in the telephone again.]* You little goniff—I smell a mices! Sure! I'll tell Sarah. Goodbye, Abie, goodbye. *[He hangs up receiver. They* ALL *sit waiting for him to tell them everything.]* Ha, ha, peoples, my Abie's got a girl. Maybe the good Rabbi will soon officiate at a wedding. Eh? *[Crosses to Center. He is delighted.]*

COHEN. Is she Hebrew?

SOLOMON. Of course. Hebrew. Jewish Hebrew. *[He is delighted. He nudges* COHEN.*]* Abie! says, vait till I see her! *[Turns to* RABBI.*]* Doctor Samuels—"Lieber Freund"—Maybe we'll all be goin' to a vedding soon! Yes! *[Crosses to back of table Left Center.]*

COHEN. Solomon, why are you trying to get Abie married? He's happy.

MRS. COHEN. You mean to say he wouldn't be happy if he was married?

COHEN. Mama, can't I talk at all?

RABBI. Oh, Isaac didn't mean to infer he isn't happy. He is happy, aren't you, Isaac?

COHEN. Perfectly.

SOLOMON. No, it isn't the idea that I want my Abie married exactly, but I want his grandchildren. *[Crosses Center.]*

COHEN. You don't want him to get married. But you want him to have children. Mama listen to that.

MRS. COHEN. Isaac, you don't know what Solomon means.

COHEN. Sure, I do, he—

MRS. COHEN. You don't understand a word he says—

COHEN. Concentrate, Mama, concentrate.

SOLOMON. Yes, Isaac, I want grandchildren—dozens of them. *[Crosses to* COHEN.*]*

COHEN. Right away you talk wholesale.

SOLOMON. You see before my Abie was born, Rebecca and I we always used to plan for him. I wanted him to be a politician. Rebecca says, "No, Solomon. I want my boy—our son—to stay close by his father."

COHEN. And he certainly has.

SOLOMON. Yes.

RABBI. Yes, I don't know what your business would have done without him.

SOLOMON. Neither do I. But don't you tell him I said so.

MRS. COHEN. Why don't you take him into the firm?

RABBI. Right. Solomon Levy and Son—that wouldn't sound bad at all.

SOLOMON. *That's* just exactly what I am going to do. When he's married—not before.

RABBI. Why must you wait until he's married?

SOLOMON. Did you ever see any of Abie's girls?

RABBI. No.

SOLOMON. Not one Jewish and my Abie is not going to marry anyone but a Jewish girl if I can help it.

COHEN. Maybe you won't be able to help it.

SOLOMON. Who said it, not be able to help it? Let him try and you'll see how I could help it.

MRS. COHEN. Are you sure that this new girl is the right one?

SOLOMON. Didn't he say wait till I see her? Oh, what a relief when I'll see that son of mine safely married. I must tell Sarah dinner for three— *[Crosses to door Left.]*

MRS. COHEN. *[Rises and starts to go.]* Ve must be going.

SOLOMON. Den please come back later and take a look at her.

MRS. COHEN. If ve can, ve vill.

COHEN. Vhy can't we, Mama? *[Rises, crosses to Center.]*

MRS. COHEN. *[To COHEN.]* Because I'm awfully tired and you ought to go to bed early.

COHEN. *[Crestfallen; To door Right Center.]* See—she's tired, and I got to go to bed early. *[Going out through hall followed by MRS. COHEN.]*

RABBI. *[Starting for the door. Right Center.]* I'll drop in later, Solomon.

SOLOMON. Goodbye, peoples, goodbye, and don't forget. When my Abie says a thing you can build a bank on it. *[Going to arch Right Center. To photograph on table up Center.]* Abele, Boyele meiner.

[SOLOMON takes out cigarette paper, puts in two pinches of tobacco, singing "Masseltof" as he reaches Left Center door, moistens cigarette, causes discord in song, and exits Left Center. ABIE enters the room from Right Center cautiously looking about, then he beckons to ROSE MARY who enters after him. They are both nervous and frightened. ABIE looks upstairs,

listens a moment, then comes down to door Left, opens it, listens, then closes it carefully, not making any noise. He goes to door Right and repeats business, then back to arch Right Center.]

ABIE. Well, the coast is clear. *[Crosses to* ROSE MARY, *Center.]*

ROSE MARY. *[Coming down to Abie.]* Oh, Abie, I'm so frightened!

ABIE. With a perfectly good husband to protect you?

ROSE MARY. Oh, I forgot!

ABIE. *[Takes her in his arms.]* You haven't been married long enough yet to be used to it. Let's see— *[Looks at his watch.]* Just one hour and thirty-three minutes. Do you realize, young lady, you are no longer Rose Mary Murphy? You are Mrs. Abraham Levy.

ROSE MARY. Mrs. Abraham Levy! Glory be to God!

ABIE. Isn't it wonderful?

ROSE MARY. Abie, we will both be disowned.

ABIE. Well, that's better than being separated for the rest of our lives, isn't it?

ROSE MARY. *[Hesitating over it.]* Yes.

ABIE. Why do you say it that way?

ROSE MARY. I am not so sure that they won't try to separate us.

ABIE. Oh, yes, try. But we're not going to let them. Are we?

ROSE MARY. No.

ABIE. *[Takes her in his arms.]* We were married good and tight by a nice Methodist minister.

ROSE MARY. "Till death do us part."

ABIE. *[Breaks embrace and takes her hands.]* Oh, that reminds me, why did you refuse to say "I do" to the obey me?

ROSE MARY. *[With a slight brogue, smiling.]* Shure— I'm that Irish!

ABIE. I didn't balk when he said "repeat after me, With all my worldly goods I thee endow." You know it's fifty-fifty.

ROSE MARY. To be sure it is. Faith you haven't any worldly goods and your father is liable to disown you when he finds out you haven't married a nice little Jewish girl.

ABIE. So is your father, when he finds out you haven't married a nice little Irish boy.

ROSE MARY. *[With true Irish foresight.]* That would be fifty-fifty. *[Backs to front of davenport.]*

ABIE. You know, Rose Mary, I was just thinking. *[Crosses down Left of davenport.]*

ROSE MARY. You are liable to have to do a whole lot of thinking, so you had better get into practice. *[Sits on davenport. He sits with her.]*

ABIE. No, in all seriousness, Rose Mary, you know I'm sure Father will be crazy about you.

ROSE MARY. *[Lapsing into brogue.]* He might be crazy about me all right but when he hears about "me religion" he'll be crazier.

ABIE. Silly, isn't it, to be so narrow-minded. Well, he can't any more than tell us to go, can he?

ROSE MARY. But Abie—you work for your father!

ABIE. Yep! *[Sighing.]* And if you don't make a hit with him, I'm liable to lose my job. I should worry. I'll find another.

ROSE MARY. And if you lost your job I'll have to do my own housework, and learn to cook.

ABIE. You can fry eggs, can't you?

ROSE MARY. I can, but I can't turn them over.

ABIE. *[With his arm around her.]* I'll turn them over for you. *[She cuddles close to him, forgetting for an instant what is coming.]*

ROSE MARY. Oh, Abie! Will you always be willing to do so much for me?

ABIE. Always! [ABIE *and* ROSE MARY *sigh.*]

ROSE MARY. Abie!

ABIE. *[Holding her close.]* Yes, dear?

ROSE MARY. Wouldn't it be wonderful if our fathers would take our marriage nicely!

ABIE. *[Hugging her closer.]* Wonderful!

ROSE MARY. Then we wouldn't have to worry about a thing. You could go on with your job—and—

ABIE. Now, you stop worrying about that, dear. I'm sure Father will fall in love with you as I did, on first sight.

ROSE MARY. Abie, you're a dear! You know sometimes *[Lapsing into brogue.]* I think you've a bit of the Irish tucked away in you somewhere. Faith, I believe you're half Irish.

ABIE. *[Right back at her with a brogue.]* To be sure Mavourneen, my better half is Irish.

ROSE MARY. *[Laughing.]* And my better half is Jewish. *[Puts right hand on his cheek.]*

ABIE. What could be sweeter? *[Kiss. In embrace.* SOLOMON *sings off Left.]* That's Father!

ROSE MARY. *[Frightened. Both rise.]* Oh, Abie!

ABIE. Don't weaken, dear! And no matter what he says, remember he's a peach when you get under his skin.

ROSE MARY. I hope it isn't a long way under.*

(1922)

*Copies of this play, in individual paper-covered acting editions, are available from Samuel French, Inc., 25 W. 45th St., New York, N.Y. 10036 or 7623 Sunset Blvd., Hollywood, Calif. 90046 or in Canada Samuel French (Canada) Ltd., 80 Richmond Street East, Toronto M5C 1P1, Canada.

PAPAGO WEDDING
by Mary Austin

There was a Papago woman out of Panták who had a marriage paper from a white man after she had borne him five children, and the man himself was in love with another woman. This Shuler was the first to raise cotton for selling in the Gila Valley—but the Pimas and Papagoes had raised it long before that—and the girl went with him willingly. As to the writing of marriage, it was not then understood that the white man is not master of his heart, but is mastered by it, so that if it is not fixed in writing it becomes unstable like water and is puddled in the lowest place. The Sisters at San Xavier del Bac had taught her to clean and cook. Shuler called her Susie, which was nearest to her Papago name, and was fond of the children. He sent them to school as they came along, and had carpets in the house.

In all things Susie was a good wife to him, though she had no writing of marriage and she never wore a hat. This was a mistake which she learned from the sisters. They, being holy women, had no notion of the *brujeria* which is worked in the heart of the white man by a hat. Into the presence of their God also, without that which passes for a hat, they do not go. Even after her children were old enough to notice it, Susie went about the country with a handkerchief tied over her hair, which was long and smooth on either side of her face, like the shut wings of a raven.

By the time Susie's children were as tall as their mother, there were many white ranchers in the Gila country, with their white wives, who are like Papago women in this, that if they see a man upstanding and prosperous, they think only that he might make some woman happy, and if they have a cousin or a friend, that she should be the woman. Also the white ones think it so shameful for a man to take a woman to his house without a writing that they have no scruple to take him away from her. At Rinconada there was a woman with large breasts, surpassing well looking, and with many hats. She had no husband and was new to the country, and when Shuler drove her about to look at it, she wore each time a different hat.

This the Papagoes observed, and, not having visited Susie when she was happy with her man, they went now in numbers, and by this Susie understood that it was in their hearts that she might have need of them. For it was well known that the white woman had told Shuler that it was a shame for him to have his children going about with a Papago woman who had only a handkerchief to cover her head. She said it was keeping Shuler back from being the principal man among the cotton growers of Gila Valley, to have in his house a woman who would come there without a writing. And when the other white women heard that she had said that, they said the same thing. Shuler said, "My God, this is the truth, I know it," and the woman said that she would go to Susie and tell her that she ought to go back to her own people and not be a shame to her children and Shuler. There was a man from Panták on the road, who saw them go, and turned in his tracks and went back, in case Susie should need him, for the Papagoes, when it is their kin against whom there is *brujeria* made, have in-knowing hearts. Susie sat in the best room with the woman and was polite. "If you want Shuler," she said, "you can have him, but I stay with my children." The white woman grew red in the face and went out to Shuler in the field where he was pretending to look after something, and they went away together.

After that Shuler would not go to the ranch except of necessity. He went around talking to his white friends. "My God," he kept saying, "what can I do, with my children in the hands of that Papago?" Then he sent a lawyer to Susie to say that if she would go away and not shame his children with a mother who had no marriage writing and no hat, he would give her money, so much every month. But the children all came in the room and stood by her, and Susie said, "What I want with money when I got my children and this good ranch?" Then Shuler said "My God!" again, and "What can I do?"

The lawyer said he could tell the Judge that Susie was not a proper person to have care of his children, and the Judge would take them away from Susie and give them to Shuler. But when the day came for Susie to come into court, it was seen that though she had a handkerchief on her hair, her dress was good, and the fringe of her shawl was long and fine. All the five children came also, with new clothes, well looking. "My God!" said Shuler, "I must get those kids away from that Papago and into the hands of a white woman.'' But the white people who had come to see the children taken away saw that although the five looked like Shuler, they had their mouths shut like Papagoes; so they waited to see how things turned out.

Shuler's lawyer makes a long speech about how Shuler loves his children, and how sorry he is in his heart to see them growing up like Papagoes, and water is coming out of Shuler's eyes. Then the Judge asks Susie if she has anything to say why her children shall not be taken away.

''You want to take these children away and giff them to Shuler?'' Susie asks him. ''What for you giff them to Shuler?'' says Susie, and the white people are listening. She says, ''Shuler's not the father of them. Thees children all got different fathers,'' says Susie. ''Shuler———''

Then she makes a sign with her hand. I tell you if a woman makes that sign to a Papago he could laugh himself dead but he would not laugh off that. Some of the white people who have been in the country a long time know that sign and they begin to laugh.

Shuler's lawyer jumps up. . . . ''Your Honour, I Object———''

The Judge waves his hand. ''I warn you the Court cannot go behind the testimony of the mother in such a case. . . .''

By this time everybody is laughing, so that they do not hear what the lawyer says. Shuler is trying to get out of the side door, and the Judge is shaking hands with Susie.

''You tell Shuler,'' she says, ''if he wants people to think hees the father of thees children he better giff me a writing. Then maybe I think so myself.''

''I *will*,'' said the Judge, and maybe two, three days after that he takes Shuler out to the ranch and makes the marriage writing. Then all the children come around Susie and say, ''Now, Mother, you will have to wear a hat.'' Susie, she says, ''Go, children, and ask your father.'' But it is not known to the Papagoes what happened after that.

(1925)

From

NINTH AVENUE
by Maxwell Bodenheim

They were silent for a while, reveling in the unexpected, warm nearness to each other and feeling a giddy swirl of revived faiths and hopes. Their first little rush of reassuring words had aroused all of the deferred plans and buried braveries within them, but the awakening was not yet articulate enough for spoken syllables. They longed to embrace each other with an open intensity, and the effort needed to control this desire also served to prevent them from talking. Then Blanche remembered a fear which she had experienced during the previous week.

"Eric, did you ever see a play called 'God's People Got Wings?' " she asked.

"No, but I've heard of it."

"Well, it certainly made me shiver," she said. "One of Oppendorf's friends took me down to see it, and I've never had such a dreadful time in my life. It was all about a colored man marrying a white girl. It ended up with the colored boy killing his wife and then committing suicide—think of it!—and I was just gripping the sides of my seat all the time."

"Were you afraid it might have some connection with us?" he asked, gravely.

"No, no, of course not," she answered, as she clutched his hand. "D'you think I'm silly enough to let some prejudiced man tell me whether I'm going to be happy or not? No, Eric, it wasn't that, but I did feel angry and upset, and, we-ell . . . it set me to wondering. Why do all these writers now always insist that colored and white people weren't meant to get along with each other—or, why do they?"

"Mister Shakespeare revived it with his Othello and it's been going strong ever since," he replied, with a contention of forlorn and contemptuous inflections in his voice. "It can't be argued about. Most of them are perfectly sincere, and they really believe that people of different races always hate and fear each other at the bottom. You could get yourself blue in the face telling them exceptional men and women aren't included in this rule, but it wouldn't make the slightest impression."

"But why are they so stubborn about it?" she asked.

"That's easy," he answered, wearily. "They don't want to admit that there's the smallest possibility of the races ever coming together. It's a deep, blind pride, and they simply can't get rid of it. They're hardly ever conscious of it, Blanche, but it's there just the same. Why, even Vanderin isn't free from it. Take that latest of his—Black Paradise—and what do you find? What? He's just a bystander trying to be indulgent and sympathetic. It's the old story. Negroes are primitive and sa-avage at the bottom, and white people aren't . . . white people like your brother, I suppose."

He had been unable to restrain the sarcasm of his last words because his wounds had cried out for a childish relief. She had listened to him with a fascination that was near to worship . . . what a dear, wise, eloquent boy he was! When he talked, even the ghosts of her former specters fled from her heart. Let the world call him a nigger—what did it matter? They didn't care whether he was beautiful or not—all they wanted was to "keep him in his place," these intel-li-gent people, just because he happened to have a mixture of blood within him.

"Oh, let's not talk any more about it," she said. "We're in love with each other, Eric, boysie, and . . . 'f other people don't like it they can stand on their heads, for all I care!"

He fondled her shoulder, gratefully, and an uproar was in his heart.

"Blanche, what's the use of waiting and waiting?" he asked at last. "We're only suffering and denying ourselves when there's no reason for it. Let's run off to-morrow and marry each other. If we wait too long we'll feel too helpless about it—it'll grow to be a habit with us. I can't exist any longer without you, Blanche—it's just impossible . . . impossible. I'll draw out the thousand I have in the bank and we'll hop a train for Chicago to-morrow afternoon. Don't you see it's useless to keep postponing it, Blanche?"

His eagerness, and her longing for him, expelled the last vestige of her fears.

"Yes, dear, I'll go with you to-morrow," she said.

Their hands gripped each other with the power of iron bands, and they stared hopefully out across the greenish-gray swells of water.

(1926)

From

SHOW BOAT
by Edna Ferber

A strange and terrible thing was happening. Julie had sprung from her bed. In her white nightgown and her wrapper, her long black hair all tumbled and wild about her face, a stricken and hunted thing, she clung to Steve, and he to her. There came a pounding at the door that led into the show-boat auditorium from the fore deck. Steve's eyes seemed suddenly to sink far back in his head. His cheek-bones showed gaunt and sharp as Julie's own. His jaw was set so that a livid ridge stood out on either side like bars of white-hot steel. He loosened Julie's hold almost roughly. From his pocket he whipped a great clasp-knife and opened its flashing blade. Julie did not scream, but the other women did, shriek on shriek. Captain Andy sprang for him, a mouse attacking a mastodon. Steve shook him off with a fling of his powerful shoulders.

"I'm not going to hurt her, you fool. Leave me be. I know what I'm doing." The pounding came again, louder and more insistent. "Somebody go down and let him in—but keep him there a minute."

No one stirred. The pounding ceased. The doors opened. The boots of Ike Keener, the sheriff, clattered down the aisle of the *Cotton Blossom.*

"Stop those women screeching," Steve shouted. Then, to Julie, "It won't hurt much, darling." With incredible swiftness he seized Julie's hand in his left one and ran the keen glittering blade of his knife firmly across the tip of her forefinger. A scarlet line followed it. He bent his blond head, pressed his lips to the wound, sucked it greedily. With a little moan Julie fell back on the bed. Steve snapped the blade into its socket, thrust the knife into his pocket. The boots of Sheriff Ike Keener were clattering across the stage now. The white faces clustered in the doorway—the stricken, bewildered, horrified faces—turned from the two within the room to the one approaching it. They made way for this one silently. Even Parthy was dumb. Magnolia clung to her, wide-eyed, uncomprehending, sensing tragedy though she had never before encountered it.

The lapel of his coat flung back, Ike Keener confronted the little cowed group on the stage. A star shone on his left breast. The scene was like a rehearsal of a *Cotton Blossom* thriller.

"Who's captain of this here boat?"

Andy, his fingers clutching his whiskers, stepped forward. "I am. What's wanted with him? Hawks is my name—Captain Andy Hawks, twenty years on the rivers."

He looked the sheriff of melodrama, did Ike Keener—boots, black moustaches, wide-brimmed black hat, flowing tie, high boots, and all. Steve himself, made up for the part, couldn't have done it better. "Well, Cap, kind of unpleasant, but I understand there's a miscegenation case on board."

"What?" whispered Magnolia. "What's that? What does he mean, Mom?"

"Hush!" hissed Parthy, and jerked the child's arm.

"How's that?" asked Andy, but he knew.

"Miscegenation. Case of a Negro woman married to a white man. Criminal offense in this state, as you well know."

"No such thing," shouted Andy. "No such thing on board this boat."

Sheriff Ike Keener produced a piece of paper. "Name of the white man is Steve Baker. Name of the negress"—he squinted again at the slip of paper—"name of the negress is Julie Dozier." He looked around at the group. "Which one's them?"

"Oh, my God!" screamed Elly. "Oh, my God! Oh, my God!"

"Shut up," said Schultzy, roughly.

Steve stepped to the window and threw up the shade, letting the morning light into the crowded disorderly little cubicle. On the bed lay Julie, her eyes enormous in her sallow pinched face.

"I'm Steve Baker. This is my wife."

Sheriff Ike Keener tucked the paper in his pocket. "You two better dress and come along with me."

Julie stood up. She looked an old woman. The marmoset whimpered and whined in his fur nest. She put out a hand, automatically, and plucked it from the muff and held it in the warm hollow of her breast. Her great black eyes stared at the sheriff like the wide-open unseeing eyes of a sleep walker.

Steve Baker grinned—rather, his lips drew back from his teeth in a horrid semblance of mirth. He threw a jovial arm about Julie's shrinking shoulder. For once she had no need to coach him in his part. He looked Ike Keener in the eye. "You wouldn't call a man a white man that's got Negro blood in him, would you?"

"No, I wouldn't; not in Mississippi. One drop of nigger blood makes you a nigger in these parts."

"Well, I got more than a drop of—nigger blood in me, and that's a fact. You can't make miscegenation out of that."

"You ready to swear to that in a court of law?"

"I'll swear to it any place. I'll swear it now." Steve took a step forward, one hand outstretched. "I'll do more than that. Look at all these folks here. There ain't one of them but can swear I got Negro blood in me this minute. That's how white I am."

Sheriff Ike Keener swept the crowd with his eye. Perhaps what he saw in their faces failed to convince him. "Well, I seen fairer men than you was niggers. Still, you better tell that——"

Mild, benevolent, patriarchal, the figure of old Windy stepped out from among the rest. "Guess you've known me, Ike, better part of twenty-five years. I was keelboatin' time you was runnin' around, a barefoot on the landin'. Now I'm tellin' you—me, Windy McKlain—that that white man there's got nigger blood in him. I'll take my oath to that."

(1926)

BLACK BOY
by Kay Boyle

At that time, it was the forsaken part, it was the other end of the city, and on early spring mornings there was no one about. By soft words, you could woo the horse into the foam, and ride her with the sea knee-deep around her. The waves came in and out there, as indolent as ladies, gathered up their skirts in their hands and, with a murmur, came tiptoeing in across the velvet sand.

The wooden promenade was high there, and when the wind was up the water came running under it like wild. On such days, you had to content yourself with riding the horse over the deep white drifts of dry sand on the other side of the walks; the horse's hoofs here made no sound and the sparks of sand stung your face in fury. It had no body to it, like the mile or two of sand packed hard that you could open out on once the tide was down.

My little grandfather, Puss, was alive then, with his delicate gait and ankles, and his belly pouting in his dove-gray clothes. When he saw from the window that the tide was sidling out, he put on his pearl fedora and came stepping down the street. For a minute, he put one foot on the sand, but he was not at ease there. On the boardwalk over our heads was some other kind of life in progress. If you looked up, you could see it in motion through the cracks in the timber: rolling chairs, and women in high heels proceeding, if the weather were fair.

"You know," my grandfather said, "I think I might like to have a look at a shop or two along the boardwalk." Or: "I suppose you don't feel like leaving the beach for a minute," or: "If you would go with me, we might take a chair together, and look at the hats and the dresses and roll along in the sun."

He was alive then, taking his pick of the broad easy chairs and the black boys.

"There's a nice skinny boy," he'd say. "He looks as though he might put some action into it. Here you are, sonny. Push me and the little girl down to the Million Dollar Pier and back."

The cushions were red velvet with a sheen of dew over them. And Puss settled back on them and took my hand in his. In his mind there was no hesitation about whether he would look at the shops on one side, or out on the vacant side where there was nothing shining but the sea.

"What's your name, Charlie?" Puss would say without turning his head to the black boy pushing the chair behind our shoulders.

"Charlie's my name, sir," he'd answer with his face dripping down like tar in the sun.

"What's your name, sonny?" Puss would say another time, and the black boy answered:

"Sonny's my name, sir."

"What's your name, Big Boy?"

"Big Boy's my name."

He never wore a smile on his face, the black boy. He was thin as a shadow but darker, and he was pushing and sweating, getting the chair down to the Million Dollar Pier and back again, in and out through the people. If you turned toward the sea for a minute, you could see his face out of the corner of your eye, hanging black as a bat's wing, nodding and nodding like a dark heavy flower.

But in the early morning, he was the only one who came down onto the sand and sat under the beams of the boardwalk, sitting idle there with a languor fallen on every limb. He had long bones. He sat idle there, with his clothes shrunk up from his wrists and his ankles, with his legs drawn up, looking out at the sea.

"I might be a king if I wanted to be," was what he said to me.

Maybe I was twelve years old, or maybe I was ten when we used to sit eating dog biscuits together. Sometimes when you broke them in two, a worm fell out and the black boy lifted his sharp finger and flecked it carelessly from off his knee.

"I seen kings," he said, "with a kind of cloth over they heads, and kind of jewels-like around here and here. They weren't any blacker than me, if as black," he said. "I could be almost anything I made up my mind to be."

"King Nebuchadnezzar," I said. "He wasn't a white man."

The wind was off the ocean and was filled with alien smells. It was early in the day, and no human sign was given. Overhead were the green beams of the boardwalk and no wheel or step to sound it.

"If I was a king," said the black boy with his biscuit in his fingers, "I wouldn't put much stock in hanging around here."

Great crystal jelly beasts were quivering in a hundred different colors on the wastes of sand around us. The dogs came, jumping them, and when they saw me still sitting still, they wheeled like gulls and sped back to the sea.

"I'd be traveling around," he said, "here and there. Now here, now there. I'd change most of my habits."

His hair grew all over the top of his head in tight dry rosettes. His neck was longer and more shapely than a white man's neck, and his fingers ran in and out of the sand like the blue feet of a bird.

"I wouldn't have much to do with pushing chairs around under them circumstances," he said. "I might even give up sleeping out here on the sand."

Or if you came out when it was starlight, you could see him sitting there in the clear white darkness. I could go and come as I liked, for whenever I went out the door, I had the dogs shouldering behind me. At night, they shook the taste of the house out of their coats and came down across the sand. There he was, with his knees up, sitting idle.

"They used to be all kinds of animals come down here to drink in the dark," he said. "They was a kind of a mirage came along and gave that impression. I seen tigers, lions, lambs, deer; I seen ostriches drinking down there side by side with each other. They's the Northern Lights gets crossed some way and switches the wrong picture down."

It may be that the coast has changed there, for even then it was changing. The lighthouse that had once stood far out on the white rocks near the outlet was standing then like a lighted torch in the heart of the town. And the deep currents of the sea may have altered so that the clearest water runs in another direction, and houses may have been built down as far as where the brink used to be. But the brink was so perilous then that every word the black boy spoke seemed to fall into a cavern of beauty.

"I seen camels; I seen zebras," he said, "I might have caught any one of them if I'd felt inclined."

The street was so still and wide then that when Puss stepped out of the house, I could hear him clearing his throat of the sharp salty air. He had no intention of soiling the soles of his boots, but he came down the street to find me.

"If you feel like going with me," he said, "we'll take a chair and see the fifty-seven varieties changing on the electric sign."

And then he saw the black boy sitting quiet. His voice drew up short on his tongue and he touched his white mustache.

"I shouldn't think it a good idea," he said, and he put his arm through my arm. "I saw another little oak not three inches high in the Jap's window yesterday. We might roll down the boardwalk and have a look at it. You know," said Puss, and he put his kid gloves carefully on his fingers, "that black boy might do you some kind of harm."

"What kind of harm could he do me?" I said.

"Well," said Puss with the garlands of lights hanging around him, "he might steal some money from you. He might knock you down and take your money away."

"How could he do that?" I said. "We just sit and talk there." Puss looked at me sharply.

"What do you find to sit and talk about?" he said.

"I don't know," I said. "I don't remember. It doesn't sound like much to tell it."

The burden of his words was lying there on my heart when I woke up in the morning. I went out by myself to the stable and led the horse to the door and put the saddle on her. If Puss were ill at ease for a day or two, he could look out the window in peace and see me riding high and mighty away. The day after tomorrow, I thought, or the next day, I'll sit down on the beach again and talk to the black boy. But when I rode out, I saw him seated idle there, under the boardwalk, heedless, looking away to the cool wide sea. He had been eating peanuts and the shells lay all around him. The dogs came running at the horse's heels, nipping the foam that lay along the tide.

The horse was as shy as a bird that morning, and when I drew her up beside the black boy, she tossed her head on high. Her mane went back and forth, from one side to the other, and a flight of joy in her limbs sent her forelegs like rockets into the air. The black boy stood up from the cold smooth sand, unsmiling, but a spark of wonder shone in his marble eyes. He put out his arm in the short tight sleeve of his coat and stroked her shivering shoulder.

"I was going to be a jockey once," he said, "but I changed my mind."

I slid down on one side while he climbed up the other.

"I don't know as I can ride him right," he said as I held her head. "The kind of saddle you have, it gives you nothing to grip your heels around. I ride them with their bare skin."

The black boy settled himself on the leather and put his feet in the stirrups. He was quiet and quick with delight, but he had no thought of smiling as he took the reins in his hands.

I stood on the beach with the dogs beside me, looking after the horse as she ambled down to the water. The black boy rode easily and straight, letting the horse stretch out and sneeze and canter. When they reached the jetty, he turned her casually and brought her loping back.

"Some folks licks hell out of their horses," he said. "I'd never raise a hand to one, unless he was to bite me or do something I didn't care for."

He sat in the saddle at ease, as though in a rocker, stroking her shoulder with his hand spread open, and turning in the stirrups to smooth her shining flank.

"Jockeys make a pile of money," I said.

"I wouldn't care for the life they have," said the black boy. "They have to watch their diet so careful."

His fingers ran delicately through her hair and laid her mane back on her neck.

When I was up on the horse again, I turned her toward the boardwalk.

"I'm going to take her over the jetty," I said. "You'll see how she clears it. I'll take her up under the boardwalk to give her a good start."

I struck her shoulder with the end of my crop, and she started toward the tough black beams. She was under it, galloping, when the dogs came down the beach like mad. They had chased a cat out of cover and were after it, screaming as they ran, with a wing of sand blowing wide behind them, and when the horse saw them under her legs, she jumped sidewise in sprightliness and terror and flung herself against an iron arch.

For a long time I heard nothing at all in my head except the melody of someone crying, whether it was my dead mother holding me in comfort, or the soft wind grieving over me where I had fallen. I lay on the sand asleep; I could feel it running with my tears through my fingers. I was rocked in a cradle of love, cradled and rocked in sorrow.

"Oh, my little lamb, my little lamb pie!" Oh, sorrow, sorrow, wailed the wind, or the tide, or my own kin about me. "Oh, lamb, oh, lamb!"

I could feel the long swift fingers of love untying the terrible knot of pain that bound my head. And I put my arms around him and lay close to his heart in comfort.

Puss was alive then, and when he met the black boy carrying me up to the house, he struck him square across the mouth.

(1932)

From

FATHERS AND SONS
by Ernest Hemingway

Then afterwards they sat, the three of them, listening for a black squirrel that was in the top branches where they could not see him. They were waiting for him to bark again because when he barked he would jerk his tail and Nick would shoot where he saw any movement. His father gave him only three cartridges a day to hunt with and he had a single-barrel twenty-gauge shotgun with a very long barrel.

"Son of a bitch never move," Billy said.

"You shoot, Nickie. Scare him. We see him jump. Shoot him again," Trudy said. It was a long speech for her.

"I've only got two shells," Nick said.

"Son of a bitch," said Billy.

They sat against the tree and were quiet. Nick was feeling hollow and happy.

"Eddie says he going to come some night sleep in bed with you sister Dorothy."

"What?"

"He said."

Trudy nodded.

"That's all he want do," she said. Eddie was their older half-brother. He was seventeen.

"If Eddie Gilby ever comes at night and even speaks to Dorothy you know what I'd do to him? I'd kill him like this." Nick cocked the gun and hardly taking aim pulled the trigger, blowing a hole as big as your hand in the head or belly of that half-breed bastard Eddie Gilby. "Like that. I'd kill him like that."

"He better not come then," Trudy said. She put her hand in Nick's pocket.

"He better watch out plenty," said Billy.

"He's big bluff," Trudy was exploring with her hand in Nick's pocket. "But don't you kill him. You get plenty trouble."

"I'd kill him like that," Nick said. Eddie Gilby lay on the ground with all his chest shot away. Nick put his foot on him proudly.

"I'd scalp him," he said happily.

"No," said Trudy. "That's dirty."

"I'd scalp him and send it to his mother."

"His mother dead," Trudy said. "Don't you kill him, Nickie. Don't you kill him for me."

"After I scalped him I'd throw him to the dogs."

Billy was very depressed. "He better watch out," he said gloomily.

"They'd tear him to pieces," Nick said, pleased with the picture. Then, having scalped that half-breed renegade and standing, watching the dogs tear him, his face unchanging, he fell backward against the tree, held tight around the neck, Trudy holding, choking him, and crying, "No kill him! No kill him! No kill him! No. No. No. Nickie. Nickie. Nickie!"

"What's the matter with you?"

"No kill him."

"I got to kill him."

"He just a big bluff."

"All right," Nickie said. "I won't kill him unless he comes around the house. Let go of me."

"That's good," Trudy said. "You want to do anything now? I feel good now."

"If Billy goes away." Nick had killed Eddie Gilby, then pardoned him his life, and he was a man now.

"You go, Billy. You hang around all the time. Go on."

"Son a bitch," Billy said. "I get tired this. What we come? Hunt or what?"

"You can take the gun. There's one shell."

"All right. I get a big black one all right."

"I'll holler," Nick said.

Then, later, it was a long time after and Billy was still away.

"You think we make a baby?" Trudy folded her brown legs together happily and rubbed against him. Something inside Nick had gone a long way away.

"I don't think so," he said.

"Make plenty baby what the hell."

They heard Billy shoot.

"I wonder if he got one."

"Don't care," said Trudy.

Billy came through the trees. He had the gun over his shoulder and he held a black squirrel by the front paws.

"Look," he said "Bigger than a cat. You all through?"

"Where'd you get him?"

"Over there. Saw him jump first."

"Got to go home," Nick said.

"No," said Trudy.

"I got to get there for supper."

"All right."

"Want to hunt tomorrow?"

"All right."

"You can have the squirrel."

"All right."

"Come out after supper?"

"No."

"How you feel?"

"Good."

"All right."

"Give me kiss on the face," said Trudy.

(1933)

From

DRUMS ALONG THE MOHAWK
by Walter D. Edmonds

In February there was some talk that the Massachusetts garrisons of Dayton and Herkimer were returning to their homes, having completed their service. It was said that they would leave in March. No provision was made for their replacement. Demooth and Bellinger had been down to Colonel Klock in Palatine to organize a protest. All three men were trying to have Fort Stanwix abandoned and the German Flats forts strengthened. But Congress would not listen to their arguments. Congress held that Stanwix was the strategic defense of the valley. It was intimated that they might send some troops to Cherry Valley, but that was all.

Joe shook his head about it.

"They might just as well have nobody at all. You wait till the snow leaves. You'll see."

"See what?" asked Gil.

Joe grunted. "Indians."

Adam Helmer said skeptically:—

"They got their medicine up there at Oriskany."

"That's the trouble. If they hadn't been whipped so bad, they might wait to come along with the next army. But the way it is they won't wait. They'll want to get their face back. They'll be after scalps. They won't care whose. They'll feel they've got to. Hell, boy, I've lived with the Senecas, and I know."

"You lived with them, Joe?" asked Gil.

The gangling trapper stretched himself on the hearth to kick over a log with his heel. The fire blazed upward, pouring a ruddy light across his sweating body. The room reeked of the men's smell, tobacco, and rum. It was stifling hot, making them all drowsy, and Joe's voice was pitched low.

"Oh yes, when I was young, like you lads. I used to trap up the Chinisee. I got along real good with the Senecas. I had a wife out there. She was a real nice girl, too." He stirred himself lazily. "They ain't as light as the Mohawk girls, but they're thinner."

He drank a little rum and turned his eyes thoughtfully on Gil and Adam. Outside the wind had died down with the coming of darkness, and the burning of the fire was even and fierce.

"I never knew you was married, Joe."

"Sure," said Joe. "I stayed there with her four years, without ever coming out." His reminiscent grin made his face unbelievably homely. "My God, that girl was set on me!"

Adam was crouched in front of Joe. The firelight made his big face scarlet and threw lights in his long yellow hair. He held his glass in both hands, his hands passed over his knees. The shadow of his broad shoulders filled all the opposite wall. Now he turned a facetious eye on Gil. Gil grinned.

But Joe knew what was going on in their minds. He said seriously, "You ought to have been along with me, Adam. You'd have liked it. Gil, now, he's a settled kind of man." He drew his breath, slowly, and belched. "Along in those days, a white man was just about the finest thing that could happen to an Indian girl. It made her important in her town. When I first went out there, the Indians treated any white man like he was one of their sachems. Like a big bug, see, come visiting. They gave him a house in the town and then they sent in all the best-looking girls so he could take his pick and feel comfortable while he was staying. It was a good idea. Only it wasn't so easy making your pick. Some of them girls was pretty nice." He poured himself another drink and stirred the molasses in with his finger. "Some trappers got the idea of staying and then going off for a day and coming back and beginning over. There wasn't any harm in that. It don't matter what a girl did till she got married, see? But it didn't happen that way to me. I got to the Chinisee Castle, the one they call Little Beard's town now, and they sent in eighteen handpicked ones. But right away I knew the one I wanted. I knew she'd suit me fine. I was young-and-coming, see, and I suited her too. Don't laugh, you timber beast. It's truth. She stood with the rest of them looking on the ground, the way they all done, but as soon as she made out all the rest was looking down, she just took one look at me and it fixed me. Boy, she could throw her eyes at you!"

"I believe you," Adam said.

"Go to hell. I reached out at her and I said, 'You, you me fine!' I hadn't learned the language then. But she understood all right. The others went out, leaving just her. And as soon as they'd gone she just looked up at me, kind of scared and shy. I was pretty young, I guess, but it made me feel big.

"She didn't come only to my shoulder and she had braids reaching down to the middle of her thighs. She wasn't only medium dark, too, and she was pretty in her best clothes. She had on a kind of red overdress, what they call Ah-de-a-da-we-sa, and a blue skirt with beadwork on it. She was a great hand with beadwork. It was what made her come high in marriage. And her pant things was doeskin with more beading on the foot."

"She come high?"

"I didn't know how I could pay her Ma," Joe said seriously. "I didn't have only a bare stake. No beads for trading. I needed everything I had, see? The girl's Ma was something big. One of the chief's lines. They keep their family on the female side. The way the girls act up they've got to if they're going to keep the children anywhere near straight. . . . But I've got away from me and the girl. Soon as we was alone she signed for me to set down by the fire and take off my shirt. She took a bone comb out of her belt and started combing my hair. She greased it and picked out the ticks and took pains where it was curled. She liked them curls. I had fine curly hair, you know."

Even though Joe looked so serious, they had to laugh. They stared at the shiny expanses of bare scalp between the remnants of his past beauty. Joe rolled over and turned his back and lifted his shirt to let the heat strike against the rum in his belly.

"Lord," he said over his shoulder. "When I went to bed with her it was pretty dark. But I didn't have to see her to know she was good-looking. I told her in the morning I'd like to marry her."

"I thought you said you couldn't speak the language."

Joe looked hurt. "You don't have to when you've done that to a girl. I just said so, and she caught on all right. She colored some. Most Indians don't show color, but that was one of the things about her. That and teaching her to kiss. The way she caught on. You can fool around with all the heifers between here and Albany if you want to, but you won't know just what teaching a wild Indian to kiss is like. Well, she said she'd like to fine, so I said fine, and she said what did I have to buy her with? Well, I opened my pack, and she went through it like a dog after a rabbit. She shook her head. She made it plain there wasn't anything good enough. I felt bad, and she looked sorry. Then she clapped her hands."

"Yes," said Adam, "she clapped her hands."

"God damn you, Adam. She did." Joe began to look embarrassed. "I'd been getting dressed and she come up to me and put her hands on my waist and made the motions I was to take my drawers off. I had red flannel drawers."

The two young men guffawed.

"Honest to God," said Joe. "I told the chief how I felt, and I got him to take them round to the old lady and she went near crazy over them. Later I heard she'd gone right in and tried them on. They was some tight, but they stretched enough. Though she had to rig a kind of tassel in front when she wore them in the turtle dance. She made a little bark box for them and hung them over her bed. They were still in good shape four years later when the old lady led the Okewa for Lou."

"What's that, Joe?"

"It's the woman's all-night Dead Song."

"Your girl died?"

"Yes," said Joe. He blew smoke against the logs and watched the flame snatch it up the chimney. "After we got married, I and Lou went up the Chinisee. I built us a hunting cabin up there. It was good beaver country and a wonderful range for fisher. And she was a first-rate woman for a man. Knew how to take care of me. She was the only woman I ever had around that didn't get on a man's nerves. When I felt like laughing, she was ready to bust with it herself. Never saw anybody so always happy. She wouldn't call me Joe. Just Boleo, only she couldn't ever say the B. She called it Do-le-o." Joe's face was deeply concentrated. "And when the trap lines weren't bearing so good, she didn't make a lot of talk—what a white woman would call distracting you. She minded her business. I knew she was around, that's all. She was good to have around. And she never got lonesome. Seemed as if I was good enough for her. Of course we'd go down to the Castle every once or twice a year. I had to trade my fur pack, see? . . . It was a good life. And healthy. The way she kept me healthy. Used to make me hemlock tea to keep my skin open. Her cooking was Indian cooking, but she learned a few things, to please me. I told you she learned kissing. But it was a funny thing, she never got to be like a white woman. She was always shy about the way she acted with me. She wouldn't wash with me in the crick. Sometimes it got me mad. I never saw her naked in plain light. A bear kilt her while she was berrying." Joe drank and drew a breath. "The queer thing was we never had no children."

"What's queer about that?" Gil asked.

"Why, those girls could have children easy as letting go a crock of lard. John O'Beal now. He come out there and traded; he bought my furs. He married a girl too, and had a mess of children. One of them's got to be a chief. His name's Cornplanter."

"You said John O'Beal?" Adam asked.

"Sure, he was quite a lad, too. But he soured on it. He came back here and lives down the valley somewhere."

"Near Fort Plain?" suggested Adam.

"Sure, that's the man. I ain't seen him in some time."

Joe Boleo lay full length on his back, draining his glass.

Gil asked, "What did you say her name was, Joe?"

"Well, her Indian name was Gahano. Means something like Hanging Flower. But I told you I called her Lou. You ought to have been out there in those days, Adam. You'd have got along good. But now they ain't so friendly about white men. You can marry all right. But they don't trot the girls out for you any more. I quit myself when Lou died. . . .

"But that was the way for a trapper to live. All you had to do was run your lines, and you had a nice cabin to come back to, and your dinner cooked, and a woman to mend your clothes. You just lay around, and got up warm in the morning. It didn't cost you a cent." He looked at them again. "Most trappers came home in summer. They cleared out with the furs and spent their money, and the woman took care of herself while they was gone. Some kept two families going. But those buffaloes never spent the summer the way I did. We'd take trips, her and me, and lay around fishing. We'd go off where there wasn't anybody, not even the tracks of anybody but ourselves, for three months. We'd build a summer shanty and she'd plant corn. Yes, sir. You'd just lay around listening to a big fish jump and wondering if it was worth the bother putting the worm in the water. Lou worked all the time we was on our vacation, readying hides and putting up quitcheraw against the winter. I whittled her a little press for making the cakes in, which tickled her a lot. And then she'd go berrying to make pemmican. That was when the bear got at her. An old she-one with a couple of cubs. I spent a while tracking them and I killed the lot—'' Joe paused and spat. ''But, hell,'' he went on, ''that's not what I set out to tell you. Indians ain't no good. This country would be a whole lot better off without any Indians. We'd be better off right now, I tell you. And I wouldn't be setting here listening to that drip off the roof.''

Adam Helmer stirred himself. Adam had been wishing he had been born in a good time of civilization so he could have gone out to the Indian country. His full lips were compressed and wet just thinking of it. A little lithe hard girl like Joe's Lou, right now, would suit him fine. ''Drip?'' he asked.

''Yes,'' said Joe with scorn. ''Drip. The thaw's commencing.''

Gil got to his feet. He went to the door of the cabin, opened it, and stood there, leaning out.

The wind had turned to the south. He felt it damp against his face; he could feel it even with the outrush of overheated air from the kitchen.

''You're right, Joe,'' he said over his shoulder. ''It's the thaw beginning. Sugaring ought to start early this year.''

''Shut that door!'' yelled Joe. ''Do you want to freeze us?''

(1936)

From

KITTY FOYLE
by Christopher Morley

I hadn't had a real holiday for about two years when Delphine made me take that trip to Bermuda. I didn't really know where the place was except that we named a skin lotion after it and the Main Line used to go there for Easter. This was August however so everything was pretty folksy, Bermuda had just been discovered as the stenographer's vacation. Delphine bought my ticket and saw me off, when she looked the crowd over she said ''Keety, what you better drink this trip is Bronx cocktail.'' Delphine's always a bit snobbish, but if a woman isn't a snob of some kind she's probably short on a gland. Anyway she had me fixed up in a deck cabin and private bath and a chaise lounge reserved for me. I was feeling rotten, one of those heavy summer colds, and it was hot humid weather.

It wasn't Bronx cocktail, it was Planters Punch. That was new to me then like lots of other things. I didn't even know Bermuda was British, I supposed in a sort of way it was part of Florida. As a matter of fact if you scummed off the tourists it acted a good deal like the cricket club wing of Philadelphia. I recognized the tourist bunch all right because I'd seen them stripped for action in the Catskills. The girls wore shorts up to the timber line and by the time they hit Hamilton they were as burned as grilled chickenskin. Not even our Caribbean Cream could take care of exposure like that. It was a shock to them when they landed, they found they had to get the shorts down to the knee or else really wear something. Bermuda didn't seem the least bit curious about the Upper West Side pelvis. They consoled themselves buying sun helmets.

Delphine knows all the ropes aboard shipping, she must have given the deck steward some big sweetening because while I was flopped out in my chair he came round to know what he could do for me. "I can hear all the lunch bells ringing," I said, "I guess I ought to go down and eat." The steward explained those weren't lunch gongs just the bellboys. I didn't know what they would be doing out in the water, unless warning people away from Staten Island, but I was too limp to argue. He said I could take my lunch right there in the chair. I said I would be more conscientious for my first sea voyage, I better go downstairs and eat a square meal, "feed a cold and starve a fever." Then the man in the next chair pipes up. I'd sort of half way noticed him because he was watching things as if he was amused. He was Jewish so I figured he'd probably been cruising before. "You misunderstand that," he says. "It means *if* you feed a cold you'll have to starve a fever later. Subsequently. With a cold like you got it I'm prescribing Planters Punch, maybe some jelly consommé and toast Melba."

The last thing I felt like it was starting conversations, but the steward thinks that's a good idea and brings it to me on a tray. And Dr Marcus Eisen, that being who it was in person, didn't make any attempt to carry through. He went off downstairs and got his own lunch and when he came up again I was asleep. By evening I felt better and even got into the diner. I found him at the same table with me. I just supposed maybe the seating was arranged according as the chairs were on deck. Well of course when my wits got sorted out I realized he had fixed it with the maitre d'hotel.

It was fun to be talking to a man again, just socially. It's like a good highball after a long spell of soda fountain. He was smart enough to see I wasn't in a mood for any forward passes to be thrown at me. I guess he used me for his intellect stimulus and when he wanted chicken gumbo he'd go after some of the deck tennis gals in shorts. I figured I must be a pretty sour old spinster to accept the situation like that, but Gulf Stream air just makes you let things slide. It was hot as my old bedroom under the roof in Frankford, and everything was new to me, the funny smell of a ship and that sort of anxiety in your stomach and such blue water with big yellow sponges floating. I guess the sail was only two days but it certainly seems like longer.

Of course Wyn got me so conditioned about men's clothes that I hate to see them overdressed. Mark's striped pants, creased like a knife-edge, would blackball him at any cricket club, and those black and white yachting shoes with perforated breathing holes were definitely Hollywood. What put Big Casino on the outfit was a polo shirt wide open to the fur and a blue tweed coat with a handkerchief made of the same stuff as the shirt. That's pretty terrible, because a man ought to look like he's put together by accident, not added up on purpose. Poor old Mark, you could just see he'd been spending his Saturday afternoons figuring out this cruising kit. It looked like all that bearskin robe on his chest was sapping the energy from his scalp, which was getting a bit scarce already. Then you'd notice his hands and forget about the other foolishness. Massage and chiropractic I studied out in Chicago made me observant about hands. When I learned he was working in the Children's Hospital we had lots to talk about. He was curious what kind of line was I in and I wouldn't tell him. After a couple of Planters Punches some of his stories were a bit corny, but I'm not too easily frightened that way and a few of Parry Berwyn's old Racquet Club favorites were even-Steven with his. There was a good many ways Mark would look like the answer to a maiden's prayer, if you were that kind of a maiden. What interested me was how he knew his stuff about kids. On the voyage back, two weeks later, he was on the same ship again, it was end of August and we ran into one of those hurricanes. A little boy fell downstairs and broke his collarbone and Mark and I happened to be standing right there. The ship's doctor was busy with trouble, and Mark had the child bandaged up and comfortable before you'd know it. That made a big hit with me.

We were staying different places when we got to Bermuda, and I was having fun with another crowd so I didn't see much of him. I ran into him one day over at Elbow Beach, tanned as brown as coffee, with a bunch of the G-string girls. He took me dancing on the hotel terrace one night, he's a good dancer too though he was crowding a bit more than is comfortable in Bermuda August. There's a terrace right alongside the water and the colored boatmen drift their little sailing boats up to the edge like butterflies in the moonlight. We went for a sail in the harbor, but I had to explain to him that I starved one fever successfully and I had no intention to start up another. He was so good humored about it I was a bit piqued. Of course Mark, successful and bright the way he is, can always get as many of his own kind as he'd care to whistle at. I was someone outside his routine and I had him puzzled. They certainly do like to know all about everything, and he'd lead up questions to try to get me placed. The most I would tell him was I came from Philly, and he'd say Well, it's only two hours away. I think he believed I was some kind of a trained nurse that hadn't had the advantages of a New York or John Hopkins training. If he'd known I was getting ready to move into my own apartment on Riverside he'd have had the number out of me after two Aquarium cocktails. I had to smile when he told me how he'd moved his Mother down to West End Avenue, which is their idea of Seventh Heaven. I liked the way he talked about her. That Jewish feeling about old people is all to the good. They're wonderful to children and old folks, they can be pretty tough with everybody in between.

He told me a lot about infantile paralysis, how it usually moves from South to North and comes in a kind of annual epidemic, mostly late summer and early autumn. Matter of fact he said he was taking this vacation to get good and tough for an extra number of cases when he got back. That was why he always stopped after the third snort, and I liked that in him. With a crowd he could get to be a pain in the neck, he was so damn full of high spirits, but get him by himself talking about the children and you forget that alligator belt with his initials M.E. on a gold buckle. He had an inferiority hidden away inside him that must have took a hundred generations to build up, but there wasn't any inferiority when he picked up a microscope or a sick kid. We took a picnic to one of those islands where there's an old prison and the cockroaches spring at you as big as mice. Mark was so excited about them he couldn't believe it, he caught one in an olive bottle and took it back to his hotel and dissected it up with a razor blade to see what it was all about.

I knew in a way that I was going to see him again because he could teach me a lot, but I thought it was good for his soul to stall a while and I wouldn't give him any address. What's furthermore I thought likely I'd run into him somewhere along the kosher belt on upper Broadway. He gave me his card. "Any time you get paralyzed," he said, "call me up."

(1939)

From

HELEN, THY BEAUTY IS TO ME—
by John Fante

When love came to Julio Sal, he was not prepared. Julio Sal, Filipino boy, forty cents an hour, Tokyo Fish Company, Wilmington. Her name was Helen, she wore a smooth red dress and she worked at the Angels' Ballroom, in Los Angeles. Five feet, four inches was the height of Julio Sal, but when that Helen's golden head lay on his shoulder, strength and grandeur filled his body. A dream shaped itself in his Malay brain. She sensed it, too. She always sensed that sort of thing in the Filipino customers. A gallant flame possessed them, and they bought more tickets. The dances were ten cents apiece; she got half of it.

Towering over the golden hair, Julio Sal saw half a hundred of his countrymen gazing after him, watching the serpentine undulations beneath the red dress, watching the fast-diminishing roll of tickets in Helen's left hand. The dances were one minute long. Somewhere behind the four-piece colored band, a bell clanged the end of each number. Since ten o'clock Julio Sal had danced continuously.

Now it was almost midnight. Already he had spent twelve dollars. Forty cents remained in his pocket. It meant four more minutes with the golden hair, and it meant his fare back to the canneries.

The bell clanged, the dance ended, another dance began. In the best alligator style, Julio jittered the dream toward the glass ticket box. Her hand over his shoulder tore a stub from the string and dropped it into the slot.

"Only one left," the girl panted as Julio bounced her in the corner. It was her first word in an hour. Sweat oozed from the dark face of Julio Sal. Again he gazed across the floor at the group of his countrymen.

Ten of them strained against the railing, each clutching a fat roll of tickets, ready to rush upon the golden girl the moment Julio's last ticket disappeared inside the glass box. Despair clutched the heart of Julio Sal. Resolution showed in his brown eyes.

"I get some more," he said.

The bell clanged, the dance ended, another dance began. There was a smile on the girl's white, hot face as she dropped the last ticket into the slot. This time it was a waltz, a breathing spell. Julio Sal nodded to the ticket man, who made his way through the couples, coins jingling in his money apron. Dismay seeped into the faces of the Penoys pressed against the rail. Julio's fingers dug into his watch pocket. Surprise widened the blue eyes of Helen when she saw forty cents—nickel, dime and quarter—pinched between Julio Sal's thumb and forefinger.

"Four tickets," said Julio Sal.

The ticket vendor rolled a cigar through his teeth. "Only four?"

"Please."

The bell clanged, the dance ended, another dance began. Out of the corner of his eye Julio Sal saw the dismay leave the faces of his little brown brothers. Their smiles mocked him. They had waited so long; they would gladly wait another four dances. The bell clanged, the dance ended, another dance began; again the bell clanged.

"Helen," said Julio Sal. "Helen, I love you, Helen."

"That's nice," she said, because all the Filipinos loved Helen, because all the Filipinos managed to say it when they got down to their last two or three.

"I write you letter," said Julio Sal.

"Please do." Because she always said that; because letters meant that they would be coming back on payday. "Please write."

"You write me, too?"

But the bell clanged, the dance ended and he had no more tickets. She slipped from his arms. The wicker gate opened and he was lost in an avalanche of little brown men fighting for the golden girl. Smiling weakly, he stood at the rail and watched her settle her child's face against the chest of Johnny Dellarosa, label machine, Van Camp's, San Pedro. A wave of tenderness suffocated Julio Sal. A small white doll—that was his Helen. The blissful future revealed itself in a reverie that shut out the boogy-woogy and the clanging bell— she was frying his bacon and eggs in a blue-tinted kitchen like in the movie pitch, and he came grinning from the bedroom in a green robe with a yellow sash, like in the movie pitch. "Ah, Helen," he was saying to her, "you are most wonderful cook in whole California. Pretty soon we take boat back to Luzon to meet my mama and papa."

The reverie endured through twenty-five clangs of the bell before he remembered that his pockets were empty and that it was eighteen miles to Wilmington.

On his way out, buttoning his square-cut, shoulder-padded, tight overcoat, Julio Sal paused before a huge photograph of the Angels' Ballroom Staff; forty beautiful girls, forty. She was there, his Helen, her lovely face and slim-hipped figure third from the left, front row.

"Helen, Helen, I love you."

He descended the stairs to Main Street, saw the fog flowing north like a white river. Julio Sal, well-dressed Filipino boy—black serge suit, hand-tailored overcoat, black patent-leather shoes, snappy, short-brimmed hat. Breasting the white river, he walked south on Main Street. Eighteen miles to the harbor. Good. It had been worth while. He breathed fog and cigarette smoke and smiled for his love. Mama, this is Helen; papa, this is Helen, my wife. The dream held. He couldn't marry her in California. The law said no. They would go to Reno. Or Tijuana. Or Seattle. Work a while up north. Then home to the Philippines. Mama, this is Helen. Papa, this is Helen.

Eighteen miles to Wilmington.

He arrived at six o'clock, his patent-leather shoes in ruins. Behind the cannery, in the duplexes, the five Japanese families were already up, lights from their windows a dull gold in the deep fog.

He smelled the fertilizer vats, the tar, the oil, the copra, the bananas and oranges, the bilge, the old rope, the decaying anchovies, the lumber, the rubber, the salt—the vast bouquet of the harbor. This too, was part of the dream. While working here at this spot, I met my love—I, Julio Sal.

Like one barefoot, he walked down the long veranda of the flat, salt-blackened building. They were single apartments set like cell blocks—one door, one window; one door, one window. A board creaked beneath his step, a baby wakened and cried. Babies, ah, babies. A little girl, he hoped, with a face and eyes of Mama Helen.

He lived in the last apartment; he and Silvio Lazada, Pacito Celestino, Manuel Bartolome, Delfin Denisio, Vivente Macario, Johnny Andrino, and Fred Bunda—all young men who had come to America as boys in the late twenties.

They were asleep now, the cramped room reeking with the odor of fish, bodies, burned rice, and salt air. Bunda, Lazada and Celestino were in the wall bed; Andrino lay on the davenport; Bartolome, Macario and Denisio on the floor.

Good boys. Loyal countrymen; though he had been gone all night, none had taken his bed in the bathtub.

On tiptoe he made his way over the sleepers to the bathroom. Through the gray fog-swept light he saw that someone was in the bathtub after all. The sleeper lay deep in blankets, old linen and soiled clothing, his head under the water spouts, his feet on the tub incline. Julio Sal bent down and smiled; it was Antonio Repollo. He had not seen Antonio in two years, not since the Seattle and Alaska canneries. Julio Sal whistled with pleasure. Now his letter-writing problem was solved. Antonio Repollo was a graduate of the University of Washington; he could write beautiful letters. Antonio Repello was not only a university graduate, he also wrote poetry for El Grafico in Manila.

Julio Sal bent over and shook him awake.

"Antonio, my friend. Welcome."

Repollo turned over, a laundry bag in his arms.

"Antonio, is me, Julio Sal. I have girl."

"Is American?" asked Repollo.

"Is blonde," said Julio Sal. "Is wonderful."

"Is bad," said Antonio.

"No," said Julio Sal. "Is good, very good."

"Is very bad," said Repollo. "Is worst thing possible."

"No," said Julio Sal. "Is best thing possible."

He slipped into his greasy dungarees, found a clean shirt behind the kitchen door, and put that on, too. It was Vivente Macario's turn to cook breakfast. Since 1926, at the asparagus fields, the celery fields, the canneries from Alaska to San Diego, Vivente Macario always prepared the same breakfast when his turn came—warmed-over rice, three cans of sardines stolen from the cannery, a hunk of bread and tea. They sat around the knife-scarred breakfast nook and ate quietly over a table whose surface was a mass of initials and dates of the hundreds of Filipino cannery workers who had come and gone throughout the years.

His brown face glowing from cold water, Antonio Repollo came into the kitchen. The poet, the college man. He was here, in their house, and they were honored; had even provided him with a bathtub in which to sleep. They made a place for him at the table, watched his long beautiful fingers remove sardines from the can.

"Julio Sal," he said, "what is the name of the woman?"

"Is Helen."

"Helen? No more? No Anderson, no Smith, Brown?"

"No more. Helen, all the same. Helen."

"He has girl," explained Repollo. "Name of Helen. He wish to marry this girl. American girl."

"No good," said Fred Bunda.

"Crazy," said Delfin Denisio.

"Too much trouble"—Johnny Andrino.

"Helen?" Manuel Bartolome talking. "Is not same Helen for to work Angels' Ballroom, taxi dance?"

"Ya, ya," said Julio Sal. "She is him, all the same."

Bartolome sucked his big lips tight. "Is no good, this woman. Cannot be. For to marry, I try myself. She damn liar. You give money, she take. Give you nothing."

"No, no," smiled Julio Sal. "Is another Helen. This one, she is good. This one love. She like me. She say 'write letter.' This I am do tonight."

"Gnah," said Bartolome, coughing an evil memory from his mouth. "For why you believe that? Is applesauce. I am write letter, too—six times. She take my money, give nothing. She no love you, Julio Sal. She no marry Filipino. She take his money, but she no marry. Is not love. Is business."

The strong first of Julio Sal whacked the table. "I make her love me. You wait. You see. Pretty soon, three months, cannery close down. I have money. We go for to get married. Reno, Seattle."

"Is bad," said Pacito Celestino.

"Crazy," said Vivente Macario.

"Is terrible," said Delfin Denisio. "Is awful."

"Is love," said Julio Sal. "Is wonderful!"

(1941)

From

DELTA AUTUMN
by William Faulkner

He had been asleep. The lantern was lighted now. Outside in the darkness the oldest Negro, Isham, was beating a spoon against the bottom of a tin pan and crying, "Raise up and get yo foa clock coffy. Raise up and get yo foa clock coffy," and the tent was full of low talk and of men dressing, and Legate's voice, repeating: "Get out of here now and let Uncle Ike sleep. If you wake him up, he'll go out with us. And he ain't got any business in the woods this morning."

So he didn't move. He lay with his eyes closed, his breathing gentle and peaceful, and heard them one by one leave the tent. He listened to the breakfast sounds from the table beneath the tarpaulin and heard them depart—the horses, the dogs, the last voice until it died away and there was only the sounds of the Negroes clearing breakfast away. After a while he might possibly even hear the first faint clear cry of the first hound ring through the wet woods from where the buck had bedded, then he would go back to sleep again— The tent-flap swung in and fell. Something jarred sharply against the end of the cot and a hand grasped his knee through the blanket before he could open his eyes. It was Edmonds, carrying a shotgun in place of his rifle. He spoke in a harsh, rapid voice:

"Sorry to wake you. There will be a——"

"I was awake," McCaslin said. "Are you going to shoot that shotgun today?"

"You just told me last night you want meat," Edmonds said. "There will be a——"

"Since when did you start having trouble getting meat with your rifle?"

"All right," the other said, with that harsh, restrained, furious impatience. Then McCaslin saw in his hand a thick oblong: an envelope. "There will be a message here some time this morning, looking for me. Maybe it won't come. If it does, give the messenger this and tell h— say I said No."

"A what?" McCaslin said. "Tell who?" He half rose onto his elbow as Edmonds jerked the envelope onto the blanket, already turning toward the entrance, the envelope striking solid and heavy and without noise and already sliding from the bed until McCaslin caught it, divining by feel through the paper as instantaneously and conclusively as if he had opened the envelope and looked, the thick sheaf of banknotes. "Wait," he said. "Wait:"—more than the blood kinsman, more even than the senior in years, so that the other paused, the canvas lifted, looking back, and McCaslin saw that outside it was already day. "Tell her No," he said. "Tell her." They stared at one another—the old face, wan, sleep-raddled above the tumbled bed, the dark and sullen younger one at once furious and cold. "Will Legate was right. This is what you called coonhunting. And now this." He didn't raise the envelope. He made no motion, no gesture to indicate it. "What did you promise her that you haven't the courage to face her and retract?"

"Nothing!" the other said. "Nothing! This is all of it. Tell her I said No." He was gone. The tent flap lifted on an in-waft of faint light and the constant murmur of rain, and fell again, leaving the old man still half-raised onto one elbow, the envelope clutched in the other shaking hand. Afterward it seemed to him that he had begun to hear the approaching boat almost immediately, before the other could have got out of sight even. It seemed to him that there had been no interval whatever: the tent flap falling on the same out-waft of faint and rain-filled light like the suspiration and expiration of the same breath and then in the next second lifted again—the mounting snarl of the outboard engine, increasing, nearer and nearer and louder and louder then cut short off, ceasing with the absolute instantaneity of a blown-out candle, into the lap and plop of water under the bows as the skiff slid in to the bank, the youngest Negro, the youth, raising the tent flap beyond which for that instant he saw the boat—a small skiff with a Negro man sitting in the stern beside the upslanted motor—then the woman entering, in a man's hat and a man's slicker and rubber boots, carrying the blanket-swaddled bundle on one arm and holding the edge of the unbuttoned raincoat over it with the other hand: and bringing something else, something intangible, an effluvium which he knew he would recognize in a moment because Isham had already told him, warned him, by sending the young Negro to the tent to announce the visitor instead of coming himself, the flap falling at last on the young Negro and they were alone—the face indistinct and as yet only young and with dark eyes, queerly colorless but not ill and not that of a country woman despite the garments she wore, looking down at him where he sat upright on the cot now, clutching the envelope, the soiled undergarment bagging about him and the twisted blankets huddled about his hips.

"Is that his?" he cried. "Don't lie to me!"

"Yes," she said. "He's gone."

"Yes. He's gone. You won't jump him here. Not this time. I don't reckon even you expected that. He left you this. Here." He fumbled at the envelope. It was not to pick it up, because it was still in his hand; he had never put it down. It was as if he had to fumble somehow to co-ordinate physically his heretofore obedient hand with what his brain was commanding of it, as if he had never performed such an action before, extending the envelope at last, saying again, "Here. Take it. Take it:" until he became aware of her eyes, or not the eyes so much as the look, the regard fixed now on his face with that immersed contemplation, that bottomless and intent candor, of a child. If she had ever seen either the envelope or his movement to extend it, she did not show it.

"You're Uncle Isaac," she said.

"Yes," he said. "But never mind that. Here. Take it. He said to tell you No." She looked at the envelope, then she took it. It was sealed and bore no superscription. Nevertheless, even after she glanced at the front of it, he watched her hold it in the one free hand and tear the corner off with her teeth and manage to rip it open and tilt the neat sheaf of bound notes onto the blanket without even glancing at them and look into the empty envelope and take the edge between her teeth and tear it completely open before she crumpled and dropped it.

"That's just money," she said.

"What did you expect? What else did you expect? You have known him long enough or at least often enough to have got that child, and you don't know him any better than that?"

"Not very often. Not very long. Just that week here last fall, and in January he sent for me and we went west, to New Mexico. We were there six weeks, where I could at least sleep in the same apartment where I cooked for him and looked after his clothes——"

"But not marriage," he said. "Not marriage. He didn't promise you that. Don't lie to me. He didn't have to."

"No. He didn't have to. I didn't ask him to. I knew what I was doing. I knew that to begin with, long before honor, I imagine he called it, told him the time had come to tell me in so many words what his code, I suppose he would call it, would forbid him forever to do. And we agreed. Then we agreed again before he left New Mexico, to make sure. That that would be all of it. I believed him. No, I don't mean that; I mean I believed myself. I wasn't even listening to him any more by then because by that time it had been a long time since he had had anything else to tell me for me to have to hear. By then I wasn't even listening enough to ask him to please stop talking. I was listening to myself. And I believed it. I must have believed it. I don't see how I could have helped but believe it, because he was gone then as we had agreed and he didn't write as we had agreed, just the money came to the bank in Vicksburg in my name but coming from nobody as we had agreed. So I must have believed it. I even wrote him last month to make sure again and the letter came back unopened and I was sure. So I left the hospital and rented myself a room to live in until the deer season opened so I could make sure myself and I was waiting beside the road yesterday when your car passed and he saw me and so I was sure."

"Then what do you want?" he said. "What do you want? What do you expect?"

"Yes," she said. And while he glared at her, his white hair awry from the pillow and his eyes, lacking the spectacles to focus them, blurred and iris-less and apparently pupilless, he saw again that grave, intent, speculative and detached fixity like a child watching him. "His great great— Wait a minute— great great *great* grandfather was your grandfather. McCaslin. Only it got to be Edmonds. Only it got to be more than that. Your cousin McCaslin was there that day when your father and Uncle Buddy won Tennie from Mr. Beauchamp for the one that had no name but Terrel so you called him Tomey's Terrel, to marry. But after that it got to be Edmonds." She regarded him, almost peacefully, with that unwinking and heatless fixity—the dark, wide, bottomless eyes in the face's dead and toneless pallor which to the old man looked anything but dead, but young and incredibly and even ineradicably alive—as though she were not only not looking at anything, she was not even speaking to anyone but herself. "I would have made a man of him. He's not a man yet. You spoiled him. You, and Uncle Lucas and Aunt Mollie. But mostly you."

"Me?" he said. "Me?"

"Yes. When you gave to his grandfather that land which didn't belong to him, not even half of it, by will or even law."

"And never mind that too," he said. "Never mind that too. You," he said. "You sound like you have been to college even. You sound almost like a Northerner even, not like the draggle-tailed women of these Delta pecker-woods. Yet you meet a man on the street one afternoon just because a box of groceries happened to fall out of a boat. And a month later you go off with him and live with him until he got a child on you: and then, by your own statement, you sat there while he took his hat and said goodbye and walked out. Even a Delta peckerwood would look after even a draggle-tail better than that. Haven't you got any folks at all?"

"Yes," she said. "I was living with one of them. My aunt, in Vicksburg. I came to live with her two years ago when my father died; we lived in Indianapolis then. But I got a job, teaching school here in Aluschaskuna, because my aunt was a widow, with a big family, taking in washing to sup——"

"Took in what?" he said. "Took in washing?" He sprang, still seated even, flinging himself backward onto one arm, awry-haired, glaring. Now he understood what it was she had brought into the tent with her, what old Isham had already told him by sending the youth to bring her in to him—the pale lips, the skin pallid and dead-looking yet not ill, the dark and tragic and foreknowing eyes. *Maybe in a thousand or two thousand years in America,* he thought. *But not now! Not now!* He cried, not loud, in a voice of amazement, pity, and outrage: "You're a nigger!"

"Yes," she said. "James Beauchamp—you called him Tennie's Jim though he had a name—was my grandfather. I said you were Uncle Isaac."

"And he knows?"

"No," she said. "What good would that have done?"

"But you did," he cried. "But you did. Then what do you expect here?"

"Nothing."

"Then why did you come here? You said you were waiting in Aluschaskuna yesterday and he saw you. Why did you come this morning?"

"I'm going back North. Back home. My cousin brought me up the day before yesterday in his boat. He's going to take me on to Leland to get the train."

"Then go," he said. Then he cried again in that thin not loud and grieving voice: "Get out of here! I can do nothing for you! Can't nobody do nothing for you!" She moved; she was not looking at him again, toward the entrance. "Wait," he said. She paused again, obediently still, turning. He took up the sheaf of banknotes and laid it on the blanket at the foot of the cot and drew his hand back beneath the blanket. "There," he said.

Now she looked at the money, for the first time, one brief blank glance, then away again. "I don't need it. He gave me money last winter. Besides the money he sent to Vicksburg. Provided. Honor and code too. That was all arranged."

"Take it," he said. His voice began to rise again, but he stopped it. "Take it out of my tent." She came back to the cot and took up the money; whereupon once more he said, "Wait:" although she had not turned, still stooping, and he put out his hand. But, sitting, he could not complete the reach until she moved her hand, the single hand which held the money, until she touched it. He didn't grasp it, he merely touched it—the gnarled, bloodless, bone-dry old man's fingers touching for a second the smooth young flesh where the strong old blood ran after its long lost journey back to home. "Tennie's Jim," he said. "Tennie's Jim." He drew the hand back beneath the blanket again: he said harshly now: "It's a boy, I reckon. They usually are, except that one was its own mother too."

"Yes," she said. "It's a boy." She stood for a moment longer, looking at him. Just for an instant her free hand moved as though she were about to lift the edge of the raincoat away from the child's face. But she did not. She turned again when once more he said Wait and moved beneath the blanket.

"Turn your back," he said. "I am going to get up. I ain't got my pants on." Then he could not get up. He sat in the huddled blanket, shaking, while again she turned and looked down at him in dark interrogation. "There," he said harshly, in the thin and shaking old man's voice. "On the nail there. The tent-pole."

"What?" she said.

"The horn!" he said harshly. "The horn." She went and got it, thrust the money into the slicker's side pocket as if it were a rag, a soiled handkerchief, and lifted down the horn, the one which General Compson had left him in his will, covered with the unbroken skin from a buck's shank and bound with silver.

"What?" she said.

"It's his. Take it."

"Oh," she said. "Yes. Thank you."

"Yes," he said, harshly, rapidly, but not so harsh now and soon not harsh at all but just rapid, urgent, until he knew that his voice was running away with him and he had neither intended it nor could stop it: "That's right. Go back North. Marry: a man in your own race. That's the only salvation for you—for a while yet, maybe a long while yet. We will have to wait. Marry a black man. You are young, handsome, almost white; you could find a black man who would see in you what it was you saw in him, who would ask nothing of you and expect less and get even still less than that, if it's revenge you want. Then you will forget all this, forget it ever happened, that he ever existed—" until he could stop it at last and did, sitting there in his huddle of blankets during the instant when, without moving at all, she blazed silently down at him. Then that was gone too. She stood in the gleaming and still dripping slicker, looking quietly down at him from under the sodden hat.

"Old man," she said, "have you lived so long and forgotten so much that you don't remember anything you ever knew or felt or even heard about love?"

Then she was gone too. The waft of light and the murmur of the constant rain flowed into the tent and then out again as the flap fell. Lying back once more, trembling, panting, the blanket huddled to his chin and his hands crossed on his breast, he listened to the pop and snarl, the mounting then fading whine of the motor until it died away and once again the tent held only silence and the sound of rain. And cold too: he lay shaking faintly and steadily in it, rigid save for the shaking. This Delta, he thought: This Delta. *This land which man has deswamped and denuded and derivered in two generations so that white men can own plantations and commute every night to Memphis and black men own plantations and ride in Jim Crow cars to Chicago to live in millionaire's mansions on Lake Shore Drive; where white men rent farms and live like nig-*

gers and niggers crop on shares and live like animals; where cotton is planted and grows man-tall in the very cracks of the sidewalks, and usury and mort- gage and bankruptcy and measureless wealth, Chinese and African and Aryan and Jew, all breed and spawn together until no man has time to say which one is which nor cares. . . .

(1942)

From

THE DARK STAIN
by Benjamin Appel

He strode past his mother into the foyer and over to the telephone. He put the receiver to his ear. "Hello, this is Miller," he said.

A voice answered. "You God damn white bastard, you kike! Get out of Harlem you aimen to live. All you white bastards get out of Harlem!"

"Who's this?" Sam cried. There was no answer. It was yesterday morning all over again.

"Sam, so fast? What do they want?"

"Nothing much," he said.

"Not eight o'clock and so fast they talk," she said condemningly. "Advice, they give you?"

"No."

"Don't even let you talk even."

"Mom, get me some breakfast. I'm getting washed."

"How do you want your eggs?"

"Any style."

"Scramble or whole yellows?"

"Whole yellows." He waited until she walked away into the kitchen. He heard the Frigidaire door slam and then the sputter of butter frying in a pan. He got to his feet and his legs were unsteady. He glanced at the telephone. Who could've called him? Who? He tried to recall the voice but already it was echoing out of memory. It had been hard enough hearing it. He shut his eyes, concentrated. "You God damn white bastard . . . Kike . . . Get out of Harlem . . . Aimen to live . . . *White! Kike!*" Of all the muffled words only these two now rang in his brain. He shuffled towards the bathroom, his shoulders stooped. In the bathroom mirror, he stared at his face. Like always it was. Who said his face was like always? He noticed that the color had ebbed out of his lips. He was very white, his head bent. He raised his head on a neck turned into rubber. Let it come, he thought; the dirty rats; Harlem Equality League were they; Communists were they; the dirty rats.

His mother knocked on the door. "Sam, the breakfast's ready."

"I haven't shaved yet."

"So shave later. The eggs ready, nice and brown like you like them."

"All right, I'll be out. No, mom. Put a lid over them. I may as well shave since I'm here."

"All right for you, Sam. For Suzy you shave? Your *shicksa* won't make you such eggs. Only your mother," she mumbled jealously. "Why don't you come home a lil later from your *shicksa? A* million *finer yiddischer maidels* but my Sam a *shicksa* brings home to the house."

"Mom, don't bother me."

"All right, I won't bother you. Never you mind, I won't bother you, but some day you'll be sorry. I won't bother you always."

He heard her leaving the bathroom door and she was unreal to him. This phone call, he frowned; this second phone call. He assembled his shaving set and shaved with furious strokes as if the razor were a bayonet with which he was charging the unknown blackmailer whose voice he had heard two mornings in a row. He cut his chin, used the styptic pencil. He stared at the reddened point and suddenly he groaned.

He trudged back into his bedroom and sat down on the bed. He could hear his heart pumping and he wondered if this was what fear was. To stare blankly at a wall. To feel as if in a great net that was slowly but surely closing in all around him. The wall, the room, the whole city, the whole world were in the net. His mind saw blood and the blood was his own. They were sweeping him out of life and future and love. They had trapped him in their mesh of leaflets and phone calls.

"Sam, come eat your breakfast," his mother said. "Your eggs'll be nothing worth it. Eggs must be treated respectful, Sam. They don't come for nothing. Everybody's eaten except you."

"Have they all gone?"

"Don't you live here since you come home with the cows? Papa's in the store, Rose is in Macy's, Mikey's in school. Your *shicksa* makes you forget your own family."

"In a minute, mom." But he couldn't move a muscle. It was only Wednesday, he was thinking; only Wednesday. He remembered what Johnny had said Monday night about slapping the face of a mean guy, and all his lifetime from his earliest boyhood onwards rose before him, conjured by Johnny's remark, and shockingly different as if he had never before understood his own past. All his life (but he hadn't known it until now), that mean guy had also shadowed him and called him kike, using the innocent child mouths of the kids he'd gone to public school with, using the eyes of forgotten Christians, using the questionnaires of the employment agencies. Always he had been hemmed in by the mean guy's hundred hands, all his life circled, all the horizons blackened by the cyclones of hate. That had been his life as it truly was but his eyes had been closed until now; all he'd seen and felt were the blinding joys, kissing his first girl, smashing through a line of green jerseys with a football under one arm, reading the great books for the first great time. He had been blinded by school and college, by family, by young love, by the jobs that had finally brought him into a blue uniform. But was it all a blindness, was the joy of growing and becoming and loving and being on the earth a blindness? No, no. It was good to live, to be in love with Suzy, to hold to sweet life with all one's might of heart and brain and flesh. This was true. The rest was false.

He stared down at his white ankles with their fine blue veins and hate glowed in him. What was he moping for, what was he scared for? What did his life or any man's life amount to in a world of a million lost lives, a million slaughters, a million rapes. All that mattered was to fight them, the cursed fascists, to fight them to *their* death. He felt the fire of hate in his vitals. His cheeks pinked, his eyes sharpened and the hand that he pushed through his thick brown hair was a living hand.

He dressed quickly, hurried out of his room into the kitchen. "Hello, mom, how about those eggs?"

"Sam, the *shicksa* makes you happy?" Sighingly, his mother slid the eggs out of the frying pan into a plate which she set down before him on the table.

"Her name's Suzy. Better call her Suzy, not *shicksa*."

"Why better?"

"I'm going to marry her like I told you yesterday morning."

"Marry who you want but not a *shicksa*, God forbid."

"God's got nothing to do with it." He drained the glass of orange juice and pitched into the eggs.

"Sam, don't fool your mother."

"I'm not fooling. One of these days I'll bring Suzy here and say, 'Meet my wife.' "

"Fool, I am! Rose's been telling me you mean serious but I don't believe her." She clasped her hands over her stomach. "You think the *shicksa's* mother, she will like it?"

"What counts is that Suzy and I will like it."

"*Shicksas* and Communists early in the morning," she complained. "Sam, me, I don't care so much. If she's a fine girl, I don't care so much. I'm not altogether a foolish old woman. Better a fine *shicksa* than a not so fine Jewish girl. But Sam your father'll have a stroke. His blood pressure's too high, he'll have a stroke. Your father'll drop dead. When he asks about you, I don't tell him. Sam, for you I want the best. All my life I want the best for you. If we would've had money, you would be a doctor with a nice practise and not this trouble in Harlem. But it wasn't to be. I'm not a fanatic, my golden son, like some Jews, like your own father. Hitler has *ausgefanaticked* me."

(1943)

From

FATHER AND GLORIOUS DESCENDANT
by Pardee Lowe

A vast grapevine telegraph connects the Chinatowns of the Pacific Coast from the Canadian to the Mexican border into one homogeneous society. In our case the telegraph worked overtime until the moment of our arrival on the Pacific Coast. It was the reason why kinsmen and friends who encountered us en route were so solicitous. They had reported to Father and Stepmother the progress of our trip, given intimate, critical details of my wife's appearance and social graces, and, most of all, gladdened my parents' hearts with totally unexpected news: "Your American daughter-in-law has found great favor in the eyes of the Chinese elders she has met."

That was why a typical American family welcome greeted us when we had arrived in Chinatown the night before. All doubts of the warmth of the reception we might be given were quickly dispelled. I smiled as I recalled Father's Western handclasp and hearty smile; Stepmother's open arms and the sisterly kisses and brotherly hugs. True to our own family tradition, they had been extremely un-Chinese in their enthusiasm. We were surely a family of social rebels.

A short time after we arrived, Stepmother convinced Father that it was necessary for us to follow all the old customs of Chinatown society. "Otherwise," she concluded, "how can our many anxious kinsfolk find out what sort of a wife Glorious Descendant has taken in Middle Europe?"

Like Father, I demurred, but finally accepted Stepmother's advice in good grace. After all, it would make Father happy. Besides, I decided, this was as good a way as any for gathering sociological material.

At the request of my kinsfolk my wife and I visited Mother's grave at Mount Pleasant. By reverently laying before her tombstone a bouquet of flowers, instead of the customary spirit money, prayer candles and food offerings, we symbolically announced to her and the myriad of ancestors before her that we were married. In the same spirit of filial piety, we paid ceremonial calls at the homes of various kinsfolk and relatives to acknowledge our humble membership in the Greater Family, and to express our dutiful respect to its senior members. We attended daily banquets in our honor and after two weeks of feasting, first by one kinsman and then another, were gastronomically convinced of the truth of the Chinese proverb: "Nowhere under Heaven is food more deliciously prepared than in Canton." Or, in this case, "Little Canton."

During these first weeks of our arrival the family home swarmed with friends and relatives eager to discover the virtues and defects of the new bride. Only one question obsessed the Greater Family: *Nay Geen Kwoh Ah Cheong Loh Paw Mah?''* (Have you seen Glorious Descendant's bride?)

To receive her guests properly, my wife wore a modern Chinese wedding gown, tailored in the Shanghai mode, of exquisite silk, elaborately embroidered and, most important of all, tinted with the color of everlasting happiness: a flaming crimson. Carefully tutored by Stepmother, she greeted each guest in Chinese with the felicitous title and phrase appropriate to the caller's age, sex, family ranking and station in life. After seating them properly she served dainty cups of boiling tea, fragrant with water-lily blossoms, sweetened with lumps of ice-crystal sugar and decorated with blood-red dates—all auspicious tokens of Chinese ceremonial felicity.

In deference to American custom, which was absolutely contradictory to the Chinese, my wife, even though a bride, was permitted to sit in the presence of her elders, who were perfectly willing to concede a point. *"Kiur Hay Say Yun,"* they informed Stepmother (She is a Westerner), implying that much could be overlooked. Barely able to understand a few words of Cantonese, my wife simulated complete comprehension, not realizing that the guests were questioning Stepmother about her ancestry, education, the circumstances of our marriage, and our European honeymoon. Their curiosity satisfied, they departed. Beside each emptied teacup was a gift of pure-gold jewelry, a jade ring, an opal brooch, or, as was most customary in the case of friends, a small flaming-red envelope containing a silver or gold piece. My wife smiled in appreciation. *"Taw Jeh! Taw Jeh!"* (Thank you! Thank you!) In true Chinese fashion her guests murmured over and over into her uncomprehending ears the ancient Chinese phrase which is both salutation and benediction to a newly-married couple: "Hope you add a son!"

All this time the tables seemed turned. Instead of our investigating Chinatown, Chinatown investigated us. However, the furore which attended our arrival soon subsided. We were accepted as normal members of the community. My wife felt thoroughly at home. Her understanding, tact and modest demeanor quickly won the hearts of the older generation. Her ability to use correctly the Chinese conventional greetings, such as "You are well, are you not?" "Please sit," "Pray drink tea," and "Slowly, slowly walk" (Good-by in Chinese) brought murmurs of delight from the older women, who grieved bitterly over the growing callousness of the young folk toward the customs of their ancestors.

Father was tremendously pleased. My wife was adding luster to the family honor. As a born and bred New Englander, she had become unintentionally one of the models for Chinatown's feminine etiquette, a preserver of its ancient traditions of social intercourse. "No wonder," Cousin Lawrence remarked admiringly to me, "Senior Paternal Uncle loves his American daughter-in-law."

(1943)

From

STRANGE FRUIT
by Lillian Smith

She stood at the gate, waiting; behind her, the swamp, in front of her, Colored Town, beyond it, all Maxwell. Tall and slim and white in the dusk, the girl stood there, hands on the picket gate.

"That's Nonnie Anderson," they would tell you, "that's one of the Anderson niggers. Been to college. Yeah! Whole family been to college! All right niggers though, even if they have. Had a good mother who raised her children to work hard and know their place. Anderson niggers all right. Good as we have in the county, I reckon."

"Stuck up like Almighty, Nonnie Anderson," some colored folks said, "holding her head so highty-tighty, not like Bess. Bess common as dirt, friendly with folks."

"You forgot Ern Anderson's ways?" others said. "Spittin' image of her pappy in her ways. Shut-mouth jes' like him, dat all. Pity ain' mo' like her! Too many folks lettin' off their moufs 'bout things they don' know nothin' 'bout, pokin' their noses in—"

"Biggety thing," white women said, "I wouldn't have her in my house with all her college airs." But most said it enviously, for women on College Street and the side streets knew that Mrs. Brown's servant Nonnie was the best servant in Maxwell, unless it was her sister Bess. And so good to little imbecile Boysie. Everybody knew how good she was to the little fellow.

"Sometimes I wonder," Mrs. Brown would say, "how I ever did without her! She's so good to the baby, Frank! He cries so in this hot weather and she never gets cross with him. You can tell a good nurse by her hands. Way she touches a baby. No matter how bad the poor little fellow is, Nonnie's never rough with him. Always so easy, picking him up. Wish we could pay her a little more. I'm afraid she'll leave us."

"Nonnie's a good nigger, all right," Frank would answer, "good as we'll find, I reckon. You pay her enough, three dollars plenty! Already more than anybody else on College Street. You'll have the women on you if you start raising wages."

"Her shy as a little critter," Tillie Anderson used to say, long ago. "Won't talk to nobody. Who got yo' tongue, Nonnie? Come out from behind my skirt, can't spen' yo' life apeekin' from behind yo' Ma! You know dat honey!"

And white boys whistled softly when she walked down the street, and said low words and rubbed the back of their hands across their mouths, for Nonnie Anderson was something to look at twice, with her soft, black hair blowing off her face, and black eyes set in a face that God knows by right should have belonged to a white girl. And old Cap'n Rushton, sitting out in front of Brown's Hardware Store as he liked to do when in from the turpentine farm, would rub his thick, red hand over his chin slowly as he watched her wheel drooling, lop-headed Boysie Brown in to see his papa, sit there watching the girl, rubbing his hand over his chin, watching her, until she had gone back across the railroad and turned down College Street.

Nonnie pushed her hair off her face as she looked across White Town. Strange . . . being pregnant could make you feel like this. So sure. After all the years, Bess wouldn't see it. You hated to try to explain. Bess would feel disgraced. Ruined. The Andersons ruined, Bess would say. You live in a dream world, she'd say. Sometimes I almost think you're crazy, Non! she would say. I almost wish you *were* crazy, she'd say in her bitterness.

Sharp words rattling like palmettos.

Nonnie sighed.

Across the town came the singing. A white singing to Jesus. An August singing of lost souls. A God-moaning.

August is the time folks give up their sins. August is a time of trouble.

Whiter than snow . . . yes whiter than snow . . . oh wash me and I shall be whiter than snow.

Her thoughts swung with the Gospel tune.

Around the curve from Miss Ada's, where the trees open up, clearing the path, she could see him coming, A drag of left foot, a lift of shoulder, half limp, half swagger. Limp, swagger . . .

She would tell him, now that she felt certain. Though she had known since that night at the river. Somehow she had known since then.

He would say, "You all right?" and look at her as if he saw her for the first time. And the sound of it would hurt in her throat. Funny, how you don't get used to things.

He had said it first when he picked her out of the sandspurs, long ago; so long, it seemed now as if she must have dreamed it. She had fallen when Nat pulled up her dress, pulled at her underpants. Nat's freckled hand had reached out for her and she had jerked away from him, but more from the look on his sallow face, new to six-year-old eyes. His words already old. Words scrawled on circus posters, on privies, on fences, said with a giggle, carrying no more meaning to her ears than the squawk of guineas running crazily along ditches in search of worms.

"You all right?" Tracy had said; and then, to Nat, "Beat it, She's not that kind. And don't let me catch you around here again."

"Haw, haw, haw," Nat showed tobacco-stained teeth and lolled his tongue, "I didn't know she was your'n."

"She's not mine," Tracy said and reddened. "Now git—before I knock the liver-an'-lights out of you."

Nat Ashley put his hands in his pockets, sauntered slowly away to show he wasn't afraid of nobody! Increased his nonchalance by jumping a gallberry bush. Grew in manliness by shouting to the boys on the distant ball ground, "Hi, how about some shinny?" Faded from their sight and from their lives.

The swamp had thrown deep shadows. Hounds barked in Nigger Town and beat the dust with their tails. The smell of scorched cloth from shanties clung to the sweet, near odor of honeysuckle in her hand.

Slowly, she took a step toward him. "I *am* your'n," she whispered, and held out the grubby flowers.

Twelve-year-old Tracy took them. "You'd better run home," he said. "Your mama oughtn't allow you to run round alone. What were you doin', anyways?"

"Picking flowers and—" She hesitated.

"And what?" he probed.

"And visiting." She stooped, pulled a sandspur from her foot, pushed her toes deep into sand.

"Visiting? Who?"

"Everywheres. The swamp, mostly."

He spat and studied her face. "What you do in that swamp?"

"Nothing. Just goes." She paused. "It says, 'Come here, come here, come here.' "

He squinted his eyes.

"You hear it?" she whispered.

"Nope. Nothing but frogs croaking, and dogs."

She smiled, pushed her black, wavy hair from her face, drew in a deep breath.

Tracy spat again, looked away. "Silly way to talk," he chided, "it's silly. You've got no business going near that swamp. You might get lost. Who you belong to?"

"I'se Tillie's child."

She searched for a meeting ground. "She's Miz Purviance's cook."

"Yeah, I know. Now run on before it's pitch-dark."

"Who is you?" Voice shy in its first social exploration.

"I'm Tracy Deen. Dr. Deen's son."

She looked at him gravely.

"Now run along! Ought to tell your mama on you."

She started toward the old Anderson place, walked a few steps, stopped, watched him cut through the gallberry bushes. In the dusk she could see him limp a little, could see his shoulder twist. He stooped over a bush. When he went on again his hands were empty. She sighed, began to run hard, dreading the scolding her sister Bess would give her for staying out so late.

In the dusk he stood now before her, tall, stooped. Took her hands from the gate, held them. "You all right?" His eyes searched her face, moved from her hair to her eyes, to her throat.

"Of course." She laughed softly.

"Cool. Your hands are cool, and it's hot as hell."

"I know. Boysie's cried all day."

"Boysie! How do you stand the slobbering little idiot day after—"

"I don't mind. It's a find job for a girl like me," she said and smiled at the white man.

Tracy did not smile.

"Come in," she said. "I'll fix you something cool to drink. It's better in the arbor."

"No, I promised Mother—promised a lot of people—to go to the meeting tonight. Think all Maxwell is praying for me. Goddamn 'em."

He opened the gate, came inside. Slim and white, she stood there before him in the dusk. He pulled her behind a spirea bush. "I'm too hot to touch you," he whispered. "Sweet and cool . . . always sweet and cool . . . you smell so good to me, Non," he said unhappily.

"I'm glad."

"All right. Tell me quick. What's happened?"

She looked up at him steadily. "I'm pregnant, Tracy."

She felt his hand tremble on her arm. "And I'm glad," she whispered.

"Glad? You can't be!"

"I'm glad."

"But—"

"You see," she spoke quickly, "I want it. I'll have something they—can't take away from me." Voice low, hard to hear the words.

"What do you mean?"

"It's like thinking something for a long time you can't put into words. One day you write it down. You always have it after that."

His face eased into the old, quick grin. "Might have been better this time to have written it down, Non."

He frowned, ran his fingers slowly over the fence pickets. "Let's don't think about it," he said.

"All right," she whispered. She looked at him and smiled, and he stared into her eyes as if he had not heard a word that she had ever said. "I wish you were glad," she said and felt her body shaking against his in sudden betrayal of her calm.

"Reckon we ought to talk about it, or something—" He looked out toward the swamp, forgetting his words. *In the dusk she's as white as Laura. God, if she weren't a nigger! Lord God what a mess . . .*

"No, we don't need to talk about it."

"Well, good-by, honey." He touched her hair, turned away, stopped, faced her again. "It's Mother. She—you know how it is! Nothing I've ever done has pleased her, as you know." He laughed abruptly. "Now the damned meeting's got her worked up. After dinner she—I don't know what's happened. Seems—well, she said—lot of things—about joining the church, settling down. Other things—Laura's lack of interest in church—seems disappointed in her children." He laughed. Non waited. "Nothing new as far as I'm concerned. First time I ever heard her put Laura in the red." He laughed again. "Well . . . better be going."

He stared into the evening. Turned suddenly, opened the picket gate, closed it. "I may come back tonight, late. All right?"

"All right," Nonnie whispered, knowing he would not come.

(1944)

From

THE FOXES OF HARROW
by Frank Yerby

Next to the Théâtre D'Orleans on Orleans Street between Bourbon and Royal stood the Orleans Ballroom. As Andre and Stephen rode up to it on a spring night early in 1838, it was ablaze with light, and the sound of music and laughing voices floated downward into the street. Stephen sat for a moment on his horse, looking at the low, ugly two-storied building.

" 'Tis not much to look at," he remarked.

"Wait until you see the interior," Andre said. "Come now, we'd better hurry."

"Why?" Stephen demanded.

Andre laughed.

"You'll find three quarters of the gentry of New Orleans inside," he said. "Last year, the *Cordon Bleu* conflicted with one of our own balls. I spent the entire night dancing—at Melia's suggestion—with various deserted females. The men were all here."

Stephen swung down from the horse.

"I don't share your eagerness," he smiled. "Your mixed-strain wenches don't seem particularly remarkable to me." ´

"We shall see," Andre said. "Come!"

They went in through the low wide façade. In the vestibule, they surrendered their hats, cloaks, and gloves; and Andre paid the admission fee of two dollars apiece. Then they went up the stairs into the ballroom. Stephen stopped just inside the door and looked around him. Above his head, the gigantic crystal chandeliers, almost as costly as the ones at Harrow, swung low over the dance floor. In niches around the walls stood statues which would not have disgraced a hall at Versailles, and paintings which Stephen's practiced eye recognized at once as being originals. The walls were paneled with fine woods, and inlaid with even costlier ones.

On the magnificent dance floor, constructed, Andre had told Stephen, of three thicknesses of cypress topped by a layer of quarter-sawed oak, the young, and not so young, gentlemen of New Orleans were dancing. Half a glance told Stephen that almost everyone he knew, and many men unknown to him, were here; then his gaze traveled on to their partners. He stopped, frowning.

"Lovely, aren't they?" Andre said.

Stephen stifled a yawn with the back of his hand.

"Of course they're pretty," he said. "Why shouldn't they be? Ye've been busy for generations improving the strain. I don't see how Frenchmen ever grow anything, ye're so busy in the slave cabins. Gad, what a taste for dark meat ye have!"

"I won't let you anger me," Andre grinned. "Besides, you haven't seen anything yet."

"I'm on pins," Stephen growled. "What the deuce is so enjoyable about this? 'Tis just as stuffy as some of the fashionable balls ye've taken me to. The girls are prettier, that I'll admit; but those fat old yellow mothers of theirs seem to be watching them like hawks."

"You don't understand. For them the connections they make here are as honorable as marriage. They never desert a protector or betray him. And when it comes to love—*Dieu!*—they've forgotten more than our women ever knew. Of course the mothers watch. They'd object to an unwise connection as strenuously as would a white mother to an unwise marriage."

"Let's make the rounds," Stephen said. "I'm wearied to tears with standing here."

The two of them moved off, circling the ballroom. The girls watched them from behind their fans, commenting in whispers as the two richly attired men passed. As they came abreast of the stairway, Stephen stopped, his slim fingers tightening on Andre's arm.

"I think," he said slowly, "I think I see what ye mean!"

Andre looked up. A group of quadroon and octoroon girls were coming down the stairs. There was no need for Andre to ask which one Stephen meant. The others might as well not have existed.

She was taller by half a head than any of the others, and her skin was darker, a clear, light golden color, gleaming against the ivory white tones of her companions. But it was her hair that made her stand out—instead of the usual midnight curls, spun in ringlets over each ear, she wore it loose—a tawny mane of chestnut, lightening to pure gold in the highlights, with overtones of auburn that ran like flame through the waves whenever she tossed her head.

Stephen was standing on the last step when she reached it. As she neared him, he put out his hand and touched her arm.

"Tonight," he said, "ye're dancing with me—and with none other. Ye understand that?"

She turned toward him without speaking, and the heavy lids widened over eyes that were as cool and green as the sea.

"You had better ask Madame my mother, monsieur," she said. Her voice was deep and rich. Stephen thought it sounded like the tones of a soft, golden gong.

Stephen looked her straight in the face.

"To hell with Madame your mother," he said clearly. "Ye're dancing with me."

The full, wine-red lips widened slowly into a smile and little flakes of gold danced in the sea-green eyes.

"And after tonight?" she said.

Stephen lashed her with his glance, letting his eyes wander over the gown which was cut in extreme décolleté, the sleeves falling away from the shoulder, a frill of fine old lace barely covering her breasts, the bodice clinging to every inch of her incredibly slim waist.

"Ye may call the turn," he said; "I'll play the fiddle."

He swung her away into the dance, gazing down into her face. She lifted it to his, until her lips were almost touching his throat. A perfume floated up from the chestnut, russet, golden hair; it was elusive, but subtly, insistently provocative. Stephen's thin nostrils flared. He looked down at her eyes, but they were closed, the sooty lashes curving out and away, unmoving. Stephen found these black lashes odd, in conjunction with the rest of her coloring; but as they swirled under the chandeliers, he saw them gleam golden at the roots, their darkness a trick of the light and shadow of the ballroom, so that their colors were constantly shifting. Now they were dull gold; now lightless, inky black; but most often they were a changing combination of the two.

Stephen took her arm and swept her from the dance floor. They went out on the gallery which overlooked the gardens in the rear of the Saint Louis Cathedral. The night was a clear one, a purple sky dusted over with stars. There over one of the spires of the Cathedral a thin sickle of a moon blazed silver, with a great halo of white around it.

That means rain, Stephen thought irrelevantly. And this means I am mad . . .

He caught her by both her soft, rounded shoulders and held her away from him at arm's length. The moonlight caught in her hair, in her lashes. Stephen drew his breath in sharply.

"Ye're lovely!" he said. "God, but ye're lovely!"

"Thank you, monsieur," she murmured, and the overtones of her rich, throaty voice lingered a moment after she was silent, like the echoes of a golden gong. Stephen listened to them a moment, straining his ears against the silence. Then he drew her to him.

Her face was lifted to his, and the wine-red lips softened and parted. As he kissed her, Stephen could feel the sweet young breath sighing through. The kiss was light at first, light petal soft, and lingering. She rolled her head ever so slightly upon her neck so that her lips caressed his, sweet and warm and parted. Then something like madness flamed in Stephen's veins. His arms tightened ferociously about her slim waist, until a little cry of pain was locked somewhere deep in her throat, then one hand swept upward to the back of her neck, and his fingers were bruising her flesh.

Then abruptly, he released her. But instead of stepping back, she rose on tiptoe, her arms limp at her sides, her lips touching his so lightly that almost they did not touch at all, swaying there as if suspended by a breath. Stephen put his arms again about her waist, and she lay back against them, her eyes closed, her breath sighing through the stillness.

Again Stephen drew her to him, but this time she did not lift her face, but hid it in the hollow of his neck, so that he could feel her warm breath making little whispers against his throat.

"My dear . . ." Stephen said.

"Yes, monsieur?"

"What is your name?"

"Desiree," she said. "Does monsieur like it?"

"Like it? 'Tis perfect. And now 'tis time I had a word with Madame your mother. If ye'll be so good as to conduct me . . ."

Desiree took his arm, and the two of them went back into the ballroom. The girl led him straight across it until they reached a tall, middle-aged quadroon, sitting regally in one of the great chairs. At once Stephen saw where Desiree got her beauty. The mother, though aging and putting on flesh, was still a rarely beautiful woman. She looked from Stephen to her daughter, her dark brows rising.

"This gentleman wishes a word with you, *Maman*," Desiree said. The woman turned her gaze to Stephen, waiting like a queen for him to speak. Stephen found her gaze disconcerting. To be looked at like this by a Negress— even an almost white Negress—was, to say the least, a new sensation. He hesitated. Seeing his perplexity, Andre crossed the room and stood at his friend's side.

"Permit me, Madame," he said politely, "to present my friend, Monsieur Fox. Your name is, Madame?"

"Hippolyte. Madame Hippolyte. Is Monsieur Fox of the plantation Harrow?"

"Aye," Stephen growled. "How did ye know of Harrow?"

Madame smiled.

"Everyone knows of Harrow, monsieur." She leaned forward, her smile pleasant and inviting.

Stephen cleared his throat. But this was a new thing: this shameless willingness to sell a daughter into concubinage. There were many men they could marry. He knew quadroons like the Logoasters, the Dumas, the Lascals and two dozen others who held great plantations and lived as richly among their slaves as any white. A girl like Desiree . . . any man . . . any man at all. . . .

"I take it that monsieur wishes to form a connection with my daughter," Madame Hippolyte said.

"Aye," Stephen said stiffly. "That is my intent."

"Monsieur is a man of wealth," the woman said.

"Sufficient to compensate ye for the loss of your daughter," Stephen said drily.

Madame Hippolyte flushed darkly.

"Monsieur does not understand. There is not that much money in all the world. Desiree is not for sale like a black slave. I simply wanted to assure myself that my daughter would be amply provided for."

"In that you need have no further concern," Andre told her. "Monsieur Fox is the richest man in Louisiana. Desiree will live like a princess. You will of course accept some token of his esteem . . ."

"Not one cent," Madame Hippolyte said firmly. "But if Desiree wants him . . ." She looked at her daughter. Desiree looked back at her, the sea-green eyes unclouded. Wordlessly, she nodded. Madame sighed.

"Shall we discuss the terms, gentlemen?"

"Yes," Stephen said, "anything ye will."

"Monsieur will provide a house for my daughter down by the ramparts. It must be richer and more beautiful than any other on the street. He will further provide her with a maid servant and a cook. He will see that she is suitably attired at all times. He will visit her with discretion, so that no scandal will be attached to her name or his. And any children born of this connection he will fully provide for, educating them in the same style as whites. And, further, monsieur is not to see Desiree or have any further contact with her until this house is completed. Then, I shall send her to him."

Stephen's fair brows met over his nose, and the great scar flamed on the side of his forehead.

"Ye're mad," he said.

Madame Hippolyte shrugged.

"Careful, Stephen," Andre whispered. " 'Tis best to humor her."

"Aye," Stephen said. "I can see that here ye have the whip hand. Very well, I shall abide by those conditions. Construction will begin tomorrow!"

He touched Desiree's hand and swept her away in a waltz. She followed him effortlessly, gazing intently into his face, her eyes very wide and green with the tiny flakes of gold swimming in their depths.

"Why do ye watch me so?" Stephen demanded.

"Monsieur's eyes are very blue," she said simply, "and his brows are almost white. And there is a great scar upon his forehead from a duel."

"What else?" Stephen laughed.

"His hair is like fire. And his lips make mockery. He is very handsome with a wickedness about him. You see, I wanted to remember."

"Why?"

" 'Twill be so long before I see you again. I could die almost. But then I couldn't come to you, could I? I will live for that—no matter how long it is."

"Never will a house be built faster," Stephen said. "Come out upon the gallery with me."

"No, monsieur."

"Why not, my little Desiree?"

"I do not wish to betray *Maman*. With you, I have no will."

Stephen smiled.

"I shall be patient," he said. " 'Twill be a great happiness having ye." Then, as she smiled at him, the great curving lashes closing over her eyes, he whispered: "Nay, more—'twill be a glory!"

When at last the *Bal du Cordon Bleu* was over, Stephen surrendered Desiree to her mother. Then he and Andre left the ballroom together. Outside it was very clear, and the horses' hooves rang in the silent street. Others saluted them as they rode away, grinning mockingly at Stephen as though glad to find in him at last a common weakness. But Stephen paid them no heed, sitting bent over in his saddle, the reins loose in his hands. His pale eyes were fixed on vacancy, glazed, unseeing.

Andre rocked his plump form back in his saddle and laughed aloud.

"So," he chuckled. "You've taken on the *placée* you swore you'd never have!"

"She's beautiful, Andre," Stephen said.

"Yes! In that you have right! Your Desiree is a creature to stop the breath and send the mind reeling. But you must be careful, Stephen. Odalie must never know."

"Odalie," Stephen said slowly. "Oh, yes, Odalie. Do you know, Andre, for the moment I'd forgotten her?"

"I don't doubt it. But she has no cause for complaint. You've treated her well, Stephen."

"Aye," Stephen said. " 'Twas a mistake—our marriage. But it cannot be undone now. I shall take whatever joy there is left for me in life and make the best of it. Come, lad, 'tis a long way yet."

(1946)

From

THE BIG SKY
by A. B. Guthrie, Jr.

A man could sit and let time run on while he smoked or cut on a stick with nothing nagging him and the squaws going about their business and the young ones playing, making out that they warred on the Assiniboines. He could let time run on, Boone thought while he sat and let it run, and feel his skin drink the sunshine in and watch the breeze skipping in the grass and see the moon like a bright horn in the sky by night. One day and another it was pretty much the same, and it was all good. The sun came up big in the fall mornings and climbed warm and small and got bigger again as it dropped, and the slow clouds sailed red after it had gone from sight. There was meat to spare, and beaver still to trap if a man wanted to put himself out. In the summer the Piegans went to buffalo and later pitched camp close to Fort McKenzie and traded for whisky and tobacco and blankets and cloth and moved on to the Marias or the Teton or the Sun or the Three Forks for a little trapping and the long, lazy winter.

If the beaver were few, buffalo still were plenty, for all that the Piegans slaughtered more and more of them just so's to have hides to trade. Boone had seen regular herds of them chased over the steep bluffs that the Indians called *pishkuns* and lying at the bottom afterwards with broken necks or standing or lunging on three legs while the hunters rode among them with battleaxes and bows and arrows, and then the squaws, chattering and happy, following up with their knives and getting bloody and not caring, and everybody taking a mouth of raw meat now and then and all feeling good because they had something to set by for winter.

Boone drew slow on his pipe while his eye took in the meat drying on the racks and the squaws working with the skins and the lodges pitched around. A dog came up and got a whiff of his tobacco and made a nose and backed up and by and by went on. Off a little piece Heavy Runner lay in front of his lodge with his head in his squaw's lap. The squaw was going through his hair with her fingers, looking for lice and cracking them between her teeth when she found any. In other lodges medicine men thumped on drums and shook buffalo-bladder rattles to drive the evil spirits out of the sick. They made a noise that a man got so used to that he hardly took notice of it.

It was a good life, the Piegan's life was. There were buffalo hunts and sometimes skirmishes with the Crows and Sioux, or the Nepercy who came from across the mountains to hunt Blackfoot buffalo, being as they didn't have any of their own; the sun heated a man in the summer and the winter put a chill in his bones, so that he kept close by his fire and ate jerked meat and pemmican if need be and looked often to the western sky for the low bank of clouds that would mean a warm wind was coming. Life went along one day after another as it had for five seasons now, and the days went together and lost themselves in one another. Looking back, it was as if time ran into itself and flowed over, running forward from past times and running back from now so that yesterday and today were the same. Or maybe time didn't flow at all but just stood still while a body moved around in it. A man hunted or fought, and sat smoking and talking at night, and after a while the camp went silent except for the dogs taking a notion to answer to the wolves, and so then he went in and lay with his woman, and it was all he could ask, just to be living like this, with his belly satisfied and himself free and his mind peaceful and in his lodge a woman to suit him.

Boone didn't guess, though, that Jim ever would be shut of fret the way he was, maybe because Jim never had found a squaw that wore good with him. Jim was forever pulling up and going somewhere, to Union or Pierre or St. Louis. Boone had traveled a considerable himself, but not to places where people were; he went into the mountains or across to British country or north into Canada where the Gros Ventres lived when they weren't on the move. He liked free country, with no more than some Indians about, and his squaw.

When Jim came back from a trip he was full of talk about new forts along the river and new people moving out from the settlements and the farmers in Missouri palavering about Oregon and California, as if the mountains were a prime place for plows and pigs and corn. When Jim went on too long that way, Boone cut him off, not wanting to be bothered with fool talk that stirred a man up inside.

Jim always seemed glad to be back, even if he was always setting out again. His face would light up when he saw Boone, and his hand was warm and strong and his mouth smiling. When he looked at Teal Eye it was as if he wished her double was around somewhere. Boone would catch just a gleam in his blue eye sometimes, or a kind of long, slow look that would make a man flare up if he didn't know Teal Eye so well, that maybe would put blood in his eye if Jim wasn't his friend.

Teal Eye was the woman for Boone. He reckoned he never would take a second woman in his lodge, and never have to cut Teal Eye's nose off, either, the way a Piegan did when he found his woman had lain in secret with another man. It was a sight, the squaws you saw with no end to their noses. Cut-nose women, they were called. They went around like nigger slaves, not having a man any longer or any proper home.

Teal Eye suited him all right. There wasn't any sense in a man nosing around like a bull, or wanting to cover every new woman just from being curious. One woman was enough, if she was the right one. Teal Eye never whined or scolded or tried to make a man something else than what he was by nature, but just took him and did her work and was happy. She had got a little heavier lately but was still well-turned in her body, with sharp, full breasts and a flat stomach and legs slim and quick as a deer's. Most squaws aged early, looking pretty just when the first bloom was on them and then drying up or going all to flesh, but not Teal Eye, maybe because she never had caught herself a baby. Looking at her, Boone couldn't tell much difference from five seasons back when he had found her on the Teton with Red Horn. He couldn't tell much difference, even, from the *Mandan* time, except that she was a woman now and rounded out as a woman ought to be. Her face was still slim and delicate, and her eyes melting and her spirit quick and cheerful and her body graceful. What she cared about most was to please him. She watched while he ate the meat or tried a new pair of moccasins and showed pleasure in her face when he grunted an all right. And she was always ready for him when his body was hungry, not lying still and spraddled, either, like a shot doe, but joining in, unashamed, her legs smooth and warm and strong and her breath whispering in his ear.

Boone uncrossed one leg and stretched it out before him and studied the moccasin he wore. Teal Eye had put a decoration of colored porcupine quills on it, arranged them neat and in a nice pattern. She had tanned the leather for this foot white and for the right foot yellow, so that a person not knowing Piegan ways would think the moccasins didn't match. They were slick shoes, he thought, while his mind went to wishing that Jim could come back soon from St. Louis. He felt better with Jim around. There was more spirit in him, and he laughed oftener. There wasn't anyone could find fun like Jim, or set a man's head to working so. When he thought of it, it was as if Jim was a part of all the life he liked, as if he always had been ever since they had met up on the road between Frankfort and Louisville, and Jim uneasy with the dead body in his wagon. Take Jim away and Boone felt there was something wanting, though he still wouldn't trade his way of living for any he ever knew or heard tell of. When Jim came back, it was as if all was well again. A man went with the feeling inside him that everything was right and just about as he would order it if it was his to order. Jim ought to be back soon, Boone figured, from going down the river with a boat of furs. It could be he had made up his mind to stay the winter in the settlements and to come back in the spring when the flood water would float steamboats to Fort Union and farther. Boone reckoned not, though. Jim never stayed away for a long stretch. Likely he would come overland, maybe with a party of mountain men who had spent their beaver. For all his traipsing around, Jim was a true mountain man, with the life showing in his face and in the set of his shoulders and legs and the way of his walk.

The wind was moving out of the west, as it nearly always did, sometimes hard and sometimes easy but nearly always moving. A shadow fell on the land, and lightning flickered and thunder sounded, and a big splash of rain fell on the hand Boone held his pipe with. The Piegans spent a heap of time inside their lodges. He liked to sit outside where the sun could hit him and the breeze get at him. Sometimes he put himself in mind of the menfolk back in Kentucky, sitting around the door while the day turned by, only he didn't have a hickory chair and wouldn't sit in it if he had. A man got so he didn't feel right unless seated cross-legged. The rain wouldn't be but a drop or two. Already the cloud was sailing over him, passing on east.

Boone knocked out his pipe and sat still, letting time run by. Each part of time was good in itself, if a man knew to enjoy it and didn't press for it to pass so as to get ahead to something different.

By and by Red Horn came along and sat down by him, not speaking until he got his pipe going. Red Horn's eyes seemed to get sharper with the years, and his nose higher and more hooked. The wrinkles were like cuts at the side of his mouth though he wasn't old yet. He made Boone think of an eagle, except he didn't bite or claw any more. The hand he held the pipe with lacked the joint of one finger. He had cut it off, along with his hair, when old Heavy Otter died of the smallpox.

"We have meat enough, and hides," said Red Horn, speaking the Blackfoot tongue that Boone knew almost as well as white men's talk.

"More hides than meat."

Red Horn puffed on his pipe.

"The buffalo die fast, Red Horn."

"They are plenty."

"They die fast, with hunters killing them for hides alone."

Red Horn hunched his shoulders. "They are more now than before the big sickness. We need robes to trade."

"I hope we never want for meat."

The lines in Red Horn's face deepened. He spread his hands, as if there was no use in anything. "The buffalo will last while the Indian lasts. Then we do not care. The buffalo cannot die faster than the Indian."

"We do well enough."

"The white Piegan does not know. He did not see the Piegans when their lodges were many and their warriors strong. We are a few now, and we are weak and tired, and our men drink the strong water and will not go far from the white man's trading house. They quarrel with one another. The white man's sickness kills them. We are like Sheepeaters. We are poor and sick and afraid."

"The nation will grow strong. The white man will leave us. We shall be many and have buffalo and beaver and live as the old ones lived."

Red Horn grunted and took the pipe from his lips to speak. "Strong Arm is a paleface. He will go back to his brothers when the Piegans go to the spirit land."

"No!" Boone answered in English. "Damn if ever I go back—not for good, anyways!" He switched to Blackfoot. "Strong Arm is a Piegan though his face is white."

"Already," said Red Horn, "the white hunters make ready to trap our rivers again."

"They have no right. It is Piegan land."

"We are weak. We cannot fight the Long Knives. Red Horn will not fight. He tells his people to keep the arrow from the bow and their hands from the medicine iron."

It was no use arguing with Red Horn. The spirit was dead in him, except for a sadness and an old anger that fanned up sometimes like a coal touched by wind. He couldn't see ahead. Already the white hunter was getting scarce in the mountains, finding beaver too few and too cheap and the life too risky now that the big parties were gone and he had to travel small. It would be the same with the other white men, with the traders who crowded the river and with those who figured to settle and make crops where crops wouldn't grow. Things came and went and came again.

"Red Hair should be back soon," Boone said, watching Teal Eye come toward the lodge with water from the stream and stoop and go in while the edge of her eye looked at him and her face told him he was her man. He heard her freshening the fire. The days were getting shorter. Already the sun was dipping behind the mountain rim, well to the south of its summer setting place. The breeze began to quiet, as if it couldn't blow without the sun shining on it.

"Red Hair waits at the trading house?" Red Horn asked.

"Maybe Jim is there."

"Two suns, and we go to trade."

"Good."

Red Horn got up and looked around the village, the lines cutting into his face, as if he could see how far the Piegan lodges would stand if the big sickness hadn't come along.

Boone smoked another pipe after Red Horn had gone. From inside there came the little noises that told him Teal Eye was readying the pot for him. The smell of wood smoke was in the air and of good meat cooking. A man's stomach answered to it. The water came into his mouth. High in the sky Boone could hear the whimper of nighthawks. Looking close, he spied one of them, diving crazy and crooked and whimpering as it dived.

He knocked the ash from his pipe and got up, stretching, and ducked under his medicine bundle that hung over the entrance and went in—to his lodge, to his meat, to his woman.

(1947)

From

OUR HEROINE
by James A. Michener

In strained silence the two lovers drove along the coral roads and up the hill to his plantation. They parked his car by the gate and walked slowly between the coconut palms. De Becque was silent, as if worried. Nellie's heart was pounding harder than her lungs. As they neared the end of the coconuts and the beginning of the cacaos, De Becque stopped impulsively and kissed his bride-to-be tenderly. "You are my hope," he whispered.

Nellie consciously placed her hand in his and walked with him toward the pavilion. She felt him trembling, and thought it was she. They paused a moment to watch the dipping black and white swallows. Then they stepped into the cool pavilion.

"Aloo, Nellie!" cried four young voices.

Nellie looked in astonishment at four little girls who stood behind one of the teakwood chairs. "Allo, Nellie!" they cried again. Then they came forth, in gingham frocks, pigtails, and curtsies.

Two were Tonkinese, that is, they were half Tonkinese, and they were beautiful as only Eurasian girls can be. They were seven and nine. Their almond eyes were black. Their foreheads were clean and high. They had very white teeth and golden complexions.

The two other girls were half Polynesian, daughters of that strange and proud race. They were round of face and darker than their sisters. Their eyes were black as pools at night, their hair the same, long and straight even in pigtails. They had rich mouths and splendidly proportioned bodies. They were ten and eleven.

At the end of their curtsy they said once more, "Allo, Nellie!"

"They're my daughters," De Becque said proudly. "I have four others. They all live in Luana Pori. One of them is married. I have their pictures here." From an envelope he produced a well-thumbed photograph of four tall thin, sharp-eyed girls. The first and third were exquisite beauties, lovelier than Bus Adams had painted them in his story. The second and fourth were handsome girls, and only their sisters' storybook charm made them seem plain. It was noticeable that each had a quizzical smile on her lips.

"My family!" De Becque said. He put his hand on Nellie's shoulder. "I had to tell you first," he said.

Nellie Forbush, of Otolousa, Arkansas, could not speak. She was glad that her mother had taught her never to make up her mind beforehand. Beside her was a strong, tough man. It was someone like him she had in mind when she said long ago, "I want to get out and meet people." It was not old ladies in white lace sitting by the fireside that Nellie wanted to meet. It was men and women who had courage. She looked at the picture of Latouche, De Becque's eldest daughter, and saw in her Emile's fire and determination. Yes, Latouche could kill a man and fight the entire American Army. The aviator's story was believable. Nellie thought that she would like Latouche.

But before her were other indisputable facts! Two of them! Emile De Becque, not satisfied with Javanese and Tonkinese women, had also lived with a Polynesian. A nigger! To Nellie's tutored mind any person living or dead who was not white or yellow was a nigger. And beyond that no words could go! Her entire Arkansas upbringing made it impossible for her to deny the teachings of her youth. Emile De Becque had lived with the nigger. He had nigger children. If she married him, they would be her stepdaughters.

She suffered a revulsion which her lover could never understand. Watching her shiver, he motioned to the little girls and they left the pavilion. "Nellie," he said, pulling her into a chair and standing over it, "I have no apologies. I came out here as a young man. There were no white women in this area. I lived as I could. No women ever hated me or tried to hurt me. You must believe me, Nellie. I loved those women and was kind to them. But I never married because I knew that some day you would come to this island."

He stood before her in considerable dignity. He was not crawling, and yet by every word and gesture he was fighting to have her believe in him.

"Oh! Look at that big one!" the little girls cried in French. Their soft voices drifted through the pavilion like the sound of distant music. Nellie looked at them running among the cacaos. The little Polynesians were dark, she thought. Almost black.

She swallowed hard. The pounding in her chest was still strong. "Where are their mothers?" she asked.

De Becque clasped his hands and looked away. "The Javanese are back in Java. They went a long time ago. I don't know where the Tonkinese is. She was no good. The Polynesian girl is dead."

Nellie was ashamed of herself, but a surge of joy ran through her entire body when she heard that the nigger was dead. Yet even as she entertained that thought the oldest Polynesian girl looked in at the window and cried in softest tones, *"Papa! Voilà une petite souris dans ce cacao!"* Nellie's hands went toward the window. The child had in her eager face and soft voice the qualities that made De Becque a man to love.

"Va-t-en jouer!" Emile said quietly.

"Oui, papa," the golden little girl replied.

"I don't know what to say, Emile," Nellie mumbled. "You don't understand."

"I know it's a surprise, Nellie. And a rude one. I know that."

"No!" Nellie cried in real anguish, stamping her foot. "It isn't that! It's something you don't know."

De Becque, defeated by tears, stood aside. Why Nellie thought he was incapable of understanding, it would be difficult to say. He had read of America. He knew something of its mores and shibboleths. And yet Nellie was correct in assuming that no Frenchman could understand why, to an Arkansas girl, a man who had openly lived with a nigger was beyond the pale. Utterly beyond the bounds of decency!

"I can't . . ." She stopped in her explanation. It was no use. The inescapable fact remained. She buried her head in her hands, and in the torment of conflicting thoughts and ideals started to cry.

"Please take me home," she said.

At the foot of the hill the Tonkinese cook expressed his astonishment that she was leaving. He held up his hands in horror. "Dinner all fine. He cooked. He good!" the cook protested. Moved by his appeal, Nellie agreed to have dinner and then go immediately. At a separate table the four little girls, obviously great favorites of the cook, had their dinners. They babbled quietly in French, displayed exquisite manners, and excused themselves when they went to bed. They, too, like the nigger wife, were indisputable facts. Nellie caught herself whispering, "I would be happy if my children were like that!"

(1947)

From

TOMORROW WILL BE BETTER
by Betty Smith

Salvatore took his hat off the block, looked inside it, then dented in the crown with a nod of approval.

"Okay, Boss?" asked the hat blocker. Sal made a circle with his thumb and middle finger and gestured toward the blocker. The swarthy young man smiled in pleasure. "Tried to clean it good—for your wedding day," he said.

Sal climbed into the end chair. The head shoeshine boy finished thanking a customer for a tip, then came over to work on Sal's shoes. A third boy rushed in from the street holding aloft a freshly pressed suit on a wire hanger.

"Made it, Boss," panted the boy. Sal nodded his thanks and the boy hung the suit behind a curtain at the back of the store.

With the bored but alert eye of the professional, Sal watched the shoeshiner slap pungent-smelling polish on his pointed perforated-tipped tan shoes.

Then his eyes traveled to the window of his small hole-in-the-wall store and saw the lettering in reverse: SUPERIOR SHOESHINE PARLOR. HATS BLOCKED. Underneath in small letters were the words: S. DE MUCCIO. PROP.

The Prop. meant that Sal was in business for himself. True, after he paid off three boys, paid for materials and for the rent on his cubbyhole, his profits were no larger than the salary of a clerk or factory hand. The bonus was that he didn't have to take orders from anybody. He was his own boss and that was worth a lot.

The heat caused by the friction of the rapidly moving shine cloth came through his shoes. He looked down on the bent head of the shoeshine boy and noted with approval that the boy was doing a good job—polishing the heel counters of the shoes as thoroughly as he polished the toes.

Sal, himself, had started as a shoeshine boy in a hotel barbershop after years of apprenticeship on the streets of Brooklyn. He had gotten ahead because he was ambitious and because he tried to polish shoes better than any other kid. He had taught his own apprentices little touches that he had picked up—touches that made a superior shine appreciated by customers.

That's the American Way, thought Sal, who had been born in America of Italian-born parents. Do something a little better than the next guy and you're in. The American Way.

"Okay, Boss," said the boy as he untucked the bottoms of Sal's trousers and let the cuffs down.

Sal got down from the chair and smiled reassuringly at the anxious boy. The boy was only seventeen, also the son of immigrants and also wanting to make good as an American. The way to do it, thought the boy, was to emulate his boss in all things. Sal knew that emulation wasn't enough. He often told the boys, "Don't try to copy me. Try to top me. That's the way to get ahead."

Sal wanted to put his hand on the boy's head in a gesture of appreciation and affection but he killed the impulse, saying to himself: He'll only think I'm a Goddamned fairy. He worked it out by pretending to swing a left to the boy's jaw. The boy, playing the game, grinned and ducked. He understood.

Funny, thought Sal, changing into his freshly pressed suit behind the curtain, how different nationalities go for different trades and how it starts with the kids. Take a Jewish kid: He buys something and resells it at a profit—like buying pretzels a cent each and selling 'em for two cents apiece in the park. A German kid sells what he makes himself—like lemonade at a ball park or pinwheels made out of wallpaper that he sells to other kids. Greek kids, now: They like to hang out in back of restaurants, waiting for a chance to deliver coffee to offices or factories. They move on up into dishwashing and then cooking. American kids, they go for selling newspapers. They like to be a part of what's going on. They like to holler out headlines, fold over a paper with a flip while they take the money at the same time. And the Irish?

The Irish had Sal buffaloed. The kids never seemed to work at anything. They were always fighting—with other kids and with each other. They fought to prove that something was true or to prove that something was a lie. That's what makes them good politicians, decided Sal.

Thinking of the Irish, he thought of Reenie. She was half Irish, her father having been the son of Irish immigrants. Her mother was second-generation German-American. But Reenie was mostly Irish the way she was so reckless, not giving much of a damn and always willing to take a chance.

He'd had other girls before Reenie, daughters of parents like his own, Italian born. But he fell in love with Reenie. She was all American and she had class. He fell in love with her but he hadn't wanted to marry her especially. She was all right to go dancing with and for "mushing," as the expression of the day had it. But for a wife?

He had dreamed of an ideal wife—a beautiful girl, passionate in love-making, but only so far as he was concerned, and utterly pure in heart, mind and soul. Oh, well, it had been one of those misty dreams—the kind that couldn't come true. And Reenie was all right. Maybe she had some kind of dream, too, of an ideal husband—not a shoeshining Wop.

He had put off marrying Reenie. Why, he didn't know. Unless he expected marriage to be disillusioning and humdrum and the beginning of getting ready for middle and old age. He would have liked everything to be the way it had started out: In love, dates, stolen hours of passion and utter freedom the rest of the time. He had put off marriage then, using his parents as an excuse. Sure, they wanted him to marry a Catholic. That was their religion. That was the way they'd brought him up. Certainly they wouldn't be worth a damn if they'd been able to set all that aside. However, they were humble and easily confused. They held Sal in awe and tried always not to offend him. He was American, of age, in business for himself. He could marry whom he pleased and how he pleased. His folks would come around. They were grateful as hell, he knew, that he still lived at home with them.

There had been four daughters and Sal. The girls had been born in Italy. Three had remained there when the parents—the mother pregnant with Sal— had sailed for America. They remained behind with their husbands and children. The fourth girl had married a naturalized Italian and gone out to California to live. Sal was the only one left to them. They'd agree to anything he said.

Sal enjoyed his parents' looking up to him, their American-born son in business for himself. But they don't have to look up to anyone, he thought. They got their own business, too—such as it is.

They were in the business of supplying quick full-grown lawns for newly built houses. Pasquale, the father, "rented" the grass on several vacant lots in Ozone Park for a few dollars a year. He and his wife pulled up the weeds, cut the grass short, mixed new seed in it and tended it until it was thick and springy. Then they mowed it and dug it up in two-foot squares, two inches thick, and Pasquale placed the squares side by side, like a carpet, on the strip of barren ground before a house, watered it, rolled it and lo! a lawn. All at twenty cents a square foot.

They had a sign in their window, too: DE MUCCIO. LAWNS MADE TO ORDER.

Sal stood before his three boys in his newly blocked hat, freshly pressed suit, with a white carnation in the buttonhole, in his shining shoes. The boys stood in a row and looked at him worshipfully.

"Well, do I pass?" he asked.

"You look just like Valentino," said the hat blocker. "Only not so dead pan."

There was a rattling of the doorknob. An irate customer peered through the door window. "What's the idea?" asked Sal, "locking up in the middle of the day? Are you on strike or something?"

"On strike five minutes," said the elder shoeshine boy. "To wish you a happy married life."

He and the blocker nudged the younger shoeshine boy who was standing in the middle. The boy brought out something that he had been holding behind his back and presented it to Sal, saying: "A present for you and your bride. From us."

Sal took it. It was a framed print of Mt. Vesuvius. The print had cost a quarter, maybe, but the ornate frame, filigreed and painted to look like gold, had probably cost three dollars. Sal took it, looked at it, and had to clear his throat twice before he spoke.

"You punks!" he said. "So that's how you waste the money I give you. I've a good mind to cut all your wages twenty per cent."

The boys grinned at each other. They knew their boss was tickled to death with the present.

Sal opened the door and let in the impatient customer. "Well," he said to the boys in farewell, "as the Irish say, God love you."

Walking over to City Hall, he thought: I'm lucky at that. She loves me. An American girl loves me and I'm nothing but a Wop. She must have been worried when she knew she was going to have my baby. Sure, I know it's mine. I was the first one. But if she worried, she never let me know. She trusted me. She knew I'd do the right thing. I'll try to be as good to her as I know how so that she'll never be sorry.

(1948)

From

BLOOD BROTHER
by Elliott Arnold

He stood in the deep part of the stream, the cold water reaching his waist, his head and beard covered with soap suds.

"Do not look," she said.

"I cannot look. I would get soap in my eyes. Come in."

"Turn your head. Do not look until the water covers my hips."

"I have soap in my eyes," he shouted. "I cannot see anything!"

She was naked behind a tree. She looked at his body above the water. She thought it was very white, up to his wrists and his neck. She suddenly felt ashamed of the golden color of her skin. She slipped past the tree and darted into the water behind him. The water line reached just below her breasts. She put her arms around him from behind and held him as though she were losing him. The suds got on her face and in her hair. He sat down in the water, pulling her down with him and then they both emerged, laughing and coughing.

She was greatly embarrassed. She looked around as though she thought someone might be watching her.

"Would you like me to wash your back?" he asked.

"If it would please you," she said timidly.

"It would please me very much." He worked the suds around her back and under her armpits and then around her breasts.

"Does my back come around to the front now?" she asked demurely.

He kissed her between her breasts. "It is like a wave through me," he said. He crushed her hard and kissed her again. "How much I love you."

"With the skins so different," she said.

"What skins?"

She held her arm next to his.

"What difference does that make," he demanded. He lifted her chin and looked into her eyes. "What are you thinking?"

"You are so white," she said piteously.

He lifted her out of the water and carried her to the bank. He put her down gently on a bed of pine needles. "Would you rather have an Indian for a husband? Would you like to take one of Cochise's men? Are you tired of me already?"

She put her hand over his mouth. "It is not for me that I speak and you know it. It is for you.'' She touched his beard lightly with her fingertips. ''Would you not like me to be white as you?''

He looked at her golden body lying on the green pine. Her skin was the color of honey. He felt his blood again and he was too choked to talk. He kissed her gently on each breast, and then he said, ''The smallest change, the very smallest change, would be sinful.''

''You say that to make me feel good.''

''There could be no change,'' he said reverently. ''Not the tiniest thing, not in your face, not in your eyes, not in your body. And not in your skin. It is as though the sun were shining only where you are lying.''

''You do not lie to me?''

''The color in you is sunlight. Look, look at my hands. Where the sun has been on them they are darker than any part of you, much darker. The sun has entered into all of you, just as it has touched my two hands. It has passed into all of you and finding you lovely it has stayed in you and lives there. It is in your color all the time and sometimes it comes into your eyes and sometimes it lights inside your face.''

''The thing that is in me is love,'' she said. She lifted her hand. ''Listen, it comes from my fingers. Can you hear it, husband?''

''Yes.''

She placed her hand over her heart. ''Put your head there. It is being said there too. Can you hear it?'' She pressed his face against her breast. ''I told you we would make our own language.''

(1950)

IDENTITY
IN
QUESTION
"Passing"

Reading the statistics of the registered people in Chicago, we found people of various nationalities, but we failed to find Lithuanians. Why so? Because our Lithuanians did not register as Lithuanians, they registered as Poles or Russians. . . . In order that our protest would not be in vain, every Lithuanian should not be ashamed of his nationality. Always and everywhere, must you admit that you are a Lithuanian. Do the Russians, the Poles stand higher than we?

Lietuva
March 21, 1896

Life can be bright in America
If you can fight in America.
Life is alright in America
If you're all white in America.

Stephen Sondheim
West Side Story

From

THE SOULS OF BLACK FOLK
by W. E. B. Du Bois

It is in the early days of rollicking boyhood that the revelation first bursts upon one, all in a day, as it were. I remember well when the shadow swept across me. I was a little thing, away up in the hills of New England, where the dark Housatonic winds between Hoosac and Taghkanic to the sea. In a wee wooden schoolhouse, something put it into the boys' and girls' heads to buy gorgeous visiting-cards—ten cents a package—and exchange. The exchange was merry, till one girl, a tall newcomer, refused my card,—refused it peremptorily, with a glance. Then it dawned upon me with a certain suddenness that I was different from the others; or like, mayhap, in heart and life and longing, but shut out from their world by a vast veil. I had thereafter no desire to tear down that veil, to creep through; I held all beyond it in common contempt, and lived above it in a region of blue sky and great wandering shadows. That sky was bluest when I could beat my mates at examination-time, or beat them at a foot-race, or even beat their stringy heads. Alas, with the years all this fine contempt began to fade; for the worlds I longed for, and all their dazzling opportunities, were theirs, not mine. But they should not keep these prizes, I said; some, all, I would wrest from them. Just how I would do it I could never decide: by reading law, by healing the sick, by telling the wonderful tales that swam in my head,— some way. With other black boys the strife was not so fiercely sunny: their youth shrunk into tasteless sycophancy, or into silent hatred of the pale world about them and mocking distrust of everything white; or wasted itself in a bitter cry, Why did God make me an outcast and a stranger in mine own house? The shades of the prison-house closed round about us all: walls strait and stubborn to the whitest, but relentlessly narrow, tall, and unscalable to sons of night who must plod darkly on in resignation, or beat unavailing palms against the stone, or steadily, half hopelessly, watch the streak of blue above.

After the Egyptian and Indian, the Greek and Roman, the Teuton and Mongolian, the Negro is a sort of seventh son, born with a veil, and gifted with second-sight in this American world,—a world which yields him no true self-consciousness, but only lets him see himself through the revelation of the other

101

world. It is a peculiar sensation, this double-consciousness, this sense of always looking at one's self through the eyes of others, of measuring one's soul by the tape of a world that looks on in amused contempt and pity. One ever feels his twoness,—an American, a Negro; two souls, two thoughts, two unreconciled strivings; two warring ideals in one dark body, whose dogged strength alone keeps it from being torn asunder.

The history of the American Negro is the history of this strife,—this longing to attain self-conscious manhood, to merge his double self into a better and truer self. In this merging he wishes neither of the older selves to be lost. He would not Africanize America, for America has too much to teach the world and Africa. He would not bleach his Negro soul in a flood of white Americanism, for he knows that Negro blood has a message for the world. He simply wishes to make it possible for a man to be both a Negro and an American, without being cursed and spit upon by his fellows, without having the doors of Opportunity closed roughly in his face.

(1903)

THE COMING-OUT OF MAGGIE
by O. Henry

Every Saturday night the Clover Leaf Social Club gave a hop in the hall of the Give and Take Athletic Association on the East Side. In order to attend one of these dances you must be a member of the Give and Take—or, if you belong to the division that starts off with the right foot in waltzing, you must work in Rhinegold's paper-box factory. Still, any Clover Leaf was privileged to escort or be escorted by an outsider to a single dance. But mostly each Give and Take brought the paper-box girl that he affected; and few strangers could boast of having shaken a foot at the regular hops.

Maggie Toole, on account of her dull eyes, broad mouth, and left-handed style of footwork in the two-step, went to the dances with Anna McCarty and her "fellow." Anna and Maggie worked side by side in the factory, and were the greatest chums ever. So Anna always made Jimmy Burns take her by Maggie's house every Saturday night so that her friend could go to the dance with them.

The Give and Take Athletic Association lived up to its name. The hall of the Association in Orchard Street was fitted out with muscle-making inventions. With the fibres thus builded up the members were wont to engage the police and rival social and athletic organizations in joyous combat. Between these more serious occupations the Saturday night hops with the paper-box factory girls came as a refining influence and as an efficient screen. For sometimes the tip went 'round, and if you were among the elect that tiptoed up the dark back stairway you might see as neat and satisfying a little welter-weight affair to a finish as ever happened inside the ropes.

On Saturdays Rhinegold's paper-box factory closed at 3 P.M. On one such afternoon Anna and Maggie walked homeward together. At Maggie's door Anna said, as usual: "Be ready at seven, sharp, Mag; and Jimmy and me'll come by for you."

But what was this? Instead of the customary humble and grateful thanks from the non-escorted one there was to be perceived a high-poised head, a prideful dimpling at the corners of a broad mouth, and almost a sparkle in a dull brown eye.

"Thanks, Anna," said Maggie; "but you and Jimmy needn't bother tonight. I've a gentleman friend that's coming 'round to escort me to the hop."

The comely Anna pounced upon her friend, shook her, chided and beseeched her. Maggie Toole catch a fellow! Plain, dear, loyal, unattractive Maggie, so sweet as a chum, so unsought for a two-step or a moonlit bench in the little park. How was it? When did it happen? Who was it?

"You'll see to-night," said Maggie, flushed with the wine of the first grapes she had gathered in Cupid's vineyard. "He's swell all right. He's two inches taller than Jimmy, and an up-to-date dresser. I'll introduce him, Anna, just as soon as we get to the hall."

Anna and Jimmy were among the first Clover Leafs to arrive that evening. Anna's eyes were brightly fixed upon the door of the hall to catch the first glimpse of her friend's "catch."

At 8:30 Miss Toole swept into the hall with her escort. Quickly her triumphant eye discovered her chum under the wing of her faithful Jimmy.

"Oh, gee!" cried Anna, "Mag ain't made a hit—oh, no! Swell fellow? well, I guess! Style? Look at 'um."

"Go as far as you like," said Jimmy, with sandpaper in his voice. "Cop him out if you want him. These new guys always win out with the push. Don't mind me. He don't squeeze all the limes, I guess. Huh!"

"Shut up, Jimmy. You know what I mean. I'm glad for Mag. First fellow she ever had. Oh, here they come."

Across the floor Maggie sailed like a coquettish yacht convoyed by a stately cruiser. And truly, her companion justified the encomiums of the faithful chum. He stood two inches taller than the average Give and Take athlete; his dark hair curled; his eyes and his teeth flashed whenever he bestowed his frequent smiles. The young men of the Clover Leaf Club pinned not their faith to the graces of person as much as they did to its prowess, its achievements in hand-to-hand conflicts, and its preservation from the legal duress that constantly menaced it. The member of the association who would bind a paper-box maiden to his conquering chariot scorned to employ Beau Brummel airs. They were not considered honourable methods of warfare. The swelling biceps, the coat straining at its buttons over the chest, the air of conscious conviction of the supereminence of the male in the cosmogony of creation, even a calm display of bow legs as subduing and enchanting agents in the gentle tourneys of Cupid—these were the approved arms and ammunition of the Clover Leaf gallants. They viewed, then, the genuflexions and alluring poses of this visitor with their chins at a new angle.

"A friend of mine, Mr. Terry O'Sullivan," was Maggie's formula of introduction. She led him around the room, presenting him to each new-arriving Clover Leaf. Almost was she pretty now, with the unique luminosity in her eyes that comes to a girl with her first suitor and a kitten with its first mouse.

"Maggie Toole's got a fellow at last," was the word that went round among the paper-box girls. "Pipe Mag's floor-walker"—thus the Give and Take expressed their indifferent contempt.

Usually at the weekly hops Maggie kept a spot on the wall warm with her back. She felt and showed so much gratitude whenever a self-sacrificing partner invited her to dance that his pleasure was cheapened and diminished. She had even grown used to noticing Anna joggle the reluctant Jimmy with her elbow as a signal for him to invite her chum to walk over his feet through a two-step.

But to-night the pumpkin had turned to a coach and six. Terry O'Sullivan was a victorious Prince Charming, and Maggie Toole winged her first butterfly flight. And though our tropes of fairyland be mixed with those of entomology they shall not spill one drop of ambrosia from the rose-crowned melody of Maggie's one perfect night.

The girls besieged her for introductions to her "fellow." The Clover Leaf young men, after two years of blindness, suddenly perceived charms in Miss Toole. They flexed their compelling muscles before her and bespoke her for the dance.

Thus she scored; but to Terry O'Sullivan the honours of the evening fell thick and fast. He shook his curls; he smiled and went easily through the seven motions for acquiring grace in your own room before an open window ten minutes each day. He danced like a faun; he introduced manner and style and atmosphere; his words came trippingly upon his tongue, and—he waltzed twice in succession with the paper-box girl that Dempsey Donovan brought.

Dempsey was the leader of the association. He wore a dress suit, and could chin the bar twice with one hand. He was one of "Big Mike" O'Sullivan's lieutenants, and was never troubled by trouble. No cop dared to arrest him. Whenever he broke a pushcart man's head or shot a member of the Heinrick B. Sweeney Outing and Literary Association in the kneecap, an officer would drop around and say:

"The Cap'n 'd like to see ye a few minutes round to the office whin ye have time, Dempsey, me boy."

But there would be sundry gentlemen there with large gold fob chains and black cigars; and somebody would tell a funny story, and then Dempsey would go back and work half an hour with the six-pound dumbbells. So, doing a tight-rope act on a wire stretched across Niagara was a safe terpsichorean perfor-mance compared with waltzing twice with Dempsey Donovan's paper-box girl. At 10 o'clock the jolly round face of "Big Mike" O'Sullivan shone at the door for five minutes upon the scene. He always looked in for five minutes, smiled at the girls, and handed out real perfectos to the delighted boys.

Dempsey Donovan was at his elbow instantly, talking rapidly. "Big Mike" looked carefully at the dancers, smiled, shook his head and departed.

The music stopped. The dancers scattered to the chairs along the walls. Terry O'Sullivan, with his entrancing bow, relinquished a pretty girl in blue to her partner, and started back to find Maggie. Dempsey intercepted him in the middle of the floor.

Some fine instinct that Rome must have bequeathed to us caused nearly every one to turn and look at them—there was a subtle feeling that two gladi-ators had met in the arena. Two or three Give and Takes with tight coat sleeves drew nearer.

"One moment, Mr. O'Sullivan," said Dempsey. "I hope you're enjoy-ing yourself. Where did you say you lived?"

The two gladiators were well matched. Dempsey had, perhaps, ten pounds of weight to give away. The O'Sullivan had breadth with quickness. Dempsey had a glacial eye, a dominating slit of a mouth, an indestructible jaw, a com-plexion like a belle's, and the coolness of a champion. The visitor showed more fire in his contempt and less control over his conspicuous sneer. They were enemies by the law written when the rocks were molten. They were each too splendid, too mighty, too incomparable to divide preëminence. One only must survive.

"I live on Grand," said O'Sullivan, insolently; "and no trouble to find me at home. Where do you live?"

Dempsey ignored the question.

"You say your name's O'Sullivan," he went on. "Well, 'Big Mike' says he never saw you before."

"Lots of things he never saw," said the favourite of the hop.

"As a rule," went on Dempsey, huskily sweet, "O'Sullivans in this dis-trict know one another. You escorted one of our lady members here, and we want a chance to make good. If you've got a family tree let's see a few histor-ical O'Sullivan buds come out on it. Or do you want us to dig it out of you by the roots?"

"Suppose you mind your own business," suggested O'Sullivan blandly.

Dempsey's eye brightened. He held up an inspired forefinger as though a brilliant idea had struck him.

"I've got it now," he said cordially. "It was just a little mistake. You ain't no O'Sullivan. You are a ring-tailed monkey. Excuse us for not recogniz-ing you at first."

O'Sullivan's eye flashed. He made a quick movement, but Andy Geoghan was ready and caught his arm.

Dempsey nodded at Andy and William McMahan, the secretary of the club, and walked rapidly toward a door at the rear of the hall. Two other members of the Give and Take Association swiftly joined the little group. Terry O'Sullivan was now in the hands of the Board of Rules and Social Referees. They spoke to him briefly and softly, and conducted him out through the same door at the rear.

This movement on the part of the Clover Leaf members requires a word of elucidation. Back of the association hall was a smaller room rented by the club. In this room personal difficulties that arose on the ballroom floor were settled, man to man, with the weapons of nature, under the supervision of the board. No lady could say that she had witnessed a fight at a Clover Leaf hop in several years. Its gentlemen members guaranteed that.

So easily and smoothly had Dempsey and the board done their preliminary work that many in the hall had not noticed the checking of the fascinating O'Sullivan's social triumph. Among these was Maggie. She looked about for her escort.

"Smoke up!" said Rose Cassidy. "Wasn't you on? Demps Donovan picked a scrap with your Lizzie-boy, and they've waltzed out to the slaughter room with him. How's my hair look done up this way, Mag?"

Maggie laid a hand on the bosom of her cheesecloth waist.

"Gone to fight with Dempsey!" she said, breathlessly. "They've got to be stopped. Dempsey Donovan can't fight him. Why, he'll—he'll kill him!"

"Ah, what do you care?" said Rose. "Don't some of 'em fight every hop?"

But Maggie was off, darting her zig-zag way through the maze of dancers. She burst through the rear door into the dark hall and then threw her solid shoulder against the door of the room of single combat. It gave way, and in the instant that she entered her eye caught the scene—the board standing about with open watches; Dempsey Donovan in his shirt sleeves dancing, light-footed, with the wary grace of the modern pugilist, within easy reach of his adversary; Terry O'Sullivan standing with arms folded and a murderous look in his dark eyes. And without slacking the speed of her entrance she leaped forward with a scream—leaped in time to catch and hang upon the arm of O'Sullivan that was suddenly uplifted, and to whisk from it the long, bright stiletto that he had drawn from his bosom.

The knife fell and rang upon the floor. Cold steel drawn in the rooms of the Give and Take Association! Such a thing had never happened before. Every one stood motionless for a minute. Andy Geoghan kicked the stiletto with the toe of his shoe curiously, like an antiquarian who has come upon some ancient weapon unknown to his learning.

And then O'Sullivan hissed something unintelligible between his teeth. Dempsey and the board exchanged looks. And then Dempsey looked at O'Sullivan without anger, as one looks at a stray dog, and nodded his head in the direction of the door.

"The back stairs, Giuseppi," he said, briefly. "Somebody'll pitch your hat down after you."

Maggie walked up to Dempsey Donovan. There was a brilliant spot of red in her cheeks, down which slow tears were running. But she looked him bravely in the eye.

"I knew it, Dempsey," she said, as her eyes grew dull even in their tears. "I knew he was a Guinea. His name's Tony Spinelli. I hurried in when they told me you and him was scrappin'. Them Guineas always carries knives. But you don't understand, Dempsey. I never had a fellow in my life. I got tired of comin' with Anna and Jimmy every night, so I fixed it with him to call himself O'Sullivan, and brought him along. I knew there'd be nothin' doin' for him if he came as a Dago. I guess I'll resign from the club now."

Dempsey turned to Andy Geoghan.

"Chuck that cheese slicer out of the window," he said, "and tell 'em inside that Mr. O'Sullivan has had a telephone message to go down to Tammany Hall."

And then he turned back to Maggie.

"Say, Mag," he said, "I'll see you home. And how about next Saturday night? Will you come to the hop with me if I call around for you?"

It was remarkable how quickly Maggie's eyes could change from dull to a shining brown.

"With you, Dempsey?" she stammered. "Say—will a duck swim?"

(1906)

From

GROPINGS IN LITERARY DARKNESS
by H. L. Mencken

"The Shadow," by Mary White Ovington (Harcourt), is a bad novel, but it is interesting as a first attempt by a colored writer to plunge into fiction in the grand manner.* Hitherto black America has confined itself chiefly to polemics and lyrical verse, not forgetting, of course, its high achievements in the sister art of music. James W. Johnson's "Biography of an Ex-Colored Man" is not,

---

*Mencken was mistaken about both the racial identity and the marital status of Miss Ovington.

at bottom, a novel at all, but a sort of mixture of actual biography and fantasy, with overtones of sociology. Mrs. Ovington issues a clearer challenge. Her book shows the familiar structure of the conventional novel—and a good deal of the familiar banality. At the very start she burdens herself with a highly improbable and untypical story. Perhaps she will answer that it once happened in real life. If so, the answer is no answer. I once knew a German saloon-keeper who drank sixty glasses of beer every day of his life, but a novel celebrating his life and eminent attainments would have been grossly false. The serious novel does not deal with prodigies; it deals with normalities. Who would argue that it is a normal phenomenon for a white girl to grow up unrecognized in a negro family, for her to pass over into her own race at twenty, for her to conceive a loathing for the scoundrelism and stupidity of the whites, and for her to prove it by going back to her black foster-relatives and resolving melodramatically to be "colored" herself thereafter? The thing is so hard to believe, even as a prodigy, that the whole story goes to pieces. Struggling with its colossal difficulties— they would daunt a Conrad or even a Bennett—Mrs. Ovington ends by making all of her characters mere word-machines. They have no more reality than so many clothing-store dummies or moving-picture actors.

Nevertheless, the author shows skill, observation, a civilized point of view. Let her forget her race prejudices and her infantile fables long enough to get a true, an unemotional and a typical picture of her people on paper, and she will not only achieve a respectable work of art, but also serve the cause that seems to have her devotion. As she herself points out, half of the difficulties between race and race are due to sheer ignorance. The black man, I suppose, has a fairly good working understanding of the white man; he has many opportunities to observe and note down, and my experience of him convinces me that he is a shrewd observer—that few white men ever fool him. But the white man, even in the South, knows next to nothing of the inner life of the negro. The more magnificently he generalizes, the more his ignorance is displayed. What the average Southerner believes about the negroes who surround him is chiefly nonsense. His view of them is moral and indignant, or, worse still, sentimental and idiotic. The great movements and aspirations that stir them are quite beyond his comprehension; in many cases he does not even hear of them. The thing we need is a realistic picture of this inner life of the negro by one who sees the race from within—a self-portrait as vivid and accurate as Dostoyevsky's portrait of the Russian or Thackeray's of the Englishman. The action should be kept within the normal range of negro experience. It should extend over a long enough range of years to show some development in character and circumstance. It should be presented against a background made vivid by innumerable small details. The negro author who makes such a book will dignify American literature and accomplish more for his race than a thousand propagandists and theorists. He will force the understanding that now seems so hopeless. He will blow up nine tenths of the current poppycock. But let him avoid the snares that fetched Mrs. Ovington. She went to Kathleen Norris and Gertrude Atherton for her model. The place to learn how to write novels is in the harsh but distinguished seminary kept by Prof. Dr. Dreiser.

Another somewhat defective contribution to negro literature, this time by a white author, is "The Negro Faces America," by Herbert J. Seligmann (Harper.) The author's aim is, first, to rehearse the difficulties confronting the emerging negro of the United States, particularly in the South, and, secondly, to expose the shallowness and inaccuracy of some of the current notions regarding negro capacities and negro character. Most of this balderdash, of course, originates in the South, where gross ignorance of the actual negro of today is combined with a great cocksureness. But *all* of the prevailing generalizations, even in the South, are not dubious, and Mr. Seligmann weakens his case when he hints that they are. For example, there is the generalization that the average negro is unreliable, that he has a rather lame sense of the sacredness of contract, that it is impossible to count upon him doing what he freely promises to do. This unreliability, it seems to me, is responsible for a great deal of the race feeling that smoulders in the South. The white man is forced to deal with negroes daily, and it irritates him constantly to find them so undependable. True enough, it is easy to prove that this failing is not met with in negroes of the upper classes, and it may be even argued plausibly that it is not intrinsically a negro character—that the pure and undebauched African is a model of honor. But the fact remains that the Southern whites have to deal with the actual negroes before them, and not with a theoretical race of African kings. These actual negroes show defects that are very real and very serious. The leaders of the race, engrossed by the almost unbearable injustices that it faces, are apt to forget them. Here is a chance for its white friends to do it a genuine service. What it needs most, of course, is a fair chance in the world, a square deal in its effort to rise, but what it needs after that is honest and relentless criticism. This criticism is absent from Mr. Seligmann's book. The negro he depicts is an innocent who never was on land or sea.

(1920)

WHO'S PASSING FOR WHO?
by Langston Hughes

One of the great difficulties about being a member of a minority race is that so many kindhearted, well-meaning bores gather around to help. Usually, to tell the truth, they have nothing to help with, except their company—which is often appallingly dull.

Some members of the Negro race seem very well able to put up with it, though, in these uplifting years. Such was Caleb Johnson, colored social worker, who was always dragging around with him some nondescript white person or two, inviting them to dinner, showing them Harlem, ending up at the Savoy—much to the displeasure of whatever friends of his might be out that evening for fun, not sociology.

Friends are friends and, unfortunately, overearnest uplifters are uplifters—no matter what color they may be. If it were the white race that was ground down instead of Negroes, Caleb Johnson would be one of the first to offer Nordics the sympathy of his utterly inane society, under the impression that somehow he would be doing them a great deal of good.

You see, Caleb, and his white friends, too, were all bores. Or so we who lived in Harlem's literary bohemia during the "Negro Renaissance" thought. We literary ones considered ourselves too broad-minded to be bothered with questions of color. We liked people of any race who smoked incessantly, drank liberally, wore complexion and morality as loose garments, and made fun of anyone who didn't do likewise. We snubbed and high-hatted any Negro or white luckless enough not to understand Gertrude Stein, Ulysses, Man Ray, the theremin, Jean Toomer, or George Antheil. By the end of the 1920's Caleb was just catching up to Dos Passos. He thought H. G. Wells good.

We met Caleb one night in Small's. He had three assorted white folks in tow. We would have passed him by with but a nod had he not hailed us enthusiastically, risen, and introduced us with great acclaim to his friends, who turned out to be schoolteachers from Iowa, a woman and two men. They appeared amazed and delighted to meet all at once two Negro writers and a black painter in the flesh. They invited us to have a drink with them. Money being scarce with us, we deigned to sit down at their table.

The white lady said, "I've never met a Negro writer before."

The two men added, "Neither have we."

"Why, we know any number of *white* writers," we three dark bohemians declared with bored nonchalance.

"But Negro writers are much more rare," said the lady.

"There are plenty in Harlem," we said.

"But not in Iowa," said one of the men, shaking his mop of red hair.

"There are no good *white* writers in Iowa either, are there?" we asked superciliously.

"Oh, yes, Ruth Suckow came from there."

Whereupon we proceeded to light in upon Ruth Suckow as old hat and to annihilate her in favor of Kay Boyle. The way we flung names around seemed to impress both Caleb and his white guests. This, of course, delighted us, though we were too young and too proud to admit it.

The drinks came and everything was going well, all of us drinking, and we three showing off in a high-brow manner, when suddenly at the table just behind us a man got up and knocked down a woman. He was a brownskin man. The woman was blonde. As she rose he knocked her down again. Then the red-haired man from Iowa got up and knocked the colored man down.

He said, "Keep your hands off that white woman."

The man got up and said, "She's not a white woman. She's my wife."

One of the waiters added, "She's not white, sir, she's colored."

Whereupon the man from Iowa looked puzzled, dropped his fists, and said, "I'm sorry."

The colored man said, "What are you doing up here in Harlem anyway, interfering with my family affairs?"

The white man said, "I thought she was a white woman."

The woman who had been on the floor rose and said, "Well, I'm not a white woman, I'm colored, and you leave my husband alone."

Then they both lit in on the gentleman from Iowa. It took all of us and several waiters, too, to separate them. When it was over the manager requested us to kindly pay our bill and get out. He said we were disturbing the peace. So we all left. We went to a fish restaurant down the street. Caleb was terribly apologetic to his white friends. We artists were both mad and amused.

"Why did you say you were sorry," said the colored painter to the visitor from Iowa, "after you'd hit that man—and then found out it wasn't a white woman you were defending, but merely a light colored woman who looked white?"

"Well," answered the red-haired Iowan, "I didn't mean to be butting in if they were all the same race."

"Don't you think a woman needs defending from a brute, no matter what race she may be?" asked the painter.

"Yes, but I think it's up to you to defend your own women."

"Oh, so you'd divide up a brawl according to races, no matter who was right?"

"Well, I wouldn't say that."

"You mean you wouldn't defend a colored woman whose husband was knocking her down?" asked the poet.

Before the visitor had time to answer, the painter said, "No! You just got mad because you thought a black man was hitting a *white* woman."

"But she *looked* like a white woman," countered the man.

"Maybe she was just passing for colored," I said.

"Like some Negroes pass for white," Caleb interposed.

"Anyhow, I don't like it," said the colored painter, "the way you stopped defending her when you found out she wasn't white."

"No, we don't like it," we all agreed except Caleb.

Caleb said in extenuation, "But Mr. Stubblefield is new to Harlem."

The red-haired white man said, "Yes, it's my first time here."

"Maybe Mr. Stubblefield ought to stay out of Harlem," we observed.

"I agree," Mr. Stubblefield said. "Good night."

He got up then and there and left the café. He stalked as he walked. His red head disappeared into the night.

"Oh, that's too bad," said the white couple who remained. "Stubby's temper just got the best of him. But explain to us, are many colored folks really as fair as that woman?"

"Sure, lots of them have more white blood than colored, and pass for white."

"Do they?" said the lady and gentleman from Iowa.

"You never read Nella Larsen?" we asked.

"She writes novels," Caleb explained. "She's part white herself."

"Read her," we advised. "Also read the *Autobiography of an Ex-colored Man.*" Not that we had read it ourselves—because we paid but little attention to the older colored writers—but we knew it was about passing for white.

We all ordered fish and settled down comfortably to shocking our white friends with tales about how many Negroes there were passing for white all over America. We were determined to *épater le bourgeois* real good via this white couple we had cornered, when the woman leaned over the table in the midst of our dissertations and said, "Listen, gentlemen, you needn't spread the word, but me and my husband aren't white either. We've just been *passing* for white for the last fifteen years,"

"What?"

"We're colored, too, just like you," said the husband. "But it's better passing for white because we make more money."

Well, that took the wind out of us. It took the wind out of Caleb, too. He thought all the time he was showing some fine white folks Harlem—and they were as colored as he was!

Caleb almost never cursed. But this time he said, "I'll be damned!"

Then everybody laughed. And laughed! We almost had hysterics. All at once we dropped our professionally self-conscious "Negro" manners, became natural, ate fish, and talked and kidded freely like colored folks do when there are no white folks around. We really had fun then, joking about that red-haired guy who mistook a fair colored woman for white. After the fish we went to two or three more night spots and drank until five o'clock in the morning.

Finally we put the light-colored people in a taxi heading downtown. They turned to shout a last good-by. The cab was just about to move off, when the woman called to the driver to stop.

She leaned out the window and said with a grin, "Listen, boys! I hate to confuse you again. But, to tell the truth, my husband and I aren't really colored at all. We're white. We just thought we'd kid you by passing for colored a little while—just as you said Negroes sometimes pass for white."

She laughed as they sped off toward Central Park, waving, "Good-by!"

We didn't say a thing. We just stood there on the corner in Harlem dumbfounded—not knowing now *which* way we'd been fooled. Were they really white—passing for colored? Or colored—passing for white?

Whatever race they were, they had had too much fun at our expense— even if they did pay for the drinks.

(1933)

From

CALL IT SLEEP
by Henry Roth

He had sat there a long time. Steadiness slowly returned to him. The planks of the dock stiffened and grew firm. He rose.

—Funny little lights all gone. Like when you squeeze too hard on a toilet. Better go home.

He approached the end of the dock. Voices, as he neared the cobbles made him look over to the left. Three boys, coming from Eighth Street, climbed nimbly over the snarled chaos of the open junk heap. At the sight of David, they hallooed, leapt down to level ground and raced toward him. All wore caps cocked sideways and sweaters, red and green, smeared, torn at the breast and elbows. Two were taller than David, wiry, blue-eyed, upturned noses freckled. The other, dark-skinned and runty, looked older than the rest and carried in his hand a sword made of a thin strip of metal that looked like sheet zinc and a long bolt wired across it near one end. One glance at their tough, hostile faces, smirched by the grime and rust of the junk heap and screwed up into malicious watchfulness was enough. David's eyes darted about for an opening. There was none— except back to the dock. Trapped, he stood still, his frightened gaze wavering from one menacing face to another.

"Wadda yiz doin' on 'at dock?" growled the runty one side-mouthed. The sunlight glanced along the sheet zinc sword as he pointed.

"N—Nottin. I was'n' doin' nott'n. Dey was boats dere."

"How old 're youse?"

"I'm—I'm eight already."

"Well, w'y aintchjis in school?"

"Cause id'd, cause—" But something warned him. "Cause I—cause my brudder's god measles."

"Dot's a lodda bullshit, Pedey." This from the freckled one. "He's onna hook."

"Yea. Tell 'at tuh Sweeney."

"We oughta take yiz tuh a cop," added the second freckled one.

"Betcha de cop'll tell yuh," urged David, hoping for no better fate.

"Nah! *We* know," Pedey scornfully rejected the idea. "W'ere d'yiz live?"

"Dere." He could see the very windows of his own floor. "Dat house on nint' stritt. My mudders gonna look oud righd away."

Pedey squinted in the direction David pointed.

"Dat's a sheeney block, Pedey," prompted the second freckled lieutenant with ominous eagerness.

"Yea. Yer a Jew aintchiz?"

"No I ain'!" he protested hotly. "I ain' nod a Jew!"

"Only sheenies live in dat block!" countered Pedey narrowly.

"I'm a Hungarian. My mudder 'n' fodder's Hungarian. We're de janitors."

"W'y wuz yuh lookin upstairs?"

"Cause my mudder wuz washin' de floors."

"Talk Hungarian," challenged the first lieutenant.

"Sure like dis. Abashishishabababyo tomama wawa. Like dot."

"Aa, yuh full o' shit!" sneered the second lieutenant angrily. "C'mon, Pedey, let's give 'im 'is lumps."

"Yea!" the other freckled one urged. "C'mon. He ain' w'ite. Yi! Yi! Yi!" He wagged his palms under his chin.

"Naa!" Pedey nudged his neighbor sharply. "He's awri'. Led 'im alone." And to David. "Got any dough? We'll match yiz pennies."

"No, I ain' god nodd'n. Id's all in mine house." He would have been glad to have the two pennies now if only they would let him go.

"Let's see yer pockets?"

"Hea, I'll show yuh," he hastily turned them inside out. "Nod even in duh watch pocket."

"C'mon, Pedey," urged first lieutenant, advancing.

"Lemme go!" David whimpered, shrinking back.

"Naa! Let 'im alone," ordered Pedey. "He's awright. Let's show 'im de magic. Waddayah say?"

"Yea! At's right!" The other two seconded him. "C'mon! Yuh wanna see some magic?"

"No-no. I don' wanna."

"Yuh don'!" Pedey's voice rose fiercely. The others strained at the leash.

"W—wa' kind o' magic?"

"C'mon, we'll show yiz, won' we, Weasel? Over dis way." His sword pointed across the junk-heap toward Tenth Street. "Where de car tracks is."

"So wod yuh gonna do?" he held back.

"C'mon we'll show yiz." They hemmed him in cutting off retreat. "Ah here's my sword—G'wan take it, fore we—" He thrust it into David's hands. He took it. They moved forward.

At the foot of the junk-heap, the lieutenant named Weasel stopped. "Waid a minute," he announced, "I godda take a piss."

"Me too," said the others halting as well. They unbuttoned. David edged away.

"Lager beer," chanted Pedey as he tapped forehead, mouth, chest and navel, "comes from here—"

"Ye see," Weasel pointed triumphantly at the shrinking David. "I tol' yuh he ain' w'ite. W'y don'tchiz piss?"

"Don' wanna. I peed befaw."

"Aw, hosschit." He lifted one leg.

"Phuwee!"

With a howl of glee, the other two pounced on him.

"Eli, eli, a bundle of strawr," they thumped his back. "Farting is against de lawr—"

"Leggo!" Weasel shook them off viciously.

"Well yiz farted—Hey!" Pedey swooped down on David. "Stay here, or yuh'll get a bust on de bugle! C'mon! An' don't try to duck on us."

With one on either side of him and one behind, David climbed up the junk heap and threaded his way cautiously over the savage iron morraine. Only one hope sustained him—that was to find a man on the other side to run to. Before him the soft, impartial April sunlight spilt over a hill of shattered stoves, splintered wheels, cracked drain pipes, potsherds, marine engines split along cruel and jagged edges. Eagerly, he looked beyond—only the suddenly alien, empty street and the glittering cartracks, branching off at the end.

"Peugh! Wadda stink!" Pedey spat. "Who opened his hole?"

From somewhere in the filth and ruin, the stench of mouldering flesh fouled the nostrils. A dead cat.

"C'mon, hurry up!"

As they neared the street, a rusty wire, tough root of a brutal soil, tripped David who had quickened his pace, and he fell against the sword bending it.

"He pissed in his w'iskers," guffawed the second lieutenant.

Pedey grinned. Only Weasel kept his features immobile. He seemed to take pride in never laughing.

"Hol' it, yuh dumb bassid," he barked, "yuh bent it!"

"Waid a secon'," Pedey warned them when they had reached the edge of the junk-heap. "Lemme lay putso." He slid down, and after a furtive glance toward Avenue D, "Come on! Shake! Nobody's aroun'."

They followed him.

"Now we're gonna show yiz de magic."

"Waid'll ye sees it," Weasel chimed in significantly.

"Yea, better'n movin' pitchiz!"

"Wadda yuh wan' I shul do?" Their growing excitement added to his terror.

"Hurry up an' take dat sword an' go to dem tracks and t'row it in—See like dis. In de middle."

"I don't wanna go." He began to weep.

"G'wan yuh blubber-mout'." Weasel's fist tightened.

"G'wan!" The other lieutenant's face screwed up. " 'Fore we kick de piss ouda yiz."

"G'wan, an' we'll letchiz go," promised Pedey. "G'wan! Shake!"

"If I jost pud id in?"

"Yea. Like I showed yuh."

"An' den yuh'll led me go?"

"Sure. G'wan. Id ain' gonna hoitcha. Ye'll see all de movies in de woil! An' vawderville too! G'wan before a car comes."

"Sure, an' all de angels."

"G'wan!" Their fists were drawn back.

Imploringly, his eyes darted to the west. The people on Avenue D seemed miles away. The saloon-door in the middle of the block was closed. East. No none! Not a soul! Beyond the tarry rocks of the river-shore, the wind had scattered the silver plain into rippling scales. He was trapped.

"G'wan!" Their faces were cruel, their bodies stiff with expectancy.

He turned toward the tracks. The long dark grooves between each pair looked as harmless as they had always looked. He had stepped over them hundreds of times without a thought. What was there about them now that made the others watch him so? Just drop it, they said, and they would let him go. Just drop it. He edged closer, stood tip-toe on the cobbles. The point of the sheet-zinc sword wavered before him, clicked on the stone as he fumbled, then finding the slot at last, rasped part way down the wide grinning lips like a tongue in an iron mouth. He stepped back. From open fingers, the blade plunged into darkness.

Power!

Like a paw ripping through all the stable fibres of the earth, power, gigantic, fetterless, thudded into day! And light, unleashed, terrific light bellowed out of iron lips. The street quaked and roared, and like a tortured thing, the sheet zinc sword, leapt writhing, fell back, consumed with radiance. Blinded, stunned by the brunt of brilliance, David staggered back. A moment later, he was spurting madly toward Avenue D.

(1934)

From

BROTHERS THREE
by John M. Oskison

On his return, Timmy became conscious of the change that was being wrought by the invaders of this Indian land, turning it from Indian serenity to white man turbulence. More and more alien families, unlike the first settlers on Bee Creek and Redbud Creek who were proud of a Cherokee strain on at least one side of the house, these newer comers were all white, living on land leased from Indians.

They threw up flimsy board shacks as houses; their barns were the crudest possible hay-covered sheds; and their fences, three slack wires stapled to widely spaced hackberry and cottonwood poles cut in the nearest creek bottom and certain to rot off at the ground within ten years, were parodies of stock-tight barriers. They belonged to the shiftless, drifting class, given to windy talk and indiscriminate "borrying." Loafing on the main street of Avra, they laughed inanely, spattered the sidewalk with tobacco juice. They were contemptuous of the Indians, and promised to hasten the movement for making the Indian Territory into a "white man's state." They carried on, in grotesque caricature, the tradition that the "savage red man" must, because of his incompetence, give way to the white. Their dirtiest tow-headed moron child of fifteen was taught to feel superior to such boys as Timmy—to any child however slightly "tainted" by Indian blood.

*   *   *   *   *

It was after Timmy had acquired his second touring car, and his third child, Claude Francis, was almost six months old, that the inevitable happened. He became Es-Teece's lover.

She wished to drive the new car, saying, "If it run the way you tell me, I sell mine and make papa buy one for me."

Sitting beside her, with no need to instruct her, he thought, "She's nicer than ever," and touched her shoulder with his. Then his arm went across her shoulders. When his hand found her breast, she stopped the car, leaned to him, and said, "I can't drive while you doing that."

"Want me to stop?"

She looked straight into his eyes, and asked, "You still like me, Tim? Like that?"

There was no coquetry in her tone, Timmy knew he faced a decision: either he must not be alone with her, or—he plunged, "Yes, I do, 'Steece! Do you?"

They kissed with the passion of lovers. She yielded the steering wheel to him, and sat relaxed against him as he drove along a road that, at dusk, became a dark tunnel under the trees beside Bee Creek. Before taking her home they had, as he said, "crossed the bridge."

He was remorseful, " 'Steece, that's—that's terrible! I didn't intend—"

Her lips on his, she smiled, drew away and asked, "What you mean? We both want' to do that, didn' we?"

"But we oughtn't to, that's what I mean. We've no right to—to—" he couldn't go on.

"You like me that way, you say. Me, too. I like you that way. Well?" she challenged him earnestly.

He made no answer for a time, thinking, "It must be the Indian in her that makes her take it like this."

Perhaps he was right. The Indians of that day stood between the old moral order and a new that was confusing. There was the old tribal code, in which the act of sexual intercourse had no special significance, illegitimate birth carried no reproach, and in which the consummation of love occurred without disgrace or punishment. According to that code, virginity was neither an asset nor a liability, and a woman was expected to remain true to a man only after marriage. Had Timmy asked, Es-Teece would have told him she was not a virgin, quite as frankly as many white girls said later, "Of course I've had men, why not?" She did say, "What it matter, if we like each other and want to do that?"

"But May, and my children, 'Steece. How can I ever look them in the face again?"

She said nothing, letting her hand lie limply in his.

Timmy thought, "She's years younger than I, but she seems ages older. Or maybe she just hasn't any moral sense—looks like she doesn't think any more of it than kissing."

If he could only take her view of it, how simple his course might be. He said to himself, "Anyway, I can try." His next words caused Es-Teece to smile, "Well, nobody knows but us, and if it never happens again—'Steece, it mustn't!"

Without looking at him, she said slowly, "That is for you to say, Tim."

On the way home, he tried desperately to wipe out of his mind all memory of the experience.

He need not have feared May's suspicion. The explanation he made of his late arrival she accepted with the casual comment, "I reckon you'll always have trouble with these machines." If he imagined that some taint of his act of betrayal would linger to alarm her as they lay together, and she drew him into her arms before going to sleep, there was nothing to justify it—she slept as soundly as ever.

But his night was torturing. He lay still, as though asleep, thinking, "Of course, I love May as much as ever. She loves me just the same. She's so sweet. She has that perfume on her nightgown. Never again will I have 'Steece, I'd be a fool to do it again. And I don't mean much to her anyway.'' He pictured the girl in his arms, almost passive; he saw her eyes, in the moonlight, half closed as though she were lost in a dream. There was a tense stillness about her. Her body was slender, brown even in the moonlight, and so alive. There had been no voiced raptures. "No, it can't mean much to her, and I'd be a fool—" But when they had got back into the car, she had crowded close to him, breathed a hardly audible, "Tim!" and pulled his head to her as she kissed him. What did that whisper mean? Love? Or just animal contentment? It was then that he had been slugged by remorse.

Did she expect anything more? Had she thought about May? Did she imagine he would divorce May, and marry her? No! It was absurd to let the question enter his mind.

Timmy grew indignant with himself, resentful of her power to torture him, "Why can't I stop worrying? She's just a prostitute, but not half as passionate and nice as Hattie Wilson. She won't lose any sleep thinking about me. She said there wasn't any danger of—she knows how to look after herself. Suppose we do it again, it won't mean anything. She's not cold, it's not that, only—I reckon maybe it's her way."

May moved in her sleep, sighed profoundly. She had grown plump, broadened; she had become solid, confident; mother of his children, absorbed in them, and in the Farm. Less absorbed in Timmy? He asked himself the question. Perhaps. She loved him no less, however. She would never want another man; he filled her need. But, unconsciously, her need was abating.

He had a vision, which he quickly blotted out of his mind: his wife and Es-Teece lying side by side, inviting comparison of their bodies, May's rather thick now, firm, powerful, but grown sluggish, the Indian girl's agile, lithe, restrained but hinting of its resources of savage ecstasy.

"I'm crazy!" he brought himself up fiercely.

It was bound to go on. Keeping away from Es-Teece for only a week meant a restlessness that was torture. Taking her again was joy, an excitement that was heightened by her whisper, "All the time since, Tim, I think about you."

"Why, 'Steece, I didn't know you cared; you never told me."

"I am Indian. We don't talk much about such things." She squeezed his hand quickly, released it, "You are not enough Indian to understand me."

(1935)

From

THE ODYSSEY OF A WOP
by John Fante

2

From the beginning, I hear my mother use the words Wop and Dago with such vigor as to denote violent distaste. She spits them out. They leap from her lips. To her, they contain the essence of poverty, squalor, filth. If I don't wash my teeth, or hang up my cap, my mother says: "Don't be like that. Don't be a Wop." Thus, as I begin to acquire her values, Wop and Dago to me become synonymous with things evil. But she's consistent.

My father isn't. He's loose with his tongue. His moods create his judgments. I at once notice to him Wop and Dago are without any distinct meaning, though if one not an Italian slaps them onto him, he's instantly insulted. Christopher Columbus was the greatest Wop who ever lived, says my father. So is Caruso. So is this fellow and that. But his very good friend Peter Ladonna is not only a drunken pig, but a Wop on top of it; and of course all his brothers-in-law are good-for-nothing Wops.

He pretends to hate the Irish. He really doesn't, but he likes to think so, and he warns us children against them. Our grocer's name is O'Neil. Frequently and inadvertently he makes errors when my mother is at his store. She tells my father about short weights in meats, and now and then of a stale egg.

Straightway my father grows tense, his lower lip curling. "This is the last time that Irish bum robs me!" And he goes out, goes to the grocery-store, his heels booming.

Soon he returns. He's smiling. His fists bulge with cigars. "From now on," says he, "everything's gonna be all right."

I don't like the grocer. My mother sends me to his store every day, and instantly he chokes up my breathing with the greeting: "Hello, you little Dago! What'll you have?" So I detest him, and never enter his store if other customers are to be seen, for to be called a Dago before others is a ghastly, almost a physical, humiliation. My stomach expands and contracts, and I feel naked.

I steal recklessly when the grocer's back is turned. I enjoy stealing from him—candy bars, cookies, fruit. When he goes into his refrigerator I lean on his meat scales, hoping to snap a spring; I press my toe into egg baskets. Sometimes I pilfer too much. Then, what a pleasure it is to stand on the curb, my appetite gorged, and heave *his* candy bars, *his* cookies, *his* apples into the high yellow weeds across the street! . . . . "Damn you, O'Neil, you can't call me a Dago and get away with it!"

His daughter is of my age. She's cross-eyed. Twice a week she passes our house on her way to her music lesson. Above the street, and high in the branches of an elm tree, I watch her coming down the sidewalk, swinging her violin case. When she is under me, I jeer in sing-song:

Martha's crooooooss-eyed!
Martha's crooooooss-eyed!
Martha's crooooooss-eyed!

3

As I grow older, I find out that Italians use Wop and Dago much more than Americans. My grandmother, whose vocabulary of English is confined to the commonest of nouns, always employs them in discussing contemporary Italians. The words never come forth quietly, unobtrusively. No, they bolt forth. There is a blatant intonation, and then the sense of someone being scathed, stunned.

I enter the parochial school with an awful fear that I will be called Wop. As soon as I find out why people have such things as surnames, I match my own against such typically Italian cognomens as Bianchi, Borello, Pacelli—the names of other students. I am pleasantly relieved by the comparison. After all, I think, people will say I am French. Doesn't my name sound French? Sure! So thereafter, when people ask me my nationality, I tell them I am French. A few boys begin calling me Frenchy. I like that. It feels fine.

Thus I begin to loathe my heritage. I avoid Italian boys and girls who try to be friendly. I thank God for my light skin and hair, and I choose my companions by the Anglo-Saxon ring of their names. If a boy's name is Whitney, Brown, or Smythe, then he's my pal; but I'm always a little breathless when I am with him; he may find me out. At the lunch hour I huddle over my lunch pail, for my mother doesn't wrap my sandwiches in wax paper, and she makes them too large, and the lettuce leaves protrude. Worse, the bread is homemade; not bakery bread, not "American" bread. I make a great fuss because I can't have mayonnaise and other "American" things.

The parish priest is a good friend of my father's. He comes strolling through the school grounds, watching the children at play. He calls to me and asks about my father, and then he tells me I should be proud to be studying about my great countrymen, Columbus, Vespucci, John Cabot. He speaks in a loud, humorous voice. Students gather around us, listening, and I bite my lips and wish to Jesus he'd shut up and move on.

Occasionally now I hear about a fellow named Dante. But when I find out that he was an Italian I hate him as if he were alive and walking through the classrooms, pointing a finger at me. One day I find his picture in a dictionary. I look at it and tell myself that never have I seen an uglier bastard.

We students are at the blackboard one day, and a soft-eyed Italian girl whom I hate but who insists that I am her beau stands beside me. She twitches and shuffles about uneasily, half on tiptoe, smiling queerly at me. I sneer and turn my back, moving as far away from her as I can. The nun sees the wide space separating us and tells me to move nearer the girl. I do so, and the girl draws away, nearer the student on her other side.

Then I look down at my feet, and there I stand in a wet, spreading spot. I look quickly at the girl, and she hangs her head and looks at me in a way that begs me to take the blame for her. We attract the attention of others, and the classroom becomes alive with titters. Here comes the nun. I think I am in for it again, but she embraces me and murmurs that I should have raised two fingers and of course I would have been allowed to leave the room. But, says she, there's no need for that now; the thing for me to do is go out and get the mop. I do so, and amid the hysteria I nurse my conviction that only a Wop girl, right out of a Wop home, would ever do such a thing as this.

Oh, you Wop! Oh, you Dago! You bother me even when I sleep. I dream of defending myself against tormentors. One day I learn from my mother that my father went to the Argentine in his youth, and lived in Buenos Aires for two years. My mother tells me of his experiences there, and all day I think about them, even to the time I go to sleep. That night I come awake with a jerk. In the darkness I grope my way to my mother's room. My father sleeps at her side, and I awaken her gently, so that he won't be aroused.

I whisper: "Are you sure Papa wasn't *born* in Argentina?"

"No. Your father was born in Italy."

I go back to bed, disconsolate and disgusted.

4

During a ball game on the school grounds, a boy who plays on the opposing team begins to ridicule my playing. It is the ninth inning, and I ignore his taunts. We are losing the game, but if I can knock out a hit our chances of winning are pretty strong. I am determined to come through, and I face the pitcher confidently. The tormentor sees me at the plate.

"Ho! Ho!" he shouts. "Look who's up! The Wop's up. Let's get rid of the Wop!"

This is the first time anyone at school has ever flung the word at me, and I am so angry that I strike out foolishly. We fight after the game, this boy and I, and I make him take it back.

Now school days become fighting days. Nearly every afternoon at 3:15 a crowd gathers to watch me make some guy take it back. This is fun; I am getting somewhere now, so come on, you guys, I dare you to call me a Wop! When at length there are no more boys who challenge me, insults come to me by hearsay, and I seek out the culprits. I strut down the corridors. The smaller boys admire me. "Here he comes!" they say, and they gaze and gaze. My two younger brothers attend the same school, and the smallest, a little squirt seven years old, brings his friends to me and asks me to roll up my sleeve and show them my muscles. Here you are, boys. Look me over.

My brother brings home furious accounts of my battles. My father listens avidly, and I stand by, to clear up any doubtful details. Sadly happy days! My father gives me pointers: how to hold my fist, how to guard my head. My mother, too shocked to hear more, presses her temples and squeezes her eyes and leaves the room.

I am nervous when I bring friends to my house; the place looks so Italian. Here hangs a picture of Victor Emmanuel, and over there is one of the cathedral of Milan, and next to it one of St. Peter's, and on the buffet stands a wine pitcher of medieval design; it's forever brimming, forever red and brilliant with wine. These things are heirlooms belonging to my father, and no matter who may come to our house, he likes to stand under them and brag.

So I begin to shout to him. I tell him to cut out being a Wop and be an American once in a while. Immediately he gets his razor strop and whales hell out of me, clouting me from room to room and finally out the back door. I go into the woodshed and pull down my pants and stretch my neck to examine the blue slices across my rump. A Wop, that's what my father is! Nowhere is there an American father who beats his son this way. Well, he's not going to get away with it; some day I'll get even with him.

I begin to think that my grandmother is hopelessly a Wop. She's a small, stocky peasant who walks with her wrists criss-crossed over her belly, a simple old lady fond of boys. She comes into the room and tries to talk to my friends. She speaks English with a bad accent, her vowels rolling out like hoops. When, in her simple way, she confronts a friend of mine and says, her old eyes smiling, "You lika go the Seester scola?" my heart roars. *Mannaggia!* I'm disgraced; now they all know that I'm an Italian.

My grandmother has taught me to speak her native tongue. By seven, I know it pretty well, and I always address her in it. But when friends are with me, when I am twelve and thirteen, I pretend ignorance of what she says, and smirk stiffly; my friends daren't know that I can speak any language but English. Sometimes this infuriates her. She bristles, the loose skin at her throat knits hard, and she blasphemes with a mighty blasphemy.

5

When I finish in the parochial school my people decide to send me to a Jesuit academy in another city. My father comes with me on the first day. Chiseled into the stone coping that skirts the roof of the main building of the academy is the Latin inscription: *Religioni et Bonis Artibus*. My father and I stand at a distance, and he reads it aloud and tells me what it means.

I look up at him in amazement. Is this man my father? Why, look at him! Listen to him! He reads with an Italian inflection! He's wearing an Italian mustache. I have never realized it until this moment, but he looks exactly like a Wop. His suit hangs carelessly in wrinkles upon him. Why the deuce doesn't he buy a new one? And look at his tie! It's crooked. And his shoes: they need a shine. And, for the Lord's sake, will you look at his pants! They're not even buttoned in front. And oh, damn, damn, damn, you can see those dirty old suspenders that he won't throw away. Say, Mister, are you really my father? You there, why, you're such a little guy, such a runt, such an old-looking fellow! You look exactly like one of those immigrants carrying a blanket. You can't be *my* father! Why, I thought . . . I've always thought . . .

I'm crying now, the first time I've ever cried for any reason except a licking, and I'm glad he's not crying too. I'm glad he's as tough as he is, and we say good-by quickly, and I go down the path quickly, and I do not turn to look back, for I know he's standing there and looking at me.

I enter the administration building and stand in line with strange boys who also wait to register for the autumn term. Some Italian boys stand among them. I am away from home, and I sense the Italians. We look at one another and our eyes meet in an irresistible amalgamation, a suffusive consanguinity; I look away.

A burly Jesuit rises from his chair behind the desk and introduces himself to me. Such a voice for a man! There are a dozen thunderstorms in his chest. He asks my name, and writes it down on a little card.

"Nationality?" he roars.

"American."

"Your father's name?"

I whisper it: "Guido."

"How's that? Spell it out. Talk louder."

I cough. I touch my lips with the back of my hand and spell out the name.

"Ha!" shouts the registrar. "And still they come! Another Wop! Well, young man, you'll be at home here! Yes, sir! Lots of Wops here! We've even got Kikes! And, you know this place reeks with shanty Irish!"

Dio! How I hate that priest!

He continues: "Where was your father born?"

"Buenos Aires, Argentina."

"Your mother?"

At last I can shout with the gusto of truth.

"Denver!" Aye, just like a conductor.

Casually, by the way of conversation, he asks: "You speak Italian?"

"Nah! Not a word."

"Too bad," he says.

"You're nuts," I think.

(1940)

From

WHAT MAKES SAMMY RUN?
by Budd Schulberg

Max Glickstein was a diamond cutter in the old country, proud of his trade and his religion. After the pogrom that took his first-born, Max brought his wife and other son to America. The child died in mid-ocean. "We must be brave, Momma," Max tried to console her. "Maybe God is trying to tell us that we will carry none of the troubles of the old world into the new. We will have new sons, little Americans. In America we will find a new happiness and peace."

They found Rivington Street. But no diamonds to cut. In time, Max got a job cutting glass at ten dollars a week. "Glass," he complained. "Glass any jackass can cut. But diamonds!"

For years he cut glass every day but Saturday, when he worshiped his God, and Sunday, when the Christians worshiped theirs. And his wife bore him two sons, first Israel and five years later Shmelka. The midwife did not think Shmelka would live. He weighed only five and a half pounds. *"Nebbish* such a little one," said the midwife. "Were he a little kitten we would drown him already." But survival of the fittest is a more complex process with thinking animals. Even one who thought as simply as Mama Glickstein. She pushed her great breasts into his mouth until he choked, hollered, and began to live.

Because he was puny, Mama spent so much time with him that his growth was precocious. He walked before his first birthday. Talked before his second. When he was three-and-a-half, he changed his own name. One of Israel's friends always teased him with "Whadya say yer name is, *Smell ya?"* One day Momma called, "Shmelka, come here," and he paid no attention. She called his name again.

"Shmelka isn't my name any more," he said.

"No," Momma said, "then what is it, please?"

"Sammy," he said.

Sammy was the name of an older kid across the hall whose mother was always yelling for him.

The strike came when Sammy was four. The glasscutters wanted twelve-fifty. Papa was a foreman now, making sixteen, but he remembered how it was to live on ten dollars a week. And now it was even worse with the war boom started and prices rising. He walked out with his men.

"Mr. Glickstein, don't be a dope," the owner said. "In another two, three years you will becoming maybe a partner. To cut your own throat, that is not human. And what kind of foolishness is this when I can get plenty immigrants" (the owner having been here twenty years could look down on the aliens) "to take their places?"

Papa Glick's voice was deep and sure as if he were reading from the Bible. "To be a partner in a sweatshop, such honors I can do without."

But the owner was right about one thing. There were too many others. The strike dragged on six months—a year . . . They never saw those jobs again.

Neighbors helped the Glicksteins the way Papa had always helped them. And he picked up a few pennies as the Cantor in *schule* on Saturday. But he would gladly have served for nothing and often had. There in the synagogue, a dignitary with his impressive shawl, his *yarmolka* and his great beard, there life was rich and beautiful. The rest were just the necessary motions to keep alive.

And this they barely did. Sammy played in the streets without shoes. For his fifth birthday he was given a pair that Israel had outgrown. But they were still several sizes too large for him, and the way they flapped like a clown's made the other kids laugh. Sometimes when Sammy would run after his tormentors the shoes would fly off, and Sammy would pick them up in a rage and hurl them at his nearest enemy.

Papa Glick finally gave up any hope of resuming his trade again. He was too old. America was a land for young men. Finally he got himself a pushcart like all the others. He sold shirts, neckties and socks, nothing over twenty-five cents. But there were too many pushcarts and not enough customers. So Sammy started peddling papers. He was three feet, four inches high. He wanted to play. He couldn't see why Israel shouldn't do it instead. But soon Israel was going to be *bar-mitzvah*. After school let out at three o'clock he studied in the *cheder* until supper time. Papa was so proud of him. The *Melamud* had told him Israel had the makings of a real Talmudic scholar. And it was well known that the *Melamud* was a man who never had a good word to say for anyone but God. "God has blessed my son with the heart and brains of a rabbi," Papa boasted.

Sammy lugged his papers up and down Fourteenth Street yelling about a war in Europe. He used to come home with a hoarse throat and thirty or forty cents in pennies. He would count the money and say, "God dammit, I'm yellin' my brains out for nuttin'."

Papa Glick would look up from his prayer book. "Please, in this house we do not bring such language."

"Look who's talkin'," Sammy said. "Know what Foxy Four Eyes tol' me—he says I wouldn' hafta peddle papers if you wasn't such a dope and quit your job. He says his ol' man tol' him."

"Silence," said Papa Glick.

"He says that strike screwed us up good," said Sammy.

Papa Glick's hand clapped against Sammy's cheek. It left a red imprint on his white skin but he made no sound. By the time he was six he had learned how to be sullen.

"Papa, please," Mrs. Glickstein pleaded. "He's so small, how should he know what he's saying—he hears it on the street."

"That's so he should forget what he hears," said Papa.

Several weeks later Sammy came in with a dollar seventy-eight. Papa, Momma and Israel danced around him.

"Sammy, you sold out all the papers?" said Papa in amazement.

"Yeah," Sammy said. "There's a guy on the opposite corner doin' pretty good 'cause he's yellin' 'U.S. MAY ENTER WAR.' So I asks a customer if there's anything in the paper about that. So when he says no, I figure I can pull a fast one too. So I starts hollerin' U.S. ENTERS WAR and jeez you shoulda seen the rush!"

"But that was a lie," Papa Glick said. "To sell papers like that is no better than stealing."

"All the guys make up headlines," Sammy said. "Why don't you wise up?"

Sammy worked a year before he entered school.

That first day at P.S. 15, Sheik kept staring at him. He wanted to listen to what Miss Carr was saying, but he couldn't concentrate very well because the Sheik's small black eyes kept boring into him. Everybody knew the Sheik. His old lady was Italian and his old man was Irish and the neighbors would always hear them fighting at night over who was the better Catholic. The Sheik was older than anybody else in the class because he had been left back a couple of times. The kids didn't call him the Sheik because he was handsome, but because it was whispered around that he already knew what to do with little girls. There was even a story that he had knocked one up already, but this was probably circulated by Sheik himself who was a notorious boaster and had a habit of appropriating all his big brother's achievements.

The Sheik sat there all through the hour actively hating Sammy. Sammy had taken his seat, the seat he had had for the past two years. He had told Sammy, but Sammy had refused to budge. "O.K., yuh dirty kike," Sheik whispered harshly through his teeth. "See yuh after class."

It was lunch hour. Some of the kids were getting up a game of ball. Sammy wanted to play. After school there was *cheder*. And then papers to sell. Sammy was going to be a ball player when he grew up. He had a good eye and he was fast. But now he had to fight Sheik. Sheik was two years older, half a head taller. Sammy appraised him. He would probably get the bejesus kicked out of him. But he wasn't scared. Just sorry he couldn't get into that ball game. He followed Sheik into a vacant lot across the street, all boarded up and full of old tin cans and whatever anybody had ever felt like throwing there.

As soon as they got inside the Sheik let one go. It cracked against Sammy's nose, and blood spurted. Sammy's nose felt bigger than his whole face and he couldn't see, but he moved in swinging. Sheik caught him on the nose again. Sammy went down with Sheik on top of him, kicking and swinging, spitting into the bloody face under him, his whole body quivering in a frenzy of hate; shrieking until it became a chant, "You killed Christ. You killed Christ . . ."

When Sammy finally stopped fighting back, Sheik left him there and went to eat his lunch. Sammy tried to stay there until he stopped bleeding, but it wouldn't stop, so he had to walk back to the schoolyard that way. Miss Carr ran over and dragged him into the ladies' room. While she washed off the blood he stood there terribly white and terribly silent. No tears. Just his mouth set hard and his eyes ugly. "I think your nose is broken," she said.

"It don't hurt much," said Sammy.

"You'd better come into the office and lie down."

"Jeez, look where I am! The guys better not see me in the girls' can."

She didn't know how to treat him. She was new here and she had never seen kids like this before. If he would only cry she could comfort him like an injured child. But he would not let her.

"Hey, what the hell's the matter with that guy sayin' I killed Christ? The dirty bastard."

"You must not talk like that," said Miss Carr. "Christ died so that everyone should forgive each other and live in brotherly love."

"Yeah?" said Sammy. "How about Sheik? Don't he believe in Christ?"

"Well, yes," said Miss Carr, "but . . ."

"I gotta sit down," said Sammy, "my head's spinnin'."

Miss Carr tried to put her arms around him but he drew away. He was like a little injured animal snarling at the hand that is trying to help it.

"You won't have to worry from now on," she said. "I'm going to have a talk with Sheik. And I think I'll ask some of the bigger boys to look after you."

His voice made her sympathy sound patronizing. "Who ast ya to? I'm no sissy. I c'n take care-a myself."

Sheik felt called upon to avenge Christ every day. Sammy accepted his beatings as part of the school routine. He never tried to avoid them, to sneak off after school. He just absorbed it with the terrible calm of a sparring partner. He would come home every night with his eyes swollen or his lip cut and his mother would hold him in her arms and cry, Sammele, Sammele, but he never cried with her, only held himself stiff in her arms, a stranger to her.

After a while, there was no satisfaction left in it for Sheik any more. It had become manual labor, slaughter-house work. Sheik began to look around for more responsive victims. It even left Sheik with a strange kind of fear for Sammy. Somewhere along the line it had become the victim's triumph. Sammy would talk back to Sheik any time he liked. There was nothing Sheik could do but beat him up again. All the suffering that Sammy had swallowed instead of crying out had formed a hard cold ball of novocaine in the pit of his stomach that deadened all his nerves.

Life moved faster for Sammy. He was learning. The Glicksteins' poverty possessed him, but in a different way from Israel. He was always on the look-out to make a dollar. The way the little Christians put on Jewish hats and mingled with the Jewish boys to get free hand-outs in the synagogue on the holy days gave him an idea. On Saturday he went down to the Missions on the Bowery and let the Christ-spouters convert him. At two-bits a conversion. He came home rich with seventy-five cents jingling in his pockets. His father, struggling to maintain his last shred of authority, the patriarchy of his own home, demanded to know why he was not at *cheder*. Sammy hated *cheder*. Three hours a day in a stinking back room with a sour-faced old Reb who taught you a lot of crap about the Hebrew laws. You don't go to jail if you break the Hebrew laws. Only if you got no money and get caught stealing, or don't pay your rent.

"I hadda chance to make a dollar," Sammy said.

"Sammy!" his father bellowed. "Touching money on the Sabbath! God should strike you dead!"

The old man snatched the money and flung it down the stairs.

Sammy glared at his father the way he had at Sheik, the way he was beginning to glare at the world.

"You big dope!" Sammy screamed at him, his voice shrill with rage. "You lazy son-of-a-bitch."

The old man did not respond. His eyes were closed and his lips were moving. He looked as if he had had a stroke. He was praying.

Sammy went down and searched for the money until he found it.

His mother came down and sat on the stairs above him. She could never scold Sammy. She was sorry for Papa but she was sorry for Sammy too. She understood. Here in America life moves too fast for the Jews. There is not time enough to pray and survive. The old laws like not touching money or riding on the Sabbath—it was hard to make them work. Israel might try to live by them but never Sammy. Sammy frightened her. In the old country there may have been Jews who were thieves or tightwads and rich Jews who would not talk to poor ones, but she had never seen one like Sammy. Sammy was not a real Jew any more. He was no different from the little wops and micks who cursed and fought and cheated. Sometimes she could not believe he grew out of her belly. He grew out of the belly of Rivington Street.

When Papa Glick found out how Sammy made his seventy-five cents, he went to Synagogue four times a day instead of twice. He cried for God to save Sammy.

Sammy remained a virgin until he was eleven. But no storks ever nested in his childish fancy. When he was still in his cradle he could hear the creaking of bedsprings and his parents' loud breathing in the same room. Cramped quarters forced sex into the open. When Sammy ran to find a place to hide from the Jew-hunting gangs with rock-filled stockings who roamed the streets on Hallowe'en, he bumped into a couple locked together in the shadow of the tunnel-like corridor, behind the stairs. On sticky summer nights he used to trip over their legs as he raced across the roofs. The first day in the street he learned about the painted women who called out intimate names to men they didn't know. When he was ten he used to turn out the light to watch the lady across the court get undressed. She was fat, and when she let her great flabby breasts ooze out of her brassiere they flopped down like hams as she bent over. Curiosity and then desire began to creep into Sammy's wiry, undeveloped loins.

He even went up to one of the women around the corner and offered her the quarter he had been given to buy groceries, but she just looked down at him, put her hands on her hips, and laughed.

"Send your old man around, sonny, you'd fall in."

A couple of days later Sammy was hanging around Foxy's shop when Shirley Stebbins came in. Shirley was several years older than any of them, maybe sixteen or seventeen. She was tall and thin and only needed a little more flesh to have a voluptuous figure. People said her family was having a tough time because she was going to high school when she should be working. She wasn't hard the way the other girls were hard, boisterous and suggestive. Everybody on the block called her Sourpuss because her mouth was always set in a sullen expression of contempt. Foxy Four Eyes had advanced the theory that she was frigid. He said it happened when her father climbed into her bed one night when his wife was in the hospital.

"Foxy, I'm in a jam," she said. "I need ten dollars bad."

"Bad, huh?" he said, managing to give it an off-color inflection as he put his hand on her. "A guy can do an awful lot with ten dollars."

He winked at the kids as if he had said something witty. A guy called Eddie who was fifteen and knew his way around got it first.

"I'll get in for a buck," he said.

The expression on his face left no doubt about the pun. It had started as a gag, but Foxy egged them on until the nine of them had subscribed six dollars. Foxy's cheeks burned with excitement and his cockeyes looked out at his protégés proudly.

"All right, sister, I'll be a sport," he said. "I'll throw in the other four—just to see ya oblige the boys."

She looked at all of them. They were jumping around her like frantic little gnomes. Sammy hardly reached her shoulder.

"All right," she said in a tired voice. "Let's see the money, you cheap bastards."

In the back room, when it came his turn Sammy was scared. He was sprawled across her, fidgeting foolishly. Foxy Four Eyes could hardly talk, he was laughing so loud. "Hey, fellers, lookit Sammy tryin' to get his first nookey!"

Sammy could feel the blood flushing his head, and her silent contempt, and his panicky impotence.

While he still clung to her ludicrously, she half-rose on her elbows and said, "Somebody pull this flea off me. I'm not going to make this my life's work."

Foxy and Eddie laughingly dragged him off, still struggling for her, like a little puppy pulled from its mother's teats.

Shirley counted the money carefully and left a little more bitter than she came. "Thanks, you cheap bastards," she said.

Sammy ran after her. "Hey, that ain't fair! I oughta get my four bits back."

But that was the initiation fee Sammy had to pay to be inducted into the mysteries of life.

After the war, prices went higher, but there was no change in the push-cart business. The talk at meals was always money now. The Glicksteins were behind in their rent. A newsboy's take was no longer enough to complement the 'old man's income. The boys had to find regular jobs.

Sammy and Israel both answered a call for messenger boys. There were hundreds of others. For hours they cussed and fought each other for places near the door because their parents had sent them all out with the same fight talk, spoken in English, Yiddish, Italian, and with a brogue—Sammy, Israel, Joe, Pete, Tony, Mike, if you don't get that job today we don't know what we'll do.

Israel was just ahead of Sammy. They had been waiting since six in the morning for the doors to open at eight. They were chilled outside, nervous inside.

When the doors opened at last and Israel was finally standing before the checker, he was told:

"Sorry, kid—ain't hirin' no Hebes."

As Israel hesitated there, crying inside, Sammy suddenly threw himself at him and knocked him down.

"What the hell you do that for?" said the checker.

"That dirty kike cut in ahead of me," Sammy screamed.

The checker looked at Sammy curiously. Sammy stood there, small, spiderlike, intense, snarling at Israel.

"Fer Chris'sake, you look like a Jew-boy yerself!"

"Oh, Jesus, everybody's always takin' me for one of them goddam sheenies," Sammy yelled. Then he broke into gibberish Italian.

(1941)

From

THE FACTS OF LIFE
by Paul Goodman

Childish Ronnie Morris has a wife Martha and a daughter Marcia, aged 9.

Ronnie is middle-aged, as we say of any one ten years older than ourselves, and he has invented a wonderful scheme to milk money from those who make $20,000 a year: he sells them Fine Editions with odd associations, as *The*

Golden Ass bound in donkey's hide or *The New Testament* signed by the designer in the blood of a lamb. (He is childish enough to go thru with such a profitable idea, instead of dismissing it like the rest of us fools.) He has a two-masted sailboat; he moves in the circle of his clients. In a business way, he knows Picasso and Thomas Benton, and is the expert at the Club in the trade-secrets of the Muses. In the acts of love, he is medium; he went to Dartmouth; but in fact he is only moderately fixated on the period when he was 5th oar, for he had had an even prior period of ease and lust, which has saved him for philosophy and the arts, rather than the brokerage.

Martha Morris is an Andalusian type. When she arranges flowers she keeps them under control with wires. She drives at high speeds. Her relations with Ronnie are as usual; she is her little daughter's friend, and every Xmas she and Marcia design a gift-volume for Ronnie's clientèle. She is more political than her husband and her position is slightly to the left of the right wing of the left-center: a group that finds no representation in Washington, but used to have thirty seats in Paris. I could write forever, as it would seem, about Martha's teeth as they flash under her nose. Aren't the rhythms delightful, of the description of the upper middle class?

Now little Marcia goes to the University Progressive School where many of her schoolmates have fathers in the embassies, but Marcia too has been to the Near East in search of that lamb. At school they are taught to express themselves freely. Little Marcia, when she does so—she takes after her mother—is delightful!

Marcia has a fight in school today with one of the little gentlemen her contemporaries. He breaks her photographic plate. The fight is about the nature of chickens' eggs. She stamps on his foot. Being a girl, she still has an advantage in mental age and more words to say; she says a sentence in French. He can't punch her in the nose because it is ungentlemanly. He is inhibited from drawing on his best knowledge because it is dirty; but worse, it is gloomily indistinct, and even on these matters she seems to have more definite information, is about to mention it.

"Shut up!" he argues, "shut up! you're just an old-time Jew."

This perplexing observation, of which she understands neither head nor tail, brings her to a momentary pause; for up to now, at least with Harry—tho certainly not with Terry or Larry—she has maintained a queenly advantage. But he has brought her to a pause by drawing on absolutely new information.

Now she does a reckless thing: she dismisses his remark from her mind and launches into a tirade which devastatingly combines contempt and the ability to form complete sentences, till Harry goes away in order not to cry. A reckless, a dangerous thing: because what we thus dismiss enters the regions of anxiety, of loss and unfulfilled desire, and there makes strange friends. This is the prologue to fanatic interests and to falling in love. How new and otherwise real is this observation on its next appearance!

Marcia calls her mother sometimes Momsy and sometimes Martha.

"What did Harry mean," she asks her, "when he called me an old-time shoe?"

"Jew?"

"Yes, he stated I was just an old-time Joo."

Across the woman's face passes, for ever so many reasons, the least perceptible tightening. "Oh oh!" feels Marcia along her ears and scalp; and now she is confirmed and doubly confirmed in the suspicions she did not know she had. When she now has to express herself with colored chalks, new and curious objects will swim into the foreground alongside the pool, the clock will become a grandfather's clock, and all be painted Prussian blue, even tho Miss Coyle is trying to cajole especially the little girls into using warm bright colors, because that is their natural bent.

"Well he was right, you are a Jewess," says Martha. "It's nothing to be ashamed of."

"Said Joo, not Juice."

"A Jew is a boy; a Jewess is a girl."

"Oh! there are 2 kinds!"

It's worse and worse. She never dreamed that Harry was up on anything, but perhaps even his veiled hints conceal something. She feels, it seems inescapable to her, that boys have a power, surely not obvious in school—and the grown-ups even take it for granted! She sees it every day, that these same boys when they become men are superior to the women. Yet men's clothes don't *express* anything, and actresses are better than actors. But just this *contradiction* confirms it all the more, for the explanations of contradictions are in the indistinct region—and everything there is mutually involved. Marcia is already working on a system of the mysteries. Especially when Momsy now tries to tell her some reasonable anecdote about Jewesses and Jews, just like a previous astringent account of the chickens and the flowers.

Martha never happens to have told little Marcia that they are all Jews.

"Is Ronnie a Joo?"

"Of course."

"Are Louis and Bernie Joos?"

"Louis is a Jew but Bernie is a Gentile."

It's a lie, thinks Marcia; they are both the same. (She means they are both effeminate.) Why is Martha lying to her?

"What is ser-cum-si-zhun?" asks Marcia, calling the lie.

This inquisition has now become intolerable to Martha. "Good night, Marcia," she explains.

"Is Rosina a Juice?" Marcia cries, asking about Ronnie's mistress.

"Marcia! I said good night!"

"Tell me! tell me! is Rosina Juice?"

"No."

"Ah!"

"Why Ah!?"

"Good night, Momsy," says Marcia, kissing her.

Since the habits are formed speediest where necessity constrains and yet conscious and deliberate adjustment is embarrassing or tedious, Martha has speedily and long ago learned the few adjustments belonging particularly to Jews of a certain class of money. The other hotel; not on this list; the right to more chic and modernity, but please no associations with Betsy Ross in tableaux or on committees. Of course habits learned by this mechanism are subject to amazing breaches, when submerged desire suddenly asserts itself and the son of Jacob becomes Belmont or Ronnie becomes, as he is, an honorary colonel in the militia. But on the whole, where money is so exchangeable, there are very few special adjustments; for instance, they never even came to Marcia's keen perception, especially since none of the Jews whom she is so often with without knowing it, ever mentions them. Of course, on the other hand, in the more critical social episodes, such as marriage—but forget that. And there are many other meanings, archaically forgotten.

"Since you have to put up with the handicap whether you like it or not," decides Mrs. Ronnie Morris, "why not make an advantage of it, and be proud of it?" And at once she writes out a check for a subscription to *The Menorah Journal,* the *Harper's Monthly* of reformed Jews.

"Never heard such a stupid argument in my life!" says Ronnie. He is very angry, like any one who has played the game like a perfect gentleman and then finds that the other side goes too far and calls his daughter an old-time Jew. "What's the use of *pretending* you're a Jew, when you're *not* a Jew?" he shouts.

"We are Jews. Don't shout," says Martha.

"I'll go to school and punch that brat's nose."

Martha says nothing.

"Do I pay $300 a year for him to tell Marcia that she's a Jew?"

"But we are Jews," says Martha, with a new loyalty.

"Since when?" says Ronnie scientifically. "To be a Jew means one of three things: It means first to belong to a certain Race; but there isn't any Jewish race in anthropology. Look at me, do I look like a Jewish race?"

He looks like a highly brushed and polished moujik.

"No. Secondly: it means a Nationality. But even if some Jews think they have a nationality, do I? I went to Jerusalem to pick out a Gentile lamb. Anyway, I can't speak the language. Hebrew isn't the same as Yiddish, you know, even tho it looks the same; but I can't speak that either.

"Third: it's a Religion. So you see," he concludes triumphantly, "it's not a matter of not *wanting* to be a Jew or trying to *hide* that you're a Jew, but you *can't* be a Jew if you're *not* a Jew!''

"Don't be a fool," says Martha. "A person's a Jew if his grandparents were Jews; even one's enough sometimes, depending."

"What sense does that make?"

"Do you think it's by accident," says Martha flatly, "that your mama and papa came to marry Jews and we married Jews?"

She means, thinks Ronnie, when our desire is toward Gentiles, toward retroussé noses and moon-face Hungarians. Does she mean Rosina? She means Bernie. We mean—but there is no time to think of that.

"I'll ask Louis," says Ronnie; for tho he holds sway at the luncheon club, all his ideas come from this poet.

"He's taking Marshy to the Picassos tomorrow."

"Let him tell her, then."

"What! are you going to let your daughter find out the facts from a stranger?"

(1941)

From

KINGSBLOOD ROYAL
by Sinclair Lewis

He crossed the lobby of his hotel in Minneapolis with his eyes rigidly held on the black-and-white marble of the floor, irritably noting that it *was* black and white, careful as a drunk who betrays himself by being too careful in his gait. He was wondering who might be staring at him, suspecting the Negro in him. Wilbur Feathering, who was a food-dealer in Grand Republic but who had been born in Mississippi, frequently asserted that he could catch any "Nigra" who passed for white, even if he was but a sixty-fourth black. If Wilbur did detect it, he would be nasty about it.

Right in the center of the lobby he wanted to stop and look at his hands. He remembered hearing that a Negro of any degree, though pale of face as Narcissus, is betrayed by the blue halfmoons of his fingernails. He wildly wanted to examine them. But he kept his arms rigidly down beside him (so that people did wonder at his angry stiffness and did stare at him) and marched into the elevator. He managed, with what he felt to be the most ingenious casualness, to prop himself with his hand against the side of the cage, and so to look at his nails.

No! The halfmoons were as clear as Biddy's.

——But I know now how a Negro who has just passed must feel all the time, when he's staying at a hotel like this: hoping that none of these high-and-mighty traveling men will notice him and ask the manager to throw him out. Does it keep up? All the time?

In the vast hidden lore of Being a Negro which he was to con, Neil was to learn that in many Northern states, including his own, there is a "civil rights law" which forbids the exclusion of Negroes and members of the other non-country-club races from hotels, restaurants, theaters, and that this law worked fully as well as had national prohibition.

White hotel guests snorted, "Why can't these niggers stay where they're wanted, among their own people, and not come horning in where they don't belong?" These monitors did not explain how a Negro, arriving in a strange city at midnight, was to find out precisely where he was wanted. Whenever they had been contaminated and almost destroyed by the presence of a Negro sleeping two hundred feet away, they threatened the hotel manager, who assumed that he had to earn a living and therefore devised a technique of treating the Negroes with nerve-freezing civility and with evasiveness about "accommodations."

Even on this, his first night of being a Negro, Neil knew that the night assistant-manager of the hotel might telephone up, "I'm terribly sorry, sir, but we find that the room we gave you is reserved."

He knew it already. He knew it more sensitively and acutely than he had ever known any of the complex etiquette of being an officer-and-gentleman.

He looked bulky enough and straight-shouldered enough in the refuge of his hotel room, but he felt bent and cowering as he listened for the telephone. He did not hear it, yet he heard it a hundred times.

And if he did not belong in this hotel, he thought, he would be no more welcome on the Pullman *Borup*. They could not arrest him for taking it, but he would not again be able to patronize genially the black Mac, who was now his uncle and his superior. In his hazardous future, it might be he who would hope for a condescending dollar from Mac.

He belonged with the other lepers in a day-coach—in a Southern jimcrow day-coach, foul and broken, so that his simian odor might not offend the delicate white nostrils of Curtiss Havock.

All this he thought, but he did not dare think of going back to Vestal and telling her that he had given her a Negro daughter.

He had planned to get his hair cut at the Swanson-Grand barbershop, this late afternoon.

He sat at the small desk in his room, tapping his teeth with his fingernail, occasionally looking suddenly at that nail again, a study in brooding. Whether or not he needed a haircut to the point of social peril, he had to go down to the shop, as a matter of manliness. He wasn't going to let any barber jimcrow *him!* He was a citizen and a guest; he paid his taxes and his hotel bills; he had as much right to be served in a barbershop as any white man——

He stood up wrathfully, but the wrath was against himself.

——Now for God's sake, Kingsblood, haven't you got enough real trouble in being a Negro, and having to tell Vestal, without making up imaginary troubles? That Svenska barber is no more likely to treat you as colored than anybody else ever has, these thirty-one years! Quit acting like a white boy trying to pretend to be a Negro. You *are* Negro, all right, *and* Chippewa, *and* West Indian spig, and you don't have to pretend. Funny, though, if I'm being too imaginative. Always thought I was too matter-of-fact. Everybody thought so.

——It couldn't be, could it, that what I needed, what Grand Republic needs, is a good dash of sun-warmed black blood?

He found a streak of humor in the astonishing collapse of everything that had been Neil Kingsblood; in noting that a black boy like himself could never conceivably be a banker, a golf-club member, an army captain, husband of the secure and placid Vestal, son of a Scotch-porridge dentist, intimate of the arrogant Major Rodney Aldwick. Suddenly he was nothing that he was, only he still was, and what he was, he did not know.

That the #3 barber in the Swanson-Grand Salon de Coiffeur would actually treat Mr. Kingsblood just as he always *had* treated Mr. Kingsblood was so obvious that Neil scarcely noticed that while he was still wondering whether #3 would refuse to cut his hair, #3 was already contentedly cutting it. But even in the soporific routine of the barber's shears and cool, damp hands, Neil could not ease his disquiet.

The head-barber, the girl cashier, the Negro bootblack, his #3 barber— had they guessed that he was a Negro, had they known it for years? Were they waiting for the proper time to threaten him, to blackmail him—waiting, lurking, laughing at him?

"Mighty hard to cut that curly hair of yours smooth, Captain," said the barber.

Now what was he referring to? Curly hair. Kinky hair. Negro wool.

Was his barber, standing back of him, winking at the barber at the next chair? Why had he yanked a lock of hair that way? Was the inconceivable social night already drawing in, and the black winter of blackness?

With the most itching carefulness, Neil crept one hand out from under the drab sheet covering him, scratched his nose, let the hand drop into his lap, and so was able to study his nails again. Was it this mercury vapor light, or was there really a blue tinge in the halfmoons?

He wanted to jump from the chair, flee to his safe room—no, flee to yet-unknown Negro friends who would sympathize with him, hide him, protect him.

It was no elegant green-and-ivory barber chair but the electric chair from which he was finally released. In his room, he quivered:

——Vestal's always loved to run her fingers through my hair. Will she, if she finds out what kind of hair it is? Same color as my dad's used to be, but his isn't curly. What would Vestal think? She mustn't find out, ever.

He thought constantly of new things, pleasant and customary, from which his status as Negro might bar him: Biddy's adoration. The lordly Federal Club. Dances and stag-drinking at the Heather Country Club, where once he had been chairman of the Bengali pool tournament. His college fraternity. His career in the bank. His friendship with Major Rodney Aldwick.

He repeated a slice of English doggerel that Rod Aldwick used to quote with unction:

> All the white man's memories:
> Hearths at eventide,
> The twinkling lights of Christmas nights
> And our high Imperial pride.

What had been his own picture, his own observations, of the Negroes?

——Come on, you high Imperial white man, what are we? Let's have it, Mister!

——Well, the Negroes are all sullen and treacherous, like Belfreda.

——Nonsense! Mac the porter isn't and I'm not and I'm no longer so sure about Belfreda.

——They're all black, flat-nosed, puff-lipped.

He went to the mirror, and laughed.

——What a lot I used to know that I didn't know! What a clack-mouthed parrot I was! Quoting that fool of a Georgia doctor. Negroes not quite human, eh? Kingsblood, Congoblood, you deserve anything you get—if it's bad enough. I think God turned me black to save my soul, if I have any beyond ledgers and college yells. I've got to say, "You're as blind and mean and ignorant as a white man," and that's a tough thing to take, even from myself.

——Oh, don't be so prejudiced against the white people. No doubt there's a lot of them who would be just as good as anybody else, if they had my chance of redemption.

——Captain, aren't you kind of overdoing your glee in becoming a colored boy?

——Okay. I am.

Under a decayed newspaper in the desk he found one sheet of Swanson-Grand letter-paper, with a half-tone of the hotel and the name of the proprietor in flourishing 1890 type, but with practically no space for writing, an accomplishment apparently not expected of the guests. He turned it over, took out his bankerish gold-mounted fountain pen, and drew up an altogether bankerish table of one branch of his ancestors:

> Xavier Pic, possible French and Spanish elements but counts as 100% Negro
> Sidonie, his daughter, who married Louis Payzold, was ½ Chippewa and ½ Negro
> Alexandre Payzold, their son, Gramma Julie's father, ¼ Negro
> My Grandmother, Julie Saxinar, an octoroon, ⅛ Negro
> Her daughter, my mother, 1/16 Negro

Myself, ¹⁄₃₂ Negro
Biddy, ¹⁄₆₄ Negro

——Well, I finally do have something interesting about our royal royal ancestry to report to Dad!

(1947)

From

WHY I REMAIN A NEGRO
by Walter White

I am a Negro. My skin is white, my eyes are blue, my hair is blond. The traits of my race are nowhere visible upon me. Not long ago I stood one morning on a subway platform in Harlem. As the train came in I stepped back for safety. My heel came down upon the toe of the man behind me. I turned to apologize to him. He was a Negro, and his face as he stared at me was hard and full of the piled-up bitterness of a thousand lynchings and a million nights in shacks and tenements and "nigger towns." "Why don't you look where you're going?" he said sullenly. "You white folks are always trampling on colored people." Just then one of my friends came up and asked how the fight had gone in Washington—there was a filibuster against legislation for a permanent Fair Employment Practices Commission. The Negro on whose toes I had stepped listened, then spoke to me penitently.

"Are you Walter White of the NAACP? I'm sorry I spoke to you that way. I thought you were white."

I am not white. There is nothing within my mind and heart which tempts me to think I am. Yet I realize acutely that the only characteristic which matters to either the white or the colored race—the appearance of whiteness—is mine. White is the rejection of all color; black is the absorption of every shade. There is magic in a white skin; there is tragedy, loneliness, exile, in a black skin. Why then do I insist that I am a Negro, when nothing compels me to do so but myself?

*   *   *   *   *

Many Negroes are judged as whites. Every year approximately 12,000 white-skinned Negroes disappear—people whose absence cannot be explained by death or emigration. Nearly every one of the 14 million discernible Negroes

in the United States knows at least one member of his race who is "passing"—
the magic word which means that some Negroes can get by as whites, men and
women who have decided that they will be happier and more successful if they
flee from the proscription and humiliation which the American color line im-
poses on them. Often these emigrants achieve success in business, the profes-
sions, the arts and sciences. Many of them have married white people, lived
happily with them, and produced families. Sometimes they tell their husbands
or wives of their Negro blood, sometimes not. Who are they? Mostly people
of no great importance, but some of them prominent figures, including a few
members of Congress, certain writers, and several organizers of movements to
"keep the Negroes and other minorities in their places." Some of the most ve-
hement public haters of Negroes are themselves secretly Negroes.

They do not present openly the paradox of the color line. It is I, with my
insistence, day after a day, year in and year out, that I am a Negro, who pro-
voke the reactions to which now I am accustomed: the sudden intake of breath,
the bewildered expression of the face, the confusion of the eyes, the muddled
fragmentary remarks—"But you do not look . . . I mean I would never have
known . . . of course if you didn't want to admit . . ." Sometimes the eyes
blink rapidly and the tongue, out of control, says, "Are you sure?"

I have tried to imagine what it is like to have me presented to a white
person as a Negro, by supposing a Negro were suddenly to say to me, "I am
white." But the reversal does not work, for whites can see no reason for a
white man ever wanting to be black: there is only reason for a black man wanting to be white. That is the way whites think; that is the way their values are
set up. It is the startling removal of the blackness which upsets people. Looking
at me without knowing who I am, they disassociate me from all the characteristics of the Negro. Informed that I am a Negro they find it impossible suddenly
to endow me with the skin, the odor, the dialect, the shuffle, the imbecile good
nature. Instantly they are aware that these things are *not* part of me. Then they
grope for the positive values of the race—genius at song, easy laughter, great
strength, humility, manners. Alexander Percy said that the most polite people
in the world are the American Negroes.

This shift to the virtues of the Negro is apt to be dangerous for me. Once
a Southern lady, discovering my identity, entered into a long conversation with
me, and suggested that I come to her home where we might enjoy a more intimate chat on race matters without being disturbed. She suggested a time. I
said I would surely come, and that I would bring my wife, who would be equally
interested in the discussion. The lady's attitude changed immediately. She did
not break the date then, but later she telephoned and said that she would be
unable to see us. What precisely she perceived in me of interest I do not know,
but probably it was the sudden transformation of the faithful "darky" into a
man covered with magic white skin which titillated her. Southern women have
generally been more friendly toward the Negroes than Southern men—who are
largely responsible for the chiaroscuro effects in the race—and she may have

felt that in some way I represented her faith and efforts, rather than the infidelity of her ancestors. Or she may have thought, "Are you sure?"

I am sure. There can never be a doubt. I have seen Negroes, male and female, killed by mobs in the streets of Atlanta. I stood with my father, who was a mail carrier, and watched them die. The next night they came to the Negro section, perhaps five thousand of them. Our house was just outside the section, above it, on Houston Street. It was a neat, modest home, in which my father and mother raised a family of seven children. The whites resented our prosperity; so at times, did the Negroes. The Negroes resented our white skin, and the ethical standards which my parents maintained themselves and required of their children.

In the darkened house that night there were my mother and father, four of my sisters and myself. Never before had there been guns in our house, but that night, at the insistence of friends, we were armed. My father was a deeply religious man, opposed to physical violence. As we watched the mob go by, their faces weird in the light of the torches they carried—faces made grotesque and ugly by the hate which was twisting and distorting them—my father said, "Don't shoot until the first man puts his foot on the lawn; and then don't miss."

I heard a voice cry out, a voice which I knew belonged to the son of our neighborhood grocer: "Let's burn the house of the nigger mail carrier! It's too nice a house for a nigger to live in!"

In the flickering light the mob swayed, paused, and began to flow toward us. In that instant there opened up within me a great awareness; I knew then who I was. I was colored, a human being with an invisible pigmentation which marked me a person to be hunted, hanged, abused, discriminated against, kept in poverty and ignorance, in order that those whose skin was white would have readily at hand a proof of their superiority, a proof patent and inclusive, accessible to the moron and the idiot as well as to the wise man and the genius. No matter how low a white man fell, he could always be certain that he was superior to two-thirds of the world's population, for those two-thirds were not white.

It made no difference how intelligent or talented I and my millions of brothers were, or how virtuously we lived. A curse like that of Judas was upon us, a mark of degradation fashioned with heavenly authority. There were white men who said Negroes had no souls, and who proved it by the Bible. Some of these now were approaching us, intent upon burning our house. My father had told us to kill them.

It was a violence which could not be avoided. The white men insisted upon it. War was with them a business; war and pillage, conquest and exploitation, colonization and Christianization. Later, when I was older, I thought about this and I began to see why. Theirs was a world of contrasts in values: superior and inferior, profit and loss, cooperative and non-cooperative, civilized and aboriginal, white and black. If you were on the wrong end of the

comparison, if you were inferior, if you were non-cooperative, if you were aboriginal, if you were black, then you were marked for excision, expulsion, or
extinction. I was a Negro; I was therefore that part of history which opposed
the good, the just, and the enlightened. I was a Persian, falling before the hordes
of Alexander. I was a Carthaginian, extinguished by the legions of Rome. I
was a Frenchman at Waterloo, an Anglo-Saxon at Hastings, a Confederate at
Vicksburg, a Pole at Warsaw. I was the defeated, wherever and whenever there
was a defeat.

Yet as a boy there in the darkness amid the tightening fright, I knew the
inexplicable thing—that my skin was as white as the skin of those who were
coming at me.

The mob moved toward the lawn. I tried to aim my gun, wondering what
it would feel like to kill a man. Suddenly there was a volley of shots. The mob
hesitated, stopped. Some friends of my father's had barricaded themselves in a
two-story brick building just below our house. It was they who had fired. Some
of the mobsmen, still bloodthirsty, shouted, "Let's go get the nigger." Others,
afraid now for their safety, held back. Our friends, noting the hesitation, fired
another volley. The mob broke and retreated up Houston Street.

In the quiet that followed I put my gun aside and tried to relax. But a
tension different from anything I had ever known possessed me. I was gripped
by the knowledge of my identity, and in the depths of my soul I was vaguely
aware that I was glad of it. I was sick with loathing for the hatred which had
flared before me that night and come so close to making me a killer; but I was
glad I was not one of those who hated; I was glad I was not one of those made
sick and murderous by pride. I was glad I was not one of those whose story is
in the history of the world, a record of bloodshed, rapine, and pillage. I was
glad my mind and spirit were part of the races that had not fully awakened, and
who therefore had still before them the opportunity to write a record of virtue
as a memorandum to Armageddon.

It was all just a feeling then, inarticulate and melancholy, yet reassuring
in the way that death and sleep are reassuring. Years later, when my father lay
in a dingy, cockroach-infested Jim Crow ward in an Atlanta hospital, he put it
into words for me and my brother.

"Human kindness, decency, love, whatever you wish to call it," he said,
"is the only real thing in the world. It is a dynamic, not a passive, emotion.
It's up to you two, and others like you, to use your education and talents in an
effort to make love as positive an emotion in the world as are prejudice and
hate. That's the only way the world can save itself. Don't forget that. No matter what happens, you must love, not hate." Then he died. He had been struck
by an automobile driven by a reckless driver—one of the hospital doctors.

I have remembered that. I have remembered that when, sitting in the gallery of the House or the Senate, I have heard members of our Congress rise
and spill diatribe and vilification on the Negroes. I have remembered it when
the Negroes were condemned as utter failures in soldiering. I remembered it

when, in the Pacific, where I went as a war correspondent, a white officer from the South told me that the 93rd Division, a Negro unit, had been given an easy beachhead to take at Bougainville, and had broken and run under fire. I collected the facts and presented them to him. Bougainville was invaded in November 1943. The 93rd was ordered there in April 1944. The first night it bivouacked on the beach, and motion pictures were shown.

I remembered it when I talked with my nephew for the last time, as he lay in a bitterly cold, rain-drenched tent on the edge of the Capodichina airfield near Naples. He was a Georgia boy, the youngest of four children. His father, like mine, was a mail carrier. He, like me, could have passed for a white man. By sacrifice and labor his parents provided him with a college education. He won a master's degree in economics, and the next day enlisted in the Army Air Corps, as a Negro. He went to the segregated field at Tuskegee, Alabama.

He hated war, he loathed killing. But he believed that Hitler and Mussolini represented the kind of hate he had seen exhibited in Georgia by the Ku Klux Klan and the degenerate political demagogues. He believed that the war would bring all of that hate to an end. He was a fighter pilot. He fought well. Over the Anzio beachhead he was shot down, bailing out and escaping with his right leg broken in two places. He was offered an opportunity to return home but he refused it. "I'll stick it out until the war is finished or I am," he told a friend. Later, returning from a bomber escort mission to Germany, his plane lost altitude over Hungary, was fired upon by anti-aircraft batteries, and was seen striking a tree and bursting into flames. That was the end of one of the men Senator Eastland of Mississippi described as "utter and dismal failures in combat in Europe."

It would be easy to grow bitter over such things, but in remembering my nephew and our last conversation, in which he asked me whether the war would really bring an end to prejudice and race hatred, I remember also the Negro corporal of an engineers unit, who said to me, "This is the only work they would give me, but I don't mind. We learn a trade; we do constructive work. The combat soldiers are taught how to kill. It will bother them. It will stick with them. It will have no effect on us. We will not have to unlearn it."

I could be sophisticated about the advantages of being a Negro. I am amused, for instance, at the fact that because it is considered remarkable that a Negro can write a book at all, a passing fair volume by one of my brothers is frequently hailed as a masterpiece. Everyone with the slightest sense is aware that genius has no color line. Everyone knows also that people generally choose friends and companions for their taste, manners, intelligence, and personality. Yet it does not occur to them that Negroes do likewise. Therefore he often mourns that we colored people cannot freely associate with whites, when it should be obvious that if we did have this privilege we would like no more of them for friends than he does. It is beyond the imagination of a white man to think that to a Negro he is dull.

(1947)

From
LOST BOUNDARIES
by W. L. White

Before you learn what Albert Johnston, Jr., was told at the age of sixteen and why he was not told it before, you should know something of his background. It would be dull but accurate to say that, until he was told, we are dealing with a normal New England boy. He was born in Boston in 1925 while his father was still a medical student at the University of Chicago. When Albert was four, his first memories begin in the little town of Gorham, New Hampshire, where his father was now the leading country doctor serving its 2,500 people, who live at the foot of Mount Washington to which vacationists swarm for winter skiing and summer coolness, with special trains in the fall when the maple leaves turn red and gold.

Here Albert played over the hills, learned to ski, camped out on long Boy Scout hikes, climbed Mount Washington to look down on the other rolling New England hills, made the high-school honor roll, was elected president of his high-school class, and took piano lessons. Looking back on it you would agree that, before he was told, he had the healthy background of rural New England—a normal American boy and Yankee both in his outlook and in his flat accent.

This was also true of his heredity, which had been for many generations a mingling of the old American blood stocks, with the possible exception of a great-grandfather who had come from Germany and who, according to Albert's mother, accounted for the fact that little Albert was darker than most of his high-school classmates, with brown eyes, a high, prominent nose and dark, curly hair.

When Albert was fifteen the family left Gorham, where his father had been a Mason, a Rotarian, park commissioner, and chairman of the school board, to move down to Keene, bigger than Gorham but much like it, another typical New England town with its two-hundred-year-old Congregational Church on the main square, its white spire high above the green elm leaves. Albert, like most children in rural New England, had been going to Congregational Sunday School since he could first remember. His father, who had taken a year off to study Roentgenology (of course at Harvard) was now working in Keene's leading hospital and Albert, who was planning on Dartmouth, was preparing at nearby Mount Hermon school.

It was a tolerant, cosmopolitan place, and here this little New England boy got his outlook broadened, for one of his schoolmates was a Negro, Charles Duncan.

Negroes in rural New Hampshire are a curiosity. Once a Negro tramp had been given a night's lodging in the Gorham jail, and next morning Albert, with all the other youngsters, had gone down to peer through the bars "to see the black man." Occasionally a summer visitor brought along a Negro cook. Albert had never seen any reason to question the prevailing opinion that Negroes were inferior, stupid, ignorant, and lazy, that they swept floors or were house-maids or at best played pianos. He had heard of the Negro scientist George Washington Carver, but he was the exception that proved the rule. Of course his parents, like most tolerant New Englanders, had taught him that it was impolite to use the word "nigger," and that they should be referred to as "colored people."

So Charlie Duncan, who was the son of Todd Duncan who sang in *Porgy and Bess,* and who was later to become a leader of his Dartmouth class, was a surprise to Albert. Charlie was quiet, well mannered, popular in Mount Hermon, and brilliant in his studies, winning not only the history prize but several others to become salutatorian of his class. He was also on the ski team, and a year ahead of Albert, who, toward the end of his junior year, was elected captain for the next.

But at this point there was a little incident. The Mount Hermon team was to be represented at the big meet at Meriden, but the coach ruled that only six could go, and did not include captain-elect Albert Johnston in the group.

Whereupon Charlie Duncan, who was scheduled to go, said to the team, "I think Peanut [Albert's school nickname] is a better skier than I am," and told the boys he would like to give up his place so Albert could go. In the end the coach relented and promised seven could go, so when Albert went home for the weekend he was still bubbling over this schoolboy's victory.

This home is one of the most beautiful in Keene. It sits on a large corner lot of one of Keene's finest residential streets, shaded by the ancient elms of New England, and why should it not also have been one of the most secure? Had not Dr. Johnston solidly established himself in New Hampshire? Was he not steadily moving up in his profession? What could be more stable?

But on this particular weekend there was trouble, as the boy could sense. Something about the Navy. His father, who had seen the war coming, had early answered the Navy's call for volunteers. After some time, he had been notified that he was accepted, and that a commission as lieutenant commander would presently come through.

Now there seemed to be some hitch. The Navy seemed to be out. Dad was all lathered up about it, talking a lot with Mom. Neither had told him what it was about. Dad had already had a couple of drinks.

Albert couldn't see that it mattered much. Of course Dad was probably all set on one of those nice blue uniforms and all that braid. But what difference did it make if the Navy had decided Dad was too old, or too fat, or something like that? After all, most men of his age weren't anxious to leave a good practice. Many were figuring all the angles as to how they could stay out. Anyway, maybe they would take Dad later.

Albert couldn't see that it mattered, and decided he would take a bath and then call a couple of girls to see how things were for a date tonight. Certainly it didn't matter as much as the news that he was, after all, going with the ski team.

He was to use the tub in the room which adjoined his parents' bedroom and, as he turned on the hot water, he began telling them the whole story of that ski incident, of Charlie Duncan's offer to give up his place so Al could go, how popular Charlie was and what a good athlete, how he led his whole class in studies, and how everyone liked Charlie, even if he *was* colored.

Although it happened several years ago, Albert still remembers as though it were only last night. He remembers how, as he praised Charlie Duncan, his father "beamed all up." And then said to Mom:

"I'm going to tell that boy."

And how his mother almost screamed from the bedroom:

"No! No! Don't do it! Don't ever do it!"

"I've got to do it," his father answered. Then Dad stepped back into the bedroom and when, half a minute later, he returned to the bathroom door, he had a third drink in his hand.

"Turn off the water," he said, and Albert did.

"Do you know something, boy?" he said.

"No, what?" said Albert.

"Well, you're colored."

Albert still remembers the funny sensation that went through him, and for a minute he didn't say anything. Then he said, "Well, how come?"

"I'm colored and your mother's colored."

Albert had his shirt off, but he did not continue dressing for the date, because he knew he would not want to call either of those girls tonight. He walked slowly into his parents' bedroom.

There his father explained that his own mother was colored, and also his father, although he didn't look it.

"How about Mom, is she colored too?" asked Albert, even though this had already been answered.

They explained that both Grandma and Grandpa on Mom's side were colored, although they didn't look it; in fact, all four grandparents were colored, but all could get by.

Albert didn't feel anything but dazed, he remembers.

Then they said he must not tell anyone of this, because of what it might do to Dad, and that the two younger children hadn't been told yet. They explained what "passing" was, and how Dad had had to do it, not because he was ashamed of being colored, but only to make their living.

Then his mother asked him, now that he knew, how he felt about it?

Albert said he felt proud of it, and that he hoped to do something for the Negro.

This greatly pleased his father, and he jumped up and shook Albert's hand, even though Albert was only sixteen. It was the first time this had ever happened in exactly this way, and of course it pleased Albert. But he kept feeling more and more dazed.

(1948)

TO END ALL STORIES
by Chester Himes

All of his family were very fair. The most thorough examination of any sort could not have disclosed their Negro blood. Yet in the small town in Tennessee where he was born his family were known as Negroes. This is not uncommon in the South. His family accepted their position as Negroes without obvious rancor and worked diligently to secure a comfortable living.

Following high school he attended Fisk university, and was graduated in 1931. He came to New York City seeking employment and worked for a year as a Red Cap. But he did not like the job; it was too demanding. The hours were long and the pay was short.

In the spring of 1933 he was offered a job as deck hand on a freighter bound for Italy. He took it. When the freighter docked in Lisbon, Portugal, for supplies, he jumped ship. He avoided discovery by going inland immediately.

For the following seven years he lived in Portugal, engaging in a number of casual occupations. He assumed the name of Ferdinand Cortes, and in time learned the language quite proficiently. In 1940 he forged papers, proving himself a native of Portugal, and applied for a passport and U. S. visa. He returned to this country as a Portuguese and when war broke out he enlisted and was stationed in Lisbon as an interpreter, where he remained for the duration.

After the war he got a job as an interpreter on Ellis Island and immediately applied for naturalization papers.

There was a beautiful young Spanish girl, named Lupe Rentera, who worked in his department. He was attracted to her on sight, but the knowledge that he was part Negro restrained him from making the first advance. She was also attracted to him. Finally, one day, she gave him an encouraging smile. He responded by asking her to lunch.

He learned that she roomed with a family of Mexicans on the fringe of a Spanish community in Brooklyn. Delightedly he announced that he roomed nearby. They discovered that they rode the same line to work and wondered how they had missed seeing each other. After that he waited for her in the morning and rode home with her at night. He began dating her regularly and in a month they were engaged.

Two months later they applied for their marriage license. He recorded his race as white, his nationality as Portuguese; she recorded her race as white, her nationality as American. Their fellow workers gave them an office party when they were married. They spent their honeymoon in Brooklyn looking for an apartment.

Two places were offered them, but both were in communities mixed with Negroes, and they declined. Finally they found a place in South Brooklyn that suited them and they spent all of their savings furnishing it.

They should have been blissfully happy, but there was a strain in their relationship. He was continuously fearful that his Negro blood would be discovered. Since his discharge he had been communicating with his relatives in Tennessee, but to avoid discovery he had rented a post office box where he received his mail. They did not know his assumed name, his address, nor his occupation. As soon as he read their letters he destroyed them.

But he was afraid that Lupe might discover signs of his Negro blood in his appearance. He kept himself scrupulously clean and used an after shave lotion which contained a slight bleach. Each week he got a hair cut and a massage. But fearing that the neighborhood barbers might guess his Negro origin from the texture of his hair, he patronized a Negro barbershop uptown in Harlem. Each Saturday afternoon when they returned from their half day at work, he departed for his jaunt uptown and did not return until dark. After getting his haircut and massage, he spent the rest of the time wandering about the streets of Harlem. It was the only time during the week that he felt completely relaxed.

Unknown to him, Lupe also had a problem. She, too, felt strained in their relationship for she was also part Negro. And as with him, she was fearful of his discovering it. She took the same precautions against its discovery as did he. She bathed frequently, used quantities of bleach creams, and patronized a Negro hair dresser uptown in Harlem. Each Saturday she left the house exactly a half hour after his departure, used the same transportation, and arrived at her beauty parlor at the time he was in his barbershop not more than four blocks away. She also spent part of the afternoon visiting friends in Harlem before returning, although she managed always to get home a few minutes before his arrival. But for those Saturday afternoon sessions with her Negro friends, she could not have endured the strain.

He told her he spent the time in school, taking a course in radio engineering. He never knew that she went out at all. In fact he did not know that her hair was the type that required straightening. He was too preoccupied with his own fear of discovery to notice.

To make matters worse, both exhibited extreme prejudice against Negroes. Of course, they did so in an effort to hide their identity. But the effect it had was only to increase their trepidation. As they labored more and more desperately to avoid detection, the strain between them increased. In time they became the most prejudiced people in all of New York City.

Due to his excellent war record, some of the red tape concerning his application for citizenship was avoided, and he became a naturalized citizen of the United States in December, 1947. It had an immediate effect of security on him. But her fears increased proportionately. She had visions of being discovered and put in jail for falsifying her race on the application for a marriage license. He would have the marriage annulled. He was so prejudiced against Negroes he might even kill her for deceiving him. Her days became filled with constant dread.

Shortly after this when he stopped at his box for mail he found a letter saying his mother had died. His father had died years before. It was from his elder sister. She wanted him to come home for the funeral.

He was so upset he forgot to destroy the letter. He slipped it into his side coat pocket. Then he began to scheme how he could make the trip without Lupe discovering his destination. At dinner he told her he'd have to spend a week in Cincinnati at the Philco radio plant to complete his radio course. She thought it strange but said nothing.

Then she noticed the tip of the letter extending from his pocket. This surprised her more than the other. She had never known him to receive a letter before.

That night, after he was asleep, she got out of bed and read the letter. To her complete astonishment she learned that he had Negro blood. In fact, he was from the same little town in Tennessee where she'd been born. As she continued to read she recognized his family. She had known them well. They were distantly related to her family. She even recalled having seen him when she was a child, but he was ten years older and wouldn't remember her.

She was so happy and jubilant over the discovery she awakened him. Waving the letter, laughing and crying at the same time, she cried, "I'm one, too, Ferdy! I'm one, too, darling." She fell on the bed and began kissing him passionately.

But he pushed her roughly aside and jumped to his feet. His face was white and stricken; he was shaken to the core. "One what?" he yelled. "What are you talking about?"

"I'm like you," she said, laughing at him. "See, I read the letter. I'm from Pinegap, Tennessee; I'm a Williams, too. My mama was Dora Williams. I'm Sadie. I even remember you—you're Clefus."

The color came back into his face. He sat down on the side of the bed. "Well, what do you know!" he exclaimed.

For the first few days they were jubilant over the discovery that they both had Negro blood. Now they would not have to live in a constant state of dread and apprehension. They would not have to take so many baths or spend so much on bleach preparations. They could go together uptown on Saturday afternoons, he to the barbershop, she to the hair dresser. Afterwards they could stop at the Savoy and dance to the good hot rhythm of the Negro bands.

They felt they had discovered the happy combination of being white and colored too.

Of course, he took her with him on the trip to Tennessee. They visited their families and told them the whole story. Everything worked out perfectly.

On their return they looked forward to a life of bliss. It was such great fun fooling all the white people with whom they worked. They laughed about it at night and felt like great conspirators.

But after the jubilance wore off, and they had settled down to the daily routine of living, a strange disillusionment came. They began feeling betrayed by each other. Each experienced bitter disappointment in the knowledge that the other was not "pure white." They realized that had they known of the other's Negro blood they would not have become married.

Each became furious at the other's deceit. In fact, they got so mad at each other they quit speaking and are now suing for divorce on the grounds of false pretenses.

(1948)

SIMPLE ON INDIAN BLOOD
by Langston Hughes

"Anybody can look at me and tell I am part Indian," said Simple.

"I see you almost every day," I said, "and I did not know it until now."

"I have Indian blood but I do not show it much," said Simple. "My uncle's cousin's great-grandma were a Cherokee. I only shows mine when I lose my temper—then my Indian blood boils. I am quick-tempered just like a Indian. If somebody does something to me, I always fights back. In fact, when I get mad, I am the toughest Negro God's got. It's my Indian blood. When I were a young man, I used to play baseball and steal bases just like Jackie. If the empire would rule me out, I would get mad and hit the empire. I had to stop playing. That Indian temper. Nowadays, though, it's mostly womens that riles me up, especially landladies, waitresses, and girl friends. To tell the truth, I believe in a woman keeping her place. Womens is beside themselves these days. They want to rule the roost."

"You have old-fashioned ideas about sex," I said. "In fact, your line of thought is based on outmoded economics."

"What?"

"In the days when women were dependent upon men for a living, you could be the boss. But now women make their own living. Some of them make more money than you do.''

''True,'' said Simple. ''During the war they got into that habit. But boss I am still due to be.''

''So you think. But you can't always put your authority into effect.''

''I can try,'' said Simple. ''I can say, 'Do this!' And if she does something else, I can raise my voice, if not my hand.''

''You can be sued for raising your voice,'' I stated, ''and arrested for raising your hand.''

''And she can be annihilated when I return from being arrested,'' said Simple. ''That's my Indian blood!''

''You must believe in a woman being a squaw.''

''She better not look like no squaw,'' said Simple. ''I want a woman to look sharp when she goes out with me. No moccasins. I wants high-heel shoes and nylons, cute legs—and short dresses. But I also do not want her to talk back to me. As I said, I am the man. *Mine* is the word, and she is due to hush.''

''Indians customarily expect their women to be quiet,'' I said.

''I do not expect mine to be too quiet,'' said Simple. ''I want 'em to sweet-talk me—'Sweet baby, this,' and 'Baby, that,' and 'Baby you's right, darling,' when they talk to me.''

''In other words, you want them both old-fashioned and modern at the same time,'' I said. ''The convolutions of your hypothesis are sometimes beyond cognizance.''

''Cog hell!'' said Simple. ''I just do not like no old loud backtalking chick. That's the Indian in me. My grandpa on my father's side were like that, too, an Indian. He was married five times and he really ruled his roost.''

''There are a mighty lot of Indians up your family tree,'' I said. ''Did your granddad look like one?''

''Only his nose. He was dark brownskin otherwise. In fact, he were black. And the womens! Man! They was crazy about Grandpa. Every time he walked down the street, they stuck their heads out the windows and kept 'em turned South—which was where the beer parlor was.''

''So your grandpa was a drinking man, too. That must be whom you take after.''

''I also am named after him,'' said Simple. ''Grandpa's name was Jess, too. So I am Jesse B. Semple.''

''What does the *B* stand for?''

''Nothing. I just put it there myself since they didn't give me no initial when I was born. I am really Jess Semple—which the kids changed around into a nickname when I were in school. In fact, they used to tease me when I were small, calling me 'Simple Simon.' But I was right handy with my fists, and after I beat the 'Simon' out of a few of them, they let me alone. But my friends still call me 'Simple.' ''

"In reality, you are Jesse Semple," I said, "colored."

"Part Indian," insisted Simple, reaching for his beer.

"Jess is certainly not an Indian name."

"No, it ain't," said Simple, "but we did have a Hiawatha in our family. She died."

"*She?*" I said. "Hiawatha was no *she.*"

"She was a *she* in our family. And she had long coal-black hair just like a Creole. You know, I started to marry a Creole one time when I was coach-boy on the L. & N. down to New Orleans. Them Louisiana girls are bee-oou-te-ful! Man, I mean!"

"Why didn't you marry her, fellow?"

"They are more dangerous than a Indian," said Simple, "also I do not want no pretty woman. First thing you know, you fall in love with her—then you got to kill somebody about her. She'll make you so jealous you'll bust! A pretty woman will get a man in trouble. Me and my Indian blood, quick-tempered as I is. No! I do not crave a pretty woman."

"Joyce is certainly not bad-looking," I said. "You hang around her all the time."

"She is far from a Creole. Besides, she appreciates me," said Simple. "Joyce knows I got Indian blood which makes my temper bad. But we take each other as we is. I respect her and she respects me."

"That's the way it should be with the whole world," I said. "Therefore, you and Joyce are setting a fine example in these days of trials and tribulations. Everybody should take each other as they are, white, black, Indians, Creoles. Then there would be no prejudice, nations would get along."

"Some folks do not see it like that," said Simple. "For instant, my land-lady—and my wife. Isabel could never get along with me. That is why we are not together today."

"I'm not talking personally," I said, "so why bring in your wife?"

"Getting along *starts* with persons, don't it?" asked Simple. "You *must* include my wife. That woman got my Indian blood so riled up one day I thought I would explode."

"I still say, I'm not talking personally."

"Then stop talking," exploded Simple, "because with me it is personal. Facts, I cannot even talk about my wife if I don't get personal. That's how it is if you're part Indian—everything is personal. *Heap much personal.*"

(1950)

PROTEST
AND
PROPHECY

Not everlastingly while others sleep
Shall we beguile their limbs with mellow flute,
Not always bend to some more subtle brute;
We were not made eternally to weep.

Countee Cullen
From the Dark Tower

The blow I struck
Was not in vain,
The blow I struck
Shall be struck again.

Robert Hayden
Gabriel

ON BEING CRAZY
by W. E. B. Du Bois

It was one o'clock and I was hungry. I walked into a restaurant, seated myself, and reached for the bill of fare. My table companion rose.

"Sir," said he, "do you wish to force your company on those who do not want you?"

No, said I, I wish to eat.

"Are you aware, sir, that this is social equality?"

Nothing of the sort, sir, it is hunger—and I ate.

The day's work done, I sought the theatre. As I sank into my seat, the lady shrank and squirmed.

I beg pardon, I said.

"Do you enjoy being where you are not wanted?" she asked coldly.

Oh no, I said.

"Well you are not wanted here."

I was surprised. I fear you are mistaken, I said, I certainly want the music, and I like to think the music wants me to listen to it.

"Usher," said the lady, "this is social equality."

"No, madame," said the usher, "it is the second movement of Beethoven's Fifth Symphony."

After the theatre, I sought the hotel where I had sent my baggage. The clerk scowled.

"What do you want?"

Rest, I said.

"This is a white hotel," he said.

I looked around. Such a color scheme requires a great deal of cleaning, I said, but I don't know that I object.

"We object," said he.

Then why, I began, but he interrupted.

"We don't keep niggers," he said, "we don't want social equality."

Neither do I, I replied gently, I want a bed.

I walked thoughtfully to the train. I'll take a sleeper through Texas. I'm a little bit dissatisfied with this town.

"Can't sell you one."

I only want to hire it, said I, for a couple of nights.

"Can't sell you a sleeper in Texas," he maintained. "They consider that social equality."

I consider it barbarism, I said, and I think I'll walk.

Walking, I met another wayfarer, who immediately walked to the other side of the road, where it was muddy. I asked his reason.

"Niggers is dirty," he said.

So is mud, said I. Moreover, I am not as dirty as you—yet.

"But you're a nigger, ain't you?" he asked.

My grandfather was so called.

"Well then!" he answered triumphantly.

Do you live in the South? I persisted, pleasantly.

"Sure," he growled, "and starve there."

I should think you and the Negroes should get together and vote out starvation.

"We don't let them vote."

We? Why not? I said in surprise.

"Niggers is too ignorant to vote."

But, I said, I am not so ignorant as you.

"But you're a nigger."

Yes, I'm certainly what you mean by that.

"Well then!" he returned, with that curiously inconsequential note of triumph. "Moreover," he said, "I don't want my sister to marry a nigger."

I had not seen his sister, so I merely murmured, let her say no.

"By God, you shan't marry her, even if she said yes."

But—but I don't want to marry her, I answered, a little perturbed at the personal turn.

"Why not!" he yelled, angrier than ever.

Because I'm already married and I rather like my wife.

"Is she a nigger?" he asked suspiciously.

Well, I said again, her grandmother was called that.

"Well then!" he shouted in that oddly illogical way.

I gave up.

Go on, I said, either you are crazy or I am.

"We both are," he said as he trotted along in the mud.

(1907)

From

THE SOUTHERNER
by Walter Hines Page

There were several Southern coloured students in college. I came to know one of them because he and I exchanged confidences about the extreme Bostonian intonations and inflections of the lecturer under whom we sat. Coming out of the classroom, this coloured lad would amuse us by mimicking him and then by translating parts of the lecture into good "nigger" English, which only he and I of the company could understand.

He amused other students by exaggerating our Southern drawl and inflections.

Another coloured student came into much notoriety for a time by an accident that made him a hero.

He had his room in a private house and somebody hired the house who objected to his presence because he was a Negro. This at once raised a storm of protest. It was the first display that I had seen of that sentimentality toward black persons which makes them pets—and victims—of a determined and ostentatious display of "justice."

Nobody had hitherto paid any especial attention to this fellow till it appeared that he was persecuted. Instantly the "New England conscience" became active and showed its morbidity. Everybody seemed bent on doing what nobody would naturally and normally have done before. A dozen men offered to take him as their roommate. It should never be said of them that they had suffered a man to be unjustly dealt with because of the colour of his skin. One of these generous volunteers was Cooley. He'd take him as a roommate at once.

"I suppose you'd regard it as a degradation, Worth, but I can't see that man hounded because he is black."

It was a fine spirit. But Cooley was too late in his good impulse. Another man had anticipated him. A man named Foster, who had an hereditary claim to abolitionist sensitiveness, had helped the Negro move his books and belongings into his own rooms; and for the rest of that year they lived together.

The way of the saints who fail to take every-day facts into account is still a hard way. Foster was years later black-balled in a social club in a Western (not a Southern) city, by peculiar persons to whom this generous conduct made him objectionable, for their zeal had a different tangent.

This foolish incident gave me much to think about. I had known before that we had a grave "Southern problem," which included white people and

Negroes too. It was now that I first found out that we had also a "Negro problem." For two years the Negro student had been there and no white lad had invited him to share his room. When the new tenants of the house objected to him, I could not see why it did not occur to his friends to help him find another room for himself. That is what would have happened if he had been a white boy—if anything would have happened. But, since he was black, that was not enough. Dozen of men who had not even been his friends—had not known him—felt impelled to take him into intimacy. Impelled by what? I had only a psychological interest in the incident. But that interest was, I confess, great. I asked Cooley, but he could not explain this to me very satisfactorily.

"Cooley," said I, "suppose the boy had been a German boy, and the people in the house had said that they objected to a German, would you have asked him to room with you?"

"Certainly not. Why should I?"

"If he had been a Roman Catholic, or a Jew, and objection had been raised to his religion or to his race, would you have come to his rescue?"

"Certainly not. Why should I?"

"Why, then, merely because he is a Negro? Wouldn't the German or the Roman Catholic or the Jew also be victims of 'persecution'?"

"No."

"It becomes 'persecution,' then, only when the victim is black?"

It was many years afterward that I ventured this definition of the Negro in the United States:

"A person of African blood (much or little) about whom men of English descent tell only half the truth and because of whom they do not act with frankness and sanity either toward the Negro or to one another—in a word, about whom they easily lose their common sense, their usual good judgment, and even their powers of accurate observation. The Negro-in-America, therefore, is a form of insanity that overtakes white men."

This definition may have ethnological defects, but psychologically and historically much can be said in its favour.

(1909)

From

THE MEXICAN
by Jack London

Barely noticed was Rivera as he entered the ring. Only a very slight and very scattering ripple of halfhearted handclapping greeted him. The house did not believe in him. He was the lamb led to slaughter at the hands of the great Danny. Besides, the house was disappointed, It had expected a rushing battle between Danny Ward and Billy Carthey, and here it must put up with this poor little tyro. Still further, it had manifested its disapproval of the change by betting two, and even three, to one on Danny. And where a betting audience's money is, there is its heart.

The Mexican boy sat down in his corner and waited. The slow minutes lagged by. Danny was making him wait. It was an old trick, but ever it worked on the young, new fighters. They grew frightened, sitting thus and facing their own apprehensions and a callous, tobacco-smoking audience. But for once the trick failed. Roberts was right. Rivera had no goat. He, who was more delicately coordinated, more finely nerved and strung than any of them, had no nerves of this sort. The atmosphere of foredoomed defeat in his own corner had no effect on him. His handlers were gringos and strangers. Also they were scrubs—the dirty driftage of the fight game, without honor, without efficiency. And they were chilled, as well, with certitude that theirs was the losing corner.

"Now you gotta be careful," Spider Hagerty warned him. Spider was his chief second. "Make it last as long as you can—them's my instructions from Kelly. If you don't, the papers'll call it another bum fight and give the game a bigger black eye in Los Angeles."

All of which was not encouraging. But Rivera took no notice. He despised prize fighting. It was the hated game of the hated gringo. He had taken up with it, as a chopping block for others in the training quarters, solely because he was starving. The fact that he was marvelously made for it had meant nothing. He hated it. Not until he had come in to the Junta had he fought for money, and he had found the money easy. Not first among the sons of men had he been to find himself successful at a despised vocation.

He did not analyze. He merely knew that he must win this fight. There could be no other outcome. For behind him, nerving him to this belief, were profounder forces than any the crowded house dreamed. Danny Ward fought for money and for the easy ways of life that money would bring. But the things Rivera fought for burned in his brain—blazing and terrible visions, that, with eyes wide open, sitting lonely in the corner of the ring and waiting for his tricky antagonist, he saw as clearly as he had lived them.

He saw the white-walled water-power factories of Rio Blanco. He saw the six thousand workers, starved and wan, and the little children, seven and eight years of age, who toiled long shifts for ten cents a day. He saw the perambulating corpses, the ghastly death's heads of men who labored in the dye rooms. He remembered that he had heard his father call the dye rooms the "suicide holes," where a year was death. He saw the little patio, and his mother cooking and moiling at crude housekeeping and finding time to caress and love him. And his father he saw, large, big-mustached, and deep-chested, kindly above all men, who loved all men and whose heart was so large that there was love to overflowing still left for the mother and the little *muchacho* playing in the corner of the patio. In those days his name had not been Felipe Rivera. It had been Fernández, his father's and mother's name. Him had they called Juan. Later he had changed it himself, for he had found the name of Fernández hated by prefects of police, *jefes políticos,* and *rurales.*

Big, hearty Joaquín Fernández! A large place he occupied in Rivera's visions. He had not understood at the time, but, looking back, he could understand. He could see him setting type in the little printery, or scribbling endless hasty, nervous lines on the much-cluttered desk. And he could see the strange evenings, when workmen, coming secretly in the dark like men who did ill deeds, met with his father and talked long hours where he, the *muchacho,* lay not always asleep in the corner.

As from a remote distance he could hear Spider Hagerty saying to him: "No layin' down at the start. Them's instructions. Take a beatin' an' earn your dough."

Ten minutes had passed, and he still sat in his corner. There were no signs of Danny, who was evidently playing the trick to the limit.

But more visions burned before the eye of Rivera's memory. The strike, or, rather, the lockout, because the workers of Rio Blanco had helped their striking brothers of Puebla. The hunger, the expeditions in the hills for berries, the roots and herbs that all ate and that twisted and pained the stomachs of all of them. And then the nightmare; the waste of ground before the company's store; the thousands of starving workers; General Rosalio Martínez and the soldiers of Porfirio Díaz; and the death-spitting rifles that seemed never to cease spitting, while the workers' wrongs were washed and washed again in their own blood. And that night! He saw the flatcars, piled high with the bodies of the slain, consigned to Vera Cruz, food for the sharks of the bay. Again he crawled over the grisly heaps, seeking and finding, stripped and mangled, his father and his mother. His mother he especially remembered—only her face projecting, her body burdened by the weight of dozens of bodies. Again the rifles of the soldiers of Porfirio Díaz cracked, and again he dropped to the ground and slunk away like some hunted coyote of the hills.

To his ears came a great roar, as of the sea, and he saw Danny Ward, leading his retinue of trainers and seconds, coming down the center aisle. The house was in wild uproar for the popular hero who was bound to win. Everybody proclaimed him. Everybody was for him. Even Rivera's own seconds warmed to something akin to cheerfulness when Danny ducked jauntily through the ropes and entered the ring. His face continually spread to an unending succession of smiles, and when Danny smiled he smiled in every feature, even to the laughter wrinkles of the corners of the eyes and into the depths of the eyes themselves. Never was there so genial a fighter. His face was a running advertisement of good feeling, of good-fellowship. He knew everybody. He joked, and laughed, and greeted his friends through the ropes. Those farther away, unable to suppress their admiration, cried loudly: "Oh, you Danny!" It was a joyous ovation of affection that lasted a full five minutes.

Rivera was disregarded. For all that the audience noticed, he did not exist. Spider Hagerty's bloated face bent down close to his.

"No gettin' scared," the Spider warned. "An' remember instructions. You gotta last. No layin' down. If you lay down, we got instructions to beat you up in the dressing rooms. Savvy? You just gotta fight."

The house began to applaud. Danny was crossing the ring to him. Danny bent over, caught Rivera's right hand in both his own and shook it with impulsive heartiness. Danny's smile-wreathed face was close to his. The audience yelled its appreciation of Danny's display of sporting spirit. He was greeting his opponent with the fondness of a brother. Danny's lips moved, and the audience, interpreting the unheard words to be those of a kindly-natured sport, yelled again. Only Rivera heard the low words.

"You little Mexican rat," hissed from between Danny's gaily smiling lips, "I'll fetch the yellow outa you."

Rivera made no move. He did not rise. He merely hated with his eyes.

"Get up, you dog!" some man yelled through the ropes from behind.

The crowd began to hiss and boo him for his unsportsmanlike conduct, but he sat unmoved. Another great outburst of applause was Danny's as he walked back across thg ring.

When Danny stripped, there were ohs! and ahs! of delight. His body was perfect, alive with easy suppleness and health and strength. The skin was white as a woman's, and as smooth. All grace, and resilience, and power resided therein. He had proved it in scores of battles. His photographs were in all the physical-culture magazines.

A groan went up as Spider Hagerty peeled Rivera's sweater over his head. His body seemed leaner because of the swarthiness of the skin. He had muscles, but they made no display like his opponent's. What the audience neglected to see was the deep chest. Nor could it guess the toughness of the fiber of the flesh, the instantaneousness of the cell explosions of the muscles, the fineness of the nerves that wired every part of him into a splendid fighting mechanism. All the audience saw was a brown-skinned boy of eighteen with what seemed the body of a boy. With Danny it was different. Danny was a man of twenty-four, and his body was a man's body. The contrast was still more striking as they stood together in the center of the ring receiving the referee's last instructions.

Rivera noticed Roberts sitting directly behind the newspapermen. He was drunker than usual, and his speech was corresponding slower.

"Take it easy, Rivera," Roberts drawled. "He can't kill you, remember that. He'll rush you at the go-off, but don't get rattled. You just cover up, and stall, and clinch. He can't hurt you much. Just make believe to yourself that he's choppin' out on you at the trainin' quarters."

Rivera made no sign that he had heard.

"Sullen little devil," Roberts muttered to the man next to him. "He always was that way."

But Rivera forgot to look his usual hatred. A vision of countless rifles blinded his eyes. Every face in the audience, far as he could see, to the high dollar seats, was transformed into a rifle. And he saw the long Mexican border arid and sun-washed and aching, and along it he saw the ragged bands that delayed only for the guns.

Back in his corner he waited, standing up. His seconds had crawled out through the ropes, taking the canvas stool with them. Diagonally across the squared ring, Danny faced him. The gong struck, and the battle was on. The audience howled its delight. Never had it seen a battle open more convincingly. The papers were right. It was a grudge fight. Three quarters of the distance Danny covered in the rush to get together, his intention to eat up the Mexican lad plainly advertised. He assailed with not one blow, nor two, nor a dozen. He was a gyroscope of blows, a whirlwind of destruction. Rivera was nowhere. He was overwhelmed, buried beneath avalanches of punches delivered from every angle and position by a past master in the art. He was overborne, swept back against the ropes, separated by the referee, and swept back against the ropes again.

It was not a fight. It was a slaughter, a massacre. Any audience, save a prize-fighting one, would have exhausted its emotions in that first minute. Danny was certainly showing what he could do—a splendid exhibition. Such was the certainty of the audience, as well as its excitement and favoritism, that it failed to take notice that the Mexican still stayed on his feet. It forgot Rivera. It rarely saw him, so closely was he enveloped in Danny's man-eating attack. A minute of this went by, and two minutes. Then, in a separation, it caught a clear glimpse of the Mexican. His lip was cut, his nose was bleeding. As he turned and staggered into a clinch the welts of oozing blood, from his contacts with the ropes, showed in red bars across his back. But what the audience did not notice was that his chest was not heaving and that his eyes were coldly burning as ever. Too many aspiring champions, in the cruel welter of the training camps, had practiced this man-eating attack on him. He had learned to live through for a compensation of from half a dollar a go up to fifteen dollars a week—a hard school, and he was schooled hard.

Then happened the amazing thing. The whirling, blurring mix-up ceased suddenly. Rivera stood alone. Danny, the redoubtable Danny, lay on his back. His body quivered as consciousness strove to return to it. He had not staggered and sunk down, nor had he gone over in a long slumping fall. The right hook of Rivera had dropped him in mid-air with the abruptness of death. The referee shoved Rivera back with one hand and stood over the fallen gladiator counting the seconds. It is the custom of prize-fighting audiences to cheer a clean knock-down blow. But this audience did not cheer. The thing had been too unexpected. It watched the toll of seconds in tense silence, and through this silence the voice of Roberts rose exultantly:

"I told you he was a two-handed fighter!"

By the fifth second Danny was rolling over on his face, and when seven was counted he rested on one knee, ready to rise after the count of nine and before the count of ten. If his knee still touched the floor at "ten" he was considered "down" and also "out." The instant his knee left the floor he was considered "up," and in that instant it was Rivera's right to try and put him down again. Rivera took no chances. The moment that knee left the floor he would strike again. He circled around, but the referee circled in between, and Rivera knew that the seconds he counted were very slow. All gringos were against him, even the referee.

At "nine" the referee gave Rivera a sharp thrust back. It was unfair, but it enabled Danny to rise, the smile back on his lips. Doubled partly over, with arms wrapped about face and abdomen, he cleverly stumbled into a clinch. By all the rules of the game the referee should have broken it, but he did not, and Danny clung on like a surf-battered barnacle and moment by moment recuperated. The last minute of the round was going fast. If he could live to the end he would have a full minute in his corner to revive. And live to the end he did, smiling through all desperateness and extremity.

"The smile that won't come off!" somebody yelled, and the audience laughed loudly in its relief.

"The kick that greaser's got is something God-awful," Danny gasped in his corner to his adviser while his handlers worked frantically over him.

The second and third rounds were tame. Danny, a tricky and consummate ring general, stalled and blocked and held on, devoting himself to recovering from that dazing first-round blow. In the fourth round he was himself again. Jarred and shaken, nevertheless his good condition had enabled him to regain his vigor. But he tried no man-eating tactics. The Mexican had proved a tartar. Instead he brought to bear his best fighting powers. In tricks and skill and experience he was the master, and though he could land nothing vital, he proceeded scientifically to chop and wear down his opponent. He landed three blows to Rivera's one, but they were punishing blows only, and not deadly. It was the sum of many of them that constituted deadliness. He was respectful of this two-handed dub with the amazing short-arm kicks in both his fists.

In defense Rivera developed a disconcerting straight left. Again and again, attack after attack he straight-lefted away from him with accumulated damage to Danny's mouth and nose. But Danny was protean. That was why he was the coming champion. He could change from style to style of fighting at will. He now devoted himself to in-fighting. In this he was particularly wicked, and it enabled him to avoid the other's straight left. Here he set the house wild repeatedly, capping it with a marvelous lock-break and lift of an inside uppercut that raised the Mexican in the air and dropped him to the mat. Rivera rested on one knee, making the most of the count, and in the soul of him he knew the referee was counting short seconds on him.

Again, in the seventh, Danny achieved the diabolical inside uppercut. He succeeded only in staggering Rivera, but in the ensuing moment of defenseless helplessness he smashed him with another blow through the ropes. Rivera's body bounced on the heads of the newspapermen below, and they boosted him back to the edge of the platform outside the ropes. Here he rested on one knee, while the referee raced off the seconds. Inside the ropes, through which he must duck to enter the ring, Danny waited for him. Nor did the referee intervene or thrust Danny back.

The house was beside itself with delight.

"Kill'm, Danny, kill'm!" was the cry.

Scores of voices took it up until it was like a war chant of wolves.

Danny did his best, but Rivera, at the count of eight, instead of nine, came unexpectedly through the ropes and safely into a clinch. Now the referee worked, tearing him away so that he could be hit, giving Danny every advantage that an unfair referee can give.

But Rivera lived, and the daze cleared from his brain. It was all of a piece. They were the hated gringos and they were all unfair. And in the worst of it visions continued to flash and sparkle in his brain—long lines of railroad track that simmered across the desert, *rurales* and American constables; prisons and calabooses; tramps at water tanks—all the squalid and painful panorama of his odyssey after Rio Blanco and the strike. And, resplendent and glorious, he saw the great red revolution sweeping across his land. The guns were there before him. Every hated face was a gun. It was for the guns he fought. He was the guns. He was the revolution. He fought for all Mexico.

The audience began to grow incensed with Rivera. Why didn't he take the licking that was appointed him? Of course he was going to be licked, but why should he be so obstinate about it? Very few were interested in him, and they were the certain, definite percentage of a gambling crowd that plays long shots. Believing Danny to be the winner, nevertheless they had put their money on the Mexican at four to ten and one to three. More than a trifle was up on the point of how many rounds Rivera could last. Wild money had appeared at the ringside proclaiming that he could not last seven rounds, or even six. The winners of this, now that their cash risk was happily settled, had joined in cheering on their favorite.

Rivera refused to be licked. Through the eighth round his opponent strove vainly to repeat the uppercut. In the ninth Rivera stunned the house again. In the midst of a clinch he broke the lock with a quick, lithe movement, and in the narrow space between their bodies his right lifted from the waist. Danny went to the floor and took the safety of the count. The crowd was appalled. He was being bested at his own game. His famous right uppercut had been worked back on him. Rivera made no attempt to catch him as he arose at "nine." The referee was openly blocking that play, though he stood clear when the situation was reversed and it was Rivera who was required to rise.

Twice in the tenth Rivera put through the right uppercut, lifted from waist to opponent's chin. Danny grew desperate. The smile never left his face, but he went back to his man-eating rushes. Whirlwind as he would, he could not damage Rivera, while Rivera through the blur and whirl, dropped him to the mat three times in succession. Danny did not recuperate so quickly now, and by the eleventh round he was in a serious way. But from then till the fourteenth he put up the gamest exhibition of his career. He stalled and blocked, fought parsimoniously, and strove to gather strength. Also he fought as foully as a successful fighter knows how. Every trick and device he employed, butting in the clinches with the seeming of accident, pinioning Rivera's glove between arm and body, heeling his glove on Rivera's mouth to clog his breathing. Often, in the clinches, through his cut and smiling lips he snarled insults unspeakable and vile in Rivera's ear. Everybody, from the referee to the house, was with Danny and was helping Danny. And they knew what he had in mind. Bested by this surprise box of an unknown, he was pinning all on a single punch. He offered himself for punishment, fished, and feinted, and drew, for that one opening that would enable him to whip a blow through with all his strength and turn the tide. As another and greater fighter had done before him, he might do—a right and left, to solar plexus and across the jaw. He could do it, for he was noted for the strength of punch that remained in his arms as long as he could keep his feet.

Rivera's seconds were not half caring for him in the intervals between rounds. Their towels made a showing but drove little air into his panting lungs. Spider Hagerty talked advice to him, but Rivera knew it was wrong advice. Everybody was against him. He was surrounded by treachery. In the fourteenth round he put Danny down again, and himself stood resting, hands dropped at side, while the referee counted. In the other corner Rivera had been noting suspicious whisperings. He saw Michael Kelly make his way to Roberts and bend and whisper. Rivera's ears were a cat's, desert-trained, and he caught snatches of what was said. He wanted to hear more, and when his opponent arose he maneuvered the fight into a clinch over against the ropes.

"Got to," he could hear Michael, while Roberts nodded. "Danny's got to win—I stand to lose a mint. I've got a ton of money covered—my own. If he lasts the fifteenth I'm bust. The boy'll mind you. Put something across."

And thereafter Rivera saw no more visions. They were trying to job him. Once again he dropped Danny and stood resting, his hands at his side. Roberts stood up.

"That settled him," he said. "Go to your corner."

He spoke with authority, as he had often spoken to Rivera at the training quarters. But Rivera looked hatred at him and waited for Danny to rise. Back in his corner in the minute interval, Kelly, the promoter, came and talked to Rivera.

"Throw it, damn you," he rasped in a harsh low voice. "You gotta lay down, Rivera. Stick with me and I'll make your future. I'll let you lick Danny next time. But here's where you lay down."

Rivera showed with his eyes that he heard, but he made neither sign of assent nor dissent.

"Why don't you speak?" Kelly demanded angrily.

"You lose anyway," Spider Hagerty supplemented. "The referee'll take it away from you. Listen to Kelly and lay down."

"Lay down, kid," Kelly pleaded, "and I'll help you to the championship."

Rivera did not answer.

"I will, so help me, kid."

At the strike of the gong Rivera sensed something impending. The house did not. Whatever it was, it was there inside the ring with him and very close. Danny's earlier surety seemed returned to him. The confidence of his advance frightened Rivera. Some trick was about to be worked. Danny rushed, but Rivera refused the encounter. He side-stepped away into safety. What the other wanted was a clinch. It was in some way necessary to the trick. Rivera backed and circled away, yet he knew, sooner or later the clinch and the trick would come. Desperately he resolved to draw it. He made as if to effect the clinch with Danny's next rush. Instead, at the last instant, just as their bodies should have come together, Rivera darted nimbly back. And in the same instant Danny's corner raised a cry of foul. Rivera had fooled them. The referee paused irresolutely. The decision that trembled on his lips was never uttered, for a shrill, boy's voice from the gallery piped, "Raw work!"

Danny cursed Rivera openly, and forced him, while Rivera danced away. Also Rivera made up his mind to strike no more blows at the body. In this he threw away half his chance of winning, but he knew if he was to win at all it was with the outfighting that remained to him. Given the least opportunity, they would lie a foul on him. Danny threw all caution to the winds. For two rounds he tore after and into the boy who dared not meet him at close quarters. Rivera was struck again and again; he took blows by the dozens to avoid the perilous clinch. During this supreme final rally of Danny's the audience rose to its feet and went mad. It did not understand. All it could see was that its favorite was winning after all.

"Why don't you fight?" it demanded wrathfully of Rivera. "You're yellow! You're yellow!'' ''Open up, you cur! Open up!'' ''Kill'm, Danny! Kill 'm!'' ''You sure got 'm! Kill 'm!''

In all the house, bar none, Rivera was the only cold man. By temperament and blood he was the hottest-passioned there; but he had gone through such vastly greater heats that this collective passion of ten thousand throats, rising surge on surge, was to his brain no more than the velvet cool of a summer twilight.

Into the seventeenth round Danny carried his rally. Rivera, under a heavy blow, drooped and sagged. His hands dropped helplessly as he reeled backward. Danny thought it was his chance. The boy was at his mercy. Thus Rivera, feigning, caught him off his guard, lashing out a clean drive to the mouth. Danny went down. When he arose Rivera felled him with a down-chop of the right on neck and jaw. Three times he repeated this. It was impossible for any referee to call these blows foul.

''Oh, Bill! Bill!'' Kelly pleaded to the referee.

''I can't,'' that official lamented back. ''He won't give me a chance.''

Danny, battered and heroic, still kept coming up. Kelly and others near to the ring began to cry out to the police to stop it, though Danny's corner refused to throw in the towel. Rivera saw the fat police captain starting awkwardly to climb through the ropes, and was not sure what it meant. There were so many ways of cheating in this game of the gringos. Danny, on his feet, tottered groggily and helplessly before him. The referee and the captain were both reaching for Rivera when he struck the last blow. There was no need to stop the fight, for Danny did not rise.

''Count!'' Rivera cried hoarsely to the referee.

And when the count was finished Danny's seconds gathered him up and carried him to the corner.

''Who wins?'' Rivera demanded.

Reluctantly the referee caught his gloved hand and held it aloft.

There were no congratulations for Rivera. He walked to his corner unattended, where his seconds had not yet placed his stool. He leaned backward on the ropes and looked his hatred at them, swept it on and about him till the whole ten thousand gringos were included. His knees trembled under him, and he was sobbing from exhaustion. Before his eyes the hated faces swayed back and forth in the giddiness of nausea. Then he remembered they were the guns. The guns were his. The revolution could go on.

(1911)

A BLACK MAN TALKS OF REAPING
by Arna Bontemps

I have sown beside all waters in my day.
I planted deep, within my heart the fear
That wind or fowl would take the grain away.
I planted safe against this stark, lean year.

I scattered seed enough to plant the land
In rows from Canada to Mexico,
But for my reaping only what the hand
Can hold at once is all that I can show.

Yet what I sowed and what the orchard yields
My brother's sons are gathering stalk and root,
Small wonder then my children glean in fields
They have not sown, and feed on bitter fruit.

(1927)

STRONG MEN
by Sterling A. Brown

The strong men keep coming on.
                SANDBURG.

They dragged you from homeland,
They chained you in coffles,
They huddled you spoon-fashion in filthy hatches,
They sold you to give a few gentlemen ease.

They broke you in like oxen,
They scourged you,
They branded you,

They made your women breeders,
They swelled your numbers with bastards. . . .
They taught you the religion they disgraced.

You sang:
>   *Keep a-inchin' along*
>   *Lak a po' inch worm.* . . .

You sang:
>   *Bye and bye*
>   *I'm gonna lay down dis heaby load.* . . .

You sang:
>   *Walk togedder, chillen,*
>   *Dontcha git weary.* . . .
>   The strong men keep a-comin' on
>   The strong men git stronger.

They point with pride to the roads you built for them,
They ride in comfort over the rails you laid for them.
They put hammers in your hands
And said—Drive so much before sundown.

You sang:
>   *Ain't no hammah*
>   *In dis lan',*
>   *Strikes lak mine, bebby,*
>   *Strikes lak mine.*

They cooped you in their kitchens,
They penned you in their factories,
They gave you the jobs that they were too good for,
They tried to guarantee happiness to themselves
By shunting dirt and misery to you.

You sang:
>   *Me an' muh baby gonna shine, shine*
>   *Me an' muh baby gonna shine.*
>   The strong men keep a-comin' on
>   The strong men git stronger. . . .

They bought off some of your leaders
You stumbled, as blind men will . . .
They coaxed you, unwontedly soft-voiced. . . .

You followed a way.
Then laughed as usual.

They heard the laugh and wondered;
Uncomfortable;
Unadmitting a deeper terror. . . .
   The strong men keep a-comin' on
   Gittin' stronger. . . .

What, from the slums
Where they have hemmed you,
What, from the tiny huts
They could not keep from you—
What reaches them
Making them ill at ease, fearful?
Today they shout prohibition at you
"Thou shalt not this"
"Thou shalt not that"
"Reserved for whites only"
You laugh.

One thing they cannot prohibit—
   The strong men . . . coming on
   The strong men gittin' stronger.
   Strong men. . . .
   Stronger. . . .

        (1932)

I HAVE SEEN BLACK HANDS
by Richard Wright

I

I am black and I have seen black hands, millions and millions of them—
Out of millions of bundles of wool and flannel tiny black fingers have
  reached restlessly and hungrily for life.
Reached out for the black nipples at the black breasts of black mothers,
And they've held red, green, blue, yellow, orange, white, and purple toys
  in the childish grips of possession,

And chocolate drops, peppermint sticks, lollypops, wineballs, ice cream
 cones, and sugared cookies in fingers sticky and gummy,
And they've held balls and bats and gloves and marbles and jack-knives
 and sling-shots and spinning tops in the thrill of sport and play
And pennies and nickles and dimes and quarters and sometimes on New
 Year's, Easter, Lincoln's Birthday, May Day, a brand new green
 dollar bill,
They've held pens and rulers and maps and tablets and books in palms
 spotted and smeared with ink,
And they've held dice and cards and half-pint flasks and cue sticks and
 cigars and cigarettes in the pride of new maturity . . .

II

I am black and I have seen black hands, millions and millions of them—
They were tired and awkward and calloused and grimy and covered with
 hangnails,
And they were caught in the fast-moving belts of machines and snagged
 and smashed and crushed,
And they jerked up and down at the throbbing machines massing taller
 and taller the heaps of gold in the banks of bosses,
And they piled higher and higher the steel, iron, the lumber, wheat, rye,
 the oats, corn, the cotton, the wool, the oil, the coal, the meat,
 the fruit, the glass, and the stone until there was too much to be
 used,
And they grabbed guns and slung them on their shoulders and marched
 and groped in trenches and fought and killed and conquered nations who were customers for the goods black hands had made.
And again black hands stacked goods higher and higher until there was
 too much to be used,
And then the black hands held trembling at the factory gates the dreaded
 lay-off slip,
And the black hands hung idle and swung empty and grew soft and got
 weak and bony from unemployment and starvation,
And they grew nervous and sweaty, and opened and shut in anguish and
 doubt and hesitation and irresolution . . .

III

I am black and I have seen black hands, millions and millions of them—
Reaching hesitantly out of days of slow death for the goods they had made,
 but the bosses warned that the goods were private and did not belong to them,

And the black hands struck desperately out in defence of life and there
    was blood, but the enraged bosses decreed that this too was wrong.
And the black hands felt the cold steel bars of the prison they had made,
    in despair tested their strength and found that they could neither
    bend nor break them,
And the black hands fought and scratched and held back but a thousand
    white hands took them and tied them,
And the black hands lifted palms in mute and futile supplication to the
    sodden faces of mobs wild in the revelries of sadism,
And the black hands strained and clawed and struggled in vain at the noose
    that tightened about the black throat,
And the black hands waved and beat fearfully at the tall flames that cooked
    and charred the black flesh . . .

IV

I am black and I have seen black hands
Raised in fists of revolt, side by side with the white fists of white work-
    ers,
And some day—and it is only this which sustains me—
Some day there shall be millions and millions of them,
On some red day in a burst of fists on a new horizon!

                                                (1934)

LET AMERICA BE AMERICA AGAIN
by Langston Hughes

Let America be America again
Let it be the dream it used to be.
Let it be the pioneer on the plain
Seeking a home where he himself is free.

(America never was America to me.)

Let America be the dream the dreamers dreamed—
Let it be that great strong land of love
Where never kings connive nor tyrants scheme
That any man be crushed by one above.

(It never was America to me.)

O, let my land be a land where Liberty
Is crowned with no false patriotic wreath,
But opportunity is real, and life is free,
Equality is in the air we breathe.

(There's never been equality for me,
Nor freedom in this "homeland of the free.")

Say who are you that mumbles in the dark?
And who are you that draws your veil across the stars?

I am the poor white, fooled and pushed apart,
I am the red man driven from the land.
I am the refugee clutching the hope I seek—
But finding only the same old stupid plan
Of dog eat dog, of mighty crush the weak.
I am the Negro, "problem" to you all.
I am the people, humble, hungry, mean—
Hungry yet today despite the dream.
Beaten yet today—O, Pioneers!
I am the man who never got ahead.
The poorest worker bartered through the years.
Yet I'm the one who dreamt our basic dream
In that Old World while still a serf of kings.
Who dreamt a dream so strong, so brave, so true,
That even yet its mighty daring sings
In every brick and stone, in every furrow turned
That's made America the land it has become.
O, I'm the man who sailed those early seas
In search of what I meant to be my home—
For I'm the one who left dark Ireland's shore,
And Poland's plain, and England's grassy lea,
And torn from Black Africa's strand I came
To build a "homeland of the free."

The free?
Who said the free? Not me?
Surely not me? The millions on relief today?
The millions who have nothing for our pay
For all the dreams we've dreamed
And all the songs we've sung
And all the hopes we've held

And all the flags we've hung,
The millions who have nothing for our pay—
Except the dream we keep alive today.

O, let America be America again—
The land that never has been yet—
And yet must be—the land where *every* man is free.
The land that's mine—the poor man's, Indian's, Negro's, ME—
Who made America,
Whose sweat and blood, whose faith and pain,
Whose hand at the foundry, whose plow in the rain,
Must bring back our mighty dream again.

O, yes,
I say it plain,
America never was America to me,
And yet I swear this oath—
America will be!

(1938)

From

BLACK BOY
by Richard Wright

At last we were at the railroad station with our bags, waiting for the train that would take us to Arkansas; and for the first time I noticed that there were two lines of people at the ticket window, a "white" line and a "black" line. During my visit at Granny's a sense of the two races had been born in me with a sharp concreteness that would never die until I died. When I boarded the train I was aware that we Negroes were in one part of the train and that the whites were in another. Naïvely I wanted to go and see how the whites looked while sitting in their part of the train.

"Can I go and peep at the white folks?" I asked my mother.

"You keep quiet," she said.

"But that wouldn't be wrong, would it?"

"Will you keep still?"

"But why can't I?"

"Quit talking foolishness!"

I had begun to notice that my mother became irritated when I questioned her about whites and blacks, and I could not quite understand it. I wanted to understand these two sets of people who lived side by side and never touched, it seemed, except in violence. Now, there was my grandmother . . . Was she white? Just how white was she? What did the whites think of her whiteness?

"Mama, is Granny white?" I asked as the train rolled through the darkness.

"If you've got eyes, you can see what color she is," my mother said.

"I mean, do the white folks think she's white?"

"Why don't you ask the white folks that?" she countered.

"But you know," I insisted.

"Why should I know?" she asked. "I'm not white."

"Granny looks white," I said, hoping to establish one fact, at least. "Then why is she living with us colored folks?"

"Don't you want Granny to live with us?" she asked, blunting my question.

"Yes."

"Then why are you asking?"

"I want to *know*."

"Doesn't Granny live with us?"

"Yes."

"Isn't that enough?"

"But does she *want* to live with us?"

"Why didn't you ask Granny that?" my mother evaded me again in a taunting voice.

"Did Granny become colored when she married Grandpa?"

"Will you stop asking silly questions!"

"But did she?"

"Granny didn't *become* colored," my mother said angrily. "She was *born* the color she is now."

Again I was being shut out of the secret, the thing, the reality I felt somewhere beneath all the words and silences.

"Why didn't Granny marry a white man?" I asked.

"Because she didn't want to," my mother said peevishly.

"Why don't you want to talk to me?" I asked.

She slapped me and I cried. Later, grudgingly, she told me that Granny came of Irish, Scotch, and French stock in which Negro blood had somewhere and somehow been infused. She explained it all in a matter-of-fact, offhand, neutral way; her emotions were not involved at all.

"What was Granny's name before she married Grandpa?"

"Bolden."

"Who gave her that name?"

"The white man who owned her."

"She was a slave?"

"Yes."

"And Bolden was the name of Granny's father?"

"Granny doesn't know who her father was."

"So they just gave her any name?"

"They gave her a name; that's all I know."

"Couldn't Granny find out who her father was?"

"For what, silly?"

"So she could know."

"Know for what?"

"Just to know."

"But for *what?*"

I could not say. I could not get anywhere.

"Mama, where did Father get his name?"

"From his father."

"And where did the father of my father get his name?"

"Like Granny got hers. From a white man."

"Do they know who he is?"

"I don't know."

"Why don't they find out?"

"For what?" my mother demanded harshly.

And I could think of no rational or practical reason why my father should try to find out who his father's father was.

"What has Papa got in him?" I asked.

"Some white and some red and some black," she said.

"Indian, white, and Negro?"

"Yes."

"Then what am I?"

"They'll call you a colored man when you grow up," she said. Then she turned to me and smiled mockingly and asked: "Do you mind, Mr. Wright?"

I was angry and I did not answer. I did not object to being called colored, but I knew that there was something my mother was holding back. She was not concealing facts, but feelings, attitudes, convictions which she did not want me to know; and she became angry when I prodded her. All right, I would find out someday. Just wait. All right, I was colored. It was fine. I did not know enough to be afraid or to anticipate in a concrete manner. True, I had heard that colored people were killed and beaten, but so far it all had seemed remote. There was, of course, a vague uneasiness about it all, but I would be able to handle that when I came to it. It would be simple. If anybody tried to kill me, then I would kill them first.

(1945)

ROLAND HAYES BEATEN
(Georgia: 1942)

by Langston Hughes

Negroes,
Sweet and docile,
Meek, humble, and kind:
Beware the day
They change their minds!

Wind
In the cotton fields,
Gentle breeze:
Beware the hour
It uproots trees!
                              (1948)

POTPOURRI

When racial and ethnic stereotypes are studied on a comparative basis, one is immediately impressed with their extraordinary similarity.

Carey McWilliams
A Mask for Privilege

Whence all this passion toward conformity anyway?—diversity is the word. . . . America is woven of many strands; I would recognize them and let it so remain.

Ralph Ellison
Invisible Man

From

THE HOUSE OF MIRTH
by Edith Wharton

On the landing she paused to look about her. There were a thousand chances to one against her meeting anybody, but one could never tell, and she always paid for her rare indiscretions by a violent reaction of prudence. There was no one in sight, however, but a char-woman who was scrubbing the stairs. Her own stout person and its surrounding implements took up so much room that Lily, to pass her, had to gather up her skirts and brush against the wall. As she did so, the woman paused in her work and looked up curiously, resting her clenched red fists on the wet cloth she had just drawn from her pail. She had a broad sallow face, slightly pitted with small-pox, and thin straw-coloured hair through which her scalp shone unpleasantly.

"I beg your pardon," said Lily, intending by her politeness to convey a criticism of the other's manner.

The woman, without answering, pushed her pail aside, and continued to stare as Miss Bart swept by with a murmur of silken linings. Lily felt herself flushing under the look. What did the creature suppose? Could one never do the simplest, the most harmless thing, without subjecting one's self to some odious conjecture? Half way down the next flight, she smiled to think that a char-woman's stare should so perturb her. The poor thing was probably dazzled by such an unwonted apparition. But *were* such apparitions unwonted on Selden's stairs? Miss Bart was not familiar with the moral code of bachelors' flat-houses, and her colour rose again as it occurred to her that the woman's persistent gaze implied a groping among past associations. But she put aside the thought with a smile at her own fears, and hastened downward, wondering if she should find a cab short of Fifth Avenue.

Under the Georgian porch she paused again, scanning the street for a hansom. None was in sight, but as she reached the sidewalk she ran against a small glossy-looking man with a gardenia in his coat, who raised his hat with a surprised exclamation.

"Miss Bart? Well—of all people! This *is* luck," he declared; and she caught a twinkle of amused curiosity between his screwed-up lids.

181

"Oh, Mr. Rosedale—how are you?" she said, perceiving that the irrepressible annoyance on her face was reflected in the sudden intimacy of his smile.

Mr. Rosedale stood scanning her with interest and approval. He was a plump rosy man of the blond Jewish type, with smart London clothes fitting him like upholstery, and small sidelong eyes which gave him the air of appraising people as if they were bric-a-brac. He glanced up interrogatively at the porch of the Benedick.

"Been up to town for a little shopping, I suppose?" he said, in a tone which had the familiarity of a touch.

Miss Bart shrank from it slightly, and then flung herself into precipitate explanations.

"Yes—I came up to see my dress-maker. I am just on my way to catch the train to the Trenors'."

"Ah—your dress-maker; just so," he said blandly. "I didn't know there were any dress-makers in the Benedick."

"The Benedick?" She looked gently puzzled. "Is that the name of this building?"

"Yes, that's the name: I believe it's an old word for bachelor, isn't it? I happen to own the building—that's the way I know." His smile deepened as he added with increasing assurance: "But you must let me take you to the station. The Trenors are at Bellomont, of course? You've barely time to catch the five-forty. The dress-maker kept you waiting, I suppose."

Lily stiffened under the pleasantry.

"Oh, thanks," she stammered; and at that moment her eye caught a hansom drifting down Madison Avenue, and she hailed it with a desperate gesture.

"You're very kind; but I couldn't think of troubling you," she said, extending her hand to Mr. Rosedale; and heedless of his protestations, she sprang into the rescuing vehicle, and called out a breathless order to the driver.

2

In the hansom she leaned back with a sigh.

Why must a girl pay so dearly for her least escape from routine? Why could one never do a natural thing without having to screen it behind a structure of artifice? She had yielded to a passing impulse in going to Lawrence Selden's rooms, and it was so seldom that she could allow herself the luxury of an impulse! This one, at any rate, was going to cost her rather more than she could afford. She was vexed to see that, in spite of so many years of vigilance, she had blundered twice within five minutes. That stupid story about her dress-maker was bad enough—it would have been so simple to tell Rosedale that she had been taking tea with Selden! The mere statement of the fact would have rendered it innocuous. But, after having let herself be surprised in a falsehood, it was doubly stupid to snub the witness of her discomfiture. If she had had the presence of mind to let Rosedale drive her to the station, the concession might have purchased his silence. He had his race's accuracy in the appraisal of values, and to be seen walking down the platform at the crowded afternoon hour in the company of Miss Lily Bart would have been money in his pocket, as he might himself have phrased it. He knew, of course, that there would be a large house-party at Bellomont, and the possibility of being taken for one of Mrs. Trenor's guests was doubtless included in his calculations. Mr. Rosedale was still at a stage in his social ascent when it was of importance to produce such impressions.

The provoking part was that Lily knew all this—knew how easy it would have been to silence him on the spot, and how difficult it might be to do so afterward. Mr. Simon Rosedale was a man who made it his business to know everything about every one, whose idea of showing himself to be at home in society was to display an inconvenient familiarity with the habits of those with whom he wished to be thought intimate. Lily was sure that within twenty-four hours the story of her visiting her dressmaker at the Benedick would be in active circulation among Mr. Rosedale's acquaintances. The worst of it was that she had always snubbed and ignored him. On his first appearance—when her improvident cousin, Jack Stepney, had obtained for him (in return for favours too easily guessed) a card to one of the vast impersonal Van Osburgh "crushes"—Rosedale, with that mixture of artistic sensibility and business astuteness which characterizes his race, had instantly gravitated toward Miss Bart. She understood his motives, for her own course was guided by as nice calculations. Training and experience had taught her to be hospitable to newcomers, since the most unpromising might be useful later on, and there were plenty of available *oubliettes* to swallow them if they were not. But some intuitive repugnance, getting the better of years of social discipline, had made her push Mr. Rosedale into his *oubliette* without a trial. He had left behind only the ripple of amusement which his speedy despatch had caused among her friends; and though later (to shift the metaphor) he reappeared lower down the stream, it was only in fleeting glimpses, with long submergences between.

Hitherto Lily had been undisturbed by scruples. In her little set Mr. Rosedale had been pronounced "impossible," and Jack Strepney roundedly snubbed for his attempt to pay his debts in dinner invitations. Even Mrs. Trenor, whose taste for variety had led her into some hazardous experiments, resisted Jack's attempts to disguise Mr. Rosedale as a novelty, and declared that he was the same little Jew who had been served up and rejected at the social board a dozen times within her memory; and while Judy Trenor was obdurate there was small chance of Mr. Rosedale's penetrating beyond the outer limbo of the Van Osburgh crushes. Jack gave up the contest with a laughing "You 'll see," and, sticking manfully to his guns, showed himself with Rosedale at the fashionable restaurants, in company with the personally vivid if socially obscure ladies who are available for such purposes. But the attempt had hitherto been vain, and as

Rosedale undoubtedly paid for the dinners, the laugh remained with his debtor.

Mr. Rosedale, it will be seen, was thus far not a factor to be feared—unless one put one's self in his power. And this was precisely what Miss Bart had done. Her clumsy fib had let him see that she had something to conceal; and she was sure he had a score to settle with her. Something in his smile told her he had not forgotten. She turned from the thought with a little shiver, but it hung on her all the way to the station, and dogged her down the platform with the persistency of Mr. Rosedale himself.

(1905)

From

THE JUNGLE
by Upton Sinclair

So Jurgis became one of the new "American heroes," a man whose virtues merited comparison with those of the martyrs of Lexington and Valley Forge. The resemblance was not complete, of course, for Jurgis was generously paid and comfortably clad, and was provided with a spring cot and a mattress and three substantial meals a day; also he was perfectly at ease, and safe from all peril of life and limb, save only in the case that a desire for beer should lead him to venture outside of the stockyards gates. And even in the exercise of this privilege he was not left unprotected; a good part of the inadequate police force of Chicago was suddenly diverted from its work of hunting criminals, and rushed out to serve him.

The police, and the strikers also, were determined that there should be no violence; but there was another party interested which was minded to the contrary—and that was the press. On the first day of his life as a strikebreaker Jurgis quit work early, and in a spirit of bravado he challenged three men of his acquaintance to go outside and get a drink. They accepted, and went through the big Halsted Street gate, where several policemen were watching, and also some union pickets, scanning sharply those who passed in and out. Jurgis and his companions went south on Halsted Street, past the hotel, and then suddenly half a dozen men started across the street toward them and proceeded to argue with them concerning the error of their ways. As the arguments were not taken in the proper spirit, they went on to threats; and suddenly one of them jerked off the hat of one of the four and flung it over the fence. The man started after it, and then, as a cry of "Scab!" was raised and a dozen people came running out of saloons and doorways, a second man's heart failed him and he followed. Jurgis and the fourth stayed long enough to give themselves the satisfaction of a quick exchange of blows, and then they, too, took to their heels and fled back of the hotel and into the yards again. Meantime, of course, policemen were coming on a run, and as a crowd gathered other police got excited and sent in a riot call. Jurgis knew nothing of this, but went back to "Packers' Avenue," and in front of the "Central Time Station" he saw one of his companions, breathless and wild with excitement, narrating to an ever growing throng how the four had been attacked and surrounded by a howling mob, and had been nearly torn to pieces. While he stood listening, smiling cynically, several dapper young men stood by with notebooks in their hands, and it was not more than two hours later that Jurgis saw newsboys running about with armfuls of newspapers, printed in red and black letters six inches high:

VIOLENCE IN THE YARDS!
STRIKEBREAKERS SURROUNDED
BY FRENZIED MOB!

If he had been able to buy all of the newspapers of the United States the next morning, he might have discovered that his beer-hunting exploit was being perused by some two score millions of people, and had served as a text for editorials in half the staid and solemn businessmen's newspapers in the land.

Jurgis was to see more of this as time passed. For the present, his work being over, he was free to ride into the city, by a railroad direct from the yards, or else to spend the night in a room where cots had been laid in rows. He chose the latter, but to his regret, for all night long gangs of strikebreakers kept arriving. As very few of the better class of workingmen could be got for such work, these specimens of the new American hero contained an assortment of the criminals and thugs of the city, besides Negroes and the lowest foreigners—Greeks, Roumanians, Sicilians, and Slovaks. They had been attracted more by the prospect of disorder than by the big wages; and they made the night hideous with singing and carousing, and only went to sleep when the time came for them to get up to work.

In the morning before Jurgis had finished his breakfast, "Pat" Murphy ordered him to one of the superintendents, who questioned him as to his experience in the work of the killing room. His heart began to thump with excitement, for he divined instantly that his hour had come—that he was to be a boss!

Some of the foremen were union members, and many who were not had gone out with the men. It was in the killing department that the packers had been left most in the lurch, and precisely here that they could least afford it; the smoking and canning and salting of meat might wait, and all the by-products might be wasted—but fresh meats must be had, or the restaurants and hotels and brownstone houses would feel the pinch, and then "public opinion" would take a startling turn.

An opportunity such as this would not come twice to a man; and Jurgis seized it. Yes, he knew the work, the whole of it, and he could teach it to others. But if he took the job and gave satisfaction he would expect to keep it—they would not turn him off at the end of the strike? To which the superintendent replied that he might safely trust Durham's for that—they proposed to teach these unions a lesson, and most of all those foremen who had gone back on them. Jurgis would receive five dollars a day during the strike, and twenty-five a week after it was settled.

So our friend got a pair of "slaughter pen" boots and "jeans," and flung himself at his task. It was a weird sight, there on the killing beds—a throng of stupid black Negroes, and foreigners who could not understand a word that was said to them, mixed with pale-faced, hollow-chested bookkeepers and clerks, half-fainting for the tropical heat and the sickening stench of fresh blood—and all struggling to dress a dozen or two of cattle in the same place where, twenty-four hours ago, the old killing gang had been speeding, with their marvelous precision, turning out four hundred carcasses every hour!

The Negroes and the "toughs" from the Levee did not want to work, and every few minutes some of them would feel obliged to retire and recuperate. In a couple of days Durham and Company had electric fans up to cool off the rooms for them, and even couches for them to rest on; and meantime they could go out and find a shady corner and take a "snooze," and as there was no place for any one in particular, and no system, it might be hours before their boss discovered them. As for the poor office employees, they did their best, moved to it by terror; thirty of them had been "fired" in a bunch that first morning for refusing to serve, besides a number of women clerks and typewriters who had declined to act as waitresses.

It was such a force as this that Jurgis had to organize. He did his best, flying here and there, placing them in rows and showing them the tricks; he had never given an order in his life before, but he had taken enough of them to know, and he soon fell into the spirit of it, and roared and stormed like any old stager. He had not the most tractable pupils, however. "See hyar, boss," a big black "buck" would begin, "ef you doan' like de way Ah does dis job, you kin git somebody else to do it." Then a crowd would gather and listen, muttering threats. After the first meal nearly all the steel knives had been missing, and now every Negro had one, ground to a fine point, hidden in his boots.

There was no bringing order out of such a chaos, Jurgis soon discovered; and he fell in with the spirit of the thing—there was no reason why he should wear himself out with shouting. If hides and guts were slashed and rendered useless there was no way of tracing it to any one; and if a man lay off and forgot to come back there was nothing to be gained by seeking him, for all the rest would quit in the meantime. Everything went, during the strike, and the packers paid. Before long Jurgis found that the custom of resting had suggested to some alert minds the possibility of registering at more than one place and earning more than one five dollars a day. When he caught a man at this he "fired" him, but it chanced to be in a quiet corner, and the man tendered him a ten-dollar bill and a wink, and he took them. Of course, before long this custom spread, and Jurgis was soon making quite a good income from it.

In the face of handicaps such as these the packers counted themselves lucky if they could kill off the cattle that had been crippled in transit and the hogs that had developed disease. Frequently, in the course of a two or three days' trip, in hot weather and without water, some hog would develop cholera, and die; and the rest would attack him before he had ceased kicking, and when the car was opened there would be nothing of him left but the bones. If all the hogs in this carload were not killed at once, they would soon be down with the dread disease, and there would be nothing to do but make them into lard. It was the same with cattle that were gored and dying, or were limping with broken bones stuck through their flesh—they must be killed, even if brokers and buyers and superintendents had to take off their coats and help drive and cut and skin them. And meantime, agents of the packers were gathering gangs of Negroes in the country districts of the far South, promising them five dollars a day and board, and being careful not to mention there was a strike; already carloads of them were on the way, with special rates from the railroads, and all traffic ordered out of the way. Many towns and cities were taking advantage of the chance to clear out their jails and workhouses—in Detroit the magistrates would release every man who agreed to leave town within twenty-four hours, and agents of the packers were in the courtrooms to ship them right. And meantime trainloads of supplies were coming in for their accommodation, including beer and whisky, so that they might not be tempted to go outside. They hired thirty young girls in Cincinnati to "pack fruit," and when they arrived put them at work canning corned beef, and put cots for them to sleep in a public hallway, through which the men passed. As the gangs came in day and night, under the escort of squads of police, they stowed them away in unused workrooms and storerooms, and in the car sheds, crowded so closely together that the cots touched. In some places they would use the same room for eating and sleeping, and at night the men would put their cots upon the tables, to keep away from the swarms of rats.

But with all their best efforts, the packers were demoralized. Ninety per cent of the men had walked out; and they faced the task of completely remaking their labor force—and with the price of meat up thirty per cent, and the public clamoring for a settlement. They made an offer to submit the whole question at issue to arbitration; and at the end of ten days the unions accepted it, and the strike was called off. It was agreed that all the men were to be reemployed within forty-five days, and that there was to be "no discrimination against union men."

This was an anxious time for Jurgis. If the men were taken back "without discrimination," he would lose his present place. He sought out the superintendent, who smiled grimly and bade him "wait and see." Durham's strikebreakers were few of them leaving.

Whether or not the "settlement" was simply a trick of the packers to gain time, or whether they really expected to break the strike and cripple the unions by the plan, cannot be said; but that night there went out from the office of Durham and Company a telegram to all the big packing centers, "Employ no union leaders." And in the morning, when the twenty thousand men thronged into the yards, with their dinner pails and working clothes, Jurgis stood near the door of the hog-trimming room, where he had worked before the strike, and saw a throng of eager men, with a score or two of policemen watching them; and he saw a superintendent come out and walk down the line, and pick out man after man that pleased him; and one after another came, and there were some men up near the head of the line who were never picked—they being the union stewards and delegates, and the men Jurgis had heard making speeches at the meetings. Each time, of course, there were louder murmurings and angrier looks. Over where the cattle butchers were waiting, Jurgis heard shouts and saw a crowd, and he hurried there. One big butcher, who was president of the Packing Trades Council, had been passed over five times, and the men were wild with rage; they had appointed a committee of three to go in and see the superintendent, and the committee had made three attempts, and each time the police had clubbed them back from the door. Then there were yells and hoots, continuing until at last the superintendent came to the door. "We all go back or none of us do!" cried a hundred voices. And the other shook his fist at them, and shouted, "You went out of here like cattle, and like cattle you'll come back!"

Then suddenly the big butcher president leaped upon a pile of stones and yelled: "It's off, boys. We'll all of us quit again!" And so the cattle butchers declared a new strike on the spot; and gathering their members from the other plants, where the same trick had been played, they marched down Packers' Avenue, which was thronged with a dense mass of workers, cheering wildly. Men who had already got to work on the killing beds dropped their tools and joined them; some galloped here and there on horseback, shouting the tidings, and within half an hour the whole of Packingtown was on strike again, and beside itself with fury.

There was quite a different tone in Packingtown after this—the place was a seething caldron of passion, and the "scab" who ventured into it fared badly. There were one or two of these incidents each day, the newspapers detailing them, and always blaming them upon the unions. Yet ten years before, when there were no unions in Packingtown, there was a strike, and national troops had to be called, and there were pitched battles fought at night, by the light of blazing freight trains. Packingtown was always a center of violence; in "Whisky Point," where there were a hundred saloons and one glue factory, there was always fighting, and always more of it in hot weather. Any one who had taken the trouble to consult the station house blotter would have found that there was less violence that summer than ever before—and this while twenty thousand men were out of work, and with nothing to do all day but brood upon bitter wrongs. There was no one to picture the battle the union leaders were fighting—to hold this huge army in rank, to keep it from straggling and pillaging, to cheer and encourage and guide a hundred thousand people, of a dozen different tongues, through six long weeks of hunger and disappointment and despair.

Meantime the packers had set themselves definitely to the task of making a new labor force. A thousand or two of strikebreakers were brought in every night, and distributed among the various plants. Some of them were experienced workers,—butchers, salesmen, and managers from the packers' branch stores, and a few union men who had deserted from other cities; but the vast majority were "green" Negroes from the cotton districts of the far South, and they were herded into the packing plants like sheep. There was a law forbidding the use of buildings as lodginghouses unless they were licensed for the purpose, and provided with proper windows, stairways, and fire escapes; but here, in a "paint room," reached only by an enclosed "chute," a room without a single window and only one door, a hundred men were crowded upon mattresses on the floor. Up on the third story of the "hog house" of Jones's was a storeroom, without a window, into which they crowded seven hundred men, sleeping upon the bare springs of cots, and with a second shift to use them by day. And when the clamor of the public led to an investigation into these conditions, and the major of the city was forced to order the enforcement of the law, the packers got a judge to issue an injunction forbidding him to do it!

Just at this time the mayor was boasting that he had put an end to gambling and prize fighting in the city; but here a swarm of professional gamblers had leagued themselves with the police to fleece the strikebreakers; and any night, in the big open space in front of Brown's, one might see brawny Negroes stripped to the waist and pounding each other for money, while a howling throng of three or four thousand surged about, men and women, young white girls from the country rubbing elbows with big buck Negroes with daggers in their boots, while rows of woolly heads peered down from every window of the surrounding factories. The ancestors of these black people had been savages in Africa; and since then they had been chattel slaves, or had been held down by a community ruled by the traditions of slavery. Now for the first time they were free—free to gratify every passion, free to wreck themselves. They were wanted to break a strike, and when it was broken they would be shipped away, and their present masters would never see them again; and so whisky and women were brought in by the carload and sold to them, and hell was let loose in the yards. Every night there were stabbings and shootings; it was said that the packers had blank permits, which enabled them to ship dead bodies from the city without troubling the authorities. They lodged men and women on the same floor; and with the night there began a saturnalia of debauchery—scenes such as never before had been witnessed in America. And as the women were the dregs from the brothels of Chicago, and the men were for the most part ignorant country Negroes, the nameless diseases of vice were soon rife; and this where food was being handled which was sent out to every corner of the civilized world.

The "Union Stockyards" were never a pleasant place; but now they were not only a collection of slaughterhouses, but also the camping place of an army of fifteen or twenty thousand human beasts. All day long the blazing midsummer sun beat down upon that square mile of abominations: upon tens of thousands of cattle crowded into pens whose wooden floors stank and steamed contagion; upon bare, blistering, cinder-strewn railroad tracks, and huge blocks of dingy meat factories, whose labyrinthine passages defied a breath of fresh air to penetrate them; and there were not merely rivers of hot blood, and carloads of moist flesh, and rendering vats and soap caldrons, glue factories and fertilizer tanks, that smelt like the craters of hell—there were also tons of garbage festering in the sun, and the greasy laundry of the workers hung out to dry, and dining rooms littered with food and black with flies, and toilet rooms that were open sewers.

And then at night, when this throng poured out into the streets to play—fighting, gambling, drinking and carousing, cursing and screaming, laughing and singing, playing banjoes and dancing! They were worked in the yards all the seven days of the week, and they had their prize fights and crap games on Sunday nights as well; but then around the corner one might see a bonfire blazing, and an old, gray-headed Negress, lean and witchlike, her hair flying wild and her eyes blazing, yelling and chanting of the fires of perdition and the blood of the "Lamb," while men and women lay down upon the ground and moaned and screamed in convulsions of terror and remorse.

Such were the stockyards during the strike; while the unions watched in sullen despair, and the country clamored like a greedy child for its food, and the packers went grimly on their way.

(1906)

From

THE WINNING OF BARBARA WORTH
by Harold Bell Wright

With a crash the heavy brake was set. The team stopped. As the driver half rose and turned to look back he slipped the reins to his left hand and his right dropped to his hip. With a motion too quick for the eye to follow the free arm straightened and the mountain echoed wildly to the loud report of a forty-five. By the side of the road in the rear of the wagon a rattlesnake uncoiled its length and writhed slowly in the dust.

Before the echoes of the shot had died away a mad, inarticulate roar came from the depths of the wagon box. The roar was followed by a thick stream of oaths in an unmistakably Irish voice. The driver, who was slipping a fresh cartridge into the cylinder, looked up to see a man grasping the back of the rear seat for support while rising unsteadily to his feet.

The Irishman, as he stood glaring fiercely at the man who had so rudely awakened him, was without hat or coat, and with bits of hay clinging to a soiled shirt that was unbuttoned at the hairy throat, presented a remarkable figure. His heavy body was fitted with legs like posts; his wide shoulders and deep chest, with arms to match his legs, were so huge as to appear almost grotesque; his round head, with its tumbled thatch of sandy hair, was set on a thick bull-neck; while all over the big bones of him the hard muscles lay in visible knots and bunches. The unsteady poise, the red, unshaven, sweating face, and the angry, blood-shot eyes, revealed the reason for his sleep under such uncomfortable circumstances. The silent driver gazed at his fearsome passenger with calm eyes that seemed to hold in their dark depths the mystery of many a still night under the still stars.

In a voice that rumbled up from his hairy chest—a husky, menacing growl—the Irishman demanded: ''Fwhat the hell do ye mane, dishturbin' the peace wid yer clamor? For less than a sup av wather I'd go over to ye wid me two hands.''

Calmly the other dropped his gun into its holster. Pointing to the canteen that hung over the side of the wagon fastened by its canvas strap to the seat spring, he drawled softly: ''There's the water. Help yourself, stranger.''

The gladiator, without a word, reached for the canteen and with huge, hairy paws lifted it to his lips. After a draught of prodigious length he heaved a long sigh and wiped his mouth with the back of his hand. Then he turned his fierce eyes again on the driver as if to inquire what manner of person he might be who had so unceremoniously challenged his threat.

The Irishman saw a man, tall and spare, but of a stringy, tough and supple leanness that gave him the look of being fashioned by the out-of-doors. He, too, was coatless but wore a vest unbuttoned over a loose, coarse shirt. A red bandana was knotted easily about his throat. With his wide, high-crowned hat, rough trousers tucked in long boots, laced-leather wrist guards and the loosely buckled cartridge belt with its long forty-five, his very dress expressed the easy freedom of the wild lands, while the dark, thin face, accented by jet black hair and a long, straight mustache, had the look of the wide, sun-burned plains.

With a grunt that might have expressed either approval or contempt, the Irishman turned and groping about in the wagon found a sorry wreck of a hat. Again he stooped and this time, from between the bales of hay, lifted a coat, fit companion to the hat. Carefully he felt through pocket after pocket. His search was rewarded by a short-stemmed clay pipe and the half of a match—nothing more. With an effort he explored the pockets of his trousers. Then again he searched the coat; muttering to himself broken sentences, not the less expressive because incomplete: "Where the divil—— Now don't that bate—— Well, I'll be——" With a temper not improved by his loss he threw down the garment in disgust and looked up angrily. The silent driver was holding toward him a sack of tobacco.

The Irishman, with another grunt, crawled under the empty seat and climbing heavily over the back of the seat in front, planted himself stolidly by the driver's side. Filling his pipe with care and deliberation he returned the sack to its owner and struck the half-match along one post-like leg. Shielding the tiny flame with his hands before applying the light he remarked thoughtfully: "Ye are a danged reckless fool to be so dishturbin' me honest slape by explodin' that cannon ye carry. 'Tis on me mind to discipline ye for sich outrageous conduct." The last word was followed by loud, smacking puffs, as he started the fire in the pipe-bowl under his nose.

While the Irishman was again uttering his threat, the driver, with a skillful twist, rolled a cigarette and, leaning forward just in the nick of time, he deliberately shared the half-match with his blustering companion. In that instant the blue eyes above the pipe looked straight into the black eyes above the cigarette, and a faint twinkle of approval met a serious glance of understanding.

(1911)

THE SHOVEL MAN
by Carl Sandburg

On the street
Slung on his shoulder is a handle half way across,
Tied in a big knot on the scoop of cast iron
Are the overalls faded from sun and rain in the ditches;
Spatter of dry clay sticking yellow on his left sleeve
And a flimsy shirt open at the throat,
I know him for a shovel man,
A dago working for a dollar six bits a day
And a dark-eyed woman in the old country dreams of him for one of the world's ready men with a pair of fresh lips and a kiss better than all the wild grapes that ever grew in Tuscany.

(1916)

FISH CRIER
by Carl Sandburg

I know a Jew fish crier down on Maxwell Street with a voice like a north
    wind blowing over corn stubble in January.
He dangles herring before prospective customers evincing a joy identical
    with that of Pavlova dancing.
His face is that of a man terribly glad to be selling fish, terribly glad that
    God made fish, and customers to whom he may call his wares from
    a pushcart.

(1916)

From

THE CHOSEN PEOPLE
by Sidney L. Nyburg

Philip's opportunity for conjecture came to a sudden end, for his conductress
turned suddenly from the corridor into a small office where at a study desk there
sat, apparently awaiting the Rabbi's entrance, a vigorous young doctor dressed
in the white Hospital uniform.

"You're Dr. Graetz?" he began, motioning Philip to a seat, and speaking
in brisk but not discourteous tones. He did not give Philip opportunity to reply
before going on to say:

"I'm Dr. Manning. I'm in charge here till morning. It's not such an appropriate night for being dragged across town, is it? Still, I thought I ought to
do something about this chap. He's a Hebrew." The doctor paused slightly before using the word, as though he were anxious to choose a term bearing the
least offensive significance.

At another time the minister would have explained tolerantly his prefer-
ence for the word "Jew," and repelled the idea of anyone of that race being
anxious to escape its implications; but now he merely nodded, and the physician continued:

"He's an accident case. Slipped tonight, on a crossing at Baltimore Street, and one wheel of a heavy auto-truck passed over his abdomen."

Philip struggled unsuccessfully to restrain a shudder of horror, and the man of medicine noticed it with professional contempt.

"You needn't get squeamish. You won't see anything to shock you. He's covered up all right!"

"It isn't that!" Philip protested feebly, but there was a definite lack of conviction in his tones.

"Well," Dr. Manning said, "they brought him in here and took him into the operating room, but the house surgeons said, at the first glimpse, he hadn't a chance. He's sure to 'go out' pretty soon, and meanwhile, all we can make out of him is the word 'Rabbi.' He says it over and over again. He's still conscious, but we can't learn his name or anything else. If he'd been an Italian or an Irishman and had called for a priest, he'd have got one, so I thought if he wanted a Rabbi I ought to try to find one for him."

"I thank you very much," Philip responded. "I hope I'll be able to make him more comfortable. Does it matter how long I stay?"

"Not a bit," the physician answered coolly. "He's got no chance anyhow. I took him off the ward and into a private room because I didn't want him to disturb the other patients too much. So make yourself as comfortable as you can, and if you want anything, ask Miss Watts to send for me. She'll take you to him at once."

The nurse, who had remained silently standing in the presence of her superior, and who would have been shocked rather than gratified had the doctor suggested her being seated during the interview, now betrayed prompt signs of returning animation.

She opened the office door significantly so that Philip would have had no reasonable opportunity for further questions even had he meditated them, and without delay, led him once more upon his quest.

A minute later she ushered him into a small room with one great window through which there was visible, against the cold brilliance of an electric street lamp, a great wind-tossed tree, every twig of which was covered with a beautiful garment of glistening ice. The gray walled room was utterly bare except for a bed, a chair, and a tiny table bearing upon it a glass of water and a nurse's chart.

The form upon the bed was covered to the chin with a white sheet, but a long, nervous, ill-kempt hand lay wearily on either side of the patient's body, and on the pillow was the head of a man whose every feature proclaimed the Jew. Not the Jew one would have expected to meet at Beth El Temple, or in Mrs. Frank's elegant living-room, but one who had known misery and hatred in the Old World, and who had fled from it to experience hardship, privation and grinding poverty in free and boundless America. His long and untrimmed beard was coarse and of the blackness of charred wood. It accentuated to an almost ghost-like whiteness the deathly pallor of his brow; but his eyes, in his hour of mute despair, were fine—great, dark, intelligent eyes—which seemed haunted with a tragedy the man himself could never have expressed or understood, even when he had been vigorous and full of abundant life.

The eloquent eyes rested inquiringly upon the intruders, and the nurse spoke with the slow distinct accents one uses to children, and to men who cannot comprehend the only language one can talk.

"The Rabbi," she announced, pointing to Philip,—"the Rabbi."

The dying man's eyes lighted up with an expression of eager hope, unspeakably touching to his young visitor. This broken creature was poor, helpless and unlettered. The life he was yielding up had been sordid and unbeautiful, but still this forlorn immigrant shared with himself the wonderful traditions of the Martyr Race, and in his crude way had borne all too heavy a share of its agony. He hurried to the bedside, and grasped the weak, useless hand in his own.

Then the mangled man on the bed began to talk in harsh dry tones spoken almost in a whisper, but with headlong feverish haste. The nurse was about to leave them to their confidences, but Philip stopped her with a gesture of consternation.

He was unable to understand one single phrase the poor creature was racking his soul to utter!

Why had he not thought to ask what tongue this man could speak, or why had not the Hospital authorities made sure before sending for him, of his primary qualifications for the task? Now and then Philip caught the sound of some familiar, though mispronounced, word of Teutonic origin, but the sense of what was being told to him was utterly lost.

The Rabbi spoke German—bookishly, it was true—but nevertheless, fluently. With Hebrew also he was perfectly familiar. Of the Yiddish dialect he knew nothing at all. Had this immigrant's vocabulary been composed almost entirely of words borrowed or corrupted from the Hebrew and German tongues, Philip might have succeeded in piecing together the significance of the torrent of words which issued from the lips of the sufferer. But unfortunately, Yiddish is a varied and fluid mode of speech. In the mouths of wanderers from some sections of Europe, it may easily be mistaken for an ungrammatical and degenerate form of the German language. Other Jews, however, speak the dialect with so many infusions of words and accents appropriated from the Russian, as to make it totally unintelligible to anyone uninitiated in its baffling perplexities.

The patient, who was now staring desperately into the Rabbi's face, had come to the scene of his death from the wrong Russian village!

Frantically, Philip began talking to the man in his own grammatical German and instantaneously, the light of intelligence left the patient's eyes, and a look of dumb, puzzled misunderstanding appeared in its place.

Again and again Philip tried his utmost to find some method of communication with the injured man. He only succeeded in awakening in this mind, to which he had intended to bring peace and comfort, a reflection of his own excitement. The guttural whisper became sullen,—almost angry—and the one word which the Rabbi could understand in the immigrant's outbursts of despairing protest was the contemptuous syllable "goy"—which he knew to be this dying man's pitiless judgment upon himself as one who was in truth no Jew at all—a stranger and an alien.

"It's no use," Philip said helplessly, turning to the nurse. "I can't find out what he wants to say. He speaks nothing but Yiddish. You should have sent for a downtown Rabbi—a Russian."

The nurse, quick to repel any blame which might be imputed to her in this unexpected dilemma, replied quickly:

"I had to use the telephone directory. Down-town Rabbis can't afford telelphones. Besides, I thought any Rabbi would do."

Her voice expressed a polite contempt for a religion so loosely organized to aid its distressed communicants. Had the man been a Roman Catholic the first priest she had summoned would have been fully equipped to cope with the situation, or at least to find prompt assistance, if for some reason he had found himself unprepared for his task!

"We must find him a Rabbi who is a Russian Jew, at once," Philip announced.

"I'll take you back to Dr. Manning," replied Miss Watts, evidently determined to become entangled in no further responsibilities.

The dying immigrant had relapsed once more into his former state of despairing apathy. Philip cast upon him a last glance of mingled compassion and self-reproach and returned to Dr. Manning's office. There new perplexities confronted him. The young doctor apparently considered Philip to be disgustingly ill-equipped for his duties, and had neither comprehension nor tolerance for these delicate distinctions between various kinds of Jews. To Dr. Graetz's demand that a Russian Rabbi be procured at once, the physician responded by giving him *carte blanche* to summon as many as he chose, but this permission merely disclosed another bit of deplorable ignorance on Philip's part. He was compelled to confess he did not know the name of a single minister of his own creed in the city, except those of the few fashionable up-town Temples—no one of whom he had a right to suppose more proficient in Yiddish than himself.

Dr. Manning's smile savored slightly of amused cynicism. Philip, growing more miserably embarrassed every moment, yet feeling he dared not ignore his debt to his dying brother Jew, continued to rack his brain for some available solution.

"It needn't be a Rabbi, then," he urged. "Surely there must be some one in this big Hospital who can understand Yiddish."

"There is no one of your faith on the resident staff at this time," the doctor informed him patiently, "in the day time one of the young women in the Social Service Department could interpret for you, but they're all off duty now, and even if I wanted to drag one from her home at this time of night, I wouldn't know for which one to send."

"There must be plenty of Russian Jewish patients here," Philip insisted.

"There certainly are," Dr. Manning agreed, "but we don't catalogue them by race; I can't send someone through the wards waking up sick people to ask if they can talk Yiddish. I'm afraid I've done all I can."

(1917)

RED CHANT
by Alfred Kreymborg

There are veins in my body, Fenton Johnson—
veins that sway and dance because of blood that is red;
there are veins in your body, Fenton Johnson—
veins that sway and dance because of blood that is red.
Let a master prick me with his pin—
the bubble of blood shows red.
Let a master prick you with his pin—
the bubble of blood shows red.
Let a woman love me,
let a woman love you—
the blood that rises is red.
Let my gray eye turn to yours,
let your brown eye turn to mine—
the bubble behind them is red.
Let my skin wrinkle to a grin,
let your skin wrinkle to a grin—
red blood inspired the wrinkles.
Let me think of a spirit,
let you think of a spirit—
bodies that nourished the thought are red.
Let me think of loving you,
let you think of loving me—
hearts that nourished the thought are red.
Let me say it as well—why shouldn't I?—
let you say it as well—why shouldn't you?—
the tongues that say it are red.
Let me sing you a song—is it foolish?—
let you sing me a song—is it foolish?—
songs and singers are red.

Let us go arm in arm down State Street—
let them cry, the easily horrified:
"Gods of our fathers,
look at the white man chumming with the black man!"
Let us nudge each other, you and I,
without humility or defiance:
"We are red," let us answer!

(1917–20)

From

MY ÁNTONIA
by Willa Cather

There was a curious social situation in Black Hawk. All the young men felt the attraction of the fine, well-set-up country girls who had come to town to earn a living, and, in nearly every case, to help the father struggle out of debt, or to make it possible for the younger children of the family to go to school.

Those girls had grown up in the first bitter-hard times, and had got little schooling themselves. But the younger brothers and sisters, for whom they made such sacrifices and who have had "advantages," never seem to me, when I meet them now, half as interesting or as well educated. The older girls, who helped to break up the wild sod, learned so much from life, from poverty, from their mothers and grandmothers; they had all, like Ántonia, been early awakened and made observant by coming at a tender age from an old country to a new.

I can remember a score of these country girls who were in service in Black Hawk during the few years I lived there, and I can remember something unusual and engaging about each of them. Physically they were almost a race apart, and out-of-door work had given them a vigour which, when they got over their first shyness on coming to town, developed into a positive carriage and freedom of movement, and made them conspicuous among Black Hawk women.

That was before the day of high-school athletics. Girls who had to walk more than half a mile to school were pitied. There was not a tennis-court in the town; physical exercise was thought rather inelegant for the daughters of well-to-do families. Some of the high-school girls were jolly and pretty, but they stayed indoors in winter because of the cold, and in summer because of the heat. When one danced with them, their bodies never moved inside their clothes;

their muscles seemed to ask but one thing—not to be disturbed. I remember those girls merely as faces in the schoolroom, gay and rosy, or listless and dull, cut off below the shoulders, like cherubs, by the ink-smeared tops of the high desks that were surely put there to make us round-shouldered and hollow-chested.

The daughters of Black Hawk merchants had a confident, unenquiring belief that they were "refined," and that the country girls, who "worked out," were not. The American farmers in our county were quite as hard-pressed as their neighbours from other countries. All alike had come to Nebraska with little capital and no knowledge of the soil they must subdue. All had borrowed money on their land. But no matter in what straits the Pennsylvanian or Virginian found himself, he would not let his daughters go out into service. Unless his girls could teach a country school, they sat at home in poverty.

The Bohemian and Scandinavian girls could not get positions as teachers, because they had had no opportunity to learn the language. Determined to help in the struggle to clear the homestead from debt, they had no alternative but to go into service. Some of them, after they came to town, remained as serious and as discreet in behaviour as they had been when they ploughed and herded on their father's farm. Others, like the three Bohemian Marys, tried to make up for the years of youth they had lost. But every one of them did what she had set out to do, and sent home those hard-earned dollars. The girls I knew were always helping to pay for ploughs and reapers, brood-sows, or steers to fatten.

One result of this family solidarity was that the foreign farmers in our county were the first to become prosperous. After the fathers were out of debt, the daughters married the sons of neighbours—usually of like nationality—and the girls who once worked in Black Hawk kitchens are to-day managing big farms and fine families of their own; their children are better off than the children of the town women they used to serve.

I thought the attitude of the town people toward these girls very stupid. If I told my schoolmates that Lena Lingard's grandfather was a clergyman, and much respected in Norway, they looked at me blankly. What did it matter? All foreigners were ignorant people who couldn't speak English. There was not a man in Black Hawk who had the intelligence or cultivation, much less the personal distinction, of Ántonia's father. Yet people saw no difference between her and the three Marys; they were all Bohemians, all "hired girls."

I always knew I should live long enough to see my country girls come into their own, and I have. To-day the best that a harassed Black Hawk merchant can hope for is to sell provisions and farm machinery and automobiles to the rich farms where that first crop of stalwart Bohemian and Scandinavian girls are now the mistresses.

The Black Hawk boys looked forward to marrying Black Hawk girls, and living in a brand-new little house with best chairs that must not be sat upon, and hand-painted china that must not be used. But sometimes a young fellow would look up from his ledger, or out through the grating of his father's bank, and let his eyes follow Lena Lingard, as she passed the window with her slow, undulating walk, or Tiny Soderball, tripping by in her short skirt and striped stockings.

The country girls were considered a menace to the social order. Their beauty shone out too boldly against a conventional background. But anxious mothers need have felt no alarm. They mistook the mettle of their sons. The respect for respectability was stronger than any desire in Black Hawk youth.

Our young man of position was like the son of a royal house; the boy who swept out his office or drove his delivery wagon might frolic with the jolly country girls, but he himself must sit all evening in a plush parlour where conversation dragged so perceptibly that the father often came in and made blundering efforts to warm up the atmosphere. On his way home from his dull call, he would perhaps meet Tony and Lena, coming along the sidewalk whispering to each other, or the three Bohemian Marys in their long plush coats and caps, comporting themselves with a dignity that only made their eventful histories the more piquant. If he went to the hotel to see a travelling man on business, there was Tiny, arching her shoulders at him like a kitten. If he went into the laundry to get his collars, there were the four Danish girls, smiling up from their ironing-boards, with their white throats and their pink cheeks.

The three Marys were the heroines of a cycle of scandalous stories, which the old men were fond of relating as they sat about the cigar-stand in the drug-store. Mary Dusak had been housekeeper for a bachelor rancher from Boston, and after several years in his service she was forced to retire from the world for a short time. Later she came back to town to take the place of her friend, Mary Svoboda, who was similarly embarrassed. The three Marys were considered as dangerous as high explosives to have about the kitchen, yet they were such good cooks and such admirable housekeepers that they never had to look for a place.

The Vannis' tent brought the town boys and the country girls together on neutral ground. Sylvester Lovett, who was cashier in his father's bank, always found his way to the tent on Saturday night. He took all the dances Lena Lingard would give him, and even grew bold enough to walk home with her. If his sisters or their friends happened to be among the onlookers on "popular nights," Sylvester stood back in the shadow under the cottonwood trees, smoking and watching Lena with a harassed expression. Several times I stumbled upon him there in the dark, and I felt rather sorry for him. He reminded me of Ole Benson, who used to sit on the draw-side and watch Lena herd her cattle. Later in the summer, when Lena went home for a week to visit her mother, I heard from Ántonia that young Lovett drove all the way out there to see her, and took her buggy-riding. In my ingenuousness I hoped that Sylvester would marry Lena, and thus give all the country girls a better position in the town.

Sylvester dallied about Lena until he began to make mistakes in his work; had to stay at the bank until after dark to make his books balance. He was daft about her, and everyone knew it. To escape from his predicament he ran away with a widow six years older than himself, who owned a half-section. This remedy worked, apparently. He never looked at Lena again, nor lifted his eyes as he ceremoniously tipped his hat when he happened to meet her on the sidewalk.

So that was what they were like, I thought, these white-handed, high-collared clerks and bookkeepers! I used to glare at young Lovett from a distance and only wished I had some way of showing my contempt for him.

(1918)

MEXICAN QUARTER
by John Gould Fletcher

By an alley lined with tumble-down shacks,
And street-lamps askew, half-sputtering,
Feebly glimmering on gutters choked with filth and dogs
Scratching their mangy backs:
Half-naked children are running about,
Women puff cigarettes in black doorways,
Crickets are crying.
Men slouch sullenly
Into the shadows:
Behind a hedge of cactus,
The smell of a dead horse
Mingles with the smell of tortillas frying.

And a girl in a black lace shawl
Sits in a rickety chair by the square of an unglazed window,
And sees the explosion of the stars
Softly poised on a velvet sky.
And she is humming to herself:—
"Stars, If I could reach you,
(You are so very clear that it seems as if I could reach you)
I would give you all to the Madonna's image,
On the grey-plastered altar behind the paper flowers,
So that Juan would come back to me,
And we could live again those lazy burning hours,
Forgetting the tap of my fan and my sharp words.
And I would only keep four of you,
Those two blue-white ones overhead,

To hang in my ears;
And those two orange ones yonder,
To fasten on my shoe-buckles.''

A little further along the street
A man sits stringing a brown guitar.
The smoke of his cigarette curls 'round his head,
And he too is humming, but other words:
"Think not that at your window I wait;
New love is better, the old is turned to hate.
Fate! Fate! All things pass away;
Life is forever, youth is for a day.
Love again if you may
Before the stars are blown out of the sky,
And the crickets die!

Babylon and Samarkand
Are mud walls in a waste of sand.''

(1921)

From

BOSTON

by Upton Sinclair

Cornelia lay in bed, a reaction from the long strain. The Negro maid brought her coffee and toast, but she could not eat; she lay like one dead. It was all over for her; she had done all she could, struggled all she could—so she told herself. The young people might go on, Joe might write newspaper stories, trying to rouse a heedless public; Betty might organize mass meetings and speeches on the Common, but the runaway grandmother's race was run.

She had to lie there and bring herself to face the thought of the electric chair. Through all these seven dreadful years, she had refused to face it—a game of self-deception; but Bart and Nick had been right all along—they had known that the thought must be faced, and they had done it. They had the will, and the philosophy; they had been able to talk about it and joke. Now Cornelia must do the same thing. Remember what somebody had told her—it does not hurt, because the current destroys the brain before there is time for a sensation. And when it is over, it is really over; other persons may worry for you, but you don't worry for yourself. Also, you are a martyr, you have accomplished something for the cause of love.

That was what she must manage to realize. Persuade herself that there was a new generation coming, that would care where this one was indifferent; that would count it as something that two wops had denied themselves happiness so that justice might be born into the world! Think about those young persons of the future; lie here and shut your eyes, and let them come into your presence and speak to you; feel their gentle hands upon your forehead, bidding you to rest, your tense nerves to relax and your heart to stop pounding.

Cornelia lay wrestling thus; and into her mind came drifting words of comfort. "Now we are not a failure. This is our career and our triumph." Vanzetti speaking; where had she heard him say those words? On a chair by her bedside was a scrap-book, full of letters, manuscripts, clippings. She was moved to sit up and turn the pages; here it was. Shortly after Judge Thayer had sentenced the two men to die, Cornelia had persuaded a reporter for the Northern American Newspaper Alliance to go to Dedhan with her, and see what kind of men these alleged bandits were. Now, reading the interview, Cornelia recalled every detail of the scene; the prisoners coming down from their tier of cells, getting a glimpse of sunshine in the central hall, and lighting up with it—Nick, with his "kid's" grin, Bart with his mature and gentle smile. The reporter, Phil D. Stong, a big fellow, rather blond German face, well-fed and well-groomed— on an expense account, as he told Cornelia, with a laugh; tender-hearted, with the sentimentality of his race—and struck dumb by the discovery of the two men of this transparent sincerity and fine idealism in the shadow of the electric chair, face to face with their last enemy and not afraid of him. He had listened, while the victims did the talking; then he had gone away and tried to make a picture of the scene for the readers of a chain of newspapers.

"Both men expect to die. They say so, and the conviction is written in grave, serene characters on Vanzetti's face. Tears touch the young man 'Nick's' eyes for a moment, brightly, but his voice is steady. He is married to a sweet-faced little Italian woman. They have two children.

"In a moment, Nick, with his smooth pompadour, and his boy's face, is laughing with the deputy sheriff in argument about prison fare.

"Vanzetti regards one kindly, but appraisingly. A ferocious mustache covers an expressive, smiling mouth. The stamp of thought is in every feature; the marks of the man whom strong intelligence has made an anchorite."

And then a glimpse of prison life:

"Up from the shops comes a file of gray men, arms folded, faces expressionless—a rhythm of steps and faces.

" 'They been working.' Sacco's fingers move nervously. 'God, when I cannot work I almost go crazy. My fingers used to be busy. I beg, I argue— give me something to do—I shovel coal, anything. At last, they give me a brick to clean—after three years. You see me now? I gain a pound a day for thirty days.' The deputy sheriff nods confirmation.

" 'First they give me basket to weave, like children. Better than nothing, but not much. Then I sit alone—seven years—thousands of days—and all for say man's nature can be perfect—day after day—nothing do—breathe, eat, sit up, lie down—because I think man innerly noble—not beast—'

"Vanzetti interrupts his companion gently. He knows the two visitors believe in the enforced regulations which restrain fallible humanity.

" 'We're capitalists,' he says smiling, and pointing to the line of workers. (Men under sentence of death are given no work.) 'We have home, we eat, don't do no work. We're non-producers—live off other man's work. When libertarians make speech, they calling Nick and me names.'

"Sacco gurgles with amusement. The deputy sheriff appears significantly. Suddenly one realizes that these men are to die in a straight wooden chair, just as the world begins its summer holidays.

"Nick and Vanzetti see the new expression and understand. They smile, gravely, sympathetically, as men smile at a child's troubles.

" 'If it had not been for these thing,' says Vanzetti, 'I might have live out my life, talking at street corners to scorning men. I might have die, unmarked, unknown, a failure. Now we are not a failure. This is our career and our triumph. Never in our full life can we hope to do such work for tolerance, for joostice, for man's onderstanding of man, as now we do by an accident.

" 'Our words—our lives—our pains—nothing! The taking of our lives—lives of a good shoemaker and a poor fish-peddler—all! That last moment belong to us—that agony is our triumph!'

"Not declaimed, just said simply."

(1928)

From

SHANTY IRISH
by Jim Tully

Old Hughie Tully was short and wide, with the strength of a bull.

My grandmother married him after she had inherited twenty acres of Irish ground.

With no money to buy horse and plow, they tilled the land with spades. For five years they bent their backs and starved.

The adjoining land was owned by an English lord. They watched sleek horses furrow his acres with shining plows.

They sold the land to their aristocratic neighbor and came to America during the middle of the last century.

My grandfather was a peddler of Irish linens and laces in the South for three years.

His wandering had given him knowledge and contempt for people. In the South he often sent another Irishman to visit the town ahead of him. It was that man's duty to select a beautiful girl, and dress her in excellent laces and linens. In all her glory the maiden would go to mass on Sunday. All the other women would be curious to know where she purchased such fine raiment. The girl would tell them she had met a peddler in a town nearby. Hughie, the adroit, would make his entrance in a few days and do a thriving business. His confederate would be in a town beyond making further arrangements.

"Wimmin are not all vain, indade not," his voice would raise, "some are dumb too."

My childhood was unusual in that it contained no soldier heroes. My grandfather had two distinct prejudices—he liked neither the Irish nor the negroes. His dislike of the former was based on general principles—and of the latter, because he believed that they were the souls of Methodists come back to earth—singed by hell-fire.

Believing this, he had no desire to fight for the freedom of scorched souls. The Civil War was deprived of his services.

I asked him why he had not been a soldier.

A man of nearly eighty then, his body still powerful, his sharp steel-blue eyes looking out from beneath shaggy eyebrows that had faded from red to yellowish gray, he snapped:

"If ye are in a strange nayborhood ye don't take sides—Ireland is me country—an' by the help of God may I niver see it agin!"

There was an old Irish shrew who did not like grandfather because he drank overmuch at times. She was haggard and worn. Her tongue was sharper than her features.

"The old hag, she said to me yisterday, 'Indade and if ye were me husband I'd give ye poison.'

" 'Indade and if I were, I'd take it,' I said right back."

Grandmother Tully was said to have been of better blood than he. The daughter of a country squire, she wrote verses.

Grandfather, who was never without his bottle, would often take a swig and exclaim:

"Sich blarney—makin' words jingle—indade—ye'd better be washin' the daishes."

When I told him I wanted to be a writer, he threw up his hands.

"Oh—me God, me God—git yereself a shovel like yere father—let yere grandmither do sich things—it's not for the likes of a brawny boy like ye."

When the rheumatism had forced grandfather to retire from a laborer's life to live on the sparse bounty of his children, he evolved a method that would keep an active mind from getting into a rut.

He would leave the house each morning at seven o'clock.

It was the hour the saloons opened.

There were twenty-six of them in St. Marys. Grandfather was the most charming of the village drunkards. He knew all the saloon keepers and bartenders in the place.

Many of them were Germans. Auglaize County was settled by Irish and German peasants. They were always at war.

Grandfather was the ambassador of love. Not for such a man were the squabbles of peasants.

He would lean his two hundred pound five-foot four body on the bar and pour soothing oil on the troubled waters of Irish and German—for a glass of liquor.

He was never really a cadger. He traded wit for drink. If wit were not needed, he gave consolation and advice. He had worn out several peddler's packs and many shovels. Thus equipped, he knew how to run the country, a neighbor's farm, and all affairs with women.

He was really a social appendage.

Every week he trimmed his black and white beard and mustache within a half-inch of his face.

He had never been to a dentist—had never lost a tooth. They were large and even.

He had retired at seventy.

"Indade—if a man works till three score and tin—an' rheumatiz taps at his heart an' no one kapes him—he'd better starve till they do."

His nose was large, his jaws heavy. He bit his words—between smiles.

There was only one negro in the town of St. Marys. In spite of his avowed prejudice, my grandfather was his bosom friend. The negro spent his money freely at the bar, which grandfather appreciated.

"Indade an' indade," grandfather often said to him, "a colored gintleman is better than the Irish—I know—for I'm one o' thim."

Often on the negro's day off, the two could be seen walking arm in arm from one saloon to the other.

My grandfather had a song which would make the darky laugh. He would pound the bar and stamp his feet to keep time, so he thought, with his words. All would listen.

> "The Lord made a nayger,
>   He made him in the night,
>   He made him in sich a hurry,
>   He forgot to make him white."

Grandfather was one of the first men in Ohio to allow his wife complete expression. He would not bother her for days at a time. Unless, of course, liquor had made him slightly ill. He would then sit in his large chair and hit the table with his bottle.

"Kath-u-rin—Kath-u-rin," he would shout.

Grandmother, aged, stooped and vital, with wrinkles in her face deep enough to bury matches, would draw near him holding a corncob pipe in her hand.

"Indade, Kath-u-rin—you know what it is—it's that damned licker Coffee sells—it'd eat a hole in a pipe."

"Well, it's good for ye—a man yere age—a-lettin' the licker soak yere fine brains out—what'll iver become o' ye?"

"Be still, woman, be still—be still! It's more licker I want an' not advice—indade a woman o' ould Ireland should be ashamed to talk so to her lord an' master."

"Indade an' ye'll git no more licker this day!" was the defiant rejoinder.

At this insult grandfather would hurry from the house.

But grandfather was unlike most men. Once in the saloon, no one ever heard of his troubles at home. He was a born man about town.

The saloon was his refuge from the crassness of a peasant world into which he had been accidentally born.

(1928)

From

JEWS WITHOUT MONEY
by Michael Gold

At first my mother had feared going out to work in a cafeteria among Christians. But after a few days she settled easily into the life of the polyglot kitchen, and learned to fight, scold, and mother the Poles, Germans, Italians, Irish and Negroes who worked there. They liked her, and soon called her "Momma," which made her vain.

"You should hear how a big black dishwasher named Joe, how he comes to me to-day, and says, 'Momma, I'm going to quit. Every one is against me here because I am black' he says. 'The whole world is against us black people.'

"So I said to him, 'Joe, I am not against you. Don't be foolish, don't go out to be a bum again. The trouble with you here is you are lazy. If you would work harder the others would like you, too.' So he said, 'Momma, all right I'll stay.' So that's how it is in the restaurant. They call me Momma, even the black ones."

It was a large, high-priced cafeteria for businessmen on lower Broadway. My mother was a chef's helper, and peeled and scoured tons of vegetables for cooking. Her wages were seven dollars a week.

She woke at five, cooked our breakfast at home, then had to walk a mile to her job. She came home at five-thirty, and made supper, cleaned the house, was busy on her feet until bedtime. It hurt my father's masculine pride to see his wife working for wages. But my mother liked it all; she was proud of earning money, and she liked her fights in the restaurant.

My dear, tireless, little dark-faced mother! Why did she always have to fight? Why did she have to give my father a new variety of headache with accounts of her battles for "justice" in the cafeteria? The manager there was a fat blond Swede with a *Kaiserliche* mustache, and the manners of a Mussolini. All the workers feared this bull-necked tyrant, except my mother. She told him "what was what." When the meat was rotten, when the drains were clogged and smelly, or the dishwashers overworked, she told him so. She scolded him as if he were her child, and he listened meekly. The other workers fell into the habit of telling their complaints to my mother, and she would relay them to the Swedish manager.

"It's because he needs me," said my mother proudly. "That's why he lets me scold him. I am one of his best workers; he can depend on me in the rush. And he knows I am not like the other kitchen help; they work a day or two; then quit, but I stay on. So he's afraid to fire me, and I tell him what is what."

It was one of those super-cafeterias, with flowers on the tables, a string orchestra during the lunch hour, and other trimmings. But my mother had no respect for it. She would never eat the lunch served there to the employees, but took along two cheese sandwiches from home.

"Your food is *Dreck,* it is fit only for pigs," she told the manager bluntly. And once she begged me to promise never to eat hamburger steak in a restaurant when I grew up.

"Swear it to me, Mikey!" she said. "Never, never eat hamburger!"

"I swear it, momma."

"Poison!" she went on passionately. "They don't care if they poison the people, so long as there's money in it. I've seen with my own eyes. If I could write English, I'd write a letter to all the newspapers."

"Mind your own business!" my father growled. "Such things are for Americans. It is their country and their hamburger steak."

(1930)

From

LIGHT IN AUGUST
by William Faulkner

"And he believed her. I think that is what gave him not the courage so much as the passive patience to endure and recognise and accept the one opportunity which he had to break in the middle of that crowded square, manacled, and run. But there was too much running with him, stride for stride with him. Not pursuers: but himself: years, acts, deeds omitted and committed, keeping pace with him, stride for stride, breath for breath, thud for thud of the heart, using a single heart. It was not alone all those thirty years which she did not know, but all those successions of thirty years before that which had put that stain either on his white blood or his black blood, whichever you will, and which killed him. But he must have run with believing for a while; anyway, with hope. But his blood would not be quiet, let him save it. It would not be either one or the other and let his body save itself. Because the black blood drove him first to the Negro cabin. And then the white blood drove him out of there, as it was the black blood which snatched up the pistol and the white blood·which would not let him fire it. And it was the white blood which sent him to the minister, which rising in him for the last and final time, sent him against all reason and all reality, into the embrace of a chimera, a blind faith in something read in a printed Book. Then I believe that the white blood deserted him for the moment. Just a second, a flicker, allowing the black to rise in its final moment and make him turn upon that on which he had postulated his hope of salvation. It was the black blood which swept him by his own desire beyond the aid of any man, swept him up into that ecstasy out of a black jungle where life has already ceased before the heart stops and death is desire and fulfillment. And then the black blood failed him again, as it must have in crises all his life. He did not kill the minister. He merely struck him with the pistol and ran on and crouched behind that table and defied the black blood for the last time, as he had been defying it for thirty years. He crouched behind that overturned table and let them shoot him to death, with that loaded and unfired pistol in his hand."

(1932)

From

COUNTRY FULL OF SWEDES
by Erskine Caldwell

There I was, standing in the middle of the chamber, trembling like I was coming down with the flu, and still not knowing what god-awful something had happened. In all my days in the Back Kingdom, I never heard such noises so early in the forenoon.

It was about half an hour after sun-rise, and a gun went off like a coffer-dam breaking up under ice at twenty below, and I'd swear it sounded like it wasn't any farther away than my feet are from my head. That gun shot off, pitching me six-seven inches off the bed, and, before I could come down out of the air, there was another roar like somebody coughing through a megaphone, with a two weeks' cold, right in my ear. God-helping, I hope I never get waked up like that again until I can get myself home to the Back Kingdom where I rightfully belong to stay.

I must have stood there ten-fifteen minutes shivering in my night-shirt, my heart pounding inside of me like a ram-rod working on a plugged-up bore, and listening for that gun again, if it was going to shoot some more. A man never knows what's going to happen next in the State of Maine; that's why I wish sometimes I'd never left the Back Kingdom to begin with. I was making sixty a month, with the best of bed and board, back there in the intervale; but like a God damn fool I had to jerk loose and come down here near the Bay. I'm going back where I came from, God-helping; I've never had a purely calm and peaceful day since I got here three-four years ago. This is the damnedest country for the unexpected raising of all kinds of unlooked-for hell a man is apt to run across in a lifetime of traveling. If a man's born and raised in the Back Kingdom, he ought to stay there where he belongs; that's what I'd done if I'd had the sense to stay out of this down-country near the Bay, where you don't ever know, God-helping, what's going to happen next, where, or when.

But there I was, standing in the middle of the upstairs chamber, shaking like a rag weed in an August wind-storm, and not knowing what minute, maybe right at me, that gun was going to shoot off again, for all I knew. Just then, though, I heard Jim and Mrs. Frost trip-trapping around downstairs in their bare feet. Even if I didn't know what god-awful something had happened, I knew things around the place weren't calm and peaceful, like they generally were of a Sunday morning in May, because it took a stiff mixture of heaven and hell to get Jim and Mrs. Frost up and out of a warm bed before six of a forenoon, any of the days of the week.

I ran to the window and stuck my head out as far as I could get it, to hear what the trouble was. Everything out there was as quiet and peaceful as midnight on a backroad in middlemost winter. But I knew something was up, because Jim and Mrs. Frost didn't make a practice of getting up and out of a warm bed that time of forenoon in the chillish May-time.

There wasn't any sense in me standing there in the cold air shivering in my night-shirt, so I put on my clothes, whistling all the time through my teeth to drive away the chill, and trying to figure out what God damn fool was around so early shooting off a gun of a Sunday morning. Just then I heard the downstairs door open, and up the steps, two at a time, came Jim in his breeches and his shirt-tail flying out behind him.

He wasn't long in coming up the stairs, for a man sixty-seven, but before he reached the door to my room, that gun went off again: BOOM! Just like that; and the echo came rolling back through the open window from the hills: *Boom! Boom!* Like fireworks going off with your eyes shut. Jim had busted through the door already, but when he heard that *Boom!* sound he sort of spun around, like a cock-eyed weathervane, five-six times, and ran out the door again like he had been shot in the hind parts with a moose gun. That *Boom!* so early in the forenoon was enough to scare the daylights out of any man, and Jim wasn't any different from me or anybody else in the town of East Joloppi. He just turned around and jumped through the door to the first tread on the stairway like his mind was made up to go somewhere else in a hurry, and no fooling around at the start.

I'd been hired to Jim and Mrs. Frost for all of three-four years, and I was near about as much of a Frost, excepting name, as Jim himself was. Jim and me got along first-rate together, doing chores and haying and farm work in general, because neither one of us was ever trying to make the other do more of the work. We were hitched to make a fine team, and I never had a kick coming, and Jim said he didn't either. Jim had the name of Frost, to be sure, but I wouldn't ever hold that against a man.

The echo of that gun-shot was still rolling around in the hills and coming in through the window, when all at once that god-awful cough-like whoop through a megaphone sounded again right there in the room and everywhere else, like it might have been, in the whole town of East Joloppi. The man or beast or whatever animal he was who hollered like that ought to be locked up to keep him from scaring all the women and children to death, and it wasn't any stomach-comforting sound for a grown man who's used to the peaceful calm of the Back Kingdom all his life to hear so early of a Sunday forenoon, either.

I jumped to the door where Jim, just a minute before, leaped through. He didn't stop till he got clear to the bottom of the stairs. He stood there, looking up at me like a wild-eyed cow moose surprised in the sheriff's corn field.

"Who fired that god-awful shot, Jim?" I yelled at him, leaping down the stairs quicker than a man of my years ought to let himself do.

"Good God!" Jim said, his voice hoarse, and falling all to pieces like a stump of punk-wood. "The Swedes! The Swedes are shooting, Stan!"

"What Swedes, Jim—those Swedes who own the farm and buildings across the road over there?" I said, trying to find the buttonholes in my shirt. "Have they come back here to live on that farm?"

"Good God, yes!" he said, his voice croaking deep down in his throat, like he had swallowed too much water. "The Swedes are all over the place. They're everywhere you can see, there's that many of them."

"What's their name, Jim?" I asked him. "You and Mrs. Frost never told me what their name is."

"Good God, I don't know. I never heard them called anything but Swedes, and that's what it is, I guess. It ought to be that, if it ain't."

I ran across the hall to look out a window, but it was on the wrong side of the house, and I couldn't see a thing. Mrs. Frost was stepping around in the downstairs chamber, locking things up in the drawers and closet and forgetting where she was hiding the keys. I could see her through the open door, and she was more scared-looking than Jim was. She was so scared of the Swedes she didn't know what she was doing, none of the time.

"What made those Swedes come back for, Jim?" I said to him. "I thought you said they were gone for good, this time."

"Good God, Stan," he said, "I don't know what they came back for. I guess hard times are bringing everybody back to the land, and the Swedes are always in the front rush of everything. I don't know what brought them back, but they're all over the place, shooting and yelling and raising hell. There are thirty-forty of them, looks like to me, counting everything with heads."

"What are they doing now, Jim, except yelling and shooting?"

"Good God," Jim said, looking behind him to see what Mrs. Frost was doing with his things in the downstairs chamber. "I don't know what they're not doing. But I can hear them, Stan! You hurry out right now and lock up all the tools in the barn and bring in the cows and tie them up in the stalls. I've got to hurry out now and bring in all of those new cedar fence posts across the front of the yard before they start pulling them up and carrying them off. Good God, Stan, the Swedes are everywhere you look out-doors! We've got to make haste, Stan!"

Jim ran to the side door and out the back of the house, but I took my time about going. I wasn't scared of the Swedes, like Jim and Mrs. Frost were, and I didn't aim to have Jim putting me to doing tasks and chores, or anything else, before breakfast and the proper time. I wasn't any more scared of the Swedes than I was of the Finns and Portuguese, anyway. It's a god-awful shame for Americans to let Swedes and Finns and the Portuguese scare the day-lights out of them. God-helping, they are no different than us, and you never see a Finn or a Swede scared of an American. But people like Jim and Mrs. Frost are scared to death of Swedes and other people from the old countries; Jim and Mrs. Frost and people like that never stop to think that all of us Americans came over from the old countries, one time or another, to begin with.

But there wasn't any sense in trying to argue with Jim and Mrs. Frost right then, when the Swedes, like a fired nest of yellow-headed bumble bees, were swarming all over the place as far as the eye could see, and when Mrs. Frost was scared to death that they were coming into the house and carry out all of her and Jim's furniture and household goods. So while Mrs. Frost was tying her and Jim's shoes in pillow cases and putting them out of sight in closets and behind beds, I went to the kitchen window and looked out to see what was going on around that tall yellow house across the road.

Jim and Mrs. Frost both were right about there being Swedes all over the place. God-helping, there were Swedes all over the country, near about all over the whole town of East Joloppi, for what I could see out the window. They were as thick around the barn and pump and the woodpile as if they had been a nest of yellow-headed bumble bees strewn over the countryside. There were Swedes everywhere a man could see, and the ones that couldn't be seen, could be heard yelling their heads off inside the yellow clapboarded house across the road. There wasn't any mistake about their being Swedes there, either; because I've never yet seen a man who mistakes a Swede or a Finn for an American. Once you see a Finn or a Swede you know, God-helping, that he is a Swede or a Finn, and not a Portugee or an American.

There was a Swede everywhere a man could look. Some of them were little Swedes, and women Swedes, to be sure; but little Swedes, in the end, and women Swedes too, near about, grow up as big as any of them. When you come right down to it, there's no sense in counting out the little Swedes and the women Swedes.

Out in the road in front of their house were seven-eight autos and trucks loaded down with furniture and household goods. All around, everything was Swedes. The Swedes were yelling and shouting at one another, the little Swedes and the women Swedes just as loud as the big Swedes, and it looked like none of them knew what all the shouting and yelling was for, and when they found out, they didn't give a damn about it. That was because all of them were Swedes. It didn't make any difference what a Swede was yelling about; just as long as he had leave to open his mouth, he was tickled to death about it.

I have never seen the like of so much yelling and shouting anywhere else before; but down here in the State of Maine, in the down-country on the Bay, there's no sense in being taken-back at the sights to be seen, because anything on God's green earth is likely and liable to happen between day and night, and the other way around, too.

Now, you take the Finns; there's any God's number of them around in the woods, where you least expect to see them, logging and such. When a Finn crew breaks a woods camp, it looks like there's a Finn for every tree in the whole State, but you don't see them going around making the noise that Swedes do, with all their yelling and shouting and shooting off guns. Finns are quiet about their hell-raising. The Portuguese are quiet, too; you see them tramping around, minding their own business, and working hard on a river dam or something, but you never hear them shouting and yelling and shooting off guns at five-six of a Sunday morning. There's no known likeness to the noise that a houseful of Swedes can make when they get to yelling and shouting at one another early in the forenoon.

I was standing there all that time, looking out the window at the Swedes across the road, when Jim came into the kitchen with an armful of wood and threw it into the woodbox behind the range.

"Good God, Stan," Jim said, "the Swedes are everywhere you can look out-doors. They're not going to get that armful of wood, anyway, though."

Mrs. Frost came to the door and stood looking like she didn't know it was her business to cook breakfast for Jim and me. I made a fire in the range and put on a pan of water to boil for the coffee. Jim kept running to the window to look out, and there wasn't much use in expecting Mrs. Frost to start cooking unless somebody set her to it, in the shape she was in, with all the Swedes around the place. She was so up-set, it was a downright pity to look at her. But Jim and me had to eat, and I went and took her by the arm and brought her to the range and left her standing there so close she would get burned if she didn't stir around and make breakfast.

"Good God, Stan," Jim said, "those Swedes are into everything. They're in the barn, and in the pasture running the cows, and I don't know what else they've been into since I looked last. They'll take the tools and the horses and cows, and the cedar posts, too, if we don't get out there and put everything under lock and key."

"Now, hold on, Jim," I said, looking out the window. "Them you see are little Swedes out there, and they're not going to make off with anything of yours and Mrs. Frost's. The big Swedes are busy carrying in furniture and household goods. Those Swedes aren't going to tamper with anything of yours and Mrs. Frost's. They're people just like us. They don't go around stealing everything in sight. Now, let's just sit here by the window and watch them while Mrs. Frost is getting breakfast ready."

"Good God, Stan, they're Swedes," Jim said, "and they're moving into the house across the road. I've got to put everything under lock and key be-fore——"

"Hold on, Jim," I told him. "It's their house they're moving into. God-helping, they're not moving into your and Jim's house, are they, Mrs. Frost?"

"Jim," Mrs. Frost said, shaking her finger at him and looking at me wild-eyed and sort of flustered-like, "Jim, don't you sit there and let Stanley stop you from saving the stock and tools. Stanley doesn't know the Swedes like we do. Stanley came down here from the Back Kingdom, and he doesn't know anything about Swedes."

Mrs. Frost was partly right, because I've never seen the things in my whole life that I've seen down here near the Bay; but there wasn't any sense in Americans like Jim and Mrs. Frost being scared of Swedes. I've seen enough Finns and Portuguese in my time in the Back Kingdom, up in the intervale, to know that Americans are no different from the others.

"Now, you hold on a while, Jim," I said. "Swedes are no different than Finns. Finns don't go around stealing another man's stock and tools. Up in the Back Kingdom the Finns are the finest kind of neighbors."

"That may be so up in the Back Kingdom, Stan," Jim said, "but Swedes down here near the Bay are nothing like anything that's ever been before or since. Those Swedes over there across the road work in a pulp mill over to Waterville three-four years, and when they've got enough money saved up, or when they lose it all, as the case may be, they all move back here to East Joloppi on this farm of theirs for two-three years at a time. That's what they do. And they've been doing it for the past thirty-forty years, ever since I can remember, and they haven't changed none in all that time. I can recall the first time they came to East Joloppi; they built that house across the road then, and if you've ever seen a sight like Swedes building a house in a hurry, you haven't got much else to live for. Why! Stan, those Swedes built that house in four-five days— just like that! I've never seen the equal to it. Of course now, Stan, it's the damnedest-looking house a man ever saw, because it's not a farm house, and it's not a city house, and it's no kind of a house an American would erect. Why! those Swedes threw that house together in four-five days—just like that! But whoever saw a house like that before, with three storeys to it, and only six rooms in the whole building! And painted yellow, too; Good God, Stan, white is the only color to paint a house, and those Swedes went and painted it yellow. Then on top of that, they went and painted the barn red. And of all of the shouting and yelling, at all times of the day and night, a man never saw or heard before. Those Swedes acted like they were purely crazy for the whole of four-five days, and they were, and they still are. But what gets me is the painting of it yellow, and the making of it three storeys high, with only six rooms in the whole building. Nobody but Swedes would go and do a thing like that; an American would have built a farm house, here in the country, resting square on the ground, with one storey, maybe a storey and a half, and then painted it lead-white. But Good God, Stan, those fool Swedes had to put up three storeys, to hold six rooms, and then went and painted the building yellow."

"Swedes are a little queer, sometimes," I said. "But Finns and Portuguese are too, Jim. And Americans sometimes——"

"A little queer!" Jim said. "Why! Good God, Stan, the Swedes are the queerest people on the earth, if that's the right word for them. You don't know Swedes, Stan. This is the first time you've ever seen those Swedes across the road, and that's why you don't know what they're like after being shut up in a pulpwood mill over to Waterville for four-five years. They're purely wild, I tell you, Stan. They don't stop for anything they set their heads on. If you was to walk out there now and tell them to move their autos and trucks off of the town road so the travelers could get past without having to drive around through the brush, they'd tear you apart, they're that wild, after being shut up in the pulp mill over to Waterville these three-four, maybe four-five, years.''

"Finns get that way, too," I tried to tell Jim. "After Finns have been shut up in a woods camp all winter, they make a lot of noise when they get out. Everybody who has to stay close to the job for three-four years likes to act free when he gets out from under the job. Now, Jim, you take the Portuguese—''

"Don't you sit there, Jim, and let Stanley keep you from putting the tools away," Mrs. Frost said. "Stanley doesn't know the Swedes like we do. He's lived up in the Back Kingdom most of his life, tucked away in the intervale, and he's never seen Swedes—''

"Good God, Stan," Jim said, standing up, he was that nervous and upset, "the Swedes are over-running the whole country. I'll bet there are more Swedes in the town of East Joloppi than there are in the rest of the country. Everybody knows there's more Swedes in the State of Maine than there are in the old country. Why! Jim, they take to this State like potato bugs take to——''

"Don't you sit there and let Stanley keep you back, Jim," Mrs. Frost put in again. "Stanley doesn't know the Swedes like we do. Stanley's lived up there in the Back Kingdom most of his life.''

Just then one of the big Swedes started yelling at some of the little Swedes and women Swedes. I'll swear, those big Swedes sounded like a pastureful of hoarse bulls, near the end of May, mad about the black-flies. God-helping, they yelled like they were fixing to kill all the little Swedes and women Swedes they could get their hands on. It didn't amount to anything, though; because the little Swedes and the women Swedes yelled right back at them just like they had been big Swedes too. The little Swedes and women Swedes couldn't yell hoarse bull bass, but it was close enough to it to make a man who's lived most of his life up in the Back Kingdom, in the intervale, think that the whole town of East Joloppi was full of big Swedes.

Jim was all for getting out after the tools and stock right away, but I pulled him back to the table. I wasn't going to let Jim and Mrs. Frost set me to doing tasks and chores before breakfast and the regular time. Forty dollars a month isn't much to pay a man for ten-eleven hours' work a day, including Sundays, when the stock has to be attended to like any other day, and I set myself that I wasn't going to work twelve-thirteen hours a day for them, even if I was practically one of the Frosts myself, except in name, by that time.

"Now, hold on a while, Jim," I said. "Let's just sit here by the window and watch them carry their furniture and household goods inside while Mrs. Frost's getting the cooking ready to eat. If they start taking off any of you and Mrs. Frost's things, we can see them just as good from here by the window as we could out there in the yard and road.''

"Now, Jim, I'm telling you," Mrs. Frost said, shaking all over, and not even trying to cook us a meal, "don't you sit there and let Stanley keep you from saving the stock and tools. Stanley doesn't know the Swedes like we do. He thinks they're like everybody else.''

(1933)

From

THE OX-BOW INCIDENT
by Walter Von Tilburg Clark

"Coming along, Sparks?'' he called, so the men grinned, finding that old joke funny about a nigger always being easy to scare. I hadn't noticed Sparks, but I saw him now, standing on the other side of the street with that constant look of his of pleasant but not very happy astonishment.

Sparks was a queer, slow, careful nigger, who got his living as a sort of general handy man to the village, splitting wood, shoveling snow, raking leaves, things like that; even baby tending, and slept around wherever was handiest to the jobs, in sheds or attics, though he had a sort of little shack he called his own out in the tall weeds behind the boarded-up church. He was a tall, stooped, thin, chocolate-colored man, with kinky hair, gray as if powdered, and big, limp hands and feet. When he talked his deep, easy voice always sounded anxious to please, slow but cheerful, but when he sang, which he did about most any work which had a regular rhythm, like sweeping or raking, he sang only slow, unhappy hymn tunes. He was anything but a fast worker, but he did things up thorough and neat, and he was honest to the bone, and the cleanest nigger I ever knew. He wore dungarees and a blue shirt, always like they'd just been washed, and his palms were clean tan, and clean steel-blue where they met the skin from the backs of his hands. He had a dry, clean, powdered look all over all the time. It was said that he'd been a minister back in Ohio before he came west, but he didn't talk about himself, outside of what he was doing right at the time, so nobody really knew anything about him, but they all liked him all right, and there wasn't anything they wouldn't trust him with. They made jokes about him and to him, but friendly ones, the sort they might make to any town character who was gentle and could take joking right.

When the men grinned they all looked across at Sparks. He was embarrassed.

"No, suh, Mistah Smith, ah don't guess so,'' he said, shaking his head but smiling to show he wasn't offended.

"You better come, Sparks,'' Smith yelled again. "It ain't every day we get a hanging in a town as dead as this one.''

The men stopped grinning. They didn't mind Smith joking Sparks, but that offended their present sense of indecision and secrecy. It seemed wrong to yell about a lynching. I felt it too, that someone might be listening who shouldn't hear; and that in spite of the fact that everybody in town knew.

Smith saw he'd made a mistake. When Sparks continued to look down and smile and shake his head, he yelled, "Yoh ain't afraid, is yoh, Spahks," badly imitating Sparks' drawl. "Not of a little thing like this," he cried in his own voice again. "You don't have to do anything, you know. The real work is all signed up. But I thought maybe we ought to have a reverend along. There'll be some praying to do, and maybe we ought to have a hymn or two afterward, to kind of cheer us up. You do know the cheerfullest hymns, Sparks."

The men laughed again, and Smith was emboldened.

"That is," he said loudly, "unless Mr. Osgood here is going along. He has first call, of course, being in practice."

"I'm not going, if it interests you," Osgood said, with surprising sharpness for him. "If you men choose to act in violence, and with no more recognition of what you're doing than this levity implies, I wash my hands. Willful murderers are not company for a Christian."

That stung, but not usefully. A bawling out from a man like Osgood doesn't sit well. Some of the men still grinned a little, but the sour way.

"I was afraid the shepherd would feel his flock was a bit too far astray for him to risk herding them this time," Smith lamented. Osgood was hit, and looked it. He knew the men tolerated him at best, and the knowledge, even when he could delude himself into believing it private, made it doubly difficult for him to keep trying to win them. Sometimes, as now, he was even pitiable. But he had an incurable gift of robbing himself even of pity. After a moment he answered, "I am sorry for you, all of you."

"Don't cry, parson," Smith warned him. "We'll do the best we can without you.

"I guess it's up to you, Sparks," he yelled.

Sparks surprised us. "Maybe it is, Mistah Smith," he said seriously. "Somebody ought to go along that feels the way Mistah Osgood and ah do; beggin' yoh pahdon, Mistah Osgood. If he don' feel it's raght foh him to go, it looks lahk ah'm the onlay one laift."

This unassuming conviction of duty, and its implication of distinct right and wrong, was not funny.

Quickly Smith struggled. "Maybe Mr. Osgood will lend you his Bible, Sparks, so's we can have the right kind of reading at the burial."

This was partially successful. Osgood was obviously offended to be so freely talked of by Smith, and perhaps even to have his name coupled with Sparks'. And everyone knew Sparks couldn't read.

"You will lend him your Book, won't you, Reverend," Smith asked Osgood. He had no sense for the end of a joke. Osgood had the thick, pale kind of skin that can't get red, so he got whiter, and was trembling a little.

Sparks came across the street in his slow, dragging gait. He didn't swing his arms when he walked, but let them hang down as if he had a pail of water in each hand.

When he was close enough to talk more quietly, he said, "No, thank you, Mistah Osgood," and turning to Smith told him, "Ah knows mah text to pray without the Book, Mistah Smith.

"But ah'm a slow walkah," he said, smiling especially at Winder, "you wouldn't have anothah mule ah could borrow, would you, Mistah Winder?"

Winder didn't know what to say, knowing it was still a joke except to Sparks.

Smith said, "Sure he would, Sparks. Gabe, you just trot back and get the Reverend a good saddle mule, will you? An easy one, mind; he ain't much padded."

The men were quiet.

Finally, Winder said, "Your mouth's too damn loose, Smith."

"I'm talking to Gabe," Smith said, but avoided Winder's stare.

Gabe stared back at Smith, but sat solid and appeared unmoved. He muttered something that nobody could hear.

"What's that you said, Gabe?" Smith prodded him.

Gabe got it out. "I said I ain't waitin' on no nigger," he said.

"Shut up, Smith," Winder said, before Smith could make anything of this.

Smith got red, which was remarkable for him, since he could swallow almost any insult, but with Winder staring at him he couldn't think of a retort.

"It's all right, Mistah Windah," Sparks said, "but if they is a mule at yoh place ah could borrow, ah'd be obliged. Ah can get him mahself, if thayas tahm."

"They're kidding you, Sparks," Canby said from the door. He liked the nigger.

"Ah know that, Mistah Canby," Sparks said, grinning again. "But ah think maybe Mistah Smith was accidentally right when he said ah should go."

"You really want to go?" Winder asked him.

"Yessuh, Mistah Windah, ah do."

Winder studied him, then shrugged and said, "There's a horse in the shed you can use. There's no saddle, but he's got a head-stall on, and there's a rope in the back stall you can use for a bridle.

"You'll have to get him yourself, though. You know how Gabe is," he apologized.

Gabe continued to stare heavily at Smith, but he didn't seem to hold anything against Sparks.

"Yassuh, ah undahstand," Sparks said, and turned to go. Winder felt he'd been too soft.

"Move along, or you'll get left," he said. "We're only waiting for Mr. Bartlett and his boys."

Sparks turned his head back, and grinned and nodded, and then went on down the street toward the stage depot, walking quickly for him. You could tell by his carriage that he was pleased in the way of a man doing what he ought to do.

(1940)

From

THE HISTORY OF ROME HANKS AND KINDRED MATTERS
by Joseph Stanley Pennell

The day General Grant was inaugurated Mr. Beckham came to supper with Papa, and he said it was just bully now they had a man like General Grant to run the country. The Hero of Appomattox would show these politicians what a soldier could do. As for himself, Mr. Beckham had been out of the war when General Grant took command of the Army of the Potomac, but the boys from his regiment, the Fighting Ninety-seventh Pennsylvania Zouaves, said General Grant was hunky dory. Myra liked to listen to him when he talked with his head thrown back like that and his beard so black and silky.

Papa said that, yes, General Grant would probably make a good president and that he had known General Grant both in the Mexican war and the Civil war and that he was a very unassuming man. Papa seemed to be thinking a good deal about it but not saying much. But then Papa never said much. One day Myra had heard him say to Brother Ream: Remus, always reserve judgment about any man. I will not quote the Bible to you, son, for I know young men do not like Biblical advice, but remember that man is a tentative image of a god. Myra did not quite understand what Papa meant, but my, oh, my! how she admired him and loved him. Why, she didn't believe she had ever heard Papa speak a cross word to anyone in her whole life—and the Lord knows he had had provocation often enough. And how Ring and the horses and even the silly sheep loved Papa. And it was plain to see that Mr. Beckham worshipped the ground that Papa walked on.

While they were eating supper something happened that was embarrassing in a way and made her feel kind of proud in another. That old Osage—well, he wasn't really old and not a bad-looking fella for an Indian—came up to the house with his painted up pony with the bright colored rags and stick-candy braided in his mane, and Papa had to go out to see what he wanted so he would go away. When Papa came back to his supper, he was smiling. And he smiled first at Ma and then at Myra.

Well, Lorna, he said, you almost lost a daughter, but I was too sharp a horse-trader for the chief.

Well, Mr. Hanks? Ma said, her dark eyes shining like berries.

The chief brought his best pony to trade for Myra—and when I refused that he offered me six more and a couple of squaws to boot. He said, hair like blackbird wing.

Myra blushed and said, Oh, Papa! And Mr. Beckham said, loudly, You just bet your bottom dollar the chief knew what he was doing all right! After he had said that Mr. Beckham's face got a little red, but Papa said something about General Grant's home in Galena, Illinois or somewhere and building a side walk and a house for the General that saved the situation. During the rest of the meal Myra could feel Mr. Beckham looking at her when she didn't see him.

He told about his brother who was in the Pennsylvania Cavalry during the war and said now that they'd put General Grant in the Capital maybe the old soldiers would get their rightful pensions. But Myra could see that he was thinking about her all the time. Afterwards Brother Ream said: Well, Myry, you could just land a beau in the middle of the Sahara desert. And Myra could see that Hetty was a little jealous, but she said Mr. Beckham seemed to be a fine upright young man. And Ellen looked at her kind of sad and yearning like in her eyes.

The very next morning as Papa was getting ready to go to the store the Osage came again. This time he was a-riding his painted up pony and had a whole herd of ponies—about thirty—following him. Myra saw him ride up to Papa and hold out his hand and then get off the pony under the pecan tree and talk and motion with Papa for a long time—about a half an hour. He was all in feathers and buckskin breeches and a bright blanket and he was taller than Papa and Mr. Beckham and so straight. Finally he got back on his painted up pony in a kind of stiff strained way; and Papa stood there beside the wagon in the yard looking out toward the Lombardy poplars and the silverleaf maples where the ponies were raising the dust as they followed the Indian, nickering and blowing, down the road. Papa turned and walked toward the house when the parade got a piece down the road.

He walked into the house smiling. Myra, he said, Myra, you must know how much your Papa thinks of you now. Myra laughed, feeling a funny glow all over her and kissed Papa on the whiskers that weren't as nice now as they were before he came back from that awful old Andersonville prison, but were still nicer than anybody's because they were her Papa's. Oh, no, she said. Not all them horses, Papa! Not all those ponies! That old Indian! Yes, honey, and a half dozen squaws too. I've little doubt it was everything the poor Indian owned. Papa went out and got up on the wagon smiling to himself.

And even if she *did* say that *old* Indian, she kept thinking of his dark sharp eyes and the way he looked at her—and she thought it was kind of sad, even if he was only an Indian and just a savage.

(1944)

From

KNOCK ON ANY DOOR
by Willard Motley

Butch told his story of the night of the killing. He was supposed to meet Nick and Sunshine at the Cobra Tap. Nick came in early with Mr. Grant. They had a couple of drinks and Mr. Grant left. Sunshine didn't get there until way after twelve—it musta been twelve-thirty. Sunshine was excited and told them Riley had been killed. "Well—we were scared we'd get picked up—they pick up anybody they want down there. Me and Sunshine said we was clearing out. But Nick said—that we hadn't done nothin' so why should we hide out from the cops . . . he ordered up drinks for us. We had a couple more after that. Then I said I'm going, and Nick laughed at me—he talked Sunshine into going on down to the poolroom to work—but me, I took a powder."

"What time, approximately, was it when you left the Cobra Tap?"

"About one o'clock—Sunshine and me left together. I knew the time 'cause Sunshine had to go clean the poolroom up when it closed at one o'clock."

Nick looked at Butch.

I got good friends . . . *good* friends.

"Why didn't you tell the police that Nick was with you?" Morton asked.

"I was afraid they'd frame me too—" Butch said. "You don't know them!"

Morton smiled. "That's all, thank you."

Kerman got up from his chair and stood at the bar near the jury box. "Walter Zinski—Squint—testified that you went out of the poolroom with him and around to the alley when he heard the shots fired that killed Officer Riley," he said.

"He's a liar!" Butch said. "I was with Nick at the Cobra Tap."

"Is that what Mr. Morton told you to say?"

"He told me just to tell the truth."

"Your name's Gus Pappas?"

"Yeah."

"What kind of beer were you drinking that night?"

"Budweiser."

"You're sure it was Budweiser?"

"Yeah."

"The defendant here"—Kerman jabbed his thumb over his shoulder at Nick—"is Italian. You're Greek. That—the other one was Mexican. What is that—a gang you had down there on West Madison? Why do you fellows of different nationalities hang around together down there?"

"Ain't that what America is?" Butch said.

"I'm not here to answer questions but to ask them! You had a gang, didn't you?"

"No, we didn't have no gang."

"Ever been in reform school?"

"Hey!—I ain't on trial here!" Butch flared.

Judge Drake leaned over the side of his bench. "Answer the question," he said.

"Yes," Butch said.

"How long?"

"Four and a half years," Butch said in a low voice.

"Do you work?"

"In my father's dairy."

"Oh—you work! Very unusual." Kerman swung around and pointed his red pencil at Nick. "Romano is your pal, isn't he? You want to alibi him, don't you?"

"No! I just don't want him to go to the chair for something he didn't do!"

Kerman pounded away at Butch like a boxer when he has his opponent on the ropes. "What stool at the tavern did you sit on? Oh, you don't know—then it could have been in some other tavern? What did Grant Holloway talk about? What time was it when he left? Couldn't it have been eleven-thirty?"

Kerman pounded his questions like a carpenter hammering spikes. "Was there a floor show? Just a strip tease? You don't remember whether the little lady was blond or brunette?"

"I wasn't lookin' at her hair. Look—Nick didn't do it! He was with me and Sunshine."

Good old Butch!

"Who is Sunshine?"

"A friend of Nick's and mine."

"What nationality is he?"

"Colored."

"Oh! Colored. A Negro! He was in your gang too, eh?"

"We didn't have no gang!"

"Exactly what did Sunshine say when he came into the tavern?"

"That Riley had been killed."

"Were you sorry?"

"I didn't care one way or the other."

Kerman smiled at the jury. "That's all!" he said.

MORTON CALLS SOCIAL AND SLUM
WORLD TO STAND IN ATTEMPT TO
SAVE PRETTY BOY FROM CHAIR

Sunshine raised his dark brown hand and was sworn in. "Jim Jackson—they call me 'Sunshine.' Ah'm twenty-four," he said in a slow frightened drawl. Morton questioned him in a voice that wrapped a friendly arm around Sunshine's shoulders.

From the stand Sunshine said, keeping his eyes carefully glued on Morton and his shoulders tense under his coat, that he had been in the Long Bar when someone came in and said that Riley had been killed. "What time was this, Sunshine, if you know?"

Sunshine remembered the story well. "Ah looked up at the clock—it's over the 26-girl's booth. . . . It was twenty minutes aftah twelve then. Ah started to go out and look. Then ah remembered that ah was colored and they might blame me and ah remembered ah was supposed to meet Butch and Nick . . . at the Cobra Tap. . . ."

Nick, with his head down a little, looked up at Sunshine.

Good friends.

Sunshine told the story.

Morton moved his fingers across his chin. "How did you happen to become a witness for the defense, Sunshine?"

"Ah was in the poolroom where ah was workin' and in comes Mr. Grant. Ah went right up to him and told him Nick didn't do it, Nick was with me. . . ."

Good old Sunshine!

"Mr. Grant, he says for me to come over with him to see you. You told me that ah had to stay away from West Madison because that man"—his head nodded at Kerman—"would have the police pick me up if he knew ah was for Nick and maybe have me arrested." Sunshine's voice went on, almost in a low wail, and the jurors leaned over and listened attentively. "So Mr. Grant, he says for me to come stay at his place so the police won't get me."

"Thank you, Sunshine," Morton said.

Kerman drew his chair right up to the witness stand. "Hello, Sunshine," he said condescendingly. "Are you a Christian, Sunshine?"

"Huh?" Sunshine asked, still staring at Morton for support.

"Are you a Christian?"

Sunshine shrank back against the witness chair. "Yes, sah."

"So you brought the news of the killing to Nick?"

"Yes, sah."

Kerman stood so that Sunshine couldn't see Morton. "How old are you?"

"Twenty-four."

"Minutes or days?" Kerman asked sarcastically.

"Years," Sunshine said solemnly.

"How many times have you been picked up by the police?" Sunshine hung his head. "Suspicion of strong-arming—wasn't it?"

"No—ah guess they didn't like mah color—Nick said so anyway." That got to the jury. Their eyes all came over and rested on Sunshine's face sympathetically.

"Just answer the question!" Kerman shouted. His voice dropped to softer tones. "You like Romano, don't you?"

"Yes, sah!"

"You want him to get out of this, don't you?"

"Yes, sah! He didn't do it—he was with me!"

"Where were you born and raised?"

"Jo'jah."

"Ever been in a chain gang?"

"No, sah!"

"You should have been!"

Morton stood up. "Move to strike—meant only to prejudice the jury."

"Yes—strike it, Miss Simpson," Judge Drake said.

"Did you see Officer Riley being murdered!" Kerman asked loudly.

"No," quaveringly.

"Were you sorry he was killed?"

Sunshine's sad, pouted face looked all around, up at Judge Drake, at Nick, at the jury. He looked up at Judge Drake again, "Do ah have to answer?" he asked.

"Yes!" Kerman shouted, "and you better tell the truth!"

Judge Drake pounded his gavel. "Yes, answer the question." His eyes were still narrowed on Kerman.

"No," Sunshine said.

"You were glad, weren't you?"

"Ah didn't care."

Kerman turned his face halfway to the jury. "Can you write?"

"Yes, sah."

"Read?"

"Yes, sah."

"Ever read the Bible?"

Sunshine nodded.

"Do you remember the commandment, 'Thou shalt not bear false witness'?"

Sunshine tried to look around Kerman at Morton; Kerman moved with Sunshine's head, blocking the way. "Yes, sah," Sunshine said in a low voice.

"Do you remember the commandment, 'Thou shalt not kill'? Well, do you remember it?"

"Yes," Sunshine said, hardly audible.

"Know what perjury is?"

"Yes, sah—it's when you swear to a lie in court."

"Know what happens when you lie?"

"You go to jail."

"Oh, no. The law says that. But you, you go to *hell!* You took an oath in the name of God." Kerman's eyes held Sunshine's. Kerman's thick lips lifted up off his big teeth. "Do you want your soul to writhe around in hell fire forever?" Sunshine was helpless in the stare of Kerman's muddy eyes. All the teachings and superstitions of the plantation cabin in Georgia flooded back to him, beat back at him. He opened his lips twice to speak. Perspiration stood in tiny balls on his shiny forehead. He moved his hand nervously over his wiry hair, pushing the cockscomb down. "Do you?" Kerman shouted. "Do you?"

"No, sah—no—no—"

Sunshine began to tremble. "Sunshine—unless you tell the truth you will never see God—your soul will be tortured in fire forever!" The words came in a burst of flame, then spread themselves out softly as Kerman said in a low, whispered tone, "You don't want that to happen, do you?"

"No, sah—no!"

Kerman's voice rose again, shouting in Sunshine's face, "Then why don't you tell the truth! You were standing just outside the alley, weren't you? You saw Romano come out of it, didn't you—didn't you?"

"Ah—ah—" For a terrible moment, while the courtroom waited, Sunshine sat with his quivering lips parted. Then loyalty came back, like a wave. "He was with me all that night—that's all ah know!" Sunshine tore his eyes away from Kerman's. He wiped his forehead with the sleeve of his coat.

"You saw him!" Kerman shouted. "You saw him but you don't want to testify! Isn't that true? Isn't it?—Answer me!"

Morton flung from his chair and stood at the foot of the rostrum. "We object, your Honor, to the argumentative disputation, the threatening language and the attitude of the prosecuting attorney because it is incompetent and intended only to create passion and prejudice against the defendant."

"Sustained."

On the witness chair Sunshine was saying in a long wail, "Nick was with me ah tell you—he was with me."

Kerman pointed his finger in Sunshine's face. "You lied when you answered Mr. Morton's questions, didn't you!"

"No—ah stuck to mah story."

"Oh—your story? Then it is a story?" Kerman whirled back into Sunshine's face. "What kind of beer did you drink?"

"Pabst—Nick likes it," Sunshine said.

Kerman smiled and crossed his arms. "Your friend Butch says that you drank Budweiser. He was mistaken, was he?"

"Ah thought it was Pabst—ah don't know—all ah know is Nick and Butch and me was together."

"Didn't you tell this story over and over to Mr. Morton?" Kerman said.

"Yes—but ah told him the truth all the time."

Kerman stood with his arms folded in front of the witness and thought a moment, squinting his eyes. He knew it was true of some of the taverns on Skid Row that tried to go high class. A shot in the dark, but it was worth trying. He smiled at Sunshine. "You've told the truth all the time, haven't you, Sunshine? And you were in the Cobra Tap as you say?"

"Yes, sah."

Kerman folded his arms. "Perhaps you don't know, Mr. Sunshine," he said loudly but slowly, "that Negroes are not served in the Cobra Tap! *That's all! Excused.*" Kerman crossed his legs as he sat down and leaned his head against the back of the chair. Morton's eyes blinked in the shadow of his hand . . . a mistake; a mistake . . . he should have investigated and made sure of his tavern . . . on Skid Row, of all places.

Kerman said, with his eyes closed, "Do you try to represent yourself or pass for a white man, Sunshine?" His lips smiled, his mustache bristled.

Morton was standing. "Objection! . . . This comes from my heart, your Honor. I am compelled to use the most opprobrious term that can be applied to a member of the bar—that in view of the appearance of the witness the question is designed only to insult, demean and degrade the witness and prejudice the defendant in the eyes of the jury, the question is not that of an ethical lawyer but"—his voice went into a crescendo—"of a shyster!"

(1947)

From

NAVAHO INTERLUDE
by Edmund Wilson

The Navahos live in "hogans," little huts made of logs and mud. These are either hexagonal or octagonal and built up to a mud-plastered dome. In the center of this vault is a hole, through which a stovepipe passes. The hole is much larger than the pipe, but they depend on the heat, it seems, to vaporize the rain and snow. They sleep with their feet toward the stove, raying out like the spokes of a wheel.

When you call on a Navaho, you wait for a moment outside the door. Infallibly, he has heard you coming, and this gives him a chance to get ready. These dwellings are much cosier and cleaner than you could possibly expect them to be. The ones that I saw were not cluttered, and they never smelt badly or even close. Utensils and other things are put away on a shelf that runs around the whole wall. The people sit cross-legged on sheepskins on the hard dry earthen floor. In the first of the hogans we visited, a woman—very handsome, with her regular features, like so many of the Navaho women—was sitting with a little girl, who promised also to be very good-looking. On the floor, spread out on a paper, was a quantity of hard candy that had just been brought home from the schoolhouse. The woman put her hand to her mouth as if she were screening a cough, in what my guide explained to me later was a conventional gesture of diffidence. She told him, in answer to his questions, put to her in Navaho, that her husband was taking a sweat-bath—a ceremony, performed in a group, which involves throwing water on heated stones and is accompanied by ritual singing. My attention was called to an object lying under a blanket beside me, and the woman lifted off the blanket, revealing a baby on a "cradle-board." Wrapped up and strapped to this wooden back, the children can be laid down to sleep or stood up against the wall, so that they can see what is going on, or completely got out of the way by being hung from a nail higher up. They are nursed till the next baby is on the way, sometimes two years or more. It is said that the women will nurse, also, on occasion, young lambs that have lost their mothers. These children are, it seems, well brought up, gradually and gently trained. I noticed that the little girl made no attempt to grab the candy, having evidently been told she had had enough. Neither Navaho nor Zuñi children are ever corrected by whipping, and the Navahos are shocked by our brutal methods (though, in Zuñi, the punishment of certain offenses and the initiation of adolescents involve ceremonial whippings).

We visited the various households of another and more prosperous family, dominated, I was told, by the grandfather, a prominent medicine man, and his very strong-minded daughter. The old man we found in a small log house, an advance on the primitive hogan and furnished with chairs and a bed; but he was sitting on the floor, where we joined him. He had cataracts on both eyes, one of which seemed completely blind, but otherwise—with a gray mustache— he was quite fine-looking; and he received us with a good deal of dignity, shaking hands without rising and smoking quietly as he talked. He spoke Spanish and had been to Washington, was relatively a man of the world. Later, children and grandchildren came in, and some general conversation took place, rather haltingly, between Navaho and English and Spanish. There was a big upright loom at one side, on the cords of which one of the women had started a red and white blanket, whose design of diagonal stripes was already constructing its angles. Rolls of wool lay ready for carding, and she was twisting carded wool into thread and winding it on a spindle. They all seem to keep little cats, for which they have a Spanish word, *mossi*.

They are more flexible than the Zuñis, unquestionably, in spite of their less modernized ways. My guide had been studying the effects of the war on the Navahos who had been in the services (many of them had been operating radio, for which they had the odd qualification of a language that the enemy could not decode); and it was easier to see changes in their habits of thought than in the case of the conservative Zuñis. Some, he told me, had broken in radical ways with Navaho tradition. It is one of the tribal conventions that, from the day when a man is married, he may not look at his mother-in-law or remain in a room where she is. If she even comes into the trading post before he has finished his business, he must quietly slip away. But one young man who has returned from the army has decided not to bother with this, thus outraging the mother-in-law, who feels that she is treated with disrespect. Another ex-soldier has declined to take part in either the ceremonies of the Navaho religion or the services at the Nazarene Mission, declaring that they are both "superstition"— which does not appear unnatural when one learns that the Christian priest has been putting his ministry on a level with the incantatory therapeutics of the Navahos by telling them that conversion to the cult of Christ will safeguard them from losing their sheep. On the other hand, some of those who are known to have killed Germans or Japs have submitted to the strenuous tribal rites for the exorcism of the ghosts of the slain, and one smiling young fellow I met, who had never been farther away than Texas, had managed, through boasting of overseas prowess, to get himself purified on false pretenses. It is a part of this defense against ghosts to smear the patient all over with charcoal. He is supposed to wear his black-up for many days; but one young man, who wanted to sleep with his girl, had flouted the spirit world by immediately washing his off. Another had tried on his girl a modern birth control device of which he had learned the use in the army—one way of meeting the population problem—and had provoked a spirited protest.

(1947)

THE WAR
ABROAD
The Battle at Home

Some got their medals and the plums,
Some got their fingers burnt,
But every one's a native son,
Except for those who weren't.

> Rosemary and
> Stephen Vincent Benét
> *A Book of Americans*

"The casualty lists are very thickly studded
with names like Rabinowitz and Zablowski and
Murphy and Vitello. They're not what some
people call fine old American names. But they
made fine old American soldiers and fine old
American corpses."

> Margaret Halsey
> *Some of My Best Friends Are*
> *Soldiers*

From

COUNTRY PEOPLE
by Ruth Suckow

The first years of the war didn't affect the Richland farmers very much. It seemed far away from them. *"Ach,* over there in those old countries——" August said with a kind of contemptuous blankness. The men talked about it down at the implement store and at the produce house. They said that this country would never be involved. They were opposed to that, the farmers, as they were opposed to anything that seemed unsettling. They were a conservative bunch about Richland.

August had at first only a slight German feeling. Many of the farmers around Richland were English, and there had always been a little line of cleavage between the English and the German farmers. Sometimes, when August heard old Roland Yarborough "blowing off" about how wicked the Germans were, and that they ought all to be exterminated, it made him hot for a moment, made him feel that he was a German. All the feeling that he had was naturally and instinctively on the side of Germany. But most of the farmers were agreed. "Well, they've got to fight it out among themselves. It's their business; 'tain't ours." That was the way that August felt. He went about his own business.

Grandpa was the one who got excited. The old man, so withdrawn, his inner life known now to no one but himself, buried in strange dreams and prayers and fervours, now suddenly came back to the world. It was as if all at once childhood things, which had long been buried, came surging to the surface and overwhelmed him with memories. He went back to his boyhood in that little village in Mecklenburg whose name the boys had never heard before. Now he was always talking about it—Gultberg. *"Ja,* in Gultberg den——" "Gultberg? What's that? What's he talking about?" the boys asked, half amused. This was all far away to them. It tickled them, they said, to see "grandpa get himself all worked up" over something he had painstakingly read in the paper; come tottering out from his room, in his old felt slippers and patched brown trousers, his dark, sunken eyes burning, shaking one long, bony finger and pouring out a lot of broken English and German that they could only half understand. "Are de Germans so bad, den? *Mein* oldt *Vater, mein* Uncle Carl, I remember in de old country, were dey den all such bad men? No, no.'' They would listen, grinning a little, until he was exhausted and would go back to his room, shaking his head and mourning sadly, *"Ach,* no, *nein,"* to sit in the old rocker, sadly, his hands in his lap, muttering as he used to do about the Sunday travel.

Emma tried to calm him; she was afraid that the excitement would hurt him. She couldn't see why he was so affected by this, by things so far away; but of course he was thinking about his old home.

But when this country went in, all this was changed. Then feelings that had never been known before were all about. Then the taunts, the talk about Huns and *Boche,* made farmers like August for the first time actually realize their German ancestry. August had always taken it for granted that he belonged in this country. They awoke a deep racial resentment that could not come flaring out into the open but had to remain smouldering, and that joined with the fear of change, the resentment at interference, into a combination of angry feelings.

This centered chiefly in a deep opposition to the draft. To have someone tell his boys to do this and that! To take away his help on the farm just when he needed it most! To have somebody just step in and tell them where they had to go! Was that what happened in this country? Why had his people left the old country, then, if things were going to be just the same?

Carl was twenty-three now, Johnnie twenty. Carl's was among the first three names drawn in Richland, where he had to register. It was on the list in the post office—Carl Kaetterhenry, along with Ray Powers and Jay Bennett, the preacher's son. August stormed, wanted to know what right the Government had. But Carl took it quietly. There was no use kicking, he said. His name happened to be one drawn, and that was all there was to it.

What roused August to the greatest anger was that Harlan Boggs, the banker's son in "Wapsie," should get exempt, while his boy had to go. Harlan Boggs had appealed to the board and got exemption on the grounds that he couldn't be spared from the bank because of Liberty-bond work. But it didn't matter to the board, August said, that he couldn't get help and that they should take his boy right in the midst of the harvest season. Johnnie was working for Frank that year, and Carl was the only one he had on the farm. They said, "Produce, produce," but how was he going to do it when he got no help? There was all this talk about the women working on the farms, but August didn't see many of those high-school girls from Richland coming out and offering to do his threshing for him. Where were all these women working, then?

Grandpa quieted down after he learned that this country was in the war; regarded with a hurt, sorrowing, bewildered wonder that it should be fighting Germany. That was all that mattered to him, all that he could see of it. Carl went in to say good-bye to him, embarrassed and a little afraid of what grandpa might do. The old man rose from his chair, holding it by one arm, and quietly shook Carl's hand. Then he returned to his solitary brooding. It was strange and remote, the touch of that dry, aged, bony hand, although grandpa had been there in the house ever since Carl could remember.

The train left in the early morning. August drove his family in, Emma and Carl and Marguerite. Johnnie and Frank and Frank's wife came in Frank's car; Mary and Elva and Roy in Roy's. There was a little group at the small wooden station: the other two boys and their families, a few people from town, one or two detached travelling men. The family stayed awkwardly in the depot, didn't know what to do or to say to one another. Johnnie and August went out to see if the train was in sight.

Just before the train came—the morning *Clipper,* the Chicago train, by which clocks were set and rising timed—Old Jerry McGuire the postmaster, an old Catholic who had come into office when "the Democrats came in," lined the three boys up on the station platform and read the President's Proclamation to them. It was a strange, solemn, unreal scene. Even the people who saw it didn't believe in it. The three boys standing there, their figures against the dim red of the harvest sunrise, with solemn blank faces, frowning a little to keep down any signs of emotion. One of the mothers sobbed. Emma wept only a little, effacing herself even now. Carl looked big and fresh between the other two boys, Jay Bennett, a thin boy, dissipated in a small-town way; Ray, gawky and sunburned, with a wild head of hair. Carl was such a big, sturdy boy! He had his father's fresh-coloured skin, only finer-grained, rough light hair, full boyish lips, and clear blue eyes.

The little town was silent. Away from the station stretched pastures, the dew lying wet and heavy on red clover and tall weeds. The train came bearing down upon them, puffing out blackish smoke into the pale morning sky. It went black and big into the red prairie-sunrise. The fields were left silent again. The scattered group of people on the platform got into their battered cars and drove back home to the morning chores.

When Johnnie had to go, they were more used to it.

It was a queer time at home. It was so strange to be without the boys! August was a big, vigorous man, but now he realized for the first time, now that he had everything to do alone, that he was getting older. He had never stopped working hard; but now he saw that, strong and dogged as he was, he could quite do the work he had done in those days when they first went on the farm. He didn't even think of getting Emma out into the field now. "Mamma" belonged in the house.

The feeling in the neighbourhood against the German farmers had grown to a degree that would have seemed incredible at the beginning of the war. August "got off easy" compared with some of them. He had two boys in the service, he could keep his mouth shut, he bought Liberty bonds, although he didn't like to be told to do so. If it had not been for Carl and Johnnie in the army, he might have refused, like old Rudolph Haas, out of pure Kaetterhenry stubbornness. It was the thought of Carl and Johnnie that kept him from flaring up too fiercely when the boys yelled at him, when he drove into Richland, "Hey,

Dutchy! Old Dutchman! Old Dutchy Kaetterhenry!'' Once or twice he threatened, and started after them; but usually he only glared at them, smothering his impulse to fight. Some of the other German farmers came up before the board because of things they had said, or were reported to have said. Old Haas's corncrib was burned. But nothing worse happened to August than being yelled at on the street and finding painted in crude red letters on his barn: ''Old Dutchy Kaetterhenry. Hun. Bosh. Look Out.''

They were having terrible times down around Turkey Creek, which was solidly German, and where there had been more resistance to the draft. One of August's brothers had been threatened. A mob of boys and men from ''Wapsie'' had gone down there one night and tarred and feathered the preacher at the old Turkey Creek German church.

(1924)

From

BLACK WARRIORS
by George S. Schuyler

Once, after an unusually large pay day winning, Rain-in-the-Face, our company gambling king, took a bunch of us to town to help him celebrate. We piled off the street car at the Totem Pole and our host led us into a well-appointed saloon. It was not a place frequented by the Seattle Aframericans. We bellied to the long bar, the five of us, and ordered whiskey.

The bartender surveyed us coldly and calmly waited on a white customer who had come in behind us. Finally he turned to us and asked sharply, ''Are you lookin' for Sam?''

''Who's Sam?'' asked Rain-in-the-Face. He was a smooth, black fellow of solemn mien and what apprehensive Nordics call a smart nigger. He hailed originally from Savannah and spoke fluently the geechie gibberish of Yamacraw. He boasted of a high-school education and interpreted current events at our Sunday morning barbershop forums.

''Sam's the porter,'' replied the gentleman in the white jacket, winking at the customer he had just served, ''an' he's just gone home fer th' day.''

''Well, he might come back,'' said Rain-in-the-Face, winking at us, ''so we'll have five whiskies while we're waiting.''

The bartender grimly set the drinks in front of us. We drank. Then he took the five empty glasses and one by one smashed them to pieces on the floor.

"That's what we do with our glasses when you kind o' people drink outta 'm," he explained.

"A'right," said Rain-in-the-Face, indulging in one of his infrequent grins, "we'll have another round. We don't care what you do with your glasses."

Five more glasses were filled, emptied quickly and returned to the bar. One by one they were picked up and deliberately smashed on the floor. The bartender glared at us and placed his hands on his hips.

"Make it five beers next time," Rain-in-the-Face ordered. "Th' big glasses cost more!"

The beer was served and the glasses promptly broken, but the bartender was plainly tiring of the play.

"Why don't you fellas go where yer wanted?" he asked.

"If we on'y went where we was wanted, we wouldn't go nowheres," remarked our host.

"Well, I don' care," the bartender replied. "We don' serve colored. That's the boss's orders."

"But we're soldiers in uniform," argued Rain-in-the-Face.

"Don't make no difference, yer colored."

"A'right," quoth our host, suddenly inspired with an idea, "we'll go, but we'll be back."

We filed out, much to the relief of the bartender, and assembling on the corner, Rain-in-the-Face informed us that he was going to fix that guy. Four blocks down the street he led us into a Negro saloon. It was full of soldiers from the First Battalion, most of them broke but eager for liquor. Rain-in-the-Face gathered about forty of them around him and with our gang in the van, retraced his steps to the exclusive barroom.

The forty-five of us crowded into the place and lined up with our feet on the long brass rail. The bartender was thunderstruck.

"What do you people want?" he asked weakly.

"Beer all around," ordered Rain-in-the-Face, tossing a five-dollar gold piece on the mahogany.

The bartender scratched his head, grinned a little sheepishly, and drew the foaming lager. We tossed it off, set down the glasses, and waited.

"You win," said the bartender. "Have another on the house."

(1930)

From

JOHN-JOHN CHINAMAN
by Pearl S. Buck

Young John Lim paused in his ironing of the mayor's dress shirt and looked at the clock. It was five minutes to four and the hours of peace were gone. In a few minutes the street, the wide street of a small Midwestern American town, would be full of children and among them the savage boys. How he hated them! They had tortured his own childhood.

He too had gone to the red brick school half a block away from his father's laundry. The mornings he had managed by being as late as he dared, and his teachers, eyeing him sternly through the grades, grew tolerant of him as one by one they found out that he was always easily the head of his class. He would have been the valedictorian had the faculty not felt that the tie between him and Jim Halley, the principal's son, was so close that Jim ought to have it. "After all, Jim's an American," people said.

John Lim had come home to his father that day to weep the angry tears of the Chinese boy who is not taught that a man does not cry.

"Did you not tell me I was born in America?" he asked his father in their angular Cantonese dialect.

"You were born in the great city of St. Louis," Mr. Lim replied.

"Am I not American?" John demanded again.

"According to the laws of this country, you are American," Mr. Lim replied. Then he said sadly, "But the hearts of people decide these things, not laws."

"John-John Chinaman, eat dead rat—" At that very moment their voices hooting the rude song came in through the window.

"Why did you name me John, Father?" he had asked.

"The first white man I ever knew was a good man who was named John," Mr. Lim said, "and he gave me food when I had none and helped me when I was ill, and I swore my first son should be named John." Mr. Lim had not stopped his ironing.

John had learned after a while to imitate his father and, in spite of his wrath, to go on ironing and never to lift his eyes. But today he could not.

Ever since Siu-lan, his little wife, had come, this torture had made his hatred flame with new anger. Was it not torture? Yes, he understood her fear. All during his childhood he had been afraid. He had had to pick up dead mice the white children had thrown into the laundry, sometimes into the clean clothes. He had had to scrub chalk marks from the door, crazy imitations of Chinese characters. At night the doorbell might ring and there was always the possibility that a customer might be there out of hours, though more often there was only a jeer of laughter from around the corner. In the summer idle boys came to tease and whistle through their fingers and make fun at the open door, and when the door was shut the little room with two irons going became hot beyond bearing.

Sometimes since he left school he had not been able to endure, and then he had rushed out at the boys with his iron and scattered them. But the boys were only delighted to have so roused him, and they were soon back.

"We are the foreigners here," his father had told him one day, the sweat pouring down his bare back. "In our country we think the white man the foreigner. I remember that once a white man came through our village. We all ran away across the fields, men, women, and children together, because he seemed to us so fearful and strange."

John had answered through clenched teeth, "But I am American as much as anyone else is."

"Ah," his father had said enigmatically without looking up, "what is an American? I often wonder."

Now he heard soft quick footsteps on the stairs and he looked up and saw her, his little wife, a small terrified child in her long Chinese robe. She ran past him to the window and stood hiding behind the curtain, staring out into the street.

"They are coming!" she whispered. "I am afraid."

She drew back from the open window and a shrill yell rose up from the building down the street. He was horrified to see the delicate color drain from her face until it was like creamy wax. He ran to her side, leaving the iron on the bosom of the mayor's good shirt. "Don't be afraid!" he said. "See, it's only the bad boys!"

Upon the closed door there were thumps and raps, and through it they heard the same rhyme that he had so loathed in his childhood.

"John-John Chinaman, eat dead rat—"

"At least they might make up a new one," he thought in his raging heart.

"Oh, hear—they even cry your own name!" Siu-lan gasped.

Before he could explain, a small stone flew in through the window and struck his head just above the temple. Then she screamed and he could do nothing to calm her. Blood was flowing down his cheek.

"Why do they hate us so?" she was crying. "What have we ever done? Oh, let us go home and never come here again!"

He had to find a cloth to wipe his head lest the blood stain her pretty silk gown, and she followed him. It was at this moment that they smelled the burning.

"Now they have set the house on fire!" she whispered.

But he knew the smell of burning linen and he fled to lift the iron and yet not in time to be before his father, who at this moment was already at the door. It was too late. On the shirt bosom was a brown burn.

Mr. Lim looked at his son. "It is the mayor's good shirt," he said severely.

"I know it," John said. "How I could have been so stupid!" He paused and bit his lip. "But she was afraid and I went to her."

"There is a point beyond which it is unfilial to love one's wife," Mr. Lim said. Then he laughed, seeing the small figure shrinking against the wall. "What shall I tell Mr. Bascom? Shall I say my son is so in love with his wife that he leaves the iron in the bosom of the mayor's only good shirt?"

John snatched the shirt out of his father's hand. "I will take it to him myself," he exclaimed. "I will tell him the truth—that she was so terrified by the rudeness of the boys in this city that I had to—had to—" He was suddenly unable to bear the twinkle he saw in his father's eye, and he rushed out with the shirt rolled under his arm.

* * * * *

Mr. Lim went back to his ironing and wondered why he still felt confused, and when his son came downstairs he took the letter out of his bosom and handed it to him.

"A letter from the mayor," he said. "See if you know its purpose."

John read it quickly. The words which his father had searched for in the dictionary were not hard for him. As he read them, certain things he had been taught in school came back to him. The Salute to the American Flag, the Declaration of Independence, "The Star-Spangled Banner," "My Country 'Tis of Thee," the birthdays of Washington and Lincoln, all these had something to do with this letter—patriotism, in a word! He laughed at it. What was there for him to fight for in a small dusty town whose citizens' clothes he washed and whose children had made his life hateful with their cruelties! This America!

He handed the letter back to his father. "You have always taught me that only the lowest of men become soldiers," he said. He quoted a Chinese proverb glibly, "Poor iron for nails, poor men for soldiers."

"That is true," Mr. Lim said calmly. "It is why China has never made a game of war. We despise war. On the other hand, there are robbers and thieves among nations as among men. Do you forget Japan and our own country?"

"What have I to do with that? I am an American," John said coolly.

Mr. Lim did not answer this too shrewd remark. He folded Mrs. Bascom's full petticoat with the expertness of years.

"Doubtless the mayor will tell us what he means," he said diplomatically. To himself he thought again that it was not easy for a Chinese to be the father of an American son. There was something about this country stronger than race or training. When a man was born here, a spirit was born in him that did not come from his two parents. What would his grandson be?

As for John, he began to work in silence and the American ferment in him said angrily that he would fight no wars for a country whose citizens treated him like yellow scum. So that even children kept his beautiful little wife in constant terror. If, as now appeared likely, she was going to have a child, could he bear to bring up his son as he himself had had to grow up?

"There must be something better to fight for here than the white race before I fight," he thought grimly.

. . . The mayor's letters worked like yeast in Median. There were some people for and some against them, but the Lims said nothing and did nothing, old Mr. Lim because he was thinking of many things and John because he was thinking of only the one thing—that he owed nothing to America. Meanwhile the laundry work went on, heavy with wash dresses and shirts. Summer came and school was out and the days were here that John dreaded. Idle boys, mischievous boys, a few downright bad boys, and did no one see what they did? He kept hoping the mayor would speak to them—and had Mr. Halley forgotten?

The boys in their freedom tortured the Chinese whenever they thought of it, on their way back and forth to the movies, to the swimming hole, anywhere. At the first shout, Siu-lan was flying upstairs—to stay, sometimes, until night grew late enough for peace. What could John do but rage until he could not eat? Mr. Lim could do nothing with him.

"You must try not to be frightened," Mr. Lim told his daughter-in-law one day when John was delivering clothes to old Mrs. Cole, who was an invalid. "He is too angry. Evil will come of it. The woman must be wise for the man."

"I will try," Siu-lan whispered piteously. She did try, but John saw through her at once.

"Do not pretend," he said fiercely. "I cannot bear it."

So she gave up pretending and the days went on unchanged.

Jim Halley came home, and once he passed John on the street.

"Hello, John," he said in the same careless way he had always spoken.

"Hello, Jim," John replied, careful to say no more.

He knew in the ways that everybody knew everything in this little town that Jim was the hero here this summer. When he came home the town had given him a big party, and the mayor had made a speech. "Median's honored young son," he had said of Jim, and then he had gone off to his favorite theme. He had called upon all parents of sons to consider the loss to the nation of such young men as Jim Halley. John had not been there. He had said he was too busy to go, but Mr. Lim, sitting on a narrow bench in the hot sun, had as usual listened carefully to the mayor's speech. The upshot of it, he decided, was that there was going to be a war and the nation would need its young men.

He took this thought home with him in quiet soberness.

"There is to be a war and all young men must go, mayor said today," he told his son at their evening meal.

"Not me," John said firmly. "I'm a married man."

Mr. Lim answered this by silence, and in silence the meal was finished. But upstairs that night John talked a great deal to his little wife.

"Do not think I would go to war even if I were not exempt," he told her. "I would renounce my citizenship first and go back to China."

At this she buried her head under his arm. "It is true the stove is better here than there," she said.

He pulled her out. "And do you not hate these boys as you did?"

To which she replied, "I dare not go out when they come, but now I notice also there are days they do not come. And I like very much the way the water flows out of the wall, hot and cold. In our village the bucket was small and the well deep, and my arms ached so at night that sometimes I could not sleep."

He fixed her with a sternly loving gaze.

"Do you like America?" he asked her.

"I do like America," she said honestly. "It is only the people—why do they not like us? It would be a good country if they liked us."

He shook his head. "You ask me what I cannot answer," he said. "I hate them," he added simply.

For though there are whole days and even weeks when they lived peacefully, yet there was no telling when suddenly there would be an outbreak of trouble, as for instance one morning in August when a loud harsh tapping came apparently from the outer wall. It was John who discovered at last a small metal toy stuck to the wall with a string tied to it, and at the end of the string a boy. John threw the thing at him and cut the boy's cheek and stood scowling while he ran home.

In a little while Hen Conolly, the garage mechanic, came to bang on the laundry door, and when John opened it the angry Irishman wanted to know what the hell John meant by hitting his boy on the cheek with a tick-tack-toe.

"What the hell does your son mean to put such a thing on my house?" John retorted and shut the door in his face.

Mr. Lim heard Hen's loud voice shouting in the street, "It's time these Chinks went back where they came from!"

"You should not have angered him," Mr. Lim said.

"He should not have angered *me*," John retorted. "I'm as good as he is."

Mr. Lim was silent. This, he perceived, was the American thing in John, and he sighed.

In October it became apparent to Median that their young men must register for the army and if there were to be a war they would have to go. The mayor banged the table in the city hall and shouted.

"Damn it, if I have to send our boys to war I'm going to do it fighting! We're going to have the biggest protest meeting we've ever had the day the draft is drawn, and the first boy drafted is goin' to get a purse of money and a guarantee of the best job in the city when he gets back! He's going to get paid to do the dirtiest work in the world, and don't you think money is enough! He's goin' to get our highest honor and all we can give him! He's goin' as the first American of our town. For when a young man gives himself to the country, he gives something that can't be made up to him.''

The mayor's eyes were suddenly hot with tears again. He was seeing another young man, himself, marching out of Median to another war, and nothing had made up to him for those years when he had had to kill his fellow men— had to—had to— ''By God,'' he shouted, ''let's not wait till any boy comes home crippled in soul, if he isn't in body! Let's tell him what we think of him when he's able to hear and see and feel and know it!''

The mayor was a born leader of men and he swept the town with him. The celebration planned for the first young man to be chosen from Median grew so enormous that every young man who had to register held his head higher because he might be the one. People forgot that in towns all over the nation young men would be chosen the first of the first draft. Everybody felt it was really only the one boy in Median who was to be chosen in Washington on a certain day in October.

Of this the Lims knew nothing because little Siu-lan had met with an accident. Mr. Lim, who had never missed a meeting of the town, now missed the one at which the mayor made his declaration, and this was because of Hen Conolly's boy. One night when he was coming home late from the movies he found a dead cat and, swinging it by the tail, he flung it at someone he saw at the door of the laundry. The heavy inert thing struck full across Siu-lan's narrow little waist. She fell upon the doorstep, and John, carrying her upstairs, saw at once that he must call Dr. Lane.

For a week Mr. Lim went into a silent misery of waiting to see whether there was or was not going to be a grandson. And John did no work. He did not leave Siu-lan day or night. Dr. Lane came daily and sometimes oftener, and then Mrs. Lane began to come because the doctor had said to her, ''My dear, there seems to be not another woman who ever enters the door down at Lim's laundry. It isn't a nurse that's wanted—her young husband is handy. But the little creature looks like a Chinese doll and she's so afraid of me she won't let me touch her.''

''Why on earth should she be afraid here?'' Mrs. Lane exclaimed. She was a kind good woman whom the thought of going to China would have terrified.

''I can't imagine,'' Dr. Lane said, ''but see what you can do—the baby's life depends on it.''

Mrs. Lane went, though as she stepped over the Lim threshold she felt as nervous as though she were going into an unknown country. ''I always was afraid of them, you know—their slant eyes and all,'' she told her friends.

But when Siu-lan saw Mrs. Lane she knew that here was one American whom she need not fear any more than she would her own mother.

''Has this one any boys?'' she asked John at once.

"They are childless, these two," John replied.

Siu-lan smiled at that and put out her small hands, and Mrs. Lane could not keep from taking them, and then it was no time until, as she told Mrs. Penny later, she forgot all about the pretty little thing not being like anybody else.

Together she and Dr. Lane brought Siu-lan back safely to her task of having a grandchild for the Lim family. Mr. Lim would have signed away his whole laundry business in gratitude if the white-haired doctor would have had it. But John said nothing and Dr. Lane noticed it.

"Old Lim is a pleasant kind of fellow—but young Lim is different," he told his wife.

"He doesn't seem to care for a thing unless it's that little girl," Mrs. Lane replied. "He's real nice to her, though."

"Who wouldn't be?" the doctor retorted.

"It wasn't so nice to have a dead cat thrown at you!" Mrs. Lane said.

"That sort of thing ought to be stopped," Dr. Lane agreed. "But what can you do about other people's children?" He rubbed his chin slowly. "Queer how cruel even good enough folks can be without thinking," he said.

"Ain't it!" Mrs. Lane said.

Thus when the mayor announced the day of the drawing of the draft the Lims were not as well prepared for it as were the other citizens of Median. But since all was now well with Siu-lan and she could be left in the care of the two old men, Mr. Lim told John that they must obey the mayor and attend the meeting, and that is why they were both there, not on the front seat where Jim Halley and his father and his mother sat, but just inside the door with the colored janitor.

Never, Mr. Lim thought, had he seen the city hall so beautiful. There were bright paper streamers across the ceiling and vines climbing the pillars and the platform was banked with the best potted plants in Median that in winter were nursed in sunny windows.

Mr. Lim leaned over to his son. "If we had known, we could have brought our potted bamboo."

John nodded, but he said nothing.

The mayor got up to speak. He was very red and spoke loudly.

"It is a pity the mayor excites himself," Mr. Lim whispered to his son. He watched awhile and then leaned over to his son again.

"Is the mayor angry about something?" he asked.

"He seems to be," John said carelessly. What had all this to do with him?

After that Mr. Lim listened closely, and what he heard was that America was the greatest country in the world, the most independent, the most generous, the richest, the best, and that while all Americans ought to be willing to die for their country and God knows *were* willing, yet it was to be asked why again they had to fight. Mr. Lim wanted to get up and say to the mayor, "Sir, but what if there are nations like Japan?" But he sat still, fearing this would be discourtesy. Nevertheless he rubbed his nose and pulled his ear and after a moment he leaned over to his son again. "Sometimes one *has* to fight," he whispered loudly. But John did not answer. The mayor had paused. The moment had come when at Washington the first number was to be drawn for the first draft of what might be the greatest army in the world. The mayor had planned his speech carefully to this instant. In the silence the atmosphere of the room tightened. People sat up, they leaned forward, heads turned toward the loudspeaker. On the front seat Jim Halley held his head very high, but his mother bent hers and stared at her hands, folded in her lap.

Only John Lim did not move. He sat looking out of the window near him into the cottonwood trees which filled the town square, thinking of himself, his wife, his child to come.

"I have no country," he was thinking.

At this instant the radio came on. The Voice from Washington spoke to Median, as it did to thousands of little towns like it. But not everywhere was there such waiting. On the table was a purse of money which the mayor himself had brought up to five hundred dollars, and there was a silver plaque donated by the merchants of Median to the first American boy to be chosen from their town, and the mayor stood waiting to receive from the radio the number which would tell Median. The mayor's mouth was quivering—though he had nothing but daughters, thank God!

"It takes me back," he said gravely, lifting his voice above the Voice from Washington, "it takes me back to my own young manhood. Of the four of us who went out of Median to that First World War, only I came back. Those other brave boys never knew what their folks thought of them. But today this boy and all our boys will know."

The Voice from Washington said, "The number is one five eight."

Jim Halley heard instantly that it was not his number and he stirred and coughed and pulled up very slightly the creases of his new trousers. He looked at his mother and then at his father. For the moment they felt nothing but disappointment. Since Jim would have to go anyway, sooner or later, it would have been nice if—

Then everybody was looking for a young figure rising to his feet, but none rose.

"Has anyone this number?" the mayor shouted.

There was an echo in John Lim's stunned brain. Slowly he stood up, a slight dark Oriental figure.

"It is I," he said.

The faces of the people of Median turned to him and stared, unbelieving, and he felt the red running to his cheeks as he received into his too sensitive mind what they were thinking.

"I am sorry," he stammered, "it is not my fault." He must find words to go on, to tell them that of course he would not take their—their money, or their honor. He would claim exemption. But before he could speak even the first word, his father rose at his side, his brown face shining with a light that none had ever seen on it before. Whatever the people of Median were feeling, he did not know it. The radio voice was announcing another number, but nobody heard, for the mayor reached and turned the dial.

"I wish to thank you, sir, Mr. Mayor," Mr. Lim said clearly. "Mr. Mayor, sir, please thank the President in Washington for my family. When I write to my family in Canton that this honor has come to us, that my son has been chosen to be the first to fight for this country where he was born, how shall they express their thanks?"

In speechlessness the people of Median listened.

"Father!" John's voice was a whispered outcry, but Mr. Lim would not hear it.

"Exempting we will not take," Mr. Lim said firmly. "In my country the father also supports son, wife, grandson, as long as needed. I gladly do so here."

John sat down suddenly and gripped his hands. American or Chinese? If he were American he would have the guts now to leap to his feet and speak. "I'll make my own choice, Father—you can't decide this for me!" He could not do it, and his father went on.

"It is now my chance to say how happy I am to have my son to give this country. He is my only son—therefore, most precious. He is the best I have to give. I give him gladly. For I have lived here so many years, and you have let me live here and have given me your business. There has been kindness as well as business. Trouble, too, but we are all humans and trouble is everywhere. The great thing for which I thank you at this time is that you have let me come here looking so different from you, such a skin and eyes, a Chinese. Yes, but my son is American. He is born American. This is the great thing. Whatever the skin and eyes, he can be American. Where else do all colors and kind make their own country? Shall we not fight to save this good country?"

He turned to his son. "John, get up!"

John was a Chinese at the sound of his father's voice.

"I won't go," he was saying wildly in himself, "I won't go!" But aloud he did not speak.

"Thank our friends," his father commanded him. "There is your schoolteacher and his son. Mr. Halley, when I first come here, I speaked no English, but I came to your night class and you taught me. You taught my son at a free public school. We thank you. Sir, in his time the son of such a man as you will do some good things for another like me. We thank you. Mr. Stout, sir, grocer, when business was bad for Depression, three months you let us eat and we could not pay. Could this happen somewhere? No, I think only here. Thanks, Mr. Stout. Recently we had a trouble in our family and Dr. Lane, you, sir, and Mrs. Lane, madam, helped us, how greatly! And Reverend Brown, your church sent money to China for the sick and hungry—thank you—thank you!"

One by one Mr. Lim named half the people of Median and bowed, and what could a Chinese son do but bow with his father? He bowed sullenly enough at first. Then a magic began to work in him as his father brought to life those faces before him. One by one he began to see them—to remember certain things that were not torture.

"Dead cat, hey?" Dr. Lane had said when he told him why Siu-lan had fallen.

The old doctor had looked sheepish.

"And when I was a small boy in another city," he said slowly, "I—I threw an apple core at a Greek. It hit him on the neck and he turned and gave me a look I never forgot. I wonder why I did that. I still feel ashamed."

Warmth stirred uncertainly in John in answer to another warmth he now saw upon these faces as his father recalled their kindness. Yes, there had been kindness. He saw his father sit down at last. But John was still standing. Now he must speak. The people waited kindly for what he would say. His eyes upon these plain friendly faces, he suddenly bowed a small quick bow.

"I agree with my father," he said and sat down.

Everybody clapped and men muttered to each other, "Good old fellow— the Chinese are good folks." As for the mayor, he had, while Mr. Lim was speaking, what afterward he called an old-fashioned conversion. "I suddenly saw what the whole shootin' match was about," he told his wife later. "John Lim," he said, "will you come forward?"

John slid past his father and went up the aisle and stood while the mayor made him the speech he had planned for half a dozen others, at heart secretly for Jim Halley, that handsome fellow. But the mayor was a good man and a just one and he went through the speech exactly as he had memorized it. When John had received the purse and the plaque, had heard himself called the First American of Median, had turned and bowed, the mayor motioned to the band and everybody rose and sang "The Star-Spangled Banner," and John's knees trembled, not with fear of anything except that his heart would grow too big for his bosom and his face break its calm and disgrace not him, but an American. If there were any who felt that it was a pity perhaps—and there were some—these waited until they got home to say so.

Mr. Lim and John walked home in silence. At the door, John stood aside as he always did and let his father go in first. Then he followed. Inside, Mr. Lim took off his hat and coat and tie and put on his apron.

"I will work also if she needs nothing," John said quickly.

"Do not hurry yourself," Mr. Lim said tranquilly, and spat on an iron to test it.

But John was already upstairs. She was in bed, looking so pretty that his heart all but fainted.

"Can you—When I go to war," he began, seizing her little hand.

"Do you go to war?" she gasped.

"I have been chosen," he said.

He showed her the purse, the plaque, the promise of a job if he wanted it, though of course he would come back to the laundry. She listened, her hand clinging to his, her eyes bright with pride in him. Then those eyes clouded.

"Is it safe for me when you are gone?" she asked. "For me and your child?"

He thought a moment and felt an old burden lift itself from his shoulders. What boy, what smallest boy, even, would chalk marks on the door of the first American to be chosen from Median, or would think of calling him "John-John Chinaman"?

"You will be safe here now," he said. "You and our son."

(1942)

DEFEAT
by Witter Bynner

On a train in Texas German prisoners eat
With white American soldiers, seat by seat
While black American soldiers sit apart—
The white men eating meat, the black men heart.
Now, with that other war a century done,
Not the live North but the dead South has won:
Not yet a riven nation comes awake.
Whom are we fighting this time, for God's sake?
Mark well the token of the separate seat—
It is again ourselves that we defeat.

(1944)

THE IMAGINARY JEW
by John Berryman

The second summer of the European war I spent in New York. I lived in a room just below street level on Lexington above Thirty-fourth, wrote a good deal, tried not to think about Europe, and listened to music on a small gramophone, the only thing of my own, except books, in the room. Haydn's London

Symphony, his last, I heard probably fifty times in two months. One night when excited I dropped the pickup, creating a series of knocks at the beginning of the last movement where the oboe joins the strings which still, when I hear them, bring up for me my low dark long damp room and I feel the dew of heat and smell the rented upholstery. I was trying, as one says, to come back a little, uncertain and low after an exhausting year. Why I decided to do this in New York—the enemy in summer equally of soul and body, as I had known for years—I can't remember; perhaps I didn't, but we held on merely from week to week by the motive which presently appeared in the form of a young woman met the Christmas before and now the occupation of every evening not passed in solitary and restless gloom. My friends were away; I saw few other people. Now and then I went to the zoo in lower Central Park and watched with interest the extraordinary behavior of a female badger. For a certain time she quickly paced the round of her cage. Then she would approach the side wall from an angle in a determined, hardly perceptible, unhurried trot; suddenly, when an inch away, point her nose up it, follow her nose up over her back, turning a deft and easy somersault, from which she emerged on her feet moving swiftly and unconcernedly away, as if the action had been no affair of hers, indeed she had scarcely been present. There was another badger in the cage who never did this, and nothing else about her was remarkable; but this competent disinterested somersault she enacted once every five or ten minutes as long as I watched her—quitting the wall, by the way, always at an angle in fixed relation to the angle at which she arrived at it. It is no longer possible to experience the pleasure I knew each time she lifted her nose and I understood again that she would not fail me, or feel the mystery of her absolute disclaimer—she has been taken away or died.

The story I have to tell is no further a part of that special summer than a nightmare takes its character, for memory, from the phase of the moon one noticed on going to bed. It could have happened in another year and in another place. No doubt it did, has done, will do. Still, so weak is the talent of the mind for pure relation—immaculate apprehension of *p* alone—that everything helps us, as when we come to an unknown city: architecture, history, trade practices, folklore. Even more anxious our approach to a city—like my small story—which we have known and forgotten. Yet how little we can learn! Some of the history is the lonely summer. Part of the folklore, I suppose, is which I now unwillingly rehearse, the character which experience has given to my sense of the Jewish people.

Born in a part of the South where no Jews had come, or none had stayed, and educated thereafter in states where they are numerous, I somehow arrived at a metropolitan university without any clear idea of what in modern life a Jew was—without even a clear consciousness of having seen one. I am unable now to explain this simplicity or blindness. I had not escaped, of course, a sense that humans somewhat different from ourselves, called ''Jews,'' existed as in the middle distance and were best kept there, but this sense was of the vaguest.

From what it was derived I do not know; I do not recall feeling the least curiosity about it, or about Jews; I had, simply, from the atmosphere of an advanced heterogeneous democratic society, ingathered a gently negative attitude toward Jews. This I took with me, untested, to college, where it received neither confirmation nor stimulus for two months. I rowed and danced and cut classes and was political; by mid-November I knew most of the five hundred men in my year. Then the man who rowed Number Three, in the eight of which I was bow, took me aside in the shower one afternoon and warned me not to be so chatty with Rosenblum.

I wondered why not. Rosenblum was stroke, a large handsome amiable fellow, for whose ability in the shell I felt great respect and no doubt envy. Because the fellows in the house wouldn't like it, my friend said. "What have they against him?" "It's only because he's Jewish," explained my friend, a second-generation Middle European.

I hooted at him, making the current noises of disbelief, and went back under the shower. It did not occur to me that he could be right. But next day when I was talking with Herz, the coxswain, whom I knew very well, I remembered the libel with some annoyance, and told Herz about it as a curiosity. Herz looked at me oddly, lowering his head, and said after a pause, "Why Al *is* Jewish, didn't you know that?" I was amazed. I said it was absurd, he couldn't be! "Why not?" said Herz, who must have been as astonished as I was. "Don't you know I'm Jewish?"

I did not know, of course, and ignorance has seldom cost me such humiliation. Herz did not guy me; he went off. But greater than my shame at not knowing something known, apparently, without effort to everyone else, were my emotions for what I then quickly discovered. Asking careful questions during the next week, I learned that about a third of the men I spent time with in college were Jewish; that they knew it, and the others knew it; that some of the others disliked them for it, and they knew this also; that certain houses existed *only* for Jews, who were excluded from the rest; and that what in short I took to be an idiotic state was deeply established, familiar, and acceptable to everyone. This discovery was the beginning of my instruction in social life proper— construing social life as that from which political life issues like a somatic dream.

My attitude toward my friends did not alter on this revelation. I merely discarded the notion that Jews were a proper object for any special attitude; my old sense vanished. This was in 1933. Later, as word of the German persecution filtered into this country, some sentimentality undoubtedly corrupted my no-attitude. I denied the presence of obvious defects in particular Jews, feeling that to admit them would be to side with the sadists and murderers. Accident allotting me close friends who were Jewish, their disadvantages enraged me. Gradually, and against my sense of impartial justice, I became the anomaly which only a partial society can produce, and for which it has no name known to the lexicons. In one area, not exclusively, "nigger-lover" is flung in a proximate way; but for a special sympathy and liking for Jews—which became my fate, so that I trembled when I heard one abused in talk—we have no term. In this condition I still was during the summer of which I speak. One further circumstance may be mentioned, as a product, I believe, of this curious training. I am spectacularly unable to identify Jews as Jews—by name, cast of feature, accent, or environment—and this has been true, not only of course before the college incident, but during my whole life since. Even names to anyone else patently Hebraic rarely suggest to me anything. And when once I learn that So-and-so is Jewish, I am likely to forget it. Now Jewishness—the religion or the race—may be a fact as striking and informative as someone's past heroism or his Christianity or his understanding of the subtlest human relations, and I feel sure that something operates to prevent my utilizing the plain signs by which such characters—in a Jewish man or woman—may be identified, and prevent my retaining the identification once it is made.

So to the city my summer and a night in August. I used to stop on Fourteenth Street for iced coffee, walking from the Village home (or to my room rather) after leaving my friend, and one night when I came out I wandered across to the island of trees and grass and concrete walks raised in the center of Union Square. Here men—a few women, old—sit in the evenings of summer, looking at papers or staring off or talking, and knots of them stay on, arguing, very late; these the unemployed or unemployable, the sleepless, the malcontent. There are no formal orators, as at Columbus Circle in the nineteen-thirties and at Hyde Park Corner. Each group is dominated by several articulate and strong-lunged persons who battle each other with prejudices and desires, swaying with intensity, and take on from time to time the interrupters: a forum at the bottom of the pot—Jefferson's fear, Whitman's hope, the dream of the younger Lenin. It was now about one o'clock, almost hot, and many men were still out. I stared for a little at the equestrian statue, obscure in the night on top of its pedestal, thinking that misty Rider would sweep away again all these men at his feet, whenever he liked—what symbol for power yet in a mechanical age rivals the mounted man?—and moved to the nearest group; or I plunged to it.

The dictator to the group was old, with dark cracked skin, fixed eyes in an excited face, leaning forward madly on his bench toward the half-dozen men in semicircle before him. "It's bread! It's bread!" he was saying. "It's bittersweet. All the bitter and all the sweetness. Of an overture. What else do you want? When you ask for steak and potatoes, do you want pastry with it? It's bread! It's bread! Help yourself! Help yourself!"

The listeners stood expressionless, except one who was smiling with contempt and interrupted now.

"Never a happy minute, never a happy minute!" the old man cried. "It's good to be dead! Some men should kill themselves."

"Don't you want to live?" said the smiling man.

"Of course I want to live. Everyone wants to live! If death comes, suddenly it's better. It's better!"

With pain I turned away. The next group were talking diffusely and angrily about the mayor, and I passed to a third, where a frantic olive-skinned young man with a fringe of silky beard was exclaiming:

"No restaurant in New York had the Last Supper! No. When people sit down to eat they should think of that!"

"Listen," said a white-shirted student on the rail, glancing around for approbation, "listen, if I open a restaurant and put *The Last Supper* up over the door, how much money do you think I'd lose? Ten thousand dollars?"

The fourth cluster was larger and appeared more coherent. A savage argument was in progress between a man of fifty with an oily red face, hatted, very determined in manner, and a muscular fellow half his age with heavy eyebrows, coatless, plainly Irish. Fifteen or twenty men were packed around them, and others on a bench near the rail against which the Irishman was lounging were attending also. I listened for a few minutes. The question was whether the President was trying to get us into the war—or, rather, whether this was legitimate, since the Irishman claimed that Roosevelt was a goddamned warmonger whom all the real people in the country hated, and the older man claimed that we should have gone into the f—ing war when France fell a year before, as everybody in the country knew except a few immigrant rats. Redface talked ten times as much as the Irishman, but he was not able to establish any advantage that I could see. He ranted, and then Irish either repeated shortly and fiercely what he had said last, or shifted his ground. The audience were silent—favoring whom I don't know, but evidently much interested. One or two men pushed out of the group, others arrived behind me, and I was eddied forward toward the disputants. The young Irishman broke suddenly into a tirade by the man with the hat:

"You're full of s—. Roosevelt even tried to get us in with the communists in the Spanish war. If he could have done it we'd have been burning churches down like the rest of the Reds."

"No, that's not right," I heard my own voice, and pushed forward, feeling blood in my face, beginning to tremble. "No, Roosevelt, as a matter of fact, helped Franco by non-intervention, at the same time that Italians and German planes were fighting against the Government and arms couldn't get in from France."

"What's that? What are you, a Jew?" He turned to me contemptuously, and was back at the older man before I could speak. "The only reason we weren't over there four years ago is because you can only screw us so much. Then we quit. No New Deal bastard could make us go help the goddamned communists."

"That ain't the question, it's if we want to fight *now* or *later*. Them Nazis ain't gonna sit!" shouted the red-faced man. "They got Egypt practically, and then it's India if it ain't England first. It ain't a question of the communists, the communists are on Hitler's side. I tellya we can wait and wait and chew and spit and the first thing you know they'll be in England, and then who's gonna help us when they start after us? Maybe Brazil? Get wise to the world!

Spain don't matter now one way or the other, they ain't gonna help and they can't hurt. It's Germany and Italy and Japan, and if it ain't too late now it's gonna be. Get wise to yourself. We shoulda gone in——''

"What with?" said the Irishman with disdain. "Pop, pop. Wooden machine guns?"

"We were as ready a year ago as we are now. Defense don't mean nothing, you gotta have to fight!"

"No, we're much better off now," I said, "than we were a year ago. When England went in, to keep its word to Poland, what good was it to Poland? The German Army——''

"Shut up, you Jew," said the Irishman.

"I'm not a Jew," I said to him. "What makes——''

"Listen, Pop," he said to the man in the hat, "it's O.K. to shoot your mouth off, but what the hell have you got to do with it? You aren't gonna do any fighting."

"Listen," I said.

"You sit on your big ass and talk about who's gonna fight who. Nobody's gonna fight anybody. If we feel hot, we ought to clean up some of the sons of bitches here before we go sticking our nuts anywhere to help England. We ought to clean up the sons of bitches in Wall Street and Washington before we take any ocean trips. You want to know something? You know why Germany's winning everything in this war? Because there ain't no Jews back home. There ain't no more Jews, first shouting war like this one here"—nodding at me— "and then skinning off to the synagogue with the profits. Wake up, Pop! You must have been around in the last war, you ought to know better."

I was too nervous to be angry or resentful. But I began to have a sense of oppression in breathing. I took the Irishman by the arm.

"Listen, told you I'm not a Jew."

"I don't give a damn what you are." He turned his half-dark eyes to me, wrenching his arm loose. "You talk like a Jew."

"What does that mean?" Some part of me wanted to laugh. "How does a Jew talk?"

"They talk like you, buddy."

"That's a fine argument! But if I'm not a Jew, my talk only——''

"You probably are a Jew. You look like a Jew."

"I *look* like a Jew? Listen''—I swung around eagerly to a man standing next to me—"do I look like a Jew? It doesn't matter whether I do or not—a Jew is as good as anybody and better than this son of a bitch." I was not exactly excited, I was trying to adapt my language as my need for the crowd, and sudden respect for its judgment possessed me. "But in fact I'm not Jewish and I don't look Jewish. Do I?"

The man looked at me quickly and said, half to me and half to the Irishman. "Hell, I don't know. Sure he does."

A wave of disappointment and outrage swept me almost to tears. I felt like a man betrayed by his brother. The lamps seemed brighter and vaguer, the night large. Glancing 'round, I saw sitting on a bench near me a tall, heavy, serious-looking man of thirty, well dressed, whom I had noticed earlier, and appealed to him, "Tell me, do I look Jewish?"

But he only stared up and waved his head vaguely. I saw with horror that something was wrong with him.

"You look like a Jew. You talk like a Jew. You *are* a Jew," I heard the Irishman say.

I heard murmuring among the men, but I could see nothing very clearly. It seemed very hot. I faced the Irishman again helplessly, holding my voice from rising.

"I'm *not* a Jew," I told him. "I might be, but I'm not. You have no bloody reason to think so, and you can't make me a Jew by simply repeating like an an idiot that I am."

"Don't deny it, son," said the red-faced man, "stand up to him."

"God damn it"—suddenly I was furious, whirling like a fool (was I afraid of the Irishman? had he conquered me?) on the red-faced man—"I'm *not* denying it! Or rather I am, but only because I'm not a Jew! I despise renegades, I hate Jews who turn on their people, if I were a Jew I would say so, I would be proud to be. What is the vicious opinion of a man like this to me if I were a Jew? But I'm not. Why the hell should I admit I am if I'm not?"

"Jesus, the Jew is excited," said the Irishman.

"I have a right to be excited, you son of a bitch. Suppose I call you a Jew. Yes, you're a Jew. Does that mean anything?"

"Not a damn thing." He spat over the rail past a man's head.

"Prove that you're not. I say you are."

"Now listen, you Jew. I'm a Catholic."

"So am I, or I was born one, I'm not one now. I was born a Catholic." I was a little calmer but goaded, obsessed with the need to straighten this out. I felt that everything for everyone there depended on my proving him wrong. If *once* this evil for which we have not even a name could be exposed to the rest of the men as empty—if I could *prove* I was not a Jew—it would fall to the ground, neither would anyone else be a Jew to be accused. Then it could be trampled on. Fascist America was at stake. I listened, intensely anxious for our fate.

"Yeah?" said the Irishman. "Say the Apostles' Creed."

Memory went swirling back. I could hear the little bell die as I hushed it and set it on the felt. Father Boniface looked at me tall from the top of the steps and smiled, greeting me in the darkness before dawn as I came to serve, the men pressed around me under the lamps, and I could remember nothing but *visibilium omnium, et invisibilium.*

"I don't remember it."

The Irishman laughed with his certainty.

The papers in my pocket; I thought them over hurriedly. In my wallet.

What would they prove? Details of ritual, Church history: anyone could learn them. My piece of Irish blood. Shame, shame: shame for my ruthless people. I will not be his blood. I wish I were a Jew, I would change my blood, to be able to say *Yes* and defy him.

"I'm not a Jew." I felt a fool. "You only say so. You haven't any evidence in the world."

He leaned forward from the rail, close to me. "Are you cut?"

Shock, fear ran through me before I could make any meaning out of his words. Then they ran faster, and I felt confused.

From that point nothing is clear for me. I stayed a long time—it seemed impossible to leave, showing him victor to them—thinking of possible allies and new plans of proof, but without hope. I was tired to the marrow. The arguments rushed on, and I spoke often now but seldom was heeded except by an old fat woman, very short and dirty, who listened intently to everyone. Heavier and heavier appeared to me to press upon us in the fading night our general guilt.

In the days following, as my resentment died, I saw that I had not been a victim altogether unjustly. My persecutors were right: I was a Jew. The imaginary Jew I was was as real as the imaginary Jew hunted down, on other nights and days, in a real Jew. Every murderer strikes the mirror, the lash of the torturer falls on the mirror and cuts the real image, and the real and the imaginary blood flow down together.

(1945)

From

FOCUS
by Arthur Miller

A stranger on the block could never have noticed any difference between Mr. Newman's house and the others. They stood in a flat-topped line, attached two-story brick, with the garages built in beneath the high front porches. Before each house grew a slender elm which was neither thicker nor much thinner than its neighbor, all of them having been planted in the same week some seven years ago when the development was finished. To Mr. Newman, however, there were certain vital differences. Standing for a moment beside his garbage can, he glanced up at his shutters which he had painted a light green. The other houses all had dark green shutters. Then his eye moved to his window screens, which he had hinged at the sides so that they opened like doors instead of swinging out from the top as the others on the block did. Many times he had wished, improvidently, that the house had been built of wood so that there would be more surface to paint. As it was, he could only work around his car which stood on concrete blocks in the garage. On Sundays before the war he would take the car out and go over it lightly with a waxed cloth, brush out the interior, and drive his mother to church. Without admitting it, however, he enjoyed the car much more now when it was on blocks, for it is well known that rust is a terrible menace to an unused machine. On these war Sundays he took the immaculate storage battery, which he kept in the basement, and installed it in the car and ran the engine for a few moments. And then he disconnected the battery and hauled it back into the cellar, and walked around the car looking for rust spots, and turned the wheels a little with his hands to keep the bearing grease mobile, and generally did each Sunday what the manufacturer had advised doing twice a year. At the end of the day he enjoyed washing his hands with Gre-Solvent, and sitting down to a good dinner, feeling the presence of his muscles and his good health.

Glancing at the garbage can now to be sure it was covered tightly, he walked down the street in his earnest way. But despite his even stride and the confident, straight-ahead set of his head, he felt his insides moving and to quiet himself he thought of his mother, who was sitting now in his kitchen waiting for the day maid to arrive and make her breakfast. She was paralyzed below the hips and spoke of nothing but pain and California. He tried to involve his mind in her, but as he neared the subway his abdomen became quite taut and he was glad for the necessity of halting a moment at the corner candy store where he bought his paper. He said good morning to the proprietor and paid his nickel, careful not to touch the man's hands with his own. He would not have been especially horrified to have touched them but he did not like the idea of it. He fancied a certain odor of old cooking coming from Mr. Finkelstein. He did not want to touch the odor. Mr. Finkelstein said good morning as usual and Mr. Newman walked the few yards around the corner, paused an instant to firmly grasp the handrail of the subway stairs and made his way down.

He had another nickel ready for the turnstile and inserted it after expertly feeling for the slot, although had he seen fit to lower his head he could easily have made it out. He did not like to be seen lowering his head.

Coming onto the platform he turned left and strolled leisurely, noting as he went that as usual most of the people were crowded together at the platform's center. He always went to the front end—as they should if they had the sense to observe that the first car was always emptiest. When a stretch of some twenty yards lay between him and the waiting people, he gradually slowed and came to a halt beside a steel pillar. He turned toward it unobtrusively, and stood with his face a hand's width from the indented center of the steel I-beam.

With an acute squint he screwed the pupils of his eyes into focus. Raising and lowering his head he searched the white-painted surface of the pillar. Then his movements stopped. Someone had written here. As he read, his skin began to warm with anticipation. In a penciled scrawl, hastily written between the arrival and departure of trains, was *Come LA 4-4409 beautiful and dumb.* As he had many times before, he stood wondering now whether this was actually an advertisement or a wishful joke. A breath of adventure touched him, and he visualized an apartment somewhere . . . dark and scented with women . . .

His eyes searched farther down. A well-drawn ear. Several $\sqrt{}\sqrt{}$ marks. It was a fairly fruitful pillar, he felt. Often they were washed clean before he arrived in the morning. *My name IS NOT ELSIE* caught him for a moment and he shook his head and nearly smiled. How angrily Elsie—or whatever her name was—had written that. Why were they calling her Elsie? he wondered. And where was this Elsie now? Was she asleep somewhere? Or on her way to work? Was she happy now or regretful? Mr. Newman felt a tie, an attachment with the people who wrote on these pillars, for it seemed to him that they said only what they meant. It was like opening someone's mail . . .

His head stopped moving. Above his eyes was carefully printed, *Kikes started WAR.* Below it, *Kill kikes kill ki.* Apparently the author had been interrupted by the arrival of his train. Mr. Newman swallowed and stared as though caught in the beam of a hypnotizing light. Above the fierce slogan stood the exclamation, *Fascists!,* with an arrow pointing down at the call to murder.

He turned from the pillar and stood looking down at the tracks. His heart had grown larger, his breathing came faster as a titillation of danger danced upon his mind. It was as though he had just seen a bloody fistfight. Around this pillar the air had witnessed a silent but terrible contest. While above on the street the traffic had calmly moved and people had slept through the night, here below a wild current had flowed darkly and had left its marks and was gone.

He stood unmoving, caught. Nothing he ever read gripped him so powerfully as did these scrawled threats. To him they were a kind of mute record that the city automatically inscribed in her sleep; a secret newspaper publishing what the people really thought, undiluted by fears of propriety and selfish interest. It was like finding the elusive eyes of the city and staring into her true mind. The first rumblings of an approaching train roused him.

As to a severed limb he turned again toward the pillar, and stopped when two women smelling of cherry soap halted near him. He glanced over at them. Why, he wondered, must these things always be written by such obviously ignorant hands? These two women, now—they share that slogan-writer's indignation and yet it is left for the lowest people to step forward and spell out the truth. Air began to whirl and rise around his legs as the train thrust like a piston into the cylindrical station. Mr. Newman stepped back a yard and his elbow brushed the dress of one of the women. The cherry smell was strong for an instant, and he was glad she was a well-kept woman. He liked to travel with people who were well kept.

The doors hissed open and the women went in. Mr. Newman waited an instant and then followed carefully, remembering how a week before he had started in before the doors had been fully withdawn and had collided with them. As he reached up and grasped an overhead porcelain handle his face grew pinker at the memory of that moment. His blood began to pump rapidly. He brought his arm down as the train started, and drew his white cuff out under the edge of his jacket sleeve. The train sped toward Manhattan. Relentlessly, mercilessly it carried him toward that island, and he closed his eyes for a moment as though to contain himself and his fear.

His paper was still tucked under his arm. Remembering it, he opened it and pretended to read. There was no banner headline. Everything crawled beneath his eyes. Holding the paper as though engrossed in it, he looked over its edge at the passenger seated in front of him. Ukrainian-Polish, he registered without thinking. He studied the man as well as he could. Worker's cap. Soiled windbreaker. He could not make out the man's eyes. Probably small, he supplied. Ukrainian-Polish . . . taciturn, hard-working, inclined toward strong drink and stupidity.

His eyes moved to the man sitting next to the worker. Negro. His eyes continued to the next, and held there. Contriving to move a step closer, he lost all sense of his surroundings. There sat a man whose type to him was like a rare clock to a collector. The man was staidly reading the *Times*. His skin was fair, the back of his neck flat and straight, his hair was probably blond beneath the new hat, and on squinting, Mr. Newman caught a glimpse of the Hindenburg bags under the subject's eyes. The mouth he could not see clearly, so he supplied it—broad and full-lipped. He relaxed with a certain satisfaction that always came to him when he played this secret game going to work. Probably he alone on this train knew that this gentleman with the square head and the fair skin was neither Swede, nor German, nor Norwegian, but a Jew.

He glanced again at the Negro and stared. Some day, he thought—as he always did when a Negro face confronted him—some day he must look into the various types of niggers. It was academic, he knew, for he did not need the information for his work, but still . . .

A hand touched his shoulder. Instantly his body stiffened as he turned.

"Hullo, Newman. Just looked up and seen you."

With the expression of affable condescension which changed his face whenever he encountered Fred, he asked, "How was it in your house, warm last night?"

"We always get a breeze through the back windows." Fred lived next door. "Didn't you get a breeze?" he asked, as though he lived in a breezier part of town.

"Oh certainly," Mr. Newman said, "I slept with a blanket."

"I'm putting a cot down cellar," Fred said, prodding Newman's arm. "Now that I got it all finished off down there it's cool as hell."

Newman considered. "Probably be damp down there."

"Not since it's finished off," Fred said, definitely.

Mr. Newman looked away inconclusively. For one thing Fred worked in the maintenance department of the same company, although in a different building, and wore his overalls to work as well as his overall manners. As he often did when confronted by Fred, Mr. Newman felt an irritated resolve to have his own cellar finished off whether he could afford it or not. He could never understand how this lumbering boar could be worth twice what he was to the same company, considering the importance of his own work and the exceptional nature of his talents. Neither did he enjoy being seen on the subway with Fred, who invariably jabbed him with his finger when he spoke.

"How'd you like the row on the street last night?" Fred asked. There was a suppressed smile of the risqué on his heavy jaw, which was attached to his face by two long, deep creases on either side.

"I heard it. How'd it wind up?" Mr. Newman asked, his handsome lower lip protruding judiciously as it did when he became intent.

"Oh, we went out and got Petey to bed. Boy, he was crocked."

"Was that Ahearn out there?" he whispered in surprise.

"Yeh, he was comin' home with a load on and he seen this Spic woman. She wasn't bad from what I seen of her." Fred had a habit of glancing behind him as he spoke.

"Did the police come?"

"Naa, we kicked her off the block and put Pete to bed."

The train stopped at a station and they were separated for a moment. When the doors closed Fred came back to Mr. Newman. They stood silent for several minutes. Mr. Newman kept looking up at Fred's hairy wrist which was very thick and probably powerful. He remembered how well Fred used to bowl last summer. It was strange how sometimes he enjoyed being with Fred and Fred's gang on the block and then at times like this could not bear him around. He remembered a picnic they had had at Marine Park and the fight Fred had . . .

"How do you like what's goin' on?" Fred's smile had gone but the two long creases remained like scars in his cheeks. He searched Newman's face with his puffed slit eyes.

"Going on how?" Newman asked.

"The neighborhood. They'll be movin' niggers in on us next."

"That's the way it goes, I guess."

"Everybody's been talking about the new element movin' around."

"That so."

"Only reason most of the block moved way out here was to get away from that element, and now they're trailin' us out here. You know that Finkelstein?"

"The candy store?"

"He's got all his relatives movin' into the house on the corner. The left-hand side next to the store." He glanced behind him.

This was what fascinated him about Fred. You wished he would speak more softly, but you somehow wanted him to go on for he said things you felt and dared not say. A foreboding of some sort of action always descended on him as Fred spoke. It was the same feeling he got around the pillars—something was building up inside the city, something thunderous and exhilarating.

"We're thinking of gettin' up a meeting. Jerry Buhl was talking to Petey about it."

"I thought that outfit was out."

"Out, nothin'," Fred said proudly, drawing down the corners of his mouth. In the mornings especially his lids were so puffed they nearly closed over his eyes. "Soon as the war's over and the boys get back you're goin' to see fireworks like there never was around here. We're just layin' low till the boys come home. This meetin' looks like the first start, y'know? Can't tell, the war might be over any day, the way it looks. We want to be on our feet and ready. Y'know?" He seemed to need Newman's confirmation, for his expression became uncertain.

"Uh huh," Newman muttered, waiting for him to speak on.

"You want to come? I'd take you along in the car."

"I'll leave the meetings to you fellows." Mr. Newman smiled encouragingly, as though deferring to Fred's powerful build. But actually he did not like the type of people at those meetings. Half of them were cracked and the other half looked like they hadn't had a new suit of clothes in years. "I'm not much good for meetings."

Fred nodded, unimpressed. His tongue slid over his cigar-worn teeth and he looked out a window at the lights rocketing by.

"All right," he said, blinking his eyes, rather hurt, "I thought I'd ask you. We just want to clean out the neighborhood, that's all. I thought you'd be interested. All we gotta do is make it hot for them and they'll pack up."

"Who?" Mr. Newman prompted avidly, his round face pleasantly interested.

"The Jews on our block. And then we'll help the boys across the avenue with the Spics. There'll be pushcarts on the streets before you know it." He seemed indignant at Newman. He had a pocked chin which now showed little red bumps.

Again the titillating of danger caught Mr. Newman. He was about to reply when he looked down and saw the Hindenburg Jew studying him. The man seemed about to get up and push him or something. He turned to Fred.

"I'll let you know. I may have to work late Thursday," he said quietly, turning his back on the Jew. The train was coming into his station. Fred touched his arm and said OK. The doors opened and Mr. Newman quickly stepped onto the platform. Instantly upon facing in the direction of his stairway his body began again to tremble inside. The train pulled away and he walked toward his exit, careful about his distance from the platform edge, and climbed the stairs.

On the sunny sidewalk he stood still for a moment and caught his wind. As he raised his arm to press his Panama more firmly onto his head, a cool drop of sweat fell from his armpit to his ribs. Every day of the past weeks he had halted on this corner, dreading what might await him in the office, and as always during these pauses his skin became creamy in the heat of the sun and his imagining. Walking neatly now, watchfully along the already baking sidewalk, he tried to think of his block and the houses all identical standing there like pickets on a fence. The memory of their sameness soothed his yearning for order, and he walked toward his building judiciously gathering the full force of his wits.

(1945)

From

CITY IN THE SUN
by Karon Kehoe

During the next year Tsuyo was too closely confined to her home to be aware of the growing antagonism of Californians to all things Japanese. Nor did Coke, in school, feel any unusual discrimination. But Katsuji moved in a different world. Because of his wide-flung reputation for impartial judgment he was called upon more than once to arbitrate the differences between factions of the Japanese fruit growers' associations. He came away distressed and discouraged from meetings of the Inter-Racial Council of Greater Los Angeles and he knew only too well that the voluntary affirmation of loyalty made by the Japanese-American Citizens' League—the J.A.C.L.—had been prompted as much by insecurity and apprehension as by patriotism. And Katsuji knew that the old poison of racial prejudice, administered to a gullible Coastal population by experienced politicians and irresponsible newspaper editors, was once more seeping along the arteries of commercial, political, and social cooperation. But Katsuji kept his knowledge and his suspicions from his family, discussing them only with other men as worried as he over the paralysis of half a century's effort toward assimilation. Hoping his fears were groundless, dreading they were not, he walked about Japanese Town quietly, waiting for an open break.

It came—suddenly and without warning—its repercussions shaking and even destroying the foundations of existence for all those of Japanese ancestry residing on the Coast.

For Tsuyo, and in a lesser degree for Coke, Pearl Harbor became inextricably associated with the day of the accident. Both struck with the same unforeseen swiftness, both carried the same stunning impact. Sunday, December 7, had started like any other Sunday. Breakfast—an especially good one Coke had thought—of orange juice, muffins, sour cream pancakes and melon—enjoyed by father and son in their bathrobes. Tsuyo allowed them that privilege on Sundays, providing they went upstairs immediately after breakfast and dressed for church. After church, they had come home and Tsuyo had gone to the kitchen to prepare dinner. Katsuji knelt on the floor to fix the latch on the back screen door. He called occasionally to Coke and Sandy, who were in the living room, to bring him the various tools he needed.

Coke had turned on the radio and was trying to accompany a recording of *Stardust* on his clarinet. While Sandy beat out a fast and intricate snare-drum accompaniment on the arm of the chair, the music suddenly stopped. There was a humming pause. Then the clipped voice of the announcer broke in: "We interrupt this program to bring you the latest N.B.C. news bulletin on the bombing of Pearl Harbor."

Katsuji sprang up from the floor, two nails still in the corner of his mouth. Coke stepped aside to let him tune in the station more clearly. Tsuyo came to the doorway of the kitchen, a chicken leg in one hand. She kept on pulling the skin from it as if she were turning the finger of a glove inside out. The boys stood motionless until the announcer finished, the smell of singed pin-feathers sharp in their nostrils. As the remaining bars of *Stardust* resumed, Katsuji snapped off the switch. "You know what this means?" Across the room his eyes sought Tsuyo's. They looked more serious than she had ever seen them.

"Criminy! It means we're at war with Japan!" Coke tried to encompass the enormity of what he had heard, but the news held no reality for him.

Sandy was the first to move. He looked at Mrs. Matsuki helplessly, feeling that he did not belong here, that he should go home. His own mother was frequently a trifle cool about his playing with Coke and he was sure she would object now. He pulled his sweater from the chair on which he had thrown it. "Well, good-by, Mrs. Matsuki. I guess I better be going. My mother will be worrying where I am," he added with unintentional irony.

Tsuyo nodded absently but Katsuji did not even notice the boy's embarrassed attempt to leave. He still stood looking at Tsuyo, phrases from recent conversations numbing his mind:

"If there ever is a war with Japan it's going to go hard with the Japanese and Japanese-Americans on the West Coast." . . . "You know how the California politicians use us as a scapegoat for everything that comes along—*if there ever is a war with Japan* the first thing they'll do is dig up the old labels MENACE IN OUR MIDST and YELLOW PERIL and spread them over the front page of every newspaper." . . . "They have already started to do it, hoping maybe there will be one." . . . "Hoping? They've actively worked toward that end for the last twenty years. *If there ever is a war with Japan* it won't be an accident!" . . . "After they spread the propaganda they'll start agitating for wholesale evacuation." . . . "We'll be driven from our homes and made to scurry across the country like the rats they call us, so the *white* sons and daughters of the golden West can have our farms and our lands for nothing." . . .

"They'll forget we've been here for twenty—thirty—forty years." . . . "They'll forget some of us fought in the last war—for democracy!" . . . "But they won't—they *can't*—forget our sons and daughters are American citizens." . . . "Oh, can't they? I'll wager that *if there ever is a war with Japan—*" Katsuji's eyes left Tsuyo and found Coke. What would this mean for the boy?

Coke had followed Sandy to the front door, obviously puzzled by Sandy's unusual behavior. Sandy never left until his mother had phoned at least twice.

"So long, kid, I'll see you tomorrow at school."

"Do you have to go? Gee, its only a quarter of two!"

Sandy took the steps two at a time. When he reached the sidewalk he broke into a run. He didn't look back, though Coke stood in the doorway staring after him him until his father peremptorily ordered him to help his mother with dinner.

As he counted out the knives and forks and set the table, he tried to get her to talk. "I wonder how many bombers they used? They said it happened at 7:55 this morning. We were still in bed then. Were you asleep then, Mom?"

"I don't remember, Coke."

"There are a lot of Japanese on Oahu, aren't there, Mom?"

"Yes, Coke."

"Mom, where is Oahu exactly? Have you ever been there?"

"No, I have never been there. Coke, hand me the potatomasher, please."

Coke watched her pour milk into the pan and mash the potatoes until they were as stiff as beaten egg whites. He was glad they were having chicken today. During the week the noonday meal was usually Japanese style—rice and tofu or misoshiru and occasionally tsukemono. Not bad but this was better. "He— the guy on the radio—said we were at war with Japan. Does that mean Pop will have to go?"

"I don't know."

"We could lick Japan anyday, couldn't we?"

Tsuyo wiped her hands and regarded him so queerly that Coke feared she was losing patience. She hadn't looked so cross since the day, shortly after she had come back from the hospital, when she discovered ants in the kitchen. She had sent him to the store for ant powder and on his hands and knees he had had to sprinkle it along the edge of the linoleum, behind the refrigerator and under the sink.

"Well, I bet we could!" he said defiantly, and walked into the dining room.

The grace Katsuji said was unusually long and the meal itself seemed interminable. Katsuji had gone out while dinner was still on the stove and bought an Extra. It lay on the chair beside the radio and Coke squirmed and twisted between mouthfuls, trying to read the headlines. "Hiroto, please sit straight in your chair and eat your dinner."

"But, gee, Pop—I don't see why—"

"Hiroto!"

"Well, I don't!"

"Coke, don't bother your father right now. Maybe we'll talk about it after dinner. There is a great deal that you don't understand and that I don't either but when your father is ready he will explain. Just eat your dinner now, son."

They were still sitting there, Coke so full he was content to eat his second helping of cream pudding at a normal speed, Tsuyo just finishing her first and Katsuji waiting for them, when the doorbell rang. Katsuji rose and, crossing through the living room and the hall, opened the door to a strange Caucasian voice. Coke let the last spoonful of pudding melt noiselessly in his mouth as he listened.

"Are you Mr. Walter Katsuji Matsuki?"

"Yes, I am."

"May we speak with you, please? We have come on business."

"Business? Surely." Courteously, Katsuji opened the door wider. "Won't you come in?" He stepped aside and two men preceded him into the living room. Both wore lightweight topcoats over their suits and, in addition to his hat, the taller of the two held some papers in his hand.

Neither made any move to sit down and the taller one reached into his inside topcoat pocket and, pulling out an identification card, held it toward Katsuji. "Mr. Matsuki, we represent the Federal Bureau of Investigation. My name is Webb and this is Mr. Heny." Without giving Katsuji time to acknowledge the introduction, he continued. "May we see your Alien Registration Certificate?"

Katsuji took the extended credentials and examined them carefully. "My Registration Certificate is in another suit, upstairs. I shall be glad to show it to you." He handed the card back to Webb and turned to go upstairs, but Webb detained him by putting his hand on Katsuji's arm.

Coke, who had nearly slid off his chair at the words "Federal Bureau of Investigation," now got up and stood quietly beside the table as he saw his mother doing. Real F.B.I. men! They didn't look it. They weren't any different from anybody else. He hardly blinked for fear Katsuji would send him away.

"We'll see your certificate in just a moment then." Webb paused. "Mr. Matsuki, we have a Presidential warrant for your internment."

"Internment?" Katsuji drew his breath in sharply. "Internment" was a new word. "You mean I am under arrest?"

"Shall we say the Department of Justice wishes to question you concerning your activities." The voice of the man Heny broke in, suave and as polite as Katsuji.

"I shall be glad to discuss my activities with the authorities. There are none that will not bear the most minute investigation."

"In that case, Mr. Matsuki, I am sure that after your hearing you will not be detained any longer than is absolutely necessary. Are you ready to accompany us?"

"Why—why—will they be holding hearings today?"

"I am sorry we can not tell you when your hearing will be. I am sure it will be held as soon as possible." Heny's expression was pleasantly deceptive. Katsuji knew he was speaking according to a fixed form.

"Where will I be interned?"

"It is our duty to deliver you to the Los Angeles Office of the Department of Justice immediately. I do not know where they intend to have you await your hearing."

Tsuyo had kept as quiet as Coke, but now she nearly upset the chair in her efforts to sit down again—quickly—before she fell down. The three men turned toward her. Her face had gone as pale as the cream pudding still in her dish and the well-healed scars stood out with grim clarity. Katsuji went to her side and chafed her hands.

"My wife has been sick. She was in a bad accident last year and has not entirely recovered." His manner was civil but his voice was cold and angry. "We have been very careful not to shock her."

"I am sorry, Mr. Matsuki; I did not realize that or I would have broken the news to you privately." Webb took Tsuyo's napkin from the table and dipped it in her drinking water. "Put this on the back of her neck. It might help her."

Tsuyo withdrew her hand from Katsuji's and raised it to her head. "I am all right now. I was just terribly dizzy for a moment." She turned to her husband. "Katsuji, I do not understand anything. First the news of the war and now these strange men come to take you away. What for? Why should you be arrested or that other word they said? What have you done?"

"I have not done anything, Tsuyo. And I am sure I shall not have any trouble proving that." He motioned to Coke to come closer. "Hiroto, I want you to take care of your mother until I come back."

"When will you be back?" The color in Tsuyo's face slowly returned and the scars receded.

Katsuji turned to the men. "When will I be back?"

Heny exchanged glances with Webb. "Mr. Matsuki, we can not answer that question but I wouldn't plan on it being right away—"

"Not right away? What does that mean? A few hours? A day? Two days?"

Webb and Heny were silent.

"What shall I do about my wife? She should not be left alone."

"I don't know, Mr. Matsuki. Isn't there someone you could call in? We are really very sorry—we don't like doing this either." The taller man's voice was not unkind. "The last place we went the woman was going to have a baby within a week"—he looked suddenly at Coke and quickly away—"and she had two other small children."

Tsuyo forced a smile to her lips, pride refusing to let these strangers see any more of her weakness—and tell it at the next place they invaded! "Katsuji, I can call in Laura Gordon if I need her and I have Coke." She put her arm around the boy. "Don't *you* worry."

Heny gave her a long, measuring look and Tsuyo's courage rose to the admiration it held. "Well, then, Mr. Matsuki, Mr. Webb will go with you up-stairs to check while you get your Alien Registration Certificate and pack a few things, and I'll have a look around down here, if you don't mind." He took out a notebook and moved about the room, stopping first before the radio. "This is short wave, I see. Are there any other radios in the house?"

Coke gulped as he thought of his own radio wired into the box he had spent so much time making. "Yes, sir, upstairs," he said under the pressure of his mother's arm. "But it's not short wave," he added quickly.

Heny made no reply. He moved swiftly from rooom to room, nothing escaping his notice, neither the picture on the piano of Katsuji's father and mother in Japan, nor any of the contents of Katsuji's desk. He asked Coke to show him what flashlights they had and he examined Katsuji's tool chest with inter-est. Coke found himself comparing this man with the many agents of the Ge-stapo he had seen in the movies. Those men always wore uniforms and carried guns, though. But maybe these men had guns, too. He studied Heny's stocky bulk, trying to find the tell-tale bulge that would reveal a weapon. Probably under his arm in a holster. He waited for Heny to raise or stretch his arm, but even when he did, to unclamp the top catch in the book case, Coke could detect nothing.

When Katsuji came down again he had a small suitcase with him. "In the event that I must remain overnight," he explained to Tsuyo.

"You will phone, Katsuji?"

"At the first possible opportunity. And, Hiroto, remember what I said."

"You mean about taking care of Mom? I sure will." He moved over to the radio and allied himself with his mother.

Mr. Heny and Mr. Webb walked toward the door, their backs turned to allow the Matsukis some slight privacy in parting. Both Katsuji and Tsuyo felt that these outsiders had seen quite enough of the intimacy of their home life so showed no more emotion than if they had been on a public thoroughfare.

"Tsuyo, I have taken most of the cash we have in the house. When you need more go to the bank."

"Yes, Katsuji."

"I shall be back as soon as I can. Good-by, son."

As the front door clicked, Coke looked at the clock and walked over to the window. No more than ten minutes had elapsed since the door bell had rung.

He peered through the curtains. So often he had dashed to this same place to see if his father were coming home. But not this time. He watched the three figures walking toward the gray Chevvy sedan, his father in the middle. In an-other minute they would drive away. Where were they going? What were they going to do with him?

"Look, they've got a gray Chevvy. It's got white side-walls, too. Mom, where are they taking Pop? And why wouldn't they say when he would be back? Mom—"

Tsuyo didn't answer so he turned from the window. She was still standing in the same place, the little bravado with which she had rallied to the occasion giving way to a stunned vagueness.

"Mom! Mom! Are you all right?" Coke frantically looked out the window, thinking to call to his father for help, but the sedan was just pulling away from the curb.

"Mom? You all right?" Her face was once more white. "Can I get you some water or an aspirin or—" If she would only speak, not just stand there looking at him but not seeing him. "Mom, I'll get you a chair." He brought an upright dining room chair, not so much to make her comfortable as to stave off by action the fear that had come with Katsuji's departure.

"Oh, Hiroto—"

"Yes, Mom?" His bravery leaped as she spoke to him.

"Oh, Hiroto—"

"What is it, Mom? What is it you want?"

"Oh, Hiroto—"

Why did she keep saying that over and over?

"Oh, Hiroto—"

(1946)

ACT OF FAITH
by Irwin Shaw

"Present it in a pitiful light," Olson was saying, as they picked their way through the mud toward the orderly room tent. "Three combat-scarred veterans, who fought their way from Omaha Beach to—what was the name of the town we fought our way to?"

"Konigstein." Seeger said.

"Konigstein." Olson lifted his right foot heavily out of a puddle and stared admiringly at the three pounds of mud clinging to his overshoe. "The backbone of the army. The noncommissioned officer. We deserve better of our country. Mention our decorations in passing."

"What decorations should I mention?" Seeger asked. "The marksman's medal?"

"Never quite made it," Olson said. "I had a cross-eyed scorer at the butts. Mention the bronze star, the silver star, the Croix de Guerre, with palms, the unit citation, the Congressional Medal of Honor."

"I'll mention them all." Seeger grinned. "You don't think the CO'll notice that we haven't won most of them, do you?"

"Gad, sir," Olson said with dignity, "do you think that one Southern military gentleman will dare doubt the word of another Southern military gentleman in the hour of victory?"

"I come from Ohio," Seeger said.

"Welch comes from Kansas," Olson said, coolly staring down a second lieutenant who was passing. The lieutenant made a nervous little jerk with his hand as though he expected a salute, then kept it rigid, as a slight superior smile of scorn twisted at the corner of Olson's mouth. The lieutenant dropped his eyes and splashed on through the mud. "You've heard of Kansas," Olson said. "Magnolia-scented Kansas."

"Of course," said Seeger. "I'm no fool."

"Do your duty by your men, Sergeant." Olson stopped to wipe the rain off his face and lectured him. "Highest ranking noncom present took the initiative and saved his comrades, at great personal risk, above and beyond the call of you-know-what, in the best traditions of the American army."

"I will throw myself in the breach," Seeger said.

"Welch and I can't ask more," said Olson, approvingly.

They walked heavily through the mud on the streets between the rows of tents. The camp stretched drearily over the Rheims plain, with the rain beating on the sagging tents. The division had been there over three weeks by now, waiting to be shipped home, and all the meager diversions of the neighborhood had been sampled and exhausted, and there was an air of watchful suspicion and impatience with the military life hanging over the camp now, and there was even reputed to be a staff sergeant in C Company who was laying odds they would not get back to America before July Fourth.

"I'm redeployable," Olson sang. "It's so enjoyable . . ." It was a jingle he had composed to no recognizable melody in the early days after the victory in Europe, when he had added up his points and found they only came to 63. "Tokyo, wait for me . . ."

They were going to be discharged as soon as they got back to the States, but Olson persisted in singing the song, occasionally adding a mournful stanza about dengue fever and brown girls with venereal disease. He was a short, round boy who had been flunked out of air cadets' school and transferred to the infantry, but whose spirits had not been damaged in the process. He had a high, childish voice and a pretty baby face. He was very good-natured, and had a girl waiting for him at the University of California, where he intended to finish his course at government expense when he got out of the army, and he was just the type who is killed off early and predictably and sadly in motion pictures about the war, but he had gone through four campaigns and six major battles without a scratch.

Seeger was a large, lanky boy, with a big nose, who had been wounded at Saint Lô, but had come back to his outfit in the Siegfried Line, quite unchanged. He was cheerful and dependable, and he knew his business and had broken in five or six second lieutenants who had been killed or wounded and the CO had tried to get him commissioned in the field, but the war had ended while the paperwork was being fumbled over at headquarters.

They reached the door of the orderly tent and stopped. "Be brave, Sergeant," Olson said. "Welch and I are depending on you."

"O.K.," Seeger said, and went in.

The tent had the dank, army-canvas smell that had been so much a part of Seeger's life in the past three years. The company clerk was reading a July, 1945, issue of the *Buffalo Courier-Express,* which had just reached him, and Captain Taney, the company CO, was seated at a sawbuck table he used as a desk, writing a letter to his wife, his lips pursed with effort. He was a small, fussy man, with sandy hair that was falling out. While the fighting had been going on, he had been lean and tense and his small voice had been cold and full of authority. But now he had relaxed, and a little pot belly was creeping up under his belt and he kept the top button of his trousers open when he could do it without too public loss of dignity. During the war Seeger had thought of him as a natural soldier, tireless, fanatic about detail, aggressive, severely anxious to kill Germans. But in the past few months Seeger had seen him relapsing gradually and pleasantly into a small-town wholesale hardware merchant, which he had been before the war, sedentary and a little shy, and, as he had once told Seeger, worried, here in the bleak champagne fields of France, about his daughter, who had just turned twelve and had a tendency to go after the boys and had been caught by her mother kissing a fifteen-year-old neighbor in the hammock after school.

"Hello, Seeger," he said, returning the salute in a mild, offhand gesture. "What's on your mind?"

"Am I disturbing you, sir?"

"Oh, no. Just writing a letter to my wife. You married, Seeger?" He peered at the tall boy standing before him.

"No, sir."

"It's very difficult," Taney sighed, pushing dissatisfiedly at the letter before him. "My wife complains I don't tell her I love her often enough. Been married fifteen years. You'd think she'd know by now." He smiled at Seeger. "I thought you were going to Paris," he said. "I signed the passes yesterday."

"That's what I came to see you about, sir."

"I suppose something's wrong with the passes." Taney spoke resignedly, like a man who has never quite got the hang of army regulations and has had requisitions, furloughs, requests for court-martial returned for correction in a baffling flood.

"No, sir," Seeger said. "The passes're fine. They start tomorrow. Well, it's just . . ." He looked around at the company clerk, who was on the sports page.

"This confidential?" Taney asked.

"If you don't mind, sir."

"Johnny," Taney said to the clerk, "go stand in the rain some place."

"Yes, sir," the clerk said, and slowly got up and walked out.

Taney looked shrewdly at Seeger, spoke in a secret whisper. "You pick up anything?" he asked.

Seeger grinned. "No, sir, haven't had my hands on a girl since Strasbourg."

"Ah, that's good." Taney leaned back, relieved, happy he didn't have to cope with the disapproval of the Medical Corps.

"It's—well," said Seeger, embarrassed, "it's hard to say—but it's money."

Taney shook his head sadly. "I know."

"We haven't been paid for three months, sir, and . . ."

"Damn it!" Taney stood up and shouted furiously. "I would like to take every bloody chair-warming old lady in the Finance Department and wring their necks."

The clerk stuck his head into the tent. "Anything wrong? You call for me, sir?"

"No," Taney shouted. "Get out of here."

The clerk ducked out.

Taney sat down again. "I suppose," he said, in a more normal voice, "they have their problems. Outfits being broken up, being moved all over the place. But it is rugged."

"It wouldn't be so bad," Seeger said. "But we're going to Paris tomorrow. Olson, Welch and myself. And you need money in Paris."

"Don't I know it." Taney wagged his head. "Do you know what I paid for a bottle of champagne on the Place Pigalle in September . . . ?" He paused significantly. "I won't tell you. You won't have any respect for me the rest of your life."

Seeger laughed. "Hanging," he said, "is too good for the guy who thought up the rate of exchange."

"I don't care if I never see another franc as long as I live." Taney waved his letter in the air, although it had been dry for a long time.

There was silence in the tent and Seeger swallowed a little embarrassedly, watching the CO wave the flimsy sheet of paper in regular sweeping movements. 'Sir," he said, "the truth is, I've come to borrow some money for Welch, Olson and myself. We'll pay it back out of the first pay we get, and that can't be too long from now. If you don't want to give it to us, just tell me and I'll understand and get the hell out of here. We don't like to ask, but you might just as well be dead as be in Paris broke."

Taney stopped waving his letter and put it down thoughtfully. He peered at it, wrinkling his brow, looking like an aged bookkeeper in the single gloomy light that hung in the middle of the tent.

"Just say the word, Captain," Seeger said, "and I'll blow . . ."

"Stay where you are, son," said Taney. He dug in his shirt pocket and took out a worn, sweat-stained wallet. He looked at it for a moment. "Alligator,'' he said, with automatic, absent pride. "My wife sent it to me when we were in England. Pounds don't fit in it. However . . ." He opened it and took out all the contents. There was a small pile of francs on the table in front of him. He counted them. "Four hundred francs," he said. "Eight bucks."

"Excuse me," Seeger said humbly. "I shouldn't have asked."

"Delighted," Taney said vigorously. "Absolutely delighted." He started dividing the francs into two piles. "Truth is, Seeger, most of my money goes home in allotments. And the truth is, I lost eleven hundred francs in a poker game three nights ago, and I ought to be ashamed of myself. Here . . ." He shoved one pile toward Seeger. "Two hundred francs."

Seeger looked down at the frayed, meretricious paper, which always seemed to him like stage money, anyway. "No, sir," he said, "I can't take it."

"Take it," Taney said. "That's a direct order."

Seeger slowly picked up the money, not looking at Taney. "Some time, sir," he said, "after we get out, you have to come over to my house and you and my father and my brother and I'll go on a real drunk."

"I regard that," Taney said, gravely, "as a solemn commitment."

They smiled at each other and Seeger started out.

"Have a drink for me," said Taney, "at the Café de la Paix. A small drink." He was sitting down to write his wife he loved her when Seeger went out of the tent.

Olson fell into step with Seeger and they walked silently through the mud between the tents.

"Well, *mon vieux?*" Olson said finally.

"Two hundred francs," said Seeger.

Olson groaned. "Two hundred francs! We won't be able to pinch a whore's behind on the Boulevard des Capucines for two hundred francs. That miserable, penny-loving Yankee!"

"He only had four hundred," Seeger said.

"I revise my opinion," said Olson.

They walked disconsolately and heavily back toward their tent.

Olson spoke only once before they got there. "These raincoats," he said, patting his. "Most ingenious invention of the war. Highest saturation point of any modern fabric. Collect more water per square inch, and hold it, than any material known to man. All hail the quartermaster!"

Welch was waiting at the entrance of their tent. He was standing there peering excitedly and short-sightedly out at the rain through his glasses, looking angry and tough, like a big-city hack-driver, individual and incorruptible even in the ten-million colored uniform. Every time Seeger came upon Welch unexpectedly, he couldn't help smiling at the belligerent stance, the harsh stare through the steel-rimmed GI glasses, which had nothing at all to do with the way Welch really was. "It's a family inheritance," Welch had once explained. "My whole family stands as though we were getting ready to rap a drunk with a beer glass. Even my old lady." Welch had six brothers, all devout, according to Welch, and Seeger from time to time idly pictured them standing in a row, on Sunday mornings in church, seemingly on the verge of general violence, amid the hushed Latin and Sabbath millinery.

"How much?" Welch asked loudly.

"Don't make us laugh," Olson said, pushing past him into the tent.

"What do you think I could get from the French for my combat jacket?" Seeger said. He went into the tent and lay down on his cot.

Welch followed them in and stood between the two of them, a superior smile on his face. "Boys," he said, "on a man's errand."

"I can just see us now," Olson murmured, lying on his cot with his hands clasped behind his head, "painting Montmartre red. Please bring on the naked dancing girls. Four bucks worth."

"I am not worried," Welch announced.

"Get out of here." Olson turned over on his stomach.

"I know where we can put our hands on sixty-five bucks." Welch looked triumphantly first at Olson, then at Seeger.

Olson turned over slowly and sat up. "I'll kill you," he said, "if you're kidding."

"While you guys are wasting your time," Welch said, "fooling around with the infantry, I used my head. I went into Reems and used my head."

"Rance," Olson said automatically. He had had two years of French in college and he felt, now that the war was over, that he had to introduce his friends to some of his culture.

"I got to talking to a captain in the air force," Welch said eagerly. "A little fat old paddle-footed captain that never got higher off the ground than the second floor of Com Z headquarters, and he told me that what he would admire to do more than anything else is take home a nice shiny German Luger pistol with him to show to the boys back in Pacific Grove, California."

Silence fell on the tent and Welch and Olson looked tentatively at Seeger.

"Sixty-five bucks for a Luger, these days," Olson said, "is a very good figure."

"They've been sellin' for as low as thirty-five," said Welch hesitantly. "I'll bet," he said to Seeger, "you could sell yours now and buy another one back when you get some dough, and make a clear twenty-five on the deal."

Seeger didn't say anything. He had killed the owner of the Luger, an enormous SS major, in Coblenz, behind some paper bales in a warehouse, and the major had fired at Seeger three times with it, once knicking his helmet, before Seeger hit him in the face at twenty feet. Seeger had kept the Luger, a long, heavy, well-balanced gun, very carefully since then, lugging it with him, hiding it at the bottom of his bedroll, oiling it three times a week, avoiding all opportunities of selling it, although he had been offered as much as a hundred dollars for it and several times eighty and ninety, while the war was still on, before German weapons became a glut on the market.

"Well," said Welch, "there's no hurry. I told the captain I'd see him tonight around 8 o'clock in front of the Lion D'Or Hotel. You got five hours to make up your mind. Plenty of time.''

"Me," said Olson, after a pause. "I won't say anything."

Seeger looked reflectively at his feet and the other two men avoided looking at him. Welch dug in his pocket. "I forgot," he said. "I picked up a letter for you." He handed it to Seeger.

"Thanks," Seeger said. He opened it absently, thinking about the Luger.

"Me," said Olson, "I won't say a bloody word. I'm just going to lie here and think about that nice fat air force captain."

Seeger grinned a little at him and went to the tent opening to read the letter in the light. The letter was from his father, and even from one glance at the handwriting, scrawly and hurried and spotted, so different from his father's usual steady, handsome, professorial script, he knew that something was wrong.

"Dear Norman," it read, "sometime in the future, you must forgive me for writing this letter. But I have been holding this in so long, and there is no one here I can talk to, and because of your brother's condition I must pretend to be cheerful and optimistic all the time at home, both with him and your mother, who has never been the same since Leonard was killed. You're the oldest now, and although I know we've never talked very seriously about anything before, you have been through a great deal by now, and I imagine you must have matured considerably, and you've seen so many different places and people. . . . Norman, I need help. While the war was on and you were fighting, I kept this to myself. It wouldn't have been fair to burden you with this. But now the war is over, and I no longer feel I can stand up under this alone. And you will have to face it some time when you get home, if you haven't faced it already, and perhaps we can help each other by facing it together. . . .''

"I'm redeployable," Olson was singing softly, on his cot. "It's so enjoyable, In the Pelilu mud, With the tropical crud . . .'' He fell silent after his burst of song.

Seeger blinked his eyes, at the entrance of the tent, in the wan rainy light, and went on reading his father's letter, on the stiff white stationery with the University letterhead in polite engraving at the top of each page.

"I've been feeling this coming on for a long time," the letter continued, "but it wasn't until last Sunday morning that something happened to make me feel it in its full force. I don't know how much you've guessed about the reason for Jacob's discharge from the army. It's true he was pretty badly wounded in the leg at Metz, but I've asked around, and I know that men with worse wounds were returned to duty after hospitalization. Jacob got a medical discharge, but I don't think it was from the shrapnel wound in his thigh. He is suffering now from what I suppose you call combat fatigue, and he is subject to fits of depression and hallucinations. Your mother and I thought that as time went by and the war and the army receded, he would grow better. Instead, he is growing worse. Last Sunday morning when I came down into the living room from upstairs he was crouched in his old uniform, next to the window, peering out . . .''

"What the hell," Olson was saying, "if we don't get the sixty-five bucks we can always go to the Louvre. I understand the Mona Lisa is back."

"I asked Jacob what he was doing," the letter went on. "He didn't turn around. 'I'm observing,' he said. 'V-1's and V-2's. Buzz-bombs and rockets. They're coming in by the hundreds.' I tried to reason with him and he told me to crouch and save myself from flying glass. To humor him I got down on the floor beside him and tried to tell him the war was over, that we were in Ohio, 4,000 miles away from the nearest spot where bombs had fallen, that America had never been touched. He wouldn't listen. 'These're the new rocket bombs,' he said, 'for the Jews.' "

"Did you ever hear of the Pantheon?" Olson asked loudly.

"No," said Welch.

"It's free."

"I'll go," said Welch.

Seeger shook his head a little and blinked his eyes before he went back to the letter.

"After that," his father went on, "Jacob seemed to forget about the bombs from time to time, but he kept saying that the mobs were coming up the street armed with bazookas and Browning automatic rifles. He mumbled incoherently a good deal of the time and kept walking back and forth saying, 'What's the situation? Do you know what the situation is?' And he told me he wasn't worried about himself, he was a soldier and he expected to be killed, but he was worried about Mother and myself and Leonard and you. He seemed to forget that Leonard was dead. I tried to calm him and get him back to bed before your mother came down, but he refused and wanted to set out immediately to rejoin his division. It was all terribly disjointed and at one time he took the ribbon he got for winning the Bronze star and threw it in the fireplace, then he got down on his hands and knees and picked it out of the ashes and made me pin it on him again, and he kept repeating, 'This is when they are coming for the Jews.' "

"The next war I'm in," said Olson, "they don't get me under the rank of colonel."

It had stopped raining by now and Seeger folded the unfinished letter and went outside. He walked slowly down to the end of the company street, and facing out across the empty, soaked French fields, scarred and neglected by various armies, he stopped and opened the letter again.

"I don't know what Jacob went through in the army," his father wrote, "that has done this to him. He never talks to me about the war and he refuses to go to a psychoanalyst, and from time to time he is his own bouncing, cheerful self, playing in tennis tournaments, and going around with a large group of girls. But he has devoured all the concentration camp reports, and I have found him weeping when the newspapers reported that a hundred Jews were killed in Tripoli some time ago.

"The terrible thing is, Norman, that I find myself coming to believe that it is not neurotic for a Jew to behave like this today. Perhaps Jacob is the normal one, and I, going about my business, teaching economics in a quiet class-room, pretending to understand that the world is comprehensible and orderly, am really the mad one. I ask you once more to forgive me for writing you a letter like this, so different from any letter or any conversation I've ever had with you. But it is crowding me, too. I do not see rockets and bombs, but I see other things.

"Wherever you go these days—restaurants, hotels, clubs, trains—you seem to hear talk about the Jews, mean, hateful, murderous talk. Whatever page you turn to in the newspapers you seem to find an article about Jews being killed somewhere on the face of the globe. And there are large, influential newspapers and well-known columnists who each day are growing more and more out-spoken and more popular. The day that Roosevelt died I heard a drunken man yelling outside a bar, 'Finally, they got the Jew out of the White House.' And some of the people who heard him merely laughed and nobody stopped him. And on V-E Day, in celebration, hoodlums in Los Angeles savagely beat a Jewish writer. It's difficult to know what to do, whom to fight, where to look for allies.

"Three months ago, for example, I stopped my Thursday night poker game, after playing with the same men for over ten years. John Reilly happened to say that the Jews were getting rich out of this war, and when I demanded an apology, he refused, and when I looked around at the faces of the men who had been my friends for so long, I could see they were not with me. And when I left the house no one said good night to me. I know the poison was spreading from Germany before the war and during it, but I had not realized it had come so close.

"And in my economics class, I find myself idiotically hedging in my lec-tures. I discover that I am loath to praise any liberal writer or any liberal act and find myself somehow annoyed and frightened to see an article of criticism of existing abuses signed by a Jewish name. And I hate to see Jewish names on important committees, and hate to read of Jews fighting for the poor, the oppressed, the cheated and hungry. Somehow, even in a country where my family has lived a hundred years, the enemy has won this subtle victory over me—he has made me disfranchise myself from honest causes by calling them foreign, Communist, using Jewish names connected with them as ammunition against them.

"And, most hateful of all, I find myself looking for Jewish names in the casualty lists and secretly being glad when I discover them there, to prove that there at least, among the dead and wounded, we belong. Three times, thanks to you and your brothers, I have found our name there, and, may God forgive me, at the expense of your blood and your brother's life, through my tears, I have felt that same twitch of satisfaction. . . .

"When I read the newspapers and see another story that Jews are still being killed in Poland, or Jews are requesting that they be given back their homes in France, or that they be allowed to enter some country where they will not be murdered, I am annoyed with them, I feel they are boring the rest of the world with their problems, they are making demands upon the rest of the world by being killed, they are disturbing everyone by being hungry and asking for the return of their property. If we could all fall through the crust of the earth and vanish in one hour, with our heroes and poets and prophets and martyrs, perhaps we would be doing the memory of the Jewish race a service. . . .

"This is how I feel today, son. I need some help. You've been to the war, you've fought and killed men, you've seen the people of other countries. Maybe you understand things that I don't understand. Maybe you see some hope somewhere. Help me. Your loving father."

Seeger folded the letter slowly, not seeing what he was doing because the tears were burning his eyes. He walked slowly and aimlessly across the dead autumn grass of the empty field, away from the camp.

He tried to wipe away his tears, because with his eyes full and dark, he kept seeing his father and brother crouched in the old-fashioned living room in Ohio and hearing his brother, dressed in the old, discarded uniform, saying, "These're the new rocket bombs. For the Jews."

He sighed, looking out over the bleak, wasted land. Now, he thought, now I have to think about it. He felt a slight, unreasonable twinge of anger at his father for presenting him with the necessity of thinking about it. The army was good about serious problems. While you were fighting, you were too busy and frightened and weary to think about anything, and at other times you were relaxing, putting your brain on a shelf, postponing everything to that impossible time of clarity and beauty after the war. Well, now, here was the impossible, clear, beautiful time, and here was his father, demanding that he think. There are all sorts of Jews, he thought, there are the sort whose every waking moment is ridden by the knowledge of Jewishness, who see signs against the Jew in every smile on a streetcar, every whisper, who see pogroms in every newspaper article, threats in every change of the weather, scorn in every handshake, death behind each closed door. He had not been like that. He was young, he was big and healthy and easy-going and people of all kinds had seemed to like him all his life, in the army and out. In America, especially, what was going on in Europe had seemed remote, unreal, unrelated to him. The chanting, bearded old men burning in the Nazi furnaces, and the dark-eyed women screaming prayers in Polish and Russian and German as they were pushed naked into the gas chambers had seemed as shadowy and almost as unrelated to him as he trotted out onto the Stadium field for a football game, as they must have been to the men named O'Dwyer and Wickersham and Poole who played in the line beside him.

They had seemed more related in Europe. Again and again in the towns that had been taken back from the Germans, gaunt, gray-faced men had stopped him humbly, looking searchingly at him, and had asked, peering at his long, lined, grimy face, under the anonymous helmet, "Are you a Jew?" Sometimes they asked it in English, sometimes French, or Yiddish. He didn't know French or Yiddish, but he learned to recognize the phrase. He had never understood exactly why they had asked the question, since they never demanded anything from him, rarely even could speak to him, until, one day in Strasbourg, a little bent old man and a small, shapeless woman had stopped him, and asked, in English, if he was Jewish.

"Yes," he said, smiling at them.

The two old people had smiled widely, like children. "Look," the old man had said to his wife. "A young American soldier. A Jew. And so large and strong." He had touched Seeger's arm reverently with the tips of his fingers, then had touched the Garand he was carrying. "And such a beautiful rifle . . ."

And there, for a moment, although he was not particularly sensitive, Seeger got an inkling of why he had been stopped and questioned by so many before. Here, to these bent, exhausted old people, ravaged of their families, familiar with flight and death for so many years, was a symbol of continuing life. A large young man in the uniform of the liberator, blood, as they thought, of their blood, but not in hiding, not quivering in fear and helplessness, but striding secure and victorious down the street, armed and capable of inflicting terrible destruction on his enemies.

Seeger had kissed the old lady on the cheek and she had wept and the old man had scolded her for it, while shaking Seeger's hand fervently and thankfully before saying good-bye.

And, thinking back on it, it was silly to pretend that, even before his father's letter, he had been like any other American soldier going through the war. When he had stood over the huge dead SS major with the face blown in by his bullets in the warehouse in Coblenz, and taken the pistol from the dead hand, he had tasted a strange little extra flavor of triumph. How many Jews, he'd thought, has this man killed, how fitting it is that I've killed him. Neither Olson nor Welch, who were like his brothers, would have felt that in picking up the Luger, its barrel still hot from the last shots its owner had fired before dying. And he had resolved that he was going to make sure to take this gun back with him to America, and plug it and keep it on his desk at home, as a kind of vague, half-understood sign to himself that justice had once been done and he had been its instrument.

Maybe, he thought, maybe I'd better take it back with me, but not as a memento. Not plugged, but loaded. America by now was a strange country for him. He had been away a long time and he wasn't sure what was waiting for him when he got home. If the mobs were coming down the street toward his house, he was not going to die singing and praying.

When he was taking basic training he'd heard a scrawny, clerk-like-looking soldier from Boston talking at the other end of the PX bar, over the watered beer. "The boys at the office," the scratchy voice was saying, "gave me a party before I left. And they told me one thing. 'Charlie,' they said, 'hold onto your bayonet. We're going to be able to use it when you get back. On the Yids.' "

He hadn't said anything then, because he'd felt it was neither possible nor desirable to fight against every random overheard voice raised against the Jews from one end of the world to another. But again and again, at odd moments, lying on a barracks cot, or stretched out trying to sleep on the floor of a ruined French farmhouse, he had heard that voice, harsh, satisfied, heavy with hate and ignorance, saying above the beery grumble of apprentice soldiers at the bar, "Hold onto your bayonet. . . ."

And the other stories—Jews collected stories of hatred and injustice and inklings of doom like a special, lunatic kind of miser. The story of the naval officer, commander of a small vessel off the Aleutians, who, in the officers' wardroom, had complained that he hated the Jews because it was the Jews who had demanded that the Germans be beaten first and the forces in the Pacific had been starved in consequence. And when one of his junior officers, who had just come aboard, had objected and told the commander that he was a Jew, the commander had risen from the table and said, "Mister, the Constitution of the United States says I have to serve in the same navy with Jews, but it doesn't say I have to eat at the same table with them." In the fogs and the cold, swelling Arctic seas off the Aleutians, in a small boat, subject to sudden, mortal attack at any moment . . .

And the two young combat engineers in an attached company on D Day, when they were lying off the coast right before climbing down into the landing barges. "There's France," one of them had said.

"What's it like?" the second one had asked, peering out across the miles of water toward the smoking coast.

"Like every place else," the first one had answered. "The Jews've made all the dough during the war."

"Shut up!" Seeger had said, helplessly thinking of the dead, destroyed, wandering, starving Jews of France. The engineers had shut up, and they'd climbed down together into the heaving boat, and gone into the beach together.

And the million other stories. Jews, even the most normal and best adjusted of them, became living treasuries of them, scraps of malice and bloodthirstiness, clever and confusing and cunningly twisted so that every act by every Jew became suspect and blameworthy and hateful. Seeger had heard the stories, and had made an almost conscious effort to forget them. Now, holding his father's letter in his hand, he remembered them all.

He stared unseeingly out in front of him. Maybe, he thought, maybe it would've been better to have been killed in the war, like Leonard. Simpler. Leonard would never have to face a crowd coming for his mother and father. Leonard would not have to listen and collect these hideous, fascinating little stories that made of every Jew a stranger in any town, on any field, on the face of the earth. He had come so close to being killed so many times, it would have been so easy, so neat and final.

Seeger shook his head. It was ridiculous to feel like that, and he was ashamed of himself for the weak moment. At the age of twenty-one, death was not an answer.

"Seeger!" It was Olson's voice. He and Welch had sloshed silently up behind Seeger, standing in the open field. "Seeger, *mon vieux,* what're you doing—grazing?"

Seeger turned slowly to them. "I wanted to read my letter," he said.

Olson looked closely at him. They had been together so long, through so many things, that flickers and hints of expression on each other's faces were recognized and acted upon. "Anything wrong?" Olson asked.

"No," said Seeger. "Nothing much."

"Norman," Welch said, his voice young and solemn. "Norman, we've been talking, Olson and me. We decided—you're pretty attached to that Luger, and maybe—if you—well . . ."

"What he's trying to say," said Olson, "is we withdraw the request. If you want to sell it, O.K. If you don't, don't do it for our sake. Honest."

Seeger looked at them, standing there, disreputable and tough and familiar. "I haven't made up my mind yet," he said.

"Anything you decide," Welch said oratorically, "is perfectly all right with us. Perfectly."

They walked aimlessly and silently across the field, away from camp. As they walked, their shoes making a wet, sliding sound in the damp, dead grass, Seeger thought of the time Olson had covered him in the little town outside Cherbourg, when Seeger had been caught going down the side of a street by four Germans with a machine gun on the second story of a house on the corner and Olson had had to stand out in the middle of the street with no cover at all for more than a minute, firing continuously, so that Seeger could get away alive. And he thought of the time outside Saint Lô when he had been wounded and had lain in a minefield for three hours and Welch and Captain Taney had come looking for him in the darkness and had found him and picked him up and run for it, all of them expecting to get blown up any second.

And he thought of all the drinks they'd had together and the long marches and the cold winter together, and all the girls they'd gone out with together, and he thought of his father and brother crouching behind the window in Ohio waiting for the rockets and the crowds armed with Browning automatic rifles.

"Say," he stopped and stood facing them. "Say, what do you guys think of the Jews?"

Welch and Olson looked at each other, and Olson glanced down at the letter in Seeger's hand.

"Jews?" Olson said finally. "What're they? Welch, you ever hear of the Jews?"

Welch looked thoughtfully at the gray sky. "No," he said. "But remember, I'm an uneducated fellow."

"Sorry, Bud," Olson said, turning to Seeger. "We can't help you. Ask us another question. Maybe we'll do better."

Seeger peered at the faces of his friends. He would have to rely upon them, later on, out of uniform, on their native streets, more than he had ever relied on them on the bullet-swept street and in the dark minefield in France. Welch and Olson stared back at him, troubled, their faces candid and tough and dependable.

"What time," Seeger asked, "did you tell that captain you'd meet him?"

"Eight o'clock," Welch said. "But we don't have to go. If you have any feeling about that gun . . ."

"We'll meet him," Seeger said. "We can use that sixty-five bucks."

"Listen," Olson said, "I know how much you like that gun and I'll feel like a heel if you sell it."

"Forget it," Seeger said, starting to walk again. "What could I use it for in America?"

(1946)

From

FROM AFRICA TO AMERICA
by Alfred Kreymborg

And then he heard a sound,
Not from the earth or air but more profound:
A human sound, a truly human sound,
And traced it to where it silenced every drum:
A youth in a sailor suit sitting alone:
A Negro in blue sitting there and weeping,
Who raised his head and finding a man nearby,
Wiped his dark eyes and sat up straight again,
Or just as though he were no longer there.

The man was too embarrassed to approach
Or back away and so he hesitated.
Here was a color he loved who drew no shade
Between himself and the darkest Africa
America still harbored like a slave.
Yet though he loved the Negro gods and prophets
And poets and daring men from Douglass to
Robeson the saint who resembled Saint Paul,
He never knew just how one could efface
The difference he seldom felt but must have shown

To those who feared advances might betray
The white man's trade, or white man's colored shade.
And "Sometimes I feel like a motherless child" myself,
Or "Steal away, steal away to Jesus,"
Or "Steal away, steal away home,"
Whenever I wish to speak and only say
A word or two betraying an awkward mood
I never meant to convey. I touch no heart
Or communion in these sensitive people
Beyond a courteous interval and so
Take my dilemma to the past or hear,
"I been rebuked and I been scorned. .
I been rebuked and I been scorned. .
Chillun, I been rebuked and I been scorned,
I's had a hard time, sho's you born."

"Do you mind," said the man, "if I sit down?"
The sailor looked at him and first he frowned.
Then he moved as if he needed moving
Over and said, "No sir, I don't mind."
But then he seemed to wish rise. .
And the man said, "Do you have to go. ."
The man said, "Do you have to go
Just because I came along?"
"No sir, no, I'm all right now. .
No, sir, yes, I'm all right now. ."
And looked at the man who must have smiled. .
And turned again like a lost child
Of Africa, America. .
And said, "I've had some trouble, sir. ."
And said, "I didn't think I'd find. .
Here in the north, if you don't mind. ."
"But I am not a Northerner. .
And I'm not a Southerner. .
Go right ahead!"
                        And the sailor told
A tale as simple and as old
As the Pyramids in a quiet tone
That showed he no longer felt alone. . . .

He was riding along and feeling good
On top of a bus and feeling good
Because he had a holiday

To do what he felt like doing now.
He'd felt that way all morning too
And felt that way all afternoon,
Never so happy anywhere
Sitting up front all by himself:
The happiest day he'd ever known
So far from home, far from home,
Free in his sailor uniform.
And proud of that blue uniform,
Watched the crowds move back and forth
On the avenue, Fifth Avenue,
The greatest crowd he'd ever seen
With nothing between, nothing between—
When suddenly he heard a man,
A Southerner in uniform,
Call from the rear, "You come back here!
Here, Nigger's where you belong!"
He knew the language and the drawl,
And, as the whole blue sky caved in
And he tried to rise, some woman cried—
"No, you stay right where you are!
This country's free and so are we:
We don't go in for Jim Crow here!"

The woman was white. He was terrified
And hurried away to the rear where he
Was surrounded by other women who
Also clamored and all he could do
Was to stagger down the swaying stair
And beg the conductor, Stop the car!
And he'd been walking quite a while
Not knowing just where to go
When he saw the trees and a park bench.
And this was just about as far
As he could go—about this far. . . .

And the white man said, "What an outrage, Man!
What a dirty, filthy American!"
"I wouldn't say that, sir, that's his way—
It'll always be that way down there."
"Where do you come from?"
                              "Tuskegee, sir—
Booker Washington's school—"
                              "I know."

"And I was in the senior class
When I heard the call—"
                    "And you answered that?"
"I couldn't leave my country flat."
"Your country?—"
                    "Yes sir, I enlisted.
They sent me to a training camp
And there I trained with a colored crew
From morning to dark—"
                    "And you came to this?"
"Yes, I came to this city where
Our crew was attached to a submarine
That settled down for a day or two
Where I'm not allowed to say—
But you can imagine!" The lad smiled,
Or no longer looked like a lost child. . . .

What could he say or do, the man
Who glanced at this strange American
And found in his eyes (that looked elsewhere)
Something he couldn't understand?
He thought of the land and of the sea
Through which the slave ships came ashore
Over three hundred years ago,
And men and women were brought like cattle
And even their children turned to chattel;
And then he heard the old chains rattle
As North and South went forth to battle,
A battle that might be fought again.
And yet this Negro had more blood
To shed in the name of his native land
And took his Bible and song in hand,
Much more steadfast than any White
Who made him cross the railroad tracks
And attached a poll-tax to his vote
As a kind of careful antidote
In case he fancied equality
Was meant for him. Must they always free
Nothing at all from slavery?

The dark lad stirred—"I'd better be going."
"What's your hurry—you're on leave?"
He stood up tall but didn't reply.

"How long have you got?"
                              "Till sunset now."
"But that's an hour or two away?"
"Yes, but somehow I feel today
I belong on the ship—if you don't mind."
"Why should I mind? You're at home down there,
Aren't you now?"
                    "Yes, I'm at home."
The man arose and said, "Good luck
To you—" and stuck out a hand
The Negro glanced at, strangely took
For a moment or so, and then slipped by.
But not before he made a speech
Or tried to make a speech that said,
"And thank you, sir— You may be white—
But you have the heart of a colored man,"
And possibly frightened a little, ran
Two or three steps; then settled down
To a regular pace and moved away
From the blue, the Blue and Gray again. . . .

                                        (1946)

From

THE SIDE OF THE ANGELS
by Robert McLaughlin

"Have you done any boxing in the Army?" his uncle asked anxiously.

"Only once," said Tom. "They put a ring up between the barracks and I got patsied into it."

"How did you make out? Who was the guy you fought?"

"He was a Fancy Dan. We spent most of our time in clinches."

"It must have looked lousy," said Uncle Ed, with feeling. "What with you bulling in the way you do, and him tying you up. I'm surprised they didn't throw you both out of the ring."

"They just about did."

"Well, you can take care of yourself, that's the main thing," said his uncle. "How about a glass of beer, boy, or would you prefer something stronger?"

"Beer's fine," said Tom. "Do you still have a ball club? Or are they a war casualty?"

Uncle Ed grinned with pleasure. "No, we've still got a team. It's not like the old days, of course. A lot of the boys are gone now. But we took a nice little four-to-one game from National Fiber this morning."

His uncle went on to tell him about the ball club, about new players and what had happened to the old ones. Uncle Ed's company had a team in an industrial league in Queens, and his fierce partisanship of the team that represented the Egan Construction Company was one of the consuming passions of his life. And he was a bleeder. If his team lost a Sunday game, he wasn't fit to live with. When they won, you could get almost anything from him.

Uncle Ed went to the kitchen for the beer and returned accompanied by his dog, Daniel, a mean-tempered animal who was given to vomiting and fainting. Daniel skittered frantically around the room before he began ducking and darting at Tom, who cuffed him amiably. Then the dog, tongue-hanging and breathing hard, went over to Uncle Ed and slavered a little on the cuff of his trousers.

Uncle Ed gave Tom a résumé of the morning's game. "I've got a pretty clever little bunch this year," he said, "but they're awful sad at the plate. There isn't a one of them who can be depended on to get the ball out of the infield. But they're fast and they play tight defensive ball, and I guess we'll do all right this season."

"Are you still keeping the records for the entire league?" Tom asked.

"Sure, why not?" Uncle Ed answered, with a slight embarrassment, and Tom could remember him sitting at the dining-room table, surrounded by box scores and ledgers in which he kept the batting and pitching records of all the players. The mathematics of batting averages gave him an intense pleasure. Now he said: "Rosen Drug has a pretty good team this year. They look like the ones who'll give us the most trouble. I'll have to watch Ikey Rosen and see he doesn't try to run in some ringers on me."

"If there're any ringers around, they'll be playing in the majors, won't they?" asked Tom.

Uncle Ed thought that was a good one and laughed heartily. Then he said: "Say, speaking of our Semitic friends, have you seen 'The First American'?"

"The what?"

"I've got it right here," said his uncle, feeling in his pockets. "No, damn it, I guess it's in my room."

Aunt Loretta announced that dinner was ready. Uncle Ed said: "You go on in, boy, I want to find that," and went on down the hall to his room.

"My, it's good to see you again, Tom," said his aunt. "You've put on some weight, haven't you?"

Tom said yes, about ten pounds, and told her he'd run into Clark at the races. She brightened and then said with regret that they hadn't seen Clark in ages. But it was obvious that his memory was bright, and Tom marveled at his brother's effortless charming of people.

"You know, Tom," said Aunt Loretta, "Clark and Peggy Muller should never have broken up. Little Peggy was the right girl for Clark and I think he knows it now. But he was just too wild in those days; no matter how hard she tried, poor girl, she just couldn't domesticate him.'' This in the face of the evidence, which was that Peggy married another man two days after her divorce from Clark.

Uncle Ed came into the dining-room, said: "Here it is. Have you seen this boy?'' and, sitting down, passed a mimeographed sheet to Tom.

Tom read:

The First American

The first American to kill a Jap soldier was
MIKE MURPHY.
The first American bomber to sink a Jap battleship was
COLIN KELLY.
The first American flier to bag a Jap plane was
EDWARD O'HARE.
The first American Coast Guard to detect a German spy was
JOHN CULLEN.
The first American to be eulogized by the President for bravery was
JOHN PATRICK POWER.
The first American to get Four New Tires was
NATHAN GOLDSTEIN.

Tom passed it back. "Very funny,'' he said, flatly.

Uncle Ed laughed. "It is funny, damn it. And it's true, too. Tell me— how many Jews have you seen in the Army?''

"Quite a lot,'' said Tom.

"Well, by God,'' said his uncle, "I'm damned if I know where they're coming from. It's a cinch they're not coming from New York. Just take a look around you; they're all still walking the streets, fat and prosperous, and pushing everyone else off the sidewalk.''

"Oh, Christ,'' thought Tom. He said: "You don't think all the draft boards have been bribed, do you?''

"I don't know how the hell they do it. But they're slippery customers, you know that. Pat Donlan's boy—you remember him, don't you?—he went in a couple of weeks ago. He said a lot of Jews left his draft board with him and went down to Grand Central with him, but when he showed up to be shipped off to Fort Dix, there wasn't a one of them around. They'd gotten out of it somewhere along the line.''

"Will you have some more chicken, darling?'' asked Aunt Loretta. "Ed, give Tom another helping of chicken.''

"Sure, boy. Pass your plate.''

"No, thanks.''

But Ed reached over, took his plate, heaped more chicken on it.

"Why do you hate the Jews?'' Tom asked curiously.

"Hate the Jews! God, boy, I don't hate 'em. I admire them. Look how they've got the whole world fighting their battle against Germany for them.'' He shook his head with heavy humor. "They're just too smart for us, that's all.''

Tom said: "As far as percentages go, more Jews have been killed in this war than any other group."

"What do you mean?" demanded his uncle.

"In concentration camps—"

"Oh, atrocities," said his Uncle Ed. "We heard a lot about them in the last war, too, and after it was over we found out it was a lot of propaganda." Then he looked sharply at Tom. "Why are you getting so steamed up about the Jews, sonny? What have they ever done for you that you're standing up for them?"

For the sake of the effect, Tom said: "I'm going to marry a Jew."

"Why, Tom!" cried his aunt. "Why, I didn't even know you had a special girl, much less thinking about marrying."

Uncle Ed frowned thoughtfully. He said: "Well, that's your funeral, Tom, my boy. I've never seen it work out, but maybe you can do it." He buttered a slice of bread. "What's your girl's name?"

Tom decided Rodia Martin would call for too many complicated explanations. He said: "Ruth Goldberg."

Uncle Ed shook his head. "I wish you all the luck. You'll need it, I'm thinking."

Aunt Loretta said: "Do you have her picture, Tom? Does she live here in New York? I'd love to meet her."

Tom said to his uncle: "You can see why I'm interested in Jews. And I'd still like to know why you hate them."

Uncle Ed pushed back a little from the table. "If you'd ever been in business, Tom, you wouldn't have to ask a question like that. No disrespect to your future bride, boy, but you just can't trust a Jew."

Tom said calmly: "Then if they'd just change their business ethics, you'd think they were all right, is that it?"

"They'd have to change a lot more than that," said his uncle. "Their ethics, their faces—"

"All right," said Tom, "their faces. Do you think you can always tell a Jew from an Italian or a Greek or an Irishman? What about old Mr. Haggerty? Doesn't he look like your conception of a Jew—a hooked nose, dark skin, stoop-shouldered."

"I can tell 'em apart often enough," said his uncle. Then he went on angrily: "What I chiefly don't like about them is that they never stand on their own two feet. Someone else always has to do their fighting for them. They ought to get tough and have ordinary self-respect. If little Ikey or Moe gets slugged by the bad boys on the corner, instead of running for mamma or the police, he ought to get a few friends together and do some slugging back. I get so sick of all this pap I read about de-moc-ra-cy," he drew the word out. "Democracy doesn't mean running squeaking to the courts every time your toe gets stepped on. You've got to stand up for your rights in the street, too."

"When Jews do that, you complain that they're pushing you off the sidewalk," Tom said.

His uncle ignored that. "Hell, the Irish have been through much the same thing. I see the ads in the paper now: 'Restricted' and 'Select Clientele' and 'Gentiles only,' and I know that back in my father's time they were a lot tougher about it. The ads said: 'No Irish need apply,' and they weren't fooling, either.

"Why, it wasn't more than fifty or sixty years ago that mobs were pouring through Irishtowns in Boston and Philadelphia, burning and sacking the churches, not just sneaking around painting swastikas on the door like they do to synagogues now. Anti-Irishism was beaten right where it started—right in the streets. It was beaten by tough Micks knocking tough Know-Nothings and APA's on the head. After a while the bully-boys found it wasn't so much fun ganging up on the Irish because the Irish ganged up on them in return. Life's tough work, Tom, and races adjust to it just like individuals do."

Tom said: "I agree there are a lot of similarities between the position of the Jews in America today, and that of the Irish a generation ago. But instead of helping you to understand the Jews, it makes you hate them. The Irish are becoming assimilated. There aren't any Irishtowns in the big cities any more. That will happen with the Jews, too."

Uncle Ed chuckled. "You're going to have to do a lot of assimilating to destroy the curve of a Jew's proboscis."

Tom shrugged. "You get mad if anyone thinks the Irish resemble the old character of the stage Irishman—the ape-faced Mick of *Punch*. But you're a sucker for another myth—the *Der Stürmer* Jew. All Jews don't have hooked noses and accents. Lots of them have been in America longer than we have."

"What do you mean?" cried his uncle. "Don't you know that over sixty per cent of George Washington's army was Irish?"

Tom saw that they were on a merry-go-round and that nothing would be accomplished. By dinner's end both he and his uncle were tight-lipped and unforgiving.

(1947)

From

THE NAKED AND THE DEAD
by Norman Mailer

Goldstein and Martinez were talking about America. By chance they had chosen cots next to each other, and they spent the afternoon lying on them, their ponchos drawn over their bodies. Goldstein was feeling rather happy. He had never been particularly close to Martinez before, but they had been chatting for

several hours and their confidences were becoming intimate. Goldstein was always satisfied if he could be friendly with someone; his ingenuous nature was
always trusting. One of the main reasons for this wretchedness in the platoon
was that his friendships never seemed to last. Men with whom he would have
long amiable conversations would wound him or disregard him the next day,
and he never understood it. To Goldstein, men were friends or they weren't
friends; he could not comprehend any variations or disloyalties. He was unhappy because he felt continually betrayed.

Yet he never became completely disheartened. Essentially he was an active man, a positive man. If his feelings were bruised, if another friend had
proved himself undependable, Goldstein would nurse his pains, but almost always he would recover and sally out again. The succession of rebuffs he had
suffered in the platoon had made him more wily, more cautious in what he said
and did. But still, Goldstein was too affectionate to possess any real defenses;
at the first positive hint of friendship he was ready to forget all his grievances
and respond with warmth and simplicity. Now he felt he knew Martinez. If he
had phrased his opinion he would have said to himself, Martinez is a very fine
fellow. He's a little quiet but he's a nice guy. Very democratic for a sergeant.

"You know in America," Martinez was saying, "lots of opportunity."

"Oh, there is," Goldstein nodded sagely. "I know I've got plans for setting up my own business, because I've considered it a lot, and a man has to
strike out for himself if he wants to get ahead. There's a lot to be said for steady
wages and security, but I'd rather be my own boss."

Martinez nodded. "Lots of money in your own business, huh?"

"Sometimes."

Martinez considered this. Money! A little perspiration formed on his palms.
He thought for a moment of a man named Ysidro Juaninez, a brothelkeeper
who had always fascinated him when he was a child. He shivered as he remembered the way Ysidro would hold a thick sheaf of dollar bills in his hand. "After
the war maybe I get out of the Army."

"You certainly ought to," Goldstein said. "I mean you're an intelligent
fellow and you're dependable."

Martinez sighed. "Still . . . ." He did not know how to say it. He was
always embarrassed at mentioning the fact that he was a Mexican. He thought
it was bad manners as if he were blaming the man he told it to, implying that
it was his fault there were no good jobs for him. Besides, there was always the
irrational hope he might be taken for a pure Spaniard.

"Still, I'm no educated," he said.

Goldstein shook his head in commiseration. "That's an obstacle, it's true.
I've always wanted a college education, and I feel its absence. But for business
a good head can carry you through. I really believe in being honest and sincere
in business; all the really big men got where they are through decency."

Martinez nodded. He wondered how big a room a very rich man needed
to hold his money. Images of rich clothing, of shoeshines and hand-painted ties,

a succession of tall blonde women with hard cold grace and brittle charm languished in his head. "A rich man do anything he damn well feel like it," Martinez said with admiration.

"Well, if I were rich I'd like to be charitable. And . . . what I want is to be well off, and have a nice house, some security . . . Do you know New York?"

"No."

"Anyway there's a suburb I'd like to live in," Goldstein said, nodding his head. "It's really a fine place, and nice people in it, cultured, refined. I wouldn't like my son to grow up the way I did."

Martinez nodded sagely. He never possessed any definite convictions or ambitions, and he always felt humble when he talked to a man who had sharp complete plans. "America's a good country," he said sincerely. He had a glow of righteous patriotism for a moment; half-remembered was his image of a schoolroom and the children singing "My Country 'Tis of Thee." For the first time in many years he thought of being an aviator, and felt a confused desire. "I learn to read good in school," he said. "The teacher thought I was smart."

"I'm sure she did," Goldstein said with conviction.

The water was less rough, and the spray had become infrequent. Martinez looked about the boat, listened for a moment to the random sounds of conversation, and shrugged again. "Long trip," he said.

Gallagher had come back to his cot, which was adjacent to Martinez's, and he lay down without saying anything. Goldstein was uncomfortable; he had not spoken to Gallagher for over a month. "It's a wonder none of the men are seasick," Goldstein said at last. "These boats aren't good for traveling."

"Roth, Wyman, they're sick," Martinez said.

Goldstein shrugged proudly. "I don't mind it. I'm used to being on boats. A friend of mine had a sailboat on Long Island, and in the summer I used to go out with him a lot. I enjoyed it thoroughly." He thought of the Sound and the pale dunes that surrounded it. "It was beautiful there. You know you can't beat America for beautiful country."

"You can say that again, brother," Gallagher snorted suddenly.

It was just his way of talking, Goldstein decided. He didn't mean any harm. "Did you ever go out on boats, Gallagher?" he asked mildly.

Gallagher raised himself on an elbow. "Aaah, I went canoeing once in a while out on the Charles, past West Roxbury. Used to go with my wife." He said it first, and then thought about it. His face altered for an instant, assumed a numb stricken cast.

"Oh, I'm sorry," Goldstein breathed.

"That's all right." Gallagher felt some irritation at getting sympathy from a Jew. "Forget it," he added, a little meaninglessly. But he was becoming tender again, dissolving in a bath of self-pity and pleasant gentle sorrow. "Look," he said abruptly, "you got a kid, ain't ya?"

Goldstein nodded. "Oh, yes," he answered eagerly. "My boy is three years old now. Wait, I'll show you a picture of him.'' With some effort, he rolled over on the cot and withdrew his wallet from his back pocket. ''This isn't a good picture of him,'' Goldstein apologized, ''he's really one of the handsomest children you could imagine. We've got a big picture at home of him that we had a professional photographer take, and honestly you couldn't beat it. It could win a prize.''

Gallagher stared at the picture. ''Yeah . . . yeah, he's a cute kid, all right.'' He was a little bewildered, uncomfortable with the praise that welled clumsily out of his mouth. He looked at the picture again, seeing it really for the first time, and he sighed. In the one letter he had written home since Mary died he had asked for a picture of his child. He had been waiting with increasing impatience for it ever since, and it had become an important need in his life. He would idle away many dull inactive hours daydreaming about his child, wondering what it looked like. Although he had not been told, he assumed it was a boy. ''That's a real cute kid,'' he said in a rough voice. He fingered the side of the cot for a moment. Surmounting his embarrassment, he blurted, ''Hey, what is it like, havin' a kid?''

Goldstein debated for a moment, as if to give the definitive answer. ''Oh, it's a lot of . . . of joy.'' He had been about to say *''nochis.''* ''But there's a lot of heartaches in it too. You worry about them a lot, and of course there are the economic difficulties.''

''Yeah.'' Gallagher nodded his head in agreement.

Goldstein went on talking. He had some constraint, for Gallagher was the man he had hated most in the platoon. The warmth and friendliness he felt toward him now were perplexing. Goldstein was self-conscious when he saw himself as a Jew talking to a Gentile; then every action, every word, was dictated to a great extent by his desire to make a good impression. Although he was gratified when people liked him, part of his satisfaction came from the idea that they were liking a Jew. And so he tried to say only the things that would please Gallagher.

Yet in talking about his family, Goldstein experienced once more an automatic sense of loss and longing. Wistful images of the beatitudes of married life drifted in his head. He remembered a night when his wife and he had giggled together in the darkness and listened to the quaint pompous snoring of their baby. ''Children are what makes life worth while,'' he said sincerely.

Martinez realized with a start that he was a father too. He remembered Rosalie's pregnancy for the first time in years. He shrugged. Seven years now? Eight years? He had lost count. Goddam, he said to himself. Once he had been free of the girl he had remembered her only as a source of trouble and worry.

The fact that he had begotten a child made him vain. Goddam, I'm okay, he said to himself. He felt like laughing. Martinez make a kid and run away. It gave him a malicious glee, as though he were a child tormenting a dog. What the hell she do with it? Knock her up. Goddam! His vanity swelled like a bloated belly. He mused with naïve delight about his potency, his attraction for women.

That the child was illegitimate increased his self-esteem; somehow it made his role more extravagant, of greater magnitude.

He felt a tolerant, almost condescending affection for Goldstein. Before this afternoon he had been a little afraid of him and quite uneasy. They had had an argument one day and Goldstein had disagreed with him. Whenever that happened, Martinez would react inevitably like a frightened schoolboy reprimanded by his teacher. There had never been a time when he was comfortable as a sergeant. But now he had been bathed in Goldstein's affection; he no longer felt Goldstein had despised him that day. Goldstein, he is okay, Martinez said to himself.

He became conscious of the vibration of the boat, its slow pitching advance through the swells. It was almost dark now, and he yawned and curled his body down farther beneath the poncho. He was slightly hungry. Lazily, he debated whether to open a ration or merely to lie still. He thought of the patrol, and the quick fear it roused made him alert again. Oh. He expelled his breath. No think about it, no think about it, he repeated to himself.

He became conscious abruptly that Gallagher and Goldstein were no longer talking. He looked up, and saw nearly all the men in the boat standing on their cots or chinning themselves on the starboard bulkhead. "What're they lookin' at?" Gallagher asked.

"It's the sunset, I think," Goldstein said.

"Sunset?" Martinez gazed at the sky above him. It was almost black, clotted with ugly leaden rain clouds. "Where the sunset?" He stood up on his cot, straddling his feet on the side poles, and stared into the west.

(1948)

From

GUARD OF HONOR
by James Gould Cozzens

"It is always the same," Colonel Ross said. "It is the standing trouble. You read about it in books, where it is often tragic. In life, as well as tragic, it tends to be tedious. A number of Negro officers came in on a project, and Mowbray assigned a separate officers' club for them. They considered it racial discrimination; and a few of them tried yesterday afternoon to use the Area Officers' Club. It is off limits for them. There was a very moderate fuss; no real violence; Johnny Sears's men arrested five or six of them. We didn't know quite what was going to happen, then; now, I think, nothing is. I have talked to the officer who is in line to be their group commander, and he is co-operative. He happened to be in the Hospital when this happened; but he is getting out now. I think he can manage them. There weren't many of them, and, of those there were, I doubt if more than one or two wanted to do it.''

Mrs. Ross said: "I should think they would all want to! It seems to me that if a man is qualified to be an officer, he is qualified to go to the Club. I don't see how he can be one and not the other.''

Colonel Ross said: "If you'll confront our condition instead of your theory, you'll see. This is how he can be one and not the other. For reasons of justice and decency; and also for reasons of political policy, the War Department decided that colored men must be given a chance to qualify as officers. We have about a thousand of them in the Air Force. In the Air Force, we have now somewhere around three hundred thousand white officers. A certain number of these, I don't know how many, but in relation to the whole, a proportion infinitely larger than that of colored to white officers, an unmanageably large number, hold that a nigger is a nigger. They will not have anything to do with him socially. That is their decision, inculcated in them from their first conscious moments, handed down to them with the sanctions of use and interest. I don't say this couldn't be changed, or that it won't ever be; but it won't change today, tomorrow, this week. A man cannot choose to see what he cannot see.''

"It is outrageous!" Mrs. Ross said. "I don't doubt there are quite a number of ignorant and prejudiced young louts, like Colonel Carricker, who feel that way. There must be many more, a big majority, who feel that a Negro is a human being, and who want to see him treated fairly. Why does what the majority wants make no difference?''

(1948)

"KING PREJUDICE"

Do we call this the land of the free? What is it to be free from King George and continue the slaves of King Prejudice?

Henry David Thoreau
Life without Principle

When the police picked the wounded strikers off the field, they loaded Ephraim into a wagon with other wounded, and that wagon stopped at a hospital, and some of the worst wounded were lifted out, but when it came his turn, he heard them say: "Uh-uh. Better take the jig somewhere else." They kept him in the wagon and drove a long time. He knew he was getting weaker. But the hospital was not a place where a man like him could go in.

Meyer Levin
Citizens

THE BOOKER WASHINGTON INCIDENT

by Finley Peter Dunne

"What ails th' prisidint havin' a coon to dinner at th' White House?" asked Mr. Hennessy.

"He's a larned man," said Mr. Dooley.

"He's a coon," said Mr. Hennessy.

"Well, annyhow," said Mr. Dooley, "it's goin' to be th' roonation iv Prisidint Tiddy's chances in th' South. Thousan's iv men who wudden't have voted f'r him undher anny circumstances has declared that under no circumstances wud they now vote f'r him. He's lost near ivry state in th' South. Th' gran' ol' commonwealth iv Texas has deserted th' banner iv th' raypublican party an' Mississippi will cast her unanimous counted vote again him. Onless he can get support fr'm Matsachoosetts or some other state where th' people don't care annything about th' naygur excipt to dislike him, he'll be beat sure.

"I don't suppose he thought iv it whin he ast me cultured but swarthy frind Booker T. They'd been talkin' over th' race problem an' th' Cubian war, an' th' prospects iv th' race an' th' Cubian war, an' th' future iv th' naygro an' th' Cubian war, an' findin' Booker T. was inthrested in important public subjects like th' Cubian war, th' prisidint ast him to come up to th' White House an' ate dinner an' have a good long talk about th' Cubian war. 'Ye'll not be th' first Wash'nton that's et here,' he says. 'Th' other was no rilitive, or at laste,' says Booker T., 'he'd hardly own me,' he says. 'He might,' says th' prisidint, 'if ye'd been in th' neighborhood iv Mt. Vernon in his time,' he says. 'Annyhow,' he says, 'come up. I'm goin' to thry an experiment,' he says. 'I want to see will all th' pitchers iv th' prisidints befure Lincoln fall out iv th' frames whin ye come in,' he says. An' Booker wint. So wud I. So wud annywan. I'd go if I had to black up.

"I didn't hear that th' guest done annything wrong at th' table. Fr'm all I can larn, he hung his hat on th' rack an' used proper discrimination between th' knife an' th' fork an' ast f'r nawthin' that had to be sint out f'r. They was no mark on th' table cloth where his hands rested an' an inventory iv th' spoons after his departure showed that he had used gintlemanly resthraint. At th' conclusion iv th' fistivities he wint away, lavin' his ilusthrees friend standin' on

297

th' top iv San Joon hill an' thought no more about it. Th' ghost iv th' other Wash'nton didn't appear to break a soop tureen over his head. P'raps where George is he has to assocyate with manny mimbers iv th' Booker branch on terms iv akequality. I don't suppose they have partitions up in th' other wurruld like th' kind they have in th' cars down south. They can't be anny Crow Hivin. I wondher how they keep up race supreemacy. Maybe they get on without it. Annyhow I was n't worrid about Booker T. I have me own share iv race prejudice, Hinnissy. Ne'er a man an' brother had darkened this threshold since I've had it or will but th' whitewasher. But I don't mind sayin' that I'd rather ate with a coon thin have wan wait on me. I'd sooner he'd handle his own food thin mine. F'r me, if anny thumb must be in th' gravy, lave it be white if ye please. But this was n't my dinner an' it was n't my house an' I hardly give it a thought.

"But it hit th' Sunny Southland. No part iv th' counthry can be more gloomy whin it thries thin th' Sunny Southland an' this here ivint sint a thrill iv horror through ivery newspaper fr'm th' Pattymack to th' Sugar Belt. 'Fr'm time immemoryal,' says wan paper I read, 'th' sacred rule at th' White House has been, whin it comes to dinner, please pass th' dark meat. It was a wise rule an' founded on thrue principles. Th' supreemacy iv th' white depinds on socyal supeeryority an' socyal supeeryority depinds on makin' th' coon ate in th' back iv th' house. He raises our food f'r us, cooks it, sets th' table an' brings in th' platter. We are liberal an' we make no attimpt to supplant him with more intilligent an' wage labor. We encourage his industhry because we know that f'r a low ordher iv intilligence, labor is th' on'y panacee. It is no good f'r a thoughtful man. We threat him right. He has plenty to do an' nawthin' to bother him an' if he isn't satisfied he be hanged. We are slowly givin him an' idjacation. Ivry year wan or more naygurs is given a good idjacation an' put on a north bound freight with a warnin'. But whin it comes to havin' him set down at th' table with us, we dhraw th' color line an' th' six shooter. Th' black has manny fine qualities. He is joyous, lighthearted, an' aisily lynched. But as a fellow bong vivant, not be anny means. We have th' highest rayspict f'r Booker T. Wash'nton. He's an idjacated coon. He is said to undherstand Latin an' Greek. We do not know. But we know that to feed him at th' White House was an insult to ivry honest man an' fair woman in th' Sunny Southland an' a blow at white supremacy. That must be avinged. Th' las' enthrinchmint iv socyal supeeryority in th' South is th' dinin' room an' there we will defind it with our sacred honor. We will not on'y defind our own dinin' room but ivry other man's, so that in time, if th' prisidint iv th' United States wants to ate with a naygur, he'll have to put on a coat iv burnt cork an' go to th' woodshed. Manetime we hear that th' white man in Alabama that voted f'r Rosenfelt las' year has come out again him. Th' tide has turned.'

"So there ye are. An' f'r th' life iv me, I can't tell which is right. But I think th' prisidint's place is a good dale like mine. I believe that manny an honest heart bates beneath a plaid vest, but I don't like a naygur. Howiver,

Hinnissy, if Fate, as Hogan said, had condemned me to start in business on th' Levee, I'd sarve th' black man that put down th' money as quick as I wud th' white. I feel I wudden't, but I know I wud. But bein' that I'm up here in this Cowcasyan neighborhood, I spurn th' dark coin. They'se very little iv it annyhow an' if anny iv me proud customers was f'r to see an unshackled slave lanin' again this bar, it'd go hard with him an' with me. Me frinds has no care f'r race supeeryority. A raaly supeeryor race niver thinks iv that. But black an' white don't mix, Hinnissy' an' if it wint th' rounds that Dooley was handin' out rayfrishmint to th' colored popylation, I might as well change me license. So be th' prisidint. They'se nawthin' wrong in him havin' me frind Booker T. up to dinner. That's a fine naygur man, an' if me an' th' presidint was in a private station, d 'ye mind, we cud f'rget th' color iv th' good man an' say, 'Booker T. stretch ye'er legs in front iv th' fire, while I go to th' butcher's f'r a pound iv pork chops.' But bein' that I—an' th' prisidint—is public sarvants an' manny iv our customers has onrais'nable prejoodices, an' afther all 't is to thim I've got to look f'r me support, I put me hand on his shouldher an' says I: 'Me colored frind, I like ye an' ye're idjacation shows ye 're a credit to th' South that it don't desarve, an' I wud swear black was white f'r ye; but swearin' it wudden't make it so, an' I know mos' iv me frinds thinks th' thirteenth amindmint stops at th' dure shtep, so if ye don't mind, I'll ast ye to leap through th' dure with ye'er hat on whin th' clock sthrikes sivin.' 'T is not me that speaks, Hinnissy, 't is th' job. Dooley th' plain citizen says, 'Come in, Rastus.' Dooley's job says: 'If ye come, th' r-rest will stay away.' An' I'd like to do something f'r th' naygur, too."

"What wud ye do?" asked Mr. Hennessy.

"Well," said Mr. Dooley, "I'd take away his right to vote an' his right to ate at th' same table an' his right to ride on th' cars an' even his sacred right to wurruk. I'd take thim all away an' give him th' on'y right he needs nowadays in th' South."

"What's that?"

"Th' right to live," said Mr. Dooley. "If he cud start with that he might make something iv himsilf."

(1901)

From

THE 'GENIUS'
by Theodore Dreiser

Another thing, fortunate for Eugene at this time, was that he changed his work. There came to the shop one day an Irish foreman, Timothy Deegan, master of a score of "guineas," as he called the Italian day laborers who worked for him, who took Eugene's fancy greatly. He was of medium height, thick of body and neck, with a cheerful, healthy red face, a keen, twinkling gray eye, and stiff, closely cropped gray hair and mustache. He had come to lay the foundation for a small dynamo in the engine room at Speonk, which was to supply the plant with light in case of night work, and a car of his had been backed in, a tool car, full of boards, barrows, mortar boards, picks and shovels. Eugene was amused and astonished at his insistent, defiant attitude and the brisk manner in which he was handing out orders to his men.

"Come, Matt! Come, Jimmie! Get the shovels now! Get the picks!" he heard him shout. "Bring some sand here! Bring some stone! Where's the cement now? Where's the cement? Jasus Christ! I must have some cement. What arre ye all doing? Hurry now, hurry! Bring the cement."

"Well, he knows how to give orders," commented Eugene to Big John, who was standing near. "He certainly does," replied the latter.

To himself Eugene observed, hearing only the calls at first, "the Irish brute." Later he discovered a subtle twinkle in Deegan's eyes as he stood brazenly in the door, looking defiantly about. There was no brutality in it, only self-confidence and a hearty Irish insistence on the necessity of the hour.

"Well, you're a dandy!" commented Eugene boldly after a time, and laughed.

"Ha! ha! ha!" mocked Deegan in return. "If you had to work as harred as these men you wouldn't laugh."

"I'm not laughing at them. I'm laughing at you," explained Eugene.

"Laugh," said Deegan. "Shure you're as funny to me as I am to you."

Eugene laughed again. The Irishman agreed with himself that there was humor in it. He laughed too. Eugene patted his big rough shoulder with his hands and they were friends immediately. It did not take Deegan long to find out from Big John why he was there and what he was doing.

"An arrtist!" he commented. "Shewer he'd better be outside than in. The loikes of him packin' shavin's and him laughin' at me."

Big John smiled.

"I believe he wants to get outside," he said.

"Why don't he come with me, then? He'd have a foine time workin' with the guineas. Shewer 'twould make a man av him—a few months of that"— and he pointed to Angelo Esposito shoveling clay.

Big John thought this worth reporting to Eugene. He did not think that he wanted to work with the guineas, but he might like to be with Deegan. Eugene saw his opportunity. He liked Deegan.

"Would you like to have an artist who's looking for health come and work for you, Deegan?" Eugene asked genially. He thought Deegan might refuse, but it didn't matter. It was worth the trial.

"Shewer!" replied the latter.

"Will I have to work with the Italians?"

"There'll be plenty av work for ye to do without ever layin' yer hand to pick or shovel unless ye want to. Shewer that's no work fer a white man to do."

"And what do you call them, Deegan? Aren't they white?"

"Shewer they're naat."

"What are they, then? They're not black."

"Nagurs, of coorse."

"But they're not negroes."

"Will, begad, they're naat white. Any man kin tell that be lookin' at thim."

Eugene smiled. He understood at once the solid Irish temperament which could draw this hearty conclusion. There was no malice in it. Deegan did not underestimate these Italians. He liked his men, but they weren't white. He didn't know what they were exactly, but they weren't white. He was standing over them a moment later shouting, "Up with it! Up with it! Down with it! Down with it!" as though his whole soul were intent on driving the last scrap of strength out of these poor underlings, when as a matter of fact they were not working very hard at all.

(1915)

THE VANISHING RED
by Robert Frost

He is said to have been the last Red Man
In Acton. And the Miller is said to have laughed—
If you like to call such a sound a laugh.
But he gave no one else a laugher's license.
For he turned suddenly grave as if to say,
"Whose business,—if I take it on myself,

Whose business—but why talk round the barn?—
When it's just that I hold with getting a thing done with."
You can't get back and see it as he saw it.
It's too long a story to go into now.
You'd have to have been there and lived it.
Then you wouldn't have looked on it as just a matter
Of who began it between the two races.

Some guttural exclamation of surprise
The Red Man gave in poking about the mill
Over the great big thumping shuffling mill-stone
Disgusted the Miller physically as coming
From one who had no right to be heard from.
"Come, John," he said, "you want to see the wheel pit?"

He took him down below a cramping rafter,
And showed him, through a manhole in the floor,
The water in desperate straits like frantic fish,
Salmon and sturgeon, lashing with their tails.
Then he shut down the trap door with a ring in it
That jangled even above the general noise,
And came up stairs alone—and gave that laugh,
And said something to a man with a meal-sack
That the man with the meal-sack didn't catch—then.
Oh, yes, he showed John the wheel pit all right.

(1916)

BURBANK WITH A BAEDEKER: BLEISTEIN WITH A CIGAR
by T. S. Eliot

Tra-la-la-la-la-la-laire—nil nisi divinum stabile est; caetera fumus—the gondola stopped, the old palace was there, how charming its grey and pink—goats and monkeys, with such hair too!—so the countess passed on until she came through the little park, where Niobe presented her with a cabinet, and so departed.

BURBANK crossed a little bridge
    Descending at a small hotel;
Princess Volupine arrived,
    They were together, and he fell.

Defunctive music under sea
    Passed seaward with the passing bell
Slowly: the God Hercules
    Had left him, that had loved him well.

The horses, under the axletree
    Beat up the dawn from Istria
With even feet. Her shuttered barge
    Burned on the water all the day.

But this or such was Bleistein's way:
    A saggy bending of the knees
And elbows, with the palms turned out,
    Chicago Semite Viennese.

A lustreless protrusive eye
    Stares from the protozoic slime
At a perspective of Canaletto.
    The smoky candle end of time

Declines. On the Rialto once.
    The rats are underneath the piles.
The jew is underneath the lot.
    Money in furs. The boatman smiles,

Princess Volupine extends
    A meagre, blue-nailed, phthisic hand
To climb the waterstair. Lights, lights,
    She entertains Sir Ferdinand

Klein. Who clipped the lion's wings
    And flea'd his rump and pared his claws?
Thought Burbank, meditating on
    Time's ruins, and the seven laws.

                  (1920)

From

DARK LAUGHTER
by Sherwood Anderson

Heat! Bruce Dudley had just come down river. June, July, August, September in New Orleans. You can't make a place something it won't be. It was slow work getting down river. Few or no boats. Often whole days idling about in river towns. You can take a train and go where you please, but what's the hurry?

Bruce at that time, when he had just left Bernice and his newspaper job, had something in mind that expressed itself in the phrase—"What's your hurry?" He sat in the shade of trees by the river-bank, got a ride once on a barge, rode on little local packets, sat in front of stores in river towns, slept, dreamed. People talked with a slow drawling speech, niggers were hoeing cotton, other niggers fished for catfish in the river.

The niggers were something for Bruce to look at, think about. So many black men slowly growing brown. Then would come the light brown, the velvet-browns, Caucasian features. The brown women tending up to the job—getting the race lighter and lighter. Soft Southern nights, warm dusky nights. Shadows flitting at the edge of cotton-fields, in dusky roads by sawmill towns. Soft voices laughing, laughing.

> Oh, ma banjo dog,
> Oh, ho, ma banjo dog.
> An' I ain't go'na give you
> None of ma jelly roll.

. . . . .

So much of that sort of thing in American life. If you are a thinking man—and Bruce was—you make half acquaintances—half friendships—Frenchmen, Germans, Italians, Englishmen—Jews. The Middle Western intellectual circles along the edge of which Bruce had played—watching Bernice plunge more boldly in—were filled with men not American at all. There was a young Polish sculptor, an Italian sculptor, a French dilettante. Was there such a thing as an American? Perhaps Bruce was the thing himself. He was reckless, afraid, bold, shy.

If you are a canvas do you shudder sometimes when the painter stands before you? All the others lending their color to him. A composition being made. Himself the composition.

Could he ever really know a Jew, a German, a Frenchman, an Englishman?

And now a nigger.

Consciousness of brown men, brown women, coming more and more into American life—by that token coming into him too.

More willing to come, more avid to come than any Jew, German, Pole, Italian. Standing laughing—coming by the back door—with shuffling feet, a laugh—a dance in the body.

Facts established would have to be recognized sometime—by individuals—when they were on an intellectual jag perhaps—as Bruce was then.

In New Orleans, when Bruce got there, the long docks facing the river. On the river just ahead of him when he came the last twenty miles, a small houseboat fitted up with a gas engine. Signs on it. "JESUS WILL SAVE." Some itinerant preacher from up river starting south to save the world. "THY WILL BE DONE." The preacher, a sallow man with a dirty beard, in bare feet, at the wheel of the little boat. His wife, also in bare feet, sitting in a rocking-chair. Her teeth were black stumps. Two children in bare feet, lying on a narrow deck.

The docks of the city go around in a great crescent. Big ocean freighters coming in bringing coffee, bananas, fruits, goods, taking out cotton, lumber, corn, oils.

Niggers on the docks, niggers in the city streets, niggers laughing. A slow dance always going on. German sea-captains, French, American, Swedish, Japanese, English, Scotch. The Germans now sailing under other flags than their own. The Scotch sailing under the English flag. Clean ships, dirty tramp ships, half-naked niggers—a shadow-dance.

How much does it cost to be a good man, an earnest man? If we can't produce good earnest men, how are we ever going to make any progress? You can't ever get anywhere if you aren't conscious—in earnest. A brown woman having thirteen children—a different man for every child—going to church too, singing, dancing, broad shoulders, broad hips, soft eyes, a soft laughing voice—getting God on Sunday night—getting—what—on Wednesday night?

Men, you've got to be up and doing if you want progress.

William Allen White, Heywood Broun—passing judgment on the arts—why not—Oh, ma banjo dog—Van Wyck Brooks, Frank Crowninshield, Tallulah Bankhead, Henry Mencken, Anita Loos, Stark Young, Ring Lardner, Eva Le Gallienne, Jack Johnson, Bill Heywood, H. G. Wells write good books, don't you think? The Literary Digest, The Dial Book of Modern Art, Harry Wills.

They dance south—out of doors—whites in a pavilion in one field, blacks, browns, high browns, velvet-browns in a pavilion in the next field—but one.

We've got to have more earnest men in this country.

Grass growing in a field between.

Oh, ma banjo dog!

Song in the air, a slow dance. Heat. Brice had some money then. He might have got a job, but what was the use? Well, he might have gone uptown and tackled the New Orleans *Picayune,* or the *Item* or *States* for a job. Why not go see Jack McClure, the ballad-maker—on the *Picayune?* Give us a song, Jack—a dance—the gumbo drift. Come, the night is hot. What was the use? He still had some of the money he had slipped into his pocket when he left Chicago. In New Orleans you can get a loft in which to sleep for five dollars a month if you know how. You know how when you don't want to work—when you want to look and listen—when you want your body to be lazy while your mind works. New Orleans is not Chicago. It isn't Cleveland or Detroit. Thank God for that!

Nigger girls in the streets, nigger women, nigger men. There is a brown cat lurking in the shadow of a building. "Come, brown puss—come get your cream." The men who work on the docks in New Orleans have slender flanks like running horses, broad shoulders, loose heavy lips hanging down—faces like old monkeys sometimes—bodies like young gods—sometimes. On Sundays—when they go to church, or to a bayou baptizing, the brown girls do sure cut loose with the colors—gaudy nigger colors on nigger women making the streets flame—deep purples, reds, yellows, green like young corn-shoots coming up. They sweat. The skin colors brown, golden yellow, reddish brown, purple-brown. When the sweat runs down high brown backs the colors come out and dance before the eyes. Flash that up, you silly painters, catch it dancing. Song-tones in words, music in words—in colors too. Silly American painters! They chase a Gauguin shadow to the South Seas. Bruce wrote a few poems. Bernice had got very far away in, oh such a short time. Good thing she didn't know. Good thing no one knows how unimportant he is. We need earnest men—got to have 'em. Who'll run the show if we don't get that kind? For Bruce—for the time—no sensual feeling that need be expressed through his body.

Hot days. Sweet Mama!

Funny business, Bruce trying to write poems. When he had that job on the newspaper, where a man is supposed to write, he never wanted to write at all. Southern white men writing songs—fill themselves first with Keats and Shelley.

> I am giving out of the richness of myself to many mornings.
> At night, when the waters of the seas murmur I am murmuring.
> I have surrendered to seas and suns and days and swinging ships.
> My blood is thick with surrender.
>
> It shall be let out through wounds and shall color the seas and the earth.
> My blood shall color the earth where the seas come for the night kiss and the
>   seas shall be red.

What did that mean? Oh, laugh a little, men! What matters what it means? Or again—

> Give me the word.
> Let my throat and my lips caress the words of your lips.

Give me the word.
Give me three words, a dozen, a hundred, a history.
Give me the word.

A broken jargon of words in the head. In old New Orleans the narrow streets are filled with iron gates leading away, past damp old walls, to cool patios. It is very lovely—old shadows dancing on sweet old walls, but some day it will all be torn away to make room for factories.

Bruce lived for five months in an old house where rent was low, where cockroaches scurried up and down the walls. Nigger women lived in the building across the narrow street.

You lie naked on the bed on hot summer mornings and let the slow creeping river-wind come, if it will. Across the street, in another room, a nigger woman of twenty arises at five and stretches her arms. Bruce rolls and looks. Sometimes she sleeps alone but sometimes a brown man sleeps with her. Then they both stretch. Thin-flanked brown man. Nigger girl with slender flexible body. She knows Bruce is looking. What does it matter? He is looking as one might look at trees, at young colts playing in a pasture.

Bruce got out of his bed and went away along a narrow street to another street near the river where he got coffee and a roll of bread for five cents. Thinking of niggers! What sort of business is that? How come? Northern men so often get ugly when they think of niggers, or they get sentimental. Give pity where none is needed. The men and women of the South understand better, maybe. "Oh, hell, don't get fussy! Let things flow! Let us alone! We'll float!" Brown blood flowing, white blood flowing, deep river flowing.

A slow dance, music, ships, cotton, corn, coffee. Slow lazy laughter of niggers. Bruce remembered a line he had once seen written by a negro. "Would white poet ever know why my people walk so softly and laugh at sunrise?"

Heat. The sun coming up in a mustard-colored sky. Driving rains that came, swirled over a half-dozen blocks of city streets and in ten minutes no trace of moisture left. Too much wet warmth for a little more wet warmth to matter. The sun licking it up, taking a drink for itself. One might get clear-headed here. Clear-headed about what? Well, don't hurry. Take your time.

Bruce lay lazy in bed. The brown girl's body was like the thick waving leaf of a young banana plant. If you were a painter now, you could paint that, maybe. Paint a brown nigger girl in a broad leaf waving and send it up North. Why not sell it to a society woman of New Orleans? Get some money to loaf a while longer on. She wouldn't know, would never guess. Paint a brown laborer's narrow suave flanks onto the trunk of a tree. Send it to the Art Institute in Chicago. Send it to the Anderson Galleries in New York. A French painter went down to the South Seas. Freddy O'Brien went down. Remember when the brown woman tried to ravage him and he said how he escaped? Gauguin put a lot of pep in his book but they trimmed it for us. No one cared much, not after Gauguin was dead anyway. You get a cup of such coffee for five cents and a big roll of bread. No swill. In Chicago, morning coffee at cheap places is like swill. Niggers like good things. Good big sweet words, flesh, corn, cane. Niggers like a free throat for song. You're a nigger down South and you get some white blood in you. A little more, and a little more. Northern travelers help, they say. Oh, Lord! Oh, my banjo dog! Do you remember the night when that Gauguin came home to his little hut and there, in the bed, was the slender brown girl waiting for him? Better read that book. "Noa-Noa," they call it. Brown mysticism in the walls of a room, in the hair—of a Frenchman, in the eyes of a brown girl. Noa-Noa. Do you remember the sense of strangeness? French painter kneeling on the floor in the darkness, smelling the strangeness. The brown girl smelling the strangeness. Love? What ho! Smelling strangeness.

Go softly. Don't hurry. What's all the shooting about?

A little more white, a little more white, graying white, muddy white, thick lips—staying sometimes. Over we go!

Something lost too. The dance of bodies, a slow dance.

Bruce on a bed in a five-dollar room. Away off, broad leaves of young banana plants waving. "D'you know why my people laugh in the morning? Do you know why my people walk softly?"

Sleep again, white man. No hurry. Then along a street for coffee and a roll of bread, five cents. Sailors off ships, bleary-eyed. Old nigger women and white women going to market. They know each other, white women, nigger women. Go soft. Don't hurry!

Song—a slow dance. A white man lying still on docks, in a five-dollar-a-month bed. Heat. No hurry. When you get that hurry out of you the mind works maybe. Maybe song will start in you too.

Lord, it would be nice with Tom Wills down here. Shall I write him a letter? No, better not. After a while, when cool days come, you mosey along up North again. Come back here some day. Stay here some day. Look and listen.

Song—dance—a slow dance.

(1925)

From

THE GREAT GATSBY
by F. Scott Fitzgerald

Over the great bridge, with the sunlight through the girders making a constant flicker upon the moving cars, with the city rising up across the river in white heaps and sugar lumps all built with a wish out of non-olfactory money. The city seen from the Queensboro Bridge is always the city seen for the first time, in its first wild promise of all the mystery and the beauty in the world.

A dead man passed us in a hearse heaped with blooms, followed by two carriages with drawn blinds, and by more cheerful carriages for friends. The friends looked out at us with the tragic eyes and short upper lips of southeastern Europe, and I was glad that the sight of Gatsby's splendid car was included in their somber holiday. As we crossed Blackwell's Island a limousine passed us, driven by a white chauffeur, in which sat three modish negroes, two bucks and a girl. I laughed aloud as the yolks of their eyeballs rolled toward us in haughty rivalry.

"Anything can happen now that we've slid over this bridge," I thought; "anything at all. . . ."

Even Gatsby could happen, without any particular wonder.

Roaring noon. In a well-fanned Forty-second Street cellar I met Gatsby for lunch. Blinking away the brightness of the street outside, my eyes picked him out obscurely in the anteroom, talking to another man.

"Mr. Carraway, this is my friend Mr. Wolfsheim."

A small, flat-nosed Jew raised his large head and regarded me with two fine growths of hair which luxuriated in either nostril. After a moment I discovered his tiny eyes in the half-darkness.

"—So I took one look at him," said Mr. Wolfsheim, shaking my hand earnestly, "and what do you think I did?"

"What?" I inquired politely.

But evidently he was not addressing me, for he dropped my hand and covered Gatsby with his expressive nose.

"I handed the money to Katspaugh and I sid: 'All right, Katspaugh, don't pay him a penny till he shuts his mouth.' He shut it then and there."

Gatsby took an arm of each of us and moved forward into the restaurant, whereupon Mr. Wolfsheim swallowed a new sentence he was starting and lapsed into a somnambulatory abstraction.

"Highballs?" asked the head waiter.

"This is a nice restaurant here," said Mr. Wolfsheim, looking at the Presbyterian nymphs on the ceiling. "But I like across the street better!"

"Yes, highballs," agreed Gatsby, and then to Mr. Wolfsheim: "It's too hot over there."

"Hot and small—yes," said Mr. Wolfsheim, "but full of memories."

"What place is that?" I asked.

"The old Metropole."

"The old Metropole," brooded Mr. Wolfsheim gloomily. "Filled with faces dead and gone. Filled with friends gone now forever. I can't forget so long as I live the night they shot Rosy Rosenthal there. It was six of us at the table, and Rosy had eat and drunk a lot all evening. When it was almost morning the waiter came up to him with a funny look and says somebody wants to speak to him outside. 'All right,' says Rosy, and begins to get up, and I pulled him down in his chair.

" 'Let the bastards come in here if they want you, Rosy, but don't you, so help me, move outside this room.'

"It was four o'clock in the morning then, and if we'd of raised the blinds we'd of seen daylight."

"Did he go?" I asked innocently.

"Sure he went." Mr. Wolfsheim's nose flashed at me indignantly. "He turned around in the door and says: 'Don't let that waiter take away my coffee!' Then he went out on the sidewalk, and they shot him three times in his full belly and drove away."

"Four of them were electrocuted," I said, remembering.

"Five, with Becker." His nostrils turned to me in an interested way. "I understand you're looking for a business gonnegtion."

The juxtaposition of these two remarks was startling. Gatsby answered for me:

"Oh, no," he exclaimed, "this isn't the man."

"No?" Mr. Wolfsheim seemed disappointed.

"This is just a friend. I told you we'd talk about that some other time."

"I beg your pardon," said Mr. Wolfsheim, "I had a wrong man."

A succulent hash arrived, and Mr. Wolfsheim, forgetting the more sentimental atmosphere of the old Metropole, began to eat with ferocious delicacy. His eyes, meanwhile, roved very slowly all around the room—he completed the arc by turning to inspect the people directly behind. I think that, except for my presence, he would have taken one short glance beneath our own table.

"Look here, old sport," said Gatsby, leaning toward me, "I'm afraid I made you a little angry this morning in the car."

There was the smile again, but this time I held out against it.

"I don't like mysteries," I answered, "and I don't understand why you won't come out frankly and tell me what you want. Why has it all got to come through Miss Baker?"

"Oh, it's nothing underhand," he assured me. "Miss Baker's a great sportswoman, you know, and she'd never do anything that wasn't all right."

Suddenly he looked at his watch, jumped up, and hurried from the room, leaving me with Mr. Wolfsheim at the table.

"He has to telephone," said Mr. Wolfsheim, following him with his eyes. "Fine fellow, isn't he? Handsome to look at and a perfect gentleman."

"Yes."

"He's an Oggsford man."

"Oh!"

"He went to Oggsford College in England. You know Oggsford College?"

"I've heard of it."

"It's one of the most famous colleges in the world."

"Have you known Gatsby for a long time?" I inquired.

"Several years," he answered in a gratified way. "I made the pleasure of his acquaintance just after the war. But I knew I had discovered a man of fine breeding after I talked with him an hour. I said to myself: 'There's the kind of man you'd like to take home and introduce to your mother and sister.' " He paused. "I see you're looking at my cuff buttons."

I hadn't been looking at them, but I did now. They were composed of oddly familiar pieces of ivory.

"Finest specimens of human molars," he informed me.

"Well!" I inspected them. "That's a very interesting idea."

"Yeah." He flipped his sleeves up under his coat. "Yeah, Gatsby's very careful about women. He would never so much as look at a friend's wife."

When the subject of this instinctive trust returned to the table and sat down Mr. Wolfsheim drank his coffee with a jerk and got to his feet.

"I have enjoyed my lunch," he said, "and I'm going to run off from you two young men before I outstay my welcome."

"Don't hurry, Meyer," said Gatsby, without enthusiasm. Mr. Wolfsheim raised his hand in a sort of benediction.

"You're very polite, but I belong to another generation," he announced solemnly. "You sit here and discuss your sports and your young ladies and your—" He supplied an imaginary noun with another wave of his hand. "As for me, I am fifty years old, and I won't impose myself on you any longer."

As he shook hands and turned away his tragic nose was trembling. I wondered if I had said anything to offend him.

"He becomes very sentimental sometimes," explained Gatsby. "This is one of his sentimental days. He's quite a character around New York—a denizen of Broadway."

"Who is he, anyhow, an actor?"

"No."

"A dentist?"

"Meyer Wolfsheim? No, he's a gambler." Gatsby hesitated, then added coolly: "He's the man who fixed the World's Series back in 1919."

"Fixed the World's Series?" I repeated.

The idea staggered me. I remembered, of course, that the World's Series had been fixed in 1919, but if I had thought of it at all I would have thought of it as a thing that merely *happened,* the end of some inevitable chain. It never occurred to me that one man could start to play with the faith of fifty million people—with the single-mindedness of a burglar blowing a safe.

"How did he happen to do that?" I asked after a minute.

"He just saw the opportunity."

"Why isn't he in jail?"

"They can't get him, old sport. He's a smart man."

(1925)

From

THE SUN ALSO RISES
by Ernest Hemingway

Robert Cohn was once middleweight boxing champion of Princeton. Do not think that I am very much impressed by that as a boxing title, but it meant a lot to Cohn. He cared nothing for boxing, in fact he disliked it, but he learned it painfully and thoroughly to counteract the feeling of inferiority and shyness he had felt on being treated as a Jew at Princeton. There was a certain inner comfort in knowing he could knock down anybody who was snooty to him, although, being very shy and a thoroughly nice boy, he never fought except in the gym. He was Spider Kelly's star pupil. Spider Kelly taught all his young gentlemen to box like featherweights, no matter whether they weighed one hundred and five or two hundred and five pounds. But it seemed to fit Cohn. He was really very fast. He was so good that Spider promptly overmatched him and got his nose permanently flattened. This increased Cohn's distaste for boxing, but it gave him a certain satisfaction of some strange sort, and it certainly improved his nose. In his last year at Princeton he read too much and took to wearing spectacles. I never met any one of his class who remembered him. They did not even remember that he was middleweight boxing champion.

I mistrust all frank and simple people, especially when their stories hold together, and I always had a suspicion that perhaps Robert Cohn had never been middleweight boxing champion, and that perhaps a horse had stepped on his face, or that maybe his mother had been frightened or seen something, or that he had, maybe, bumped into something as a young child, but I finally had somebody verify the story from Spider Kelly. Spider Kelly not only remembered Cohn. He had often wondered what had become of him.

Robert Cohn was a member, through his father, of one of the richest Jewish families in New York, and through his mother of one of the oldest. At the military school where he prepped for Princeton, and played a very good end on the football team, no one had made him race-conscious. No one had ever made him feel he was a Jew, and hence any different from anybody else, until he went to Princeton. He was a nice boy, a friendly boy, and very shy, and it made him bitter. He took it out in boxing, and he came out of Princeton with painful self-consciousness and the flattened nose, and was married by the first girl who was nice to him. He was married five years, had three children, lost most of the fifty thousand dollars his father left him, the balance of the estate having gone to his mother, hardened into a rather unattractive mould under domestic unhappiness with a rich wife; and just when he had made up his mind to leave his wife she left him and went off with a miniature-painter. As he had been thinking for months about leaving his wife and had not done it because it would be too cruel to deprive her of himself, her departure was a very healthful shock.

(1926)

From

THE ISLAND WITHIN
by Ludwig Lewisohn

How was it that, before they went to school, always and always, as far back as the awakening of consciousness, the children knew that they were Jews? This was a subject on which Arthur speculated not a few times in the later years. There was in the house no visible symbol of religion and of race. Had the house been emptied of its inhabitants, to be let furnished, for instance, there would have been nothing in it to differentiate it from the house of Protestant Americans. There were a few German books of Gertrude's. But these, too, had neither Jewish content nor association. Arthur was quite sure on one point, at all events, and that point was the crucial one, that when he was old enough to understand certain definite remarks that betrayed a Jewish consciousness, he already knew, consented, was nowise astonished nor tempted to ask. Such remarks in the household were few enough. They were usually made by his father and usually amounted to this, that one must not expect too much of So-

and-so and So-and-so or trust them too completely, as far as one's most intimate affairs were concerned, because the people in question were *Goyim*. The
corresponding remark was that such and such people could be approached, such
and such a physician called in, such and such a merchant trusted because they
were *Yehudim*. And it was distinctly clear to Arthur, from the beginning of his
reasoning life on, that these judgments involved no absolute moral values. They
meant that the decentest Gentile was apt to relax his ethical vigilance in dealing
with a Jew and that the shabbiest Jew was apt to rise above his lower level
when dealing with a fellow Jew. At times Arthur was to repudiate these judgments heartily and even fiercely later on. He was sure that he had made no
mistake as to their character and quality from the beginning. He continued to
search his memory for other and outward visible methods by which the consciousness of being Jews had crept into his sister's mind and into his own. He
found none. Something he had to leave, at his most hostile and rebellious moments, to ancestral memories, to instinct, to the voice of the blood. . . .

Neither was he ever able to estimate how far these early impressions might
have been obliterated by life in a various and forgetful world. For on this one
point the world was strict and mindful from the moment of one's first contact
with it. On his second day in school, from the low form ahead of him, there
was suddenly turned a small round screwed-up gargoyle face, red, freckled,
pug-nosed, blue-eyed, with crimson tongue stuck far out and hot against the
lovely, fair chin. Then the tongue slid, like a quick little round animal, back
into its hole and he heard a hot whisper, "Sheenie!" . . . Was it again the
voice of the blood? For Arthur was sure that he had never heard that word before. But neither had he any doubt as to its meaning and character. So sure was
he, and so hurt, and so rebellious against that hurt which had leaped suddenly
at him in a world hitherto all security and tenderness and peace, that, instead
of relating the incident at home, he told his mother that there was a nice little
boy in his class whose name was Georgie Fleming. . . .

One doesn't reflect at six. But to Arthur the immense value of this incident and this childish reaction lay precisely in their unreflectiveness. The instinctive gesture involved was evidently on the part of the child that he then
was a protective and self-protective one. He didn't want this thing with its
enormous implications to be true; he wanted to shut it out. He didn't want his
mother to heal his hurt, because he didn't want her or, in truth, himself, to
know of it. And the reason for this was obviously that it wasn't a quick and
fleeting and superficial hurt of childhood. It evidently struck a chord of incon-
ceivably mighty and dolorous ancestral resonances. . . . Or was it too curious
to consider so? The fact, the fact remained . . . as well as the indelible memory of that little red gargoyle face and of that hot whispered word. . . .

Yes, that memory clung in spite of the fact that Arthur and George got
to know each other very well. And that was possible (as Arthur the child perceived and Arthur the youth recalled) because, while he remembered, little George
forgot. George was quite innocent and had a lovable nature. His liking for Ar-

thur was genuine, though casual. He did not speak to him for a whole day at school. Then he would come and kiss him in a strange, bird-like little way. Arthur felt a dim childish passion for George's blithe fairness, and the terror he had at the core of him lest the gargoyle face and the hot whisper return heightened his half-tormented devotion. He asked his mother whether he might ask George Fleming to come over and play with Hazel and himself, and she gave her consent very readily. (Over-readily, Arthur thought in the later years, a little proudly at the first moment that her children were to have a nice little Christian playmate. George's father was an alderman of the city of New York. And Arthur was retrospectively ashamed of that touch of pride in his mother and did not know how many of his own impulses in the matter of human contacts were governed by a similar emotional coloring, a similar hopeless hopefulness of escape from a fate—strange contradiction if one weighs the words!—a fate that seemed, at certain periods, a mere accident, like the blue mark of a bruise received in the dark and unwilling to fade.)

Little George Fleming came to the Levy house and at first seemed shy. He stood there twisting one foot about the other and frankly sniffing the air with uplifted and suspicious little nose. He looked into corners as though he expected something to jump at him. He was extraordinarily polite, as though he had to propitiate somebody by being on his best behavior. He finally followed to the playroom and forgot himself and began to toss the toys about and to romp in a way that made Arthur nervous. Hazel didn't like it either. But she pretended, and Arthur knew that she pretended, that she did. Georgie wanted to wrestle. He cried: "Gee! but you got a lota books!" He slid along the floor, pretending to make a base. Arthur and Hazel proposed playing their favorite game, in which Hazel was a patient and Arthur a doctor and Hazel's dolls other patients. Georgie looked at them wide-eyed. "Gee! what a funny game!" he cried. Then he said: "Gee! Arthur, I bet I could knock you outa that window!" and came very near succeeding. Then, red and panting a little from the struggle, he announced: "Gee! I guess pretty soon I'm goin' to be as strong as my Dad! I bet I will." At this point—Arthur and Hazel were beginning to feel sleepy and a little forlorn here in their own home—Mrs. Levy came in and asked the children to come downstairs for some chocolate and cake. George twisted one foot about the other again. Mrs. Levy put her white hand with the amethyst ring on the little boy's shoulder, an action which, for a moment, infuriated Arthur. . . . They all went downstairs and sat about the table in the dining-room. At first Georgie seemed afraid to touch anything. At last he took a crumb of cake—it was a home-made *Marzipantorte*—and then a mouthful, and then drank his chocolate, too. Enjoyment and elation sparkled in his beautiful blue eyes. A piece of cake in his hand, his mouth almost too full for utterance, he leaned back and kicked his boots against the table and said with deep conviction: "My Dad says theyah lotsa nice Jewish people. He did so!"

(1928)

From

THE BRIAR PATCH

by Robert Penn Warren

In 1619 twenty negroes were landed at the colony of Jamestown and sold into slavery. Probably they came from the Indies; in such case they were torn from the servitude of the Spaniard to be delivered into that of the Englishman in America. The ship that brought them—she was named the *Jesus*—touched history significantly, but only for a moment. When she again put to sea, with the price of twenty slaves added to the profits of her venture, she disappeared forever into the obscurity from which she had brought those first negroes to American shores.

The number of negroes in the country increased slowly until the eighteenth century, but they had come to stay. Long before the Civil War, when Northern philanthropy and Southern interest raised money from Sunday schools and societies to colonize the negroes in Africa and thus solve the problem which distressed the nation, the negroes, in so far as they were articulate concerning their fate, usually opposed any such scheme. They might be mobbed from their farms in Ohio or be forced to spend their days in the cotton-fields under a blazing Mississippi sun, but America, after all, was home. Here they knew where they stood; the jungle, though not many generations behind, was mysterious and deadly.

At Appomattox, in the April of 1865, Lee's infantry marched past the close Federal ranks to the place of surrender and acknowledged with muskets at carry the courtesy of the enemy's salute. The old Emancipation Proclamation was at last effective, and the negro became a free man in the country which long before he had decided was his home. When the bluecoats and bayonets disappeared, when certain gentlemen packed their carpet-bags and silently departed, and when scalawags settled down to enjoy their profits or sought them elsewhere, the year of jubilo drew to a close and the negro found himself in a jungle as puzzling and mysterious, and as little answering to his desires, as the forgotten jungles of Africa.

The negro was as little equipped to establish himself in it as he would have been to live again, with spear and breech-clout, in the Sudan or Bantu country. The necessities of life had always found their way to his back or skillet without the least thought on his part; the things had been only the bare necessities, but their coming was certain. He did not know how to make a living, or, if he did, he did not know how to take thought for the morrow. Always in the past he had been told when to work and what to do, and now, with the new-got freedom, he failed to understand the limitation which a simple contract of labor set on that freedom. It is not surprising that the idea of freedom meant eating the cake and keeping it, too. In the old scheme of things which had dwindled away at Vicksburg, Gettysburg, and Chattanooga, he had occupied an acknowledged, if limited and humble, place. Now he had to find a place, and the attempt to find it is the story of the negro since 1865.

(1930)

From

THE AUTOBIOGRAPHY OF LINCOLN STEFFENS
by Lincoln Steffens

A Chinese captain of industry kept my mind off my work. He had a method. He had worked his way up along the shore of the Sound, setting up a laundry in each place. When he had it going he appointed an agent, another Chinaman, to carry on the local business while he went on to the next place. This trust-building business was known to the natives of Cos Cob, and when Ah Sing opened a place on the inner harbor right opposite the post office we all sided with the villagers and said: "Well, let him try it. He might have conquered other, New York State sea villages; but he can't get us. No outsider can break into a good old New England community like Cos Cob. Mrs. Marshall does our washing, and no Chink shall get us away from her." Mrs. Marshall came, on both sides, from old, old families that came over on that certain ship which carried more passengers than any bottom ever floated by man except possibly the ark. Distinguished men had borne her names, and all the old New Englanders and all the visitors who stood for justice boycotted that Chinaman, who did nothing but fish. Day after day for weeks Ah Sing fished in front of his workless laundry; day after day the villagers watched him fish and asked one another how long he could hold out. He smiled, spoke pleasantly to people who would not speak to him. One day when I was getting into my boat and nobody was looking I asked him how he expected to succeed there.

"Oh," he said, "allee time just the same. Allee place no come till by-meby." And he went right on fishing.

But he fished in a curious way, and he caught lots of fish; the fish he caught were of a variety white folks didn't take, but he dried and he ate them. Everybody, especially the fishermen, were curious about it all. They laughed at first when they saw him sink a small open net on his pole, leave it, and go back later to take up a panful of fish. You'd see the fishermen walk past him to look into his catch and study his net. But they didn't report satisfactorily after such a betrayal of interest. Others tried it. One day an oysterman drew up the net; there were fishes in it, and he, looking around, saw that Ah Sing had left his pan there ready for this event. The oysterman dumped the fish out of the net into the pan and then lowered the net again into the water. Others who had seen this repeated the act of curiosity, sport, or decency, and pretty soon we saw the villagers on their way to the post office and back habitually lift the funny net and empty the funny fish into the pan. A week or so of this, and Ah Sing was seen talking to the talkative villagers. The Chink was a pleasant-spoken, genial good fellow, and his talk about fishing in China was curious. Others talked to him; everybody talked to Ah Sing; and finally, when I came back from a long trip, I found the laundry going full time and everybody having their washing done by the Chink, who was cheap, by the way. I don't know how it went with Mrs. Marshall, but Ah Sing was gone; his cousin ran his laundry, and he said that the boss was carrying on his string of chain laundries up Boston way. A fisher for men was Ah Sing, and a prophet of industry.

(1931)

THIS IS THE MAN
by John Peale Bishop

This is the man who bore his shoulders hunched
    And arched his backbone like an angry cat;
      He also wore, derisively, a hat
A low black Jewish hat, battered and punched
Out of all argument, with his ears conched
    Beneath it, small and strangely disparate;
      His lips skimmed back upon a smile that spat
Between his toothpick and a tooth. He scrunched

Along the pathway toward us and without
    Lifting his feet went past us with the smile
      Still pinned there by the toothpick and
Just at that moment turned. Semitic snout
    Returned and upturned eyes came back, and while
      I stared there speechless bent and kissed your hand.

(1933)

From

OF TIME AND THE RIVER
by Thomas Wolfe

And so Eugene recalled Abraham Jones.

This ugly, good, and loyal creature had almost forgotten his real name: the "Jones," of course, was one of those random acquisitions which, bestowed in some blind, dateless moment of the past, evoked a picture of those nameless hordes of driven and frightened people who had poured into this country within the last half-century, and whose whole lives had been determined for them by the turn of a word, the bend of a street, the drift of the crowd, or a surly and infuriated gesture by some ignorant tyrant of an official. In such a way, Abe Jones's father, a Polish Jew, without a word of Yankee English in his throat, had come to Castle Garden forty years before and, stunned and frightened by the moment's assault of some furious little swine of a customs inspector, had stood dumbly while the man snarled and menaced him: "What's yer name? . . . Huh? . . . Don't yuh know what yer name is . . . Huh? . . . Ain't yuh got a name? . . . Huh?" To all this the poor Jew had no answer but a stare of stupefaction and terror: at length a kind of frenzy seized him—a torrent of Polish, Jewish, Yiddish speech poured from his mouth, but never a word his snarling inquisitor could understand. The Jew begged, swore, wept, pleaded, prayed, entreated—a thousand tales of horror, brutal violence and tyranny swept through his terror-stricken mind, the whole vast obscene chronicle of immigration gleaned from the mouths of returned adventurers or from the letters of those who had triumphantly passed the gates of wrath: he showed his papers, he clasped his hands, he swore by all the oaths he knew that all was as it should be, that he had done all he had been told to do, that there was no trick or fraud or cheat in anything he did or said, and all the time, the foul, swollen, snarling face kept thrusting at him with the same maddening and indecipherable curse: "Yer name! . . . Yer name! . . . Fer Christ's sake don't yuh know yer own name? . . . All right!" he shouted suddenly, furiously, "If yuh ain't got a name I'll give yuh one! . . . If yuh ain't got sense enough to tell me what yer own name is, I'll find one for yuh!" The snarling face came closer: "Yer name's Jones! See! J-o-n-e-s. Jones! That's a good Amurrican name. See? I'm giving yuh a good honest Amurrican name that a lot of good decent Amurricans have got. Yuh've gotta try to live up to it and desoive it! See? Yer in Amurrica now, Jones. . . . See? . . . Yuh've gotta t'ink fer yerself, Jones. In Amurrica we know our own name. We've been trained to t'ink fer ourselves over here! . . .

See? Yer not one of them foreign dummies any more! . . . Yer Jones—Jones—Jones!'' he yelled. ''See!''—and in such a way, on the impulsion of brutal authority and idiot chance, Abe's father had been given his new name. Eugene did not know what Abe's real name was: Abe had told him once, and he remembered it as something pleasant, musical, and alien to our tongue, difficult for our mouths to shape and utter.

Already, when he had first met Abe Jones in the first class he taught, the process of mutation had carried so far that he was trying to rid himself of the accursed ''Abraham,'' reducing it to an ambiguous initial, and signing his papers with a simple unrevealing ''A. Jones,'' as whales are said to have lost through atrophy the use of legs with which they once walked across the land, but still to carry upon their bodies the rudimentary stump. Now, in the last year, he had dared to make a final transformation, shocking, comical, pitifully clumsy in its effort at concealment and deception: when Eugene had tried to find his name and number in the telephone directory a month before, among the great gray regiment of Joneses, the familiar, quaint, and homely ''Abe'' had disappeared—at length he found him coyly sheltered under the gentlemanly obscurity of A. Alfred Jones. The transformation, thus, had been complete: he was now, in name, at any rate, a member of the great Gentile aristocracy of Jones; and just as ''Jones'' had been thrust by violence upon his father, so had Abe taken violently, by theft and rape, the ''Alfred.'' There was something mad and appalling in the bravado, the effrontery, and the absurdity of the attempt: what did he hope to do with such a name? What reward did he expect to win? Was he engaged in some vast conspiracy in which all depended on the *sound* and not the *appearance* of deception? Was he using the mails in some scheme to swindle or defraud? Was he carrying on by correspondence an impassioned courtship of some ancient Christian maiden with one tooth and a million shining dollars? Or was it part of a gigantic satire on Gentile genteelness, country-club Christianity, a bawdy joke perpetrated at the expense of sixty thousand anguished and protesting Social Registerites? That he should hope actually to palm himself off as a Gentile was unthinkable, because one look at him revealed instantly the whole story of his race and origin: if all the Polish-Russian Jews that ever swarmed along the ghettoes of the earth had been compacted in a single frame the physical result might have been something amazingly like Eugene's friend, Abraham Jones.

The whole flag and banner of his race was in the enormous putty-colored nose that bulged, flared and sprouted with the disproportionate extravagance of a caricature or a dill-pickle over his pale, slightly freckled and rather meagre face; he had a wide, thin, somewhat cruel-looking mouth, dull weak eyes that stared, blinked, and grew misty with a murky, somewhat slimily ropy feeling behind his spectacles, a low, dull, and slanting forehead, almost reptilian in its ugliness, that sloped painfully back an inch or two into the fringes of unpleasantly greasy curls and coils of dark, short, screwy hair. He was about the middle height, and neither thin nor fat: his figure was rather big-boned and angular,

and yet it gave an impression of meagreness, spareness, and somewhat tal-
lowy toughness which so many city people have, as if their ten thousand days
and nights upon the rootless pavement had dried all juice and succulence out
of them, as if asphalt and brick and steel had got into the conduits of their
blood and spirit, leaving them with a quality that is tough, dry, meagre, tal-
lowy, and somewhat calloused.

(1935)

From

SERENADE
by James M. Cain

I was in the Tupinamba, having a *bizcocho* and coffee, when this girl came in.
Everything about her said Indian, from the maroon *rebozo* to the black dress
with purple flowers on it, to the swaying way she walked, that no woman ever
got without carrying pots, bundles, and baskets on her head from the time she
could crawl. But she wasn't any of the colors that Indians come in. She was
almost white, with just the least dip of *café con leche*. Her shape was Indian,
but not ugly. Most Indian women have a rope of muscle over their hips that
give them a high-waisted, mis-shapen look, thin, bunchy legs, and too much
breast-works. She had plenty in that line, but her hips were round, and her legs
had a soft line to them. She was slim, but there was something voluptuous about
her, like in three or four years she would get fat. All that, though, I only half
saw. What I noticed was her face. It was flat, like an Indian's but the nose
broke high, so it kind of went with the way she held her head, and the eyes
weren't dumb, with that shiny, shoe-button look. They were pretty big, and
black, but they leveled out straight, and had kind of a sleepy, impudent look
to them. Her lips were thick, but pretty, and of course had plenty of lipstick
on them.

It was about nine o'clock at night, and the place was pretty full, with
bullfight managers, agents, newspaper men, pimps, cops and almost everybody
you can think of, except somebody you would trust with your watch. She went
to the bar and ordered a drink, then went to a table and sat down, and I had a
stifled feeling I had had before, from the thin air up there, but that wasn't it
this time. There hadn't been any woman in my life for quite some while, and
I knew what this meant. Her drink came, and it was coca-cola and Scotch, and
I thought that over. It might mean that she was just starting the evening, and it
might mean she was just working up an appetite, and if it meant that I was

sunk. The Tupinamba is more of a café than a restaurant, but plenty of people eat there, and if that was what she expected to do, my last three pesos wouldn't go very far.

I had about decided to take a chance and go over there when she moved. She slipped over to a place about two tables away, and then she moved again, and I saw what she was up to. She was closing in on a bullfighter named Triesca, a kid I had seen a couple of times in the ring, once when he was on the card with Solorzano, that seemed to be their main ace at the time, and once after the main season was over, when he killed two bulls in a novillada they had one Sunday in the rain. He was a wow with the cape, and just moving up into the money. He had on the striped suit a Mexican thinks is pretty nifty, and a cream-colored hat. He was alone, but the managers, agents, and writers kept dropping by his table. She didn't have much of a chance, but every time three or four or five of them would shove off she would slip nearer. Pretty soon she dropped down beside him. He didn't take off his hat. That ought to have told me something, but it didn't. All I saw was a cluck too stuck on himself to know how to act. She spoke, and he nodded, and they talked a little bit, and it didn't look like she had ever seen him before. She drank out, and he let it ride for a minute, then he ordered another.

When I got it, what she was in there for, I tried to lose interest in her, but my eyes kept coming back to her. After a few minutes, I knew she felt me there, and I knew some of the other tables had tumbled to what was going on. She kept pulling her *rebozo* around her, like it was cold, and hunching one shoulder up, so she half had her back to me. All that did was throw her head up still higher, and I couldn't take my eyes off her at all. So of course a bullfighter is like any other ham, he's watching every table but his own, and he had no more sense than to see these looks that were going round. You understand, it's a dead-pan place, a big café with a lot of mugs sitting around with their hats on the back of their heads, eating, drinking, smoking, reading, and jabbering Spanish, and there wasn't any nudging, pointing, or hey-get-a-load-of-this. They strictly minded their business. Just the same, there would be a pair of eyes behind a newspaper that weren't on the newspaper, or maybe a waitress would stop by somebody, and say something, and there'd be a laugh just a little louder than a waitress's gag is generally worth. He sat there, with a kind of a foolish look on his face, snapping his fingernail against his glass, and then I felt a prickle go up my spine. He was getting up, he was coming over.

A guy with three pesos in his pocket doesn't want any trouble, and when the room froze like a stop-camera shot, I tried to tell myself to play it friendly, to get out of it without starting something I couldn't stop. But when he stood there in front of me he still had on that hat.

"My table, he interest you, ha?"

"Your—what?"

"My table. You look, you seem interest, Señor."

"Oh, now I understand."

I wasn't playing it friendly, I was playing it mean. I got up, with the best smile I could paste on my face, and waved at a chair. "Of course. I shall explain. I shall gladly explain." Down there you make it simple, because spig reception isn't any too good. "Please sit down."

He looked at me and he looked at the chair, but it looked like he had me on the run, so he sat down. I sat down. Then I did something I wanted to do for fifteen minutes. I lifted that cream hat off his head, like it was the nicest thing I knew to do for him, slipped a menu card under it, and put it on a chair. If he had moved I was going to let him have it, if they shot me for it. He didn't. It caught him by surprise. A buzz went over the room. The first round was mine.

"May I order you something, Señor?"

He blinked, and I don't think he even heard me. Then he began looking around for help. He was used to having a gallery yell Olé every time he wiped his nose, but it had walked out on him this time. It was all deadpan, what he saw, and so far as they were concerned, we weren't even there. There wasn't anything he could do but face me, and try to remember what he had come for.

"The explain. Begin, please."

I had caught him with one he wasn't looking for, and I decided to let him have another, right between the eyes. "Certainly. I did look, that is true. But not at you. Believe me, Señor, not at you. And not at the table. At the lady."

". . . You—tell me this? You tell me this thing?"

"Sure. Why not?"

Well, what was he going to do? He could challenge me to a duel, but they never heard of a duel in Mexico. He could take a poke at me, but I outweighed him by about fifty pounds. He could shoot me, but he didn't have any gun. I had broken all the rules. You're not supposed to talk like that in Mexico, and once you hand a Mexican something he never heard of, it takes him about a year to figure out the answer. He sat there blinking at me, and the red kept creeping over his ears and cheeks, and I gave him plenty of time to think of something, if he could, before I went on. "I tell you what, Señor. I have examined this lady with care, and I find her very lovely. I admire your taste. I envy your fortune. So let us put her in a lottery, and the lucky man wins. We'll each buy her a ticket, and the one holding the highest number buys her next drink. Yes?"

Another buzz went around, a long one this time. Not over half of them in there could speak any English, and it had to be translated around before they could get it. He took about four beats to think it through, and then he began to feel better. "Why I do this, please? The lady, she is with me, no? I put lady in *lotería,* what you put in, Señor? You tell me that?"

"I hope you're not afraid, Señor?"

He didn't like that so well. The red began to creep up again, but then I felt something behind me, and I didn't like that so well either. In the U.S., you feel something behind you, it's probably a waiter with a plate of soup, but in Mexico it could be anything, and the last thing you want is exactly the best bet. About half the population of the country go around with pearl-handled automatics on their hips, and the bad part about those guns is that they shoot, and after they shoot nothing is ever done about it. This guy had a lot of friends. He was a popular idol, but I didn't know of anybody that would miss me. I sat looking straight at him, afraid even to turn around.

He felt it too, and a funny look came over his face. I leaned over to brush cigarette ashes off my coat, and out of the tail of my eye I peeped. There had been a couple of lottery peddlers in there, and when he came over they must have stopped in their tracks like everybody else. They were back there now, wig-wagging him to say yes, that it was in the bag. I didn't let on. I acted impatient, and sharpened up a bit when I jogged him. "Well, Señor? Yes?"

"*Sí, sí*. We make *lotería!*"

They broke pan then, and crowded around us, forty or fifty of them. So long as we meant business, it had to be hands off, but now that it was a kind of a game, anybody could get in it, and most of them did. But even before the crowd, the two lottery peddlers were in, one shoving pink tickets at me, the other green tickets at him. You understand; there's hundreds of lotteries in Mexico, some pink, some green, some yellow, and some blue, and not many of them pay anything. Both of them went through a hocus-pocus of holding napkins over the sheets of tickets, so we couldn't see the numbers, but my man kept whispering to me, and winking, meaning that his numbers were awful high. He was an Indian, with gray hair and a face like a chocolate saint, and you would have thought he couldn't possibly tell a lie. I thought of Cortés, and how easy he had seen through their tricks, and how lousy the tricks probably were.

But I was different from Cortés, because I wanted to be taken. Through the crowd I could see the girl, sitting there as though she had no idea what was going on, and it was still her I was after, not getting the best of a dumb bullfighter. And something told me the last thing I ought to do was to win her in a lottery. So I made up my mind I was going to lose, and see what happened then.

I waved at him, meaning pick whatever one he wanted, and there wasn't much he could do but wave back. I picked the pink, and it was a peso, and I laid it down. When they tore off the ticket, they went through some more hocus-pocus of laying it down on the table, and covering it with my hat. He took the green, and it was half a peso. That was a big laugh, for some reason. They put his hat over it, and then we lifted the hats. I had No. 7. He had No. 100,000 and something. That was an Olé. I still don't get the chemistry of a Mexican. Out in the ring, when the bull comes in, they know that in exactly fifteen minutes that bull is going to be dead. Yet when the sword goes in, they yell like hell. And mind you, there's nothing as much like one dead bull as another dead bull. In that café that night there wasn't one man there that didn't know I was framed, and yet when the hats were lifted they gave him a hand, and clapped him on the shoulder, and laughed, just like Lady Luck had handed him a big victory.

"So. And now. You still look, ha?"

"Absolutely not. You've won, and I congratulate you, *de todo corazón.* Please give the lady her ticket, with my compliments, and tell her I hope she wins the Bank of Mexico."

"*Sí, sí, sí.* And so, Señor, *adiós.*"

He went back with the tickets, and I put a little more hot *leche* into my coffee, and waited. I didn't look. But there was a mirror back of the bar, so I could see if I wanted to, and just once, after he had handed her the tickets, and they had a long jibber-jabber, she looked.

It was quite a while before they started out. I was between them and the door, but I never turned my head. Then I felt them stop, and she whispered to him, and he whispered back, and laughed. What the hell? He had licked me, hadn't he? He could afford to be generous. A whiff of her smell hit me in the face, and I knew she was standing right beside me, but I didn't move till she spoke.

"Señor."

I got up and bowed. I was looking down at her, almost touching her. She was smaller than I had thought. The voluptuous lines, or maybe it was the way she held her head, fooled you.

"Señorita."

"*Gracias,* thanks, for the *billete.*"

"It was nothing, Señorita. I hope it wins for you as much as it lost for me. You'll be rich—*muy rico.*"

She liked that one. She laughed a little, and looked down, and looked up. "So. *Muchas gracias.*"

"*De nada.*"

But she laughed again before she turned away, and when I sat down my head was pounding, because that laugh, it sounded as though she had started to say something and then didn't, and I had this feeling there would be more. When I could trust myself to look around, he was still standing there near the door, looking a little sore. From the way he kept looking at the *damas,* I knew she must have gone in there, and he wasn't any too pleased about it.

In a minute, my waitress came and laid down my check. It was for sixty centavos. She had waited on me before, and she was a pretty little *mestiza,* about forty, with a wedding ring she kept flashing every time she got the chance. A wedding ring is big news in Mexico, but it still doesn't mean there's been a wedding. She pressed her belly against the table, and then I heard her voice, though her lips didn't move and she was looking off to one side: "The lady, you like her *dirección,* yes? Where she live?"

"You sure you know this *dirección?*"

"A *paraquito* have told me—just now."

"In that case, yes."

I laid a peso on the check. Her little black eyes crinkled up into a nice friendly smile, but she didn't move. I put the other peso on top of it. She took out her pencil, pulled the menu over, and started to write. She hadn't got three letters on paper before the pencil was jerked out of her hand, and he was standing there, purple with fury. He had tumbled, and all the things he had wanted to say to me, and never got the chance, he spit at her, and she spit back. I couldn't get all of it, but you couldn't miss the main points. He said she was delivering a message to me, she said she was only writing the address of a hotel I had asked for, a hotel for *Americanos*. They must like to see a guy framed in Mexico. About six of them chimed in and swore they had heard me ask her the address of a hotel, and that that was all she was giving me. They didn't fool him for a second. He was up his own alley now, and speaking his own language. He told them all where to get off, and in the middle of it, here she came, out of the *damas*. He let her have the last of it, and then he crumpled the menu card up and threw it in her face, and walked out. She hardly bothered to watch him go. She smiled at me, as though it was a pretty good joke, and I got up. "Señorita. Permit me to see you home."

That got a buzz, a laugh, and an *Olé*.

I don't think there's ever been a man so moony that a little bit of chill didn't come over him as soon as a woman said yes, and plenty of things were going through my head when she took my arm and we headed for the door of that café. One thing that was going through was that my last peso was gone at last, that I was flat broke in Mexico City with no idea what I was going to do or how I was going to do it. Another thing was that I didn't thank them for their *Olé*, that I hated Mexicans and their tricks, and hated them all the more because the tricks were all so bad you could always see through them. A Frenchman's tricks cost you three francs, but a Mexican is just dumb. But the main thing was a queer echo in that *Olé*, like they were laughing at me all the time, and I wondered, all of a sudden, which way we were going to turn when we got out that door. A girl on the make for a bullfighter, you don't exactly expect that she came out of a convent. Just the same, it hadn't occurred to me up to that second that she could be a downright piece of trade goods. I was hoping, when we reached the main street, that we would turn right. To the right lay the main part of town, and if we headed that way, she could be taking me almost anywhere. But to our left lay the Guauhtemolzin, and that's nothing but trade.

We turned left.

We turned left, but she walked so nice and talked so sweet I started hoping again. Nothing about an Indian makes any sense. He can live in a hut made of sticks and mud, and sticks and mud are sticks and mud, aren't they? You can't make anything else out of them. But he'll take you in there with the nicest manners in the world, more dignity than you'd ever get from a dozen dentists in the U.S., with stucco bungalows that cost ten thousand dollars apiece, kids in a private school, and stock in the building and loan. She went along, her hand on my arm, and if she had been a duchess she couldn't have stepped cleaner. She made a little gag out of falling in step, looked up once or twice and smiled, and then asked me if I had been long in Mexico.

"Only three or four months."

"Oh. You like?"

"Very much." I didn't, but I wanted anyway to be as polite as she was. "It's very pretty."

"Yes." She had a funny way of saying yes, like the rest of them have. She drew it out, so it was "yayse." "Many flowers."

"And birds."

"And señoritas."

"I wouldn't know about them."

"No? Just a little bit?"

"No."

An American girl would have mauled it to death, but when she saw I didn't want to go on with it, she smiled and began talking about Xochimilco, where the best flowers grew. She asked me if I had been there. I said no, but maybe some day she would take me. She looked away at that, and I wondered why. I figured I had been a little previous. Tonight was tonight, and after that it would be time to talk about Xochimilco. We got to the Guauhtemolzin. I was hoping she would cross. She turned, and we hadn't gone twenty yards before she stopped at a crib.

I don't know if you know how it works in Mexico. There's no houses, with a madame, a parlor, and an electric piano, anyway not in that part of town. There's a row of adobe huts, one story high, and washed blue, or pink, or green, or whatever it happens to be. Each hut is one room deep, and jammed up against each other in the way they are, they look like a barracks. In each hut is a door, with a half window in it, like a hat-check booth. Under the law they've got to keep that door shut, and drum up trade by leaning out the window, but if they know the cop they can get away with an open door. This door was wide open, with three girls in there, two of them around fourteen, and looking like children, the other big and fat, maybe twenty-five. She brought me right in, but then I was alone, because she and the other three went out in the street to have a palaver, and I could partly catch what it was. They all four rented the room together, so three of them had to wait outside when one of them had a customer, but I seemed to be a special case, and if I was going to spend the night, her friends had to flop somewhere else. Most of the street got in it before long, the cop, the café woman on the corner, and a flock of girls from the other cribs. Nobody sounded sore, or surprised, or made dirty cracks. A street like that is supposed to be tough, but from the way they talked, you would have thought it was the junior section of the Ladies' Aid figuring out where to bunk the minister's brother-in-law that had blown in town kind of sudden. They acted like it was the most natural thing in the world.

After a while they got it straightened out to suit them, who was to go where, and she came back and closed the door and closed the window. There was a bed in there, and a chest of drawers in the early Grand Rapids style, and a washstand with a mirror over it, and some grass mats rolled up in a corner, for sleeping purposes. Then there were a couple of chairs. I was tilted back on one, and as soon as she had given me a cigarette, she took the other. There we were. There was no use kidding myself any longer why Triesca hadn't taken off his hat. My lady love was a three-peso whore.

(1937)

From

TROPIC OF CAPRICORN
by Henry Miller

Maxie with his talk of Odessa revived something which I had lost as a child. Though I had never a very clear picture of Odessa the aura of it was like the little neighborhood in Brooklyn which meant so much to me and from which I had been torn away too soon. I get a very definite feeling of it every time I see an Italian painting without perspective; if it is a picture of a funeral procession, for example, it is exactly the sort of experience which I knew as a child, one of intense immediacy. If it is a picture of the open street, the women sitting in the windows are sitting *on* the street and not above it and away from it. Everything that happens is known immediately by everybody, just as among primitive people. Murder is in the air, chance rules.

Just as in the Italian primitives this perspective is lacking, so in the little old neighborhood from which I was uprooted as a child there were these parallel vertical planes on which everything took place and through which, from layer to layer, everything was communicated, as if by osmosis. The frontiers were sharp, clearly defined, but they were not impassable. I lived then, as a boy, close to the boundary between the north and the south side. I was just a little bit over on the north side, just a few steps from a broad thoroughfare called North Second Street, which was for me the real boundary line between the north and the south side. The actual boundary was Grand Street, which led to Broadway Ferry, but this street meant nothing to me, except that it was already beginning to be filled with Jews. No, North Second Street was the mystery street, the frontier between two worlds. I was living, therefore, between two boundaries, the one real, the other imaginary—as I have lived all my life. There was a little street, just a block long, which lay between Grand Street and North Second Street, called Fillmore Place. This little street was obliquely opposite the house my grandfather owned and in which we lived. It was the most enchanting street I have ever seen in all my life. It was the ideal street—for a boy, a lover, a maniac, a drunkard, a crook, a lecher, a thug, an astronomer, a musician, a poet, a tailor, a shoemaker, a politician. In fact this was just the sort of street it was, containing just such representatives of the human race, each one a world unto himself and all living together harmoniously and inharmoniously, *but together,* a solid corporation, a close knit human spore which could not disintegrate unless the street itself disintegrated.

So it seemed, at least. Until the Williamsburg Bridge was opened, whereupon there followed the invasion of the Jews from Delancey Street, New York. This brought about the disintegration of our little world, of the little street called Fillmore Place, which like the name itself was a street of value, of dignity, of light, of surprises. The Jews came, as I say, and like moths they began to eat into the fabric of our lives until there was nothing left but this mothlike presence which they brought with them everywhere. Soon the street began to smell bad, soon the real people moved away, soon the houses began to deteriorate and even the stoops fell away, like the paint. Soon the street looked like a dirty mouth with all the prominent teeth missing, with ugly charred stumps gaping here and there, the lips rotting, the palate gone. Soon the garbage was knee deep in the gutter and the fire escapes filled with bloated bedding, with cockroaches, with dried blood. Soon the kosher sign appeared on the shop windows and there was poultry everywhere and lox and sour pickles and enormous loaves of bread. Soon there were baby carriages in every areaway and on the stoops and in the little yards and before the shop fronts. And with the change the English language also disappeared; one heard nothing but Yiddish, nothing but this sputtering, choking, hissing tongue in which God and rotten vegetables sound alike and mean alike.

We were among the first families to move away, following the invasion. Two or three times a year I came back to the old neighborhood, for a birthday or for Christmas or Thanksgiving. With each visit I marked the loss of something I had loved and cherished. It was like a bad dream. It got worse and worse. The house in which my relatives still lived was like an old fortress going to ruin; they were stranded in one of the wings of the fortress, maintaining a forlorn, island life, beginning themselves to look sheepish, hunted, degraded. They even began to make distinctions between their Jewish neighbors, finding some of them quite human, quite decent, clean, kind, sympathetic, charitable, etc. etc. To me it was heartrending. I could have taken a machine gun and mowed the whole neighborhood down, Jew and Gentile together.

It was about the time of the invasion that the authorities decided to change the name of North Second Street to Metropolitan Avenue. This highway, which to the Gentiles had been the road to the cemeteries, now became what is called an artery of traffic, a link between two ghettos. On the New York side the river front was rapidly being transformed owing to the erection of the skyscrapers. On our side, the Brooklyn side, the warehouses were piling up and the approaches to the various new bridges created plazas, comfort stations, pool-rooms, stationery shops, ice-cream parlors, restaurants, clothing stores, hock shops, etc. In short everything was becoming *metropolitan,* in the odious sense of the word.

As long as we lived in the old neighborhood we never referred to Metropolitan Avenue: it was always North Second Street, despite the official change of name. Perhaps it was eight or ten years later, when I stood one winter's day at the corner of the street facing the river and noticed for the first time the great tower of the Metropolitan Life Insurance Building, that I realized that North Second Street was no more. The imaginary boundary of my world had changed. My glance traveled now far beyond the cemeteries, far beyond the rivers, far beyond the city of New York or the State of New York, beyond the whole United States indeed. At Point Loma, California, I had looked out upon the broad Pacific and I had felt something there which kept my face permanently screwed in another direction. I came back to the old neighborhood, I remember, one night with my old friend Stanley who had just come out of the army, and we walked the streets sadly and wistfully. A European can scarcely know what this feeling is like. Even when a town becomes modernized, in Europe, there are still vestiges of the old. In America, though there are vestiges, they are effaced, wiped out of the consciousness, trampled upon, obliterated, nulli-fied by the new. The new is, from day to day, a moth which eats into the fabric of life, leaving nothing finally but a great hole. Stanley and I, we were walking through this terrifying hole. Even a war does not bring this kind of desolation and destruction. Through war a town may be reduced to ashes and the entire population wiped out, but what springs up again resembles the old. Death is fecundating, for the soil as well as for the spirit. In America the destruction is complete, annihilating. There is no rebirth, only a cancerous growth, layer upon layer of new, poisonous tissue, each one uglier than the previous one.

We were walking through this enormous hole, as I say, and it was a win-ter's night, clear, frosty, sparkling, and as we came through the south side to-ward the boundary line we saluted all the old relics or the spots where things had once stood and where there had been once something of ourselves. And as we approached North Second Street, between Fillmore Place and North Second Street—a distance of only a few yards and yet such a rich, full area of the globe—before Mrs. O'Melio's shanty I stopped and looked up at the house where I had known what it was to really have a being. Everything had shrunk now to diminutive proportions, including the world which lay beyond the boundary line, the world which had been so mysterious to me and so terrifyingly grand, so delimited. Standing there in a trance I suddenly recalled a dream which I have had over and over, which I still dream now and then, and which I hope to dream as long as I live. It was the dream of passing the boundary line. As in all dreams the remarkable thing is the vividness of the reality, the fact that *one is in reality* and not dreaming. Across the line I am unknown and absolutely alone. Even the language has changed. In fact, I am always regarded as a stranger, a for-

eigner. I have unlimited time on my hands and I am absolutely content in saun-
tering through the streets. There is only *one* street, I must say—the continua-
tion of the street on which I lived. I come finally to an iron bridge over the
railroad yards. It is always nightfall when I reach the bridge, though it is only
a short distance from the boundary line. Here I look down upon the webbed
tracks, the freight stations, the tenders, the storage sheds, and as I gaze down
upon this cluster of strange moving substances a process of metamorphosis takes
place, *just as in a dream.* With the transformation and deformation I become
aware that this is the old dream which I have dreamed so often. I have a wild
fear that I shall wake up, and indeed I know that I will wake up shortly, just
at the moment when in the midst of a great open space I am about to walk into
the house which contains something of the greatest importance for me. Just as
I go toward this house the lot on which I am standing begins to grow vague at
the edges, to dissolve, to vanish. Space rolls in on me like a carpet and swallows me up, and with it of course the house which I never succeed in entering.

There is absolutely no transition from this, the most pleasurable dream I
know, to the heart of a book called *Creative Evolution.* In this book by Henri
Bergson, which I came to as naturally as to the dream of the land beyond the
boundary, I am again quite alone, again a foreigner, again a man of indeter-
minate age standing on an iron bridge observing a peculiar metamorphosis without
and within. If this book had not fallen into my hands at the precise moment it
did, perhaps I would have gone mad. It came at a moment when another huge
world was crumbling on my hands. If I had never understood a thing which
was written in this book, if I have preserved only the memory of one word,
creative, it is quite sufficient. This word was my talisman. With it I was able
to defy the whole world, and especially my friends.

There are times when one must break with one's friends in order to understand the meaning of friendship. It may seem strange to say so, but the discovery of this book was equivalent to the discovery of a weapon, an implement, wherewith I might lop off all the friends who surrounded me and who
no longer meant anything to me. This book became my friend because it taught
me that I had no need of friends. It gave me the courage to stand alone, and it
enabled me to appreciate loneliness. I have never understood the book; at times
I thought I was on the point of understanding, but I never really did understand.
It was more important for me not to understand. With this book in my hands,
reading aloud to my friends, questioning them, explaining to them, I was made
clearly to understand that I had no friends, that I was alone in the world. Because in not understanding the meaning of the words, neither I nor my friends,
one thing became very clear and that was that there were ways of not understanding and that the difference between the non-understanding of one individual and the non-understanding of another created a world of terra firma even
more solid than differences of understanding. Everything which once I thought
I had understood crumbled, and I was left with a clean slate. My friends, on
the other hand, entrenched themselves more solidly in the little ditch of under-

standing which they had dug for themselves. They died comfortably in their little bed of understanding, to become useful citizens of the world. I pitied them, and in short order I deserted them one by one, without the slightest regret.

What was there then in this book which could mean so much to me and yet remain obscure? I come back to the word *creative*. I am sure that the whole mystery lies in the realization of the meaning of this word. When I think of the book now, and the way I approached it, I think of a man going through the rites of initiation. The disorientation and reorientation which comes with the initiation into any mystery is the most wonderful experience which it is possible to have. Everything which the brain has labored for a lifetime to assimilate, categorize and synthesize has to be taken apart and reordered. Moving day for the soul! And of course it's not for a day, but for weeks and months that this goes on. You meet a friend on the street by chance, one whom you haven't seen for several weeks, and he has become an absolute stranger to you. You give him a few signals from your new perch and if he doesn't cotton you pass him up—*for good*. It's exactly like mopping up a battlefield: all those who are hopelessly disabled and agonizing you dispatch with one swift blow of your club. You move on, to new fields of battle, to new triumphs or defeats. But you move! And as you move the world moves with you, with terrifying exactitude. You seek out new fields of operation, new specimens of the human race whom you patiently instruct and equip with the new symbols. You choose sometimes those whom you would never have looked at before. You try everybody and everything within range, provided they are ignorant of the revelation.

It was in this fashion that I found myself sitting in the busheling room of my father's establishment, reading aloud to the Jews who were working there. Reading to them from this new Bible in the way that Paul must have talked to the disciples. With the added disadvantage, to be sure, that these poor Jew bastards could not read the English language. Primarily I was directing myself toward Bunchek the cutter, who had a rabbinical mind. Opening the book I would pick a passage at random and read it to them in a transposed English almost as primitive as pidgin English. Then I would attempt to explain, choosing for example and analogy the things they were familiar with. It was amazing to me how well they understood, how much better they understood, let me say, than a college professor or a literary man or any educated man. Naturally what they understood had nothing to do finally with Bergson's book, as a book, but was not that the purpose of such a book as this? My understanding of the meaning of a book is that the book itself disappears from sight, that it is chewed alive, digested and incorporated into the system as flesh and blood which in turn creates new spirit and reshapes the world. It was a great communion feast which we shared in the reading of this book and the outstanding feature of it was the chapter on Disorder which, having penetrated me through and through, has endowed me with such a marvelous sense of order that if a comet suddenly struck the earth and jarred everything out of place, stood everything upside down, turned everything inside out, I could orient myself to the new order in the twinkling of an eye. I have no fear or illusions about disorder any more than I have of death. The labyrinth is my happy hunting ground and the deeper I burrow into the maze the more oriented I become.

With *Creative Evolution* under my arm I board the elevated line at the Brooklyn Bridge after work and I commence the journey homeward toward the cemetery. Sometimes I get on at Delancey Street, the very heart of the ghetto, after a long walk through the crowded streets. I enter the elevated line below the ground, like a worm being pushed through the intestines. I know each time I take my place in the crowd which mills about the platform that I am the most unique individual down there. I look upon everything which is happening about me like a spectator from another planet. My language, my world, is under my arm. I am the guardian of a great secret; if I were to open my mouth and talk I would tie up traffic. What I have to say, and what I am holding in every night of my life on this journey to and from the office, is absolute dynamite. I am not ready yet to throw my stick of dynamite. I nibble at it meditatively, ruminatively, cogently. Five more years, ten more years perhaps, and I will wipe these people out utterly. If the train in making a curve gives a violent lurch I say to myself *fine! jump the track, annihilate them!* I never think of myself as being endangered should the train jump the track. We're wedged in like sardines and all the hot flesh pressed against me diverts my thoughts. I become conscious of a pair of legs wrapped around mine. I look down at the girl sitting in front of me, I look her right in the eye, and I press my knees still further into her crotch. She grows uneasy, fidgets about in her seat, and finally she turns to the girl next to her and complains that I am molesting her. The people about look at me hostilely. I look out of the window blandly and pretend I have heard nothing. Even if I wished to I can't remove my legs. Little by little though, the girl, by a violent pushing and squiggling, manages to unwrap her legs from mine. I find myself almost in the same situation with the girl next to her, the one she was addressing her complaints to. Almost at once I feel a sympathetic touch and then, to my surprise, I hear her tell the other girl that one can't help these things, that it is really not the man's fault but the fault of the company for packing us in like sheep. And again I feel the quiver of her legs against mine, a warm, human pressure, like squeezing one's hand. With my one free hand I manage to open my book. My object is two-fold: first I want her to see the kind of book I read, second, I want to be able to carry on the leg language without attracting attention. It works beautifully. By the time the train empties a bit I am able to take a seat beside her and converse with her—about the book, naturally. She's a voluptuous Jewess with enormous liquid eyes and the frankness which comes from sensuality. When it comes time to get off we walk arm in arm through the streets, toward her home. I am almost on the confines of the old neighborhood. Everything is familiar to me and yet repulsively strange. I have not walked these streets for years and now I am walking with a Jew girl from the ghetto, a beautiful girl with a strong Jewish accent. I look incongruous walking beside her. I can sense that people are staring at us behind our backs.

I am the intruder, the goy who has come down into the neighborhood to pick off a nice ripe cunt. She on the other hand seems to be proud of her conquest; she's showing me off to her friends. This is what I picked up in the train, an educated goy, a refined goy! I can almost hear her think it. Walking slowly I'm getting the lay of the land, all the practical details which will decide whether I call for her after dinner or not. There's no thought of asking her to dinner. It's a question of what time and where to meet and how will we go about it, because, as she lets drop just before we reach the door, she's got a husband who's a traveling salesman and she's got to be careful. I agree to come back and to meet her at the corner in front of the candy store at a certain hour. If I want to bring a friend along she'll bring her girl friend. No, I decide to see her alone. It's agreed. She squeezes my hand and darts off into a dirty hallway. I beat it quickly back to the elevated station and hasten home to gulp down the meal.

(1939)

From

THE LOON FEATHER
by Iola Fuller

"Cute little *chicot*," said Michel one late fall day, when he and I were tending large flakes of sturgeon drying on Marthe's rack, and Paul was playing in the gravel beside the cabin steps. Smiling at the wordless chatter of his seven months, as he tried to tell Mother what he was doing with the colored autumn leaves and scraps of birchbark in his hands, and hearing through the open door the sound of Mother's voice as she approved, I did not at first realize what Michel had said.

When I did ask about it, he told me *chicot* was the name he had always heard for those who were half one race and half another, that in the *pays d'en haut,* Canada, where his parents had come from, it was the name for the half-burned stumps in the cleared forest. It was just a new word to me. I felt no disparagement in it, and my serenity was untouched as I looked around at the sun-baked shore. Summer was already announcing her farewell in the colored leaves on the heights. The meadow grass was long, and had waves in it when the wind blew up off the water, making it look as if the water and the island were all of a piece and the fishing cabins were on a raft in the midst of the waves, a raft on which Michel and I stood and turned the drying fish.

Mother came to the door and took Paul up, smiling at us over his dark little head. Michel touched his forehead in respect.

"Quiet around here," he said when she had gone back in the cabin. "Where is Rosanne?"

"She went to the village with Jacques."

"Did he have Mother's market basket?"

I nodded. "Then you won't have to go, will you?"

"Not to the store, but I have a washing to take back to the village later on." He gathered up the smoke-dried flakes and tied them in a little bundle that could be hung from cabin rafters. As I spread fresh ones on the rack, I thought briefly about Rosanne. It had already become a natural thing for her to be with Jacques wherever he was. She had grown beautiful, with the same dark curly hair, the dark skin touched with rose and creaminess she had had as a child. The same temper she had, too, but she never showed it with Jacques and everyone marveled how he could so well manage her. Though he was only thirteen, he had already announced that when he had become a voyageur and then a brigade leader, with a comfortable home of his own in the winter camp—one of the important posts of the fur company it must be—he would marry Rosanne.

Little clouds, round and fluffy as a rabbit's tail, moved slowly through the sky above, and closer about our heads, gulls no less white than the clouds, circled out over the water and back again. The dull smoke rose in the still air. We heard throaty shouts and songs in French *patois* as canoes of traders went past. These were such accustomed sounds that for all the attention we gave, there might as well have been silence, until at once we heard a strange noise on the beach near the point. I dropped my turning-fork and ran out near the water, Michel following, until we could see what it was.

Coming down the beach was the postmaster's helper, this time leading a pony hitched to his high-wheeled cart, for it was full of bags and boxes, as many as the shallow cart could hold without tumbling them out. He came on down the beach so close that we could see his bushy eyebrows and his vacant eyes, before we saw that someone was walking behind the cart.

An old lady was coming down the beach, small and dressed like the village women, but with a difference. Her gray skirt had a black band as soft as fur around the hem. I later learned it was velvet. She was most careful to hold it up off the pebbles with one hand, while the other held a small bag of red woven goods. The dress had a high collar that seemed to be pushing her head in the air. On her head was a little cap of white, its ruffle standing up stiffly around her wrinkled face.

Many people were seen on our beach in summer that were never seen again, for the island had already become a stopping place for schooners, a place to rest overnight for travelers bound for Green Bay or the Chicago settlement at Fort Dearborn far down the lake of the Illinois. Many of these travelers strolled around our point on their way to see the mountainous bluffs beyond, the cobbler's cave, the spring, and Lover's Leap, as they had named the rock of the maiden. These always walked slowly, in groups of two or three, exclaiming and uttering admiring remarks. "Like a beautiful park set in blue water," they would say. "Such a quaint village." And, "We must all go to see the arched rock before we leave."

But no visitors had come alone, with a cartful of boxes. I looked at this old lady more closely. Her eyes were bright, and kept moving about, taking in the cabins, the rack of fish, and Michel and me. Her steps were quick and lively, so that her gray hair and wrinkles were her only sign of age. She was like a cedar that has long fought wind, snow, and hail, but at last begins dying in the top branches. She walked along as if she knew where she was going, yet by the way she looked at things I was sure she had never been on this beach before.

As we watched, one of the boxes slipped from the overloaded cart and fell to the ground. Instantly she raised the red bag and tapped the boy on the head with it as he bent to lift the box. "Don't you dare drop that!" she exclaimed in French. "That has my best spoons and china in it. *Vite, vite,* get on past these huts and to where my son lives."

The boy replaced the box and stood up, resting his hands on his hips. "He lives there," he said sulkily, twitching one shoulder toward our cabin.

"What? I believe it not!" shouted the old lady. She walked with short quick steps to where Michel and I were standing, her little silver shoe buckles catching the sun in quick flashes. She gave me only a curious look, and turned her back on me, speaking to Michel. "You tell me, lad, if you can, where does Monsieur Pierre Debans live?"

But Pierre had heard her voice and came running out of the cabin before Michel could answer. "Mother! Mother! What in the world—what are you doing here?"

She dropped her package and threw her arms around him. He gave her frail body a joyous hug, swinging her completely off the ground. Seeing them there, her wrinkled cheek against his pale white one, I saw how like they were. It was in the straightness of the nose, the height of forehead, the curl in the hair, though hers was almost as white as the cap that sat upon it. It was in the frailness of their bodies. Most of all it was in the way they held their heads up to face all the world, their backs in a straight line, and in their calmness with fun and fire beneath.

"How in the world did you get here?" Pierre asked again.

She put a wrinkled hand up to his face, fine lace falling away from her wrist as she did so. "*Mais, mon Dieu,* I got lonesome for you. And when I got your letter about your marriage, I understood you were not coming back to Quebec. So, *tout à fait,* I knew I must live here with you. Did you not get my letter about selling our house, and my plans to come?"

"No. I have had no letter from you in the whole winter."

"Maybe it was lost," Michel offered in explanation. "Do you remember, M'sieu, that one of the couriers drowned? Her letter may have been in his pack."

"It matters not about the letter," said the old lady. "I am here now. Let's have a look at you.'' She held her head on one side like a saucy wren and looked into Pierre's face. Then she threw her arms about him again, swinging around so her back was toward me. She had a row of curls all around under the cap so that from the back she looked like a little girl with her grandmother's clothes on. At once I was not shy of her, and stepped to her side.

"Bon jour, Madame,'' I said. ''I have heard Pierre speak of you.''

''Mercy on us!'' she exclaimed. ''Does this little native then speak like civilized people?''

Repulsed at her tone, I backed away, but I went on staring at her until she took her eyes away, turning back to her son. ''She calls you Pierre—do you then know some of the natives so well?'' Before he could answer, she came back to the first thing that had puzzled her. ''But how is it that you live in such a—'' She pointed to our cabin. And then a strange look came over her face. I followed the direction of her eyes. My mother had been attracted by the voices and stood looking out of the doorway. ''Pierre—*Pierre,* that is a servant?'' The old lady said it weakly, as if she already knew the truth.

''No, Mother, that is my wife.'' Pierre spoke with an effort, as if he were dragging a weight, as when one travels on snowshoes loaded with rain-softened snow. It was not as if he were ashamed, but as if he had to say something he could not make her understand.

A silence fell between them. The old lady looked as if she were suddenly ill. ''Why didn't you tell me you had taken an Indian squaw?''

Embarrassed, Michel and I turned away. I was angry at her tone, but kept silence, remembering an admonition of Marthe's, ''Say nothing that is unworthy of you.''

The boy, standing impatiently by his cart, called out, ''Want the boxes dumped here?''

''No,'' said the old lady. ''Take them right back to the village. I'll find some place to stay there until the next boat.''

''They ain't goin' to be any more boats,'' the boy said in his high voice. ''I heard the captain of this'un tell the postmaster there wouldn't be any more mail in by boat—there won't be another one through. It's too near time for the ice to come.''

''I will find you a place in the village until we can talk this over,'' said Pierre. ''Mrs. Ruggs keeps a very good boarding house.''

His mother looked like a trapped animal at the words that there wouldn't be any way to go back to Quebec.

Pierre went on. ''But of course you will live here with us. We'll arrange it somehow—we'll build you a room of your own.''

''A woman who has bowed at the court of France, to live with an Indian squaw for a daughter-in-law?'' she asked with spirit. ''Have I then made this long journey, risking my life for that? Never!''

Pierre bowed his head. ''She is good and kind, and she has made me very comfortable. And it is not unusual here—''

"Say not another word!" she said angrily. "And I suppose you've got a flock of papooses you haven't written me about, too," she stormed.

Pierre straightened up then, and turned to me, laying his hand gently on my shoulder. "This is her daughter, whom I have adopted. And we have now a son."

"A half-breed! Bringing half-breeds into the world!"

I knew suddenly that half-breed meant *chicot,* but her tone had put something shameful in it that had not been in Michel's word.

While I was thinking about it, she was still talking angrily. "I'm glad your father didn't live to see it. Could you do nothing better with your education, with one of the proudest names of France?"

She turned back to the boy, and motioned to him, commanding. He hastened to turn the pony around. Michel picked up her red package and handed it to her. *"Merci,"* she said sadly. *"Sainte Vierge, ne m'abandonnez pas,"* she sobbed as she turned away. Pierre hesitated, then took her parcel, and side by side they followed the cart around the point.

(1940)

From

SO LITTLE TIME
by John P. Marquand

The radio, too, was like Minot in that it represented his self-indulgence and his ability to get anything he wanted. The box was covered with all sorts of dials for short wave and long wave which Jeffrey could not understand, and adjustments for every sort of kilocycle. It was one of those radios which could pick up Japan as easily as a local station, and he finally saw where to turn it on. The uncanniness of a strange voice breaking the silence was stranger that afternoon than usual.

"And now this ends Jo-Jo and Mu-Mu. They'll be back again with you tomorrow, same time, same station. In fifteen seconds it will be exactly six o'clock, Lovely Watch time. L-o-v-e-l-y . . . and spelling, too, compact daintiness. Lovely Watch time. And now, friends, in these late days of March, the danger month, do you feel run-down, a little headachy, without the old pep to put things over? There's an easy answer. Mu-Mu Tablets. They work in six easy ways. At your neighborhood druggist, and remember, the letters of these two words read backwards spell 'um-um,' and that's the way they taste. And now it is six o'clock, and the friendly voice of your friendly reporter brings to you the latest flashes off the wires of the world press."

It was not decent. Jeffrey wondered why he tolerated such an intrusion on his thoughts. If he turned it off, he would not hear the news. The makers of Mu-Mu, spelt backward meaning "um-um," and of Lovely Watch, were trading on anxiety, tramping over the blood of battlefields to get the sordid anticlimax of their message home. He knew he would not like the voice of the friendly reporter, either, a fluty, cheery voice, dealing with headlines which were a distortion of fact.

". . . and now—Berlin. . . . On his arrival in Berlin from Moscow, Japan's foreign minister, Matsuoka, said in a message to the German people, 'The Japanese nation is with you, in joy or sorrow.' And he went on to say that Japan, and I quote, 'will not lag behind you in fidelity, courage, and firm determination to arrange the world on the basis of the New Order.' "

It was not hard to form an idea of what was meant. After waiting patiently, balancing everything, the government of Japan was reaching the conclusion that Germany could not help but win the war. It was possible to consider it as another piece of devious, oriental straddling, but he knew he would not have thought so if he were a Japanese. He thought of Japanese he had known, mostly salesmen in oriental stores and houseboys. Once he and Madge had employed a Japanese, an unhappy little man.

"The little bastard," Jeffrey said, and he turned off the radio. Then he heard Minot's voice behind him.

"What's the news?" Minot asked. Minot was wearing a quilted smoking jacket and patent-leather pumps.

"Japan is going to get into the Axis," Jeffrey said.

"A damn good thing if she does," Minot answered. "Let 'em come on in. You ought to hear the boys in the navy. What we won't do to Japan!"

"If we're going to convoy," Jeffrey said, "we won't have much navy in the Pacific.'

"We'll have enough," Minot said. "I'll tell you something. When I was coming North, I stopped in Washington, and I won't tell you who told me, but they're just waiting for the Japanese—I'll tell you something, Jeff, a war with Japan would be an air war, and people with Mongoloid eyes can't focus the way we can. Everybody knows they can't fly."

Minot was like everyone else, busily repeating something which someone else had said, and Jeffrey listened, as others always listened, hopefully taking that piece of gossip and trying to add it to something else.

"Gosh," Minot said, "it's gloomy here. Why haven't you turned on the lights? Where's William? Let's light a fire."

It was not so much the light that made it gloomy as those obtruding thoughts from which you could never escape. There was that tremor of insecurity again. It looked stormy outside and Jeffrey could see lights across the Park through the windows. He had loved the sensation once of standing behind the dark panes and listening to the invisible rain beat against them and hearing the roar of thunder overhead. He had loved it, because he had felt dry and secure, but now it was like standing behind a window and knowing that the rain would smash through into the room before the storm was over, and that everything would be a sodden, irreparable mess.

"Yes," Jeffrey said, "it still gets dark early."

Then the lights were on, and the whole room looked better. William had entered, with two cocktails on a silver tray.

"Well," Minot said, "happy landings!"

William touched a match to the fire and there was a sudden illusion of serenity and ease. Jeffrey raised his glass. He found it easier to take a drink that winter than it had ever been before. You could take a cocktail, and you did not care so much.

"So you're going to Hollywood," Minot said. "What do they want you for?"

Jeffrey had a suspicion that Minot looked upon Hollywood as a gay adventure, a round of yachting parties and night clubs. Jeffrey might have talked until he was blue in the face without ever convincing anyone like Minot that the work was hard.

"It's a script," Jeffrey said. "Their regular writers are bogged down with it. I have a sort of reputation for pulling things together."

Minot sat comfortably, looking at the fire.

"You won't be mad if I say something?" Minot said.

"No," Jeffrey said, "of course not," but he knew exactly what it was that Minot was going to say.

"Jeff, why don't you write something of your own instead of doing potboiling for someone else?"

It sounded exactly like Madge. That was what they always called it, "potboiling." He could not understand why that hackneyed term had such appeal for an amateur. It indicated the same type of mind that referred to writing as "scribbling," and he hoped very much that Minot would not use that term, but Minot used it.

"I mean," Minot said, "if you're going to do scribbling, why don't you do your own scribbling?"

Jeffrey hesitated. He even contrived to smile.

"I can't afford it, Minot," he said. "You see, I've got to pay the bills, and it takes a good deal of money, with the new income taxes."

When he saw Minot smile, he knew that Minot was exactly as annoyed by this explanation as he had been by Minot's reference to scribbling.

"Jeff," Minot said, "Madge has plenty of money."

"I thought you'd say that," Jeffrey answered. "Maybe it's funny of me, but I like to run my own show, while I can."

Minot nodded, and Jeffrey knew Minot was thinking that it was quite correct, that one did not take money from women.

"I know what you mean," Minot said. "Jeff, I'll tell you what I'll do. I'll stake you. You wouldn't mind that, would you?" And Minot leaned forward impulsively. "Jeff, you're too damned good. You're too good to waste your time working for a bunch of Jews in Hollywood."

"They pay for what I give them," Jeffrey said.

"God damn it," Minot said, "why do you always think about money?"

"I suppose you think it's funny of me," Jeffrey said. "There's only one thing I've ever done, and I want to keep on doing it. I want to run my own show."

Minot was silent and Jeffrey could see that he was puzzled.

"Jeff," Minot asked, "are you afraid?"

Jeffrey raised his head sharply.

"Afraid of what?" he asked.

Minot was watching him intently. Minot's knees were crossed, and he was moving one ankle nervously, so that Jeffrey could see the light from the fire reflected on Minot's patent-leather pump.

"Afraid that anything you do won't be any good."

Jeffrey sat looking at the fire. He did not want to take it, but he had to take it.

"Yes," he said, "I suppose so, in a way. Maybe, Minot, it's pretty late to try."

"It's never too late," Minot said.

The problems of human beings could not be expressed in such simple terms, but Minot did not see that.

"I don't know," Jeffrey said. "I've lived with myself for quite a while. Maybe I'll try it sometime, but I can't right now."

"You ought not to go to Hollywood," Minot said, "and work for a bunch of Jews."

"Why Jews, particularly?" Jeffrey asked. "You'd be surprised. They're about the same as anyone else."

"You know what I mean," Minot said. "It's just a figure of speech."

"Well, I wouldn't use it," Jeffrey said. "It doesn't make any sense."

Somehow, even talking to one's friends in these days you came to racial issues that bordered on a party line. Somewhere in the background, the old phrases were dangling. He could almost hear Minot saying that Jews were all right if there were not too many of them and that he was just as broad-minded as Jeffrey and that he liked Jews as individuals.

"I'm not saying anything against them," Minot said. "You know more about them than I do."

(1943)

From

GENTLEMAN'S AGREEMENT
by Laura Z. Hobson

A polite cough brought him back to the present. Miss Wales said, "Go right ahead, Mr. Green," and looked at the notes already folded neatly before him.

"Sorry, I got thinking about something. What about Jordan?"

"Well, he's telling everybody about Mr. Minify's ad and he thinks it's a wonderful thing. He's *saying*."

"Quick as that?" He snapped his fingers. Knuckling little hypocrite.

"I'd thought I'd ask you if it's true the ad says right out that—"

"Right straight out. It'll be in the papers tomorrow."

"You mean practically *inviting* any type to apply?"

"Any type? What are you driving at?"

"Oh, Mr. Green, *you* don't want things different around here either, do you? Even though you're an editor and it's different with editors?"

Finally it got through the sheath of his own good spirits that under her usual manner was something new.

"Different for editors how?"

She hesitated. She looked away. "Well, I just mean. If they just get one wrong one in, it'll come out of *us*." Her voice edged into stridency. "Don't you hate being the fall guy for the kikey ones?"

Kin to no reaction he'd ever had before, a tiny geyser seemed to shoot upward and spray out within his viscera. An image flashed into his mind of a minuscule Old Faithful. When he spoke, he did so with extreme care.

"We've got to be frank with each other," he said. "You have the right to know right off that words like kike and kikey and yid and coon and nigger just make me kind of sick, no matter who says them."

"Why, *I* just said it for a type. You know the kind of person." She was clearly astonished at being picked up on it.

"We're talking about a word, first."

"But that's nothing. Why, sometimes I even say it to myself—about me, I mean. Like, if I'm about to do something and I know I shouldn't, sort of in my head I'll say, 'Oh, don't be such a kike.' "

The minute geyser rose in stature, crowding his solar plexus. She was not improvising; this was truth she was telling him.

As if the matter were disposed of, she went on, "Just *one* of the objectionable ones in here and—"

He said, "Just a minute." She stopped. It had to be thought through a bit before he could go on. He leaned over his desk, picked up a pencil as though he were about to write. She waited, and this time he felt no compunction about letting her wait.

What made her do it? He had to know something of the answer, guess at it, find it, before he could go on speaking. Did she have so deep a hatred and fear of the word that she needed to fob it off as a light jest to exorcise it? Was it an unconscious need to beat the insulter at his own game by applying the epithet to oneself first? "This is nothing; this isn't a word that can hurt me." The man who cries out to the wife he has betrayed, "I know I'm a weakling, a bounder, a cad, anything you want," in the need to make himself immune from the words she would otherwise hurl—wasn't she doing the same thing? Or did her impulse spring from an unconscious longing, hidden and desperate, to be gentile and have the "right" to call Jews kikes?

He put down the pencil and turned back to her.

"What do you mean by 'objectionable'?" He was proud that no irritation sounded in his words.

"You know, loud, and too much rouge and all."

"They don't hire *any* girls that are loud and vulgar. What makes you think they'll suddenly start?"

"Well, it isn't *only* that." She suddenly turned on him with spirit. "You're just sort of heckling me, Mr. Green. You *know* the kind that just starts trouble in a place like this and the kind that doesn't, like you or me, so what's the sense of pinning me down?"

"You mean because we don't look especially Jewish."

"Well—" She smiled confidently.

That was it, then. They were O.K. Jews; they were "white" Jews; with them about, the issue could lie mousy and quiet.

"Look, Miss Wales," he said slowly, "I hate antisemitism and I guess I'd better tell you I hate it just as much when it comes from you as from anybody else."

"Me? Anti—why, Mr. Green!" She stood up, did nothing whatever for a space of seconds, and then walked with complete dignity from the room.

(1947)

From

THE GENTLE BUSH
by Barbara Giles

Until noon that morning Peter had thought he wouldn't go to the Mardi Gras dance. All day long he would read, even memorize some things in *The Orations of Famous Men* that Mr. DuPuy had loaned him. But when his mother called him to dinner he willingly put the book away under the counter and closed the store for the day. His yellow-and-red costume, not quite finished, lay across a chair near the dining room window, and when he looked at it he knew it would be impossible for him to stay home. All morning the weird shouts of masqueraders on the banquette had mingled with the *Orations,* making the latter twice as fatiguing. And they were fatiguing enough already, tiresome in what they had to say and full of words he didn't know. Of course he liked new words—that was what he really wanted out of the book—but they tortured him, too, until he had understood them, made them *his,* to use some day as he wanted.

"You will go?" his mother asked with timid eagerness, seeing his interest in the costume. "You will go to the party?"

He shrugged, then nodded, not too willing to please her in this respect. For he knew why she had been so eager, insisting that he was not too big for one more Mardi Gras, so he could tell her afterward what "they" (the children of the fine people) had worn and how their mammas had looked.

"*Ah-h-h!*" She expressed her joy with the one exclamation, then turned quickly to something else, as if afraid he might reconsider. "Sit, *cher;* for Papa will not wait, the *grillades* will be cold." Though her sentences ran together, there was a fluttery, jerky quality in her hurried speech. She sat down when her son did and began to dish out rice-and-gravy, white beans, and the savory beef of *grillades.* Aristide Boudreaux's family ate very well, compared with their relatives—as why shouldn't they, with a grocery store? Peter noticed that she had put out the rough, everyday china instead of the remarkable set—hand-painted, with scenes and bars of music from an opera—that old Mr. DeRoux had once thrust on Papa in payment of a bill he couldn't meet in cash. It was only when they themselves were very short of cash that Mamma took out the DeRoux plates for their salt-meat and grits. If her son hadn't known her so well, he might have thought she was making a little joke.

"What she buy, Madam Louis's granddaughter?" she inquired now, and went on without waiting for an answer, "*Mais,* but she was drassed! Avverything matching together and soch a beautiful collor; she is a pretty leetle thing. Clothes like that I have never seen, me, in Mr. Bienvenu's store!"

"Her Yankee aunt gave them, mebbe," Peter retorted.

"Mademoiselle Leonie is not herzalf a Yankee," his mother reminded him patiently. "It is her hosband."

"Quel différence? It is his money she pays with." Peter gave a short laugh. "When you remember how her father wanted to whip Papa for 'taking gold from the Carpetbaggers'!"

"Oh, *cher,*" his mother pleaded. "Nobody remambers that any more."

"No," Peter conceded, and refrained from repeating what his father had once said, which was in effect that if the Durels and their friends had tried to "remember" all the Cajuns who refused to support the Confederacy there would have been a civil war without end, worse than with the Yankees. He did not want to argue with his mother. Long ago he had found it was useless, and besides she was ill, often in pain. . . . He began to talk about other things, telling her some incidents of his stay last night at Shadowdown, and she listened with smiling absorption, occasionally asking a question to encourage him. He talked so well, her Peter, sometimes hardly like a Cajun at all! Let Raoul and Hermine and all her husband's family make fun if they wanted, or get mad and tell Aristide he should make the boy *work,* not read. That was because they were Boudreauxs and anyone could see Peter was really a Charpentier, like herself. Her own father had been able to read some English, and it wasn't the Carpetbaggers who taught him!

Her secret reflections, however, did not detract from the respect she showed her husband when he came in. (After all, a man with his own store—even the Charpentiers looked up to him.) She hurried to get his plate of food keeping warm on the back of the stove, bringing it almost as he sat down. When she put it before him he gave her a sharp, affectionate pat on the *derrière* and grinned at the little jump she made. But upon his son he turned a scowl.

"You close opp the store?" he demanded. "Already you close him opp?" He looked more like a blacksmith than his blacksmith father at Des Roses had, especially when a frown harshened his heavy features and accented his black eyebrows. There was no gray in them or in any of his hair, although he was fifty-five.

"Only three people came to buy," Peter said in indifferent defense. He knew that Papa didn't really expect the store to stay open after noon today and was only acting this way because he thought it was the way he should act. And indeed, after Aristide had shaken his head sternly and thrown a despairing glance at his wife, as if to say, "See what a foolish, lazy son we have!" he let the matter drop. There were complaints—Peter had heard them—that Aristide Boudreaux was a mean businessman, hard-fisted, greedy, and sly "even for a *Cajin.*" But it was said mostly by those who paid their bills in old china or tried not to pay at all. With such people it was good for him that he looked sly and could be mean on occasion. Among his own friends and his family he was regarded as a bluffer, although an uncommonly smart one.

"What you think, Anais!" he exclaimed after his first mouthful of rice-and-gravy, and her face brightened at the familiar phrase, a prelude to all the gossip and small news and speculation he picked up during a visit in town. Most of it Peter had heard the day before at school. He only half listened, dawdling over his fig preserves and coffee and watching with secret sympathy the zest of his father's bad table manners. Aristide ate like a man who had worked all his life for good food. The sun came in the window, revealing the polished cleanliness and all the dents in the scanty furniture, lighting up the cheap and gruesome painting of Christ on the Cross which Peter had liked when he was little because it reminded him of salt pork hanging on a hook in the pantry. Sometimes his mother's pride in her dining room sickened him. What was so grand about it, just because they didn't have to eat in the kitchen like most Cajuns? She was as good as Madam DeRoux or better, and she had more sense!

But listening to his parents' animated exchange, he felt shut out, apart from them. Sometimes they acted as if he were already grown and a stranger. It was a year now since Papa had roared at him, without bluffing, that he was making a goddog fool of himself and ruining the business with his crazy talk about the planters. His mother had cried, and Peter had promised that he would talk crazy only to them, not out of the house. But that, too, frightened his mother, and Aristide didn't encourage it. Of course he could talk to them about other things, ordinary things, but mostly when he was only with one of them. Together, they seemed to feel that he wasn't really interested, that he was moving into another world, one of strange words as well as strange ideas. Maybe they were right. . . .

And yet? When he had been quiet too long, Papa would sometimes remind him. "What was it you say to Mr. Louviere wan day?" he would ask. "I forgat, me. What you say that mek him so mad, mad?" He would grin, waiting for the answer which he remembered perfectly well. "How much you pay God for your sins?" was what Peter had said to the man who was notorious in Bienville for his vices and for his frantic eagerness when the pews were auctioned every year to purchase the one closest to the altar.

Then Aristide would roar, but with laughter this time. He himself had no great love for the planters, who had treated him like a cur during the Reconstruction just because he had taken money—honest money for honest work—from a Carpetbagger. And he loved them no better because he had finally acted like a cur, terrified of and repudiating the "nigger government," relieved after all to see the White Man's League growing with less and less interference from Washington. But what else could he have done? He too was a white man; Louis Durel's threat to whip him was nothing by his taunt that the Boudreauxs were "behaving like coons." Worse than coons. One day on the road he had met an elderly Negro who looked at him contemptuously and said *"Saloperie!"* And he, Aristide Boudreaux, had not been able to strike him, even answer him. He was too full of the shame of Louis Durel's phrase. Better in the end to behave like a cur, a white cur.

But at that point in his reasoning he usually shrugged. It was all so long ago and who cared now? He had what he wanted most, his independence and comfort—all the sweeter that he still had to scheme and work to keep them. When Louis Durel's widow came to him, three years ago, unable to meet the prices of Mr. Fuselier's big store on the main street and asking him, Aristide, for good terms (meaning long credit) he had felt a certain triumph, but he had considered the matter from a strictly business viewpoint. Yes, he would give credit, the same as he extended to all his "fine trade," those few members of the gentry who bought from him only because of credit and with whom he dealt leniently up to a point. But only to a point, for too much fine trade could ruin him. In her case, however, it had been different: she had not tried to play any tricks on him. The bills were paid, sometimes very late, but always paid. That was the way she had said it would be, in their first talk, and Aristide had been inclined to believe her then. He had never gotten over his surprise at that interview. She had come into the dining room, at Anais's excited invitation, and sat down and drunk a little coffee, even pretending a polite surprise that they were not drinking with her. And while her speech was delicate, with little hesitations and roundabout phrases, she had looked him straight in the eye without embarrassment and managed to make herself quite plain. Anais had been rather shocked—it was not the way she had expected a great lady to act!

She was more shocked now, three years later, by the rumor Aristide had to report: that "young" Mr. Agricole was trying to buy Madam Villebauve's land. And he was said to have as much land, himself, as his Uncle Louis once had.

"Non!" she cried, in disbelief and denial. To her it was unthinkable that the first Agricole, who from her in-laws' accounts was not quite a gentleman, should have left his son wealthy while Madam Louis' husband had died in debt.

The tone of her denial reminded Peter of the interview between his father and Madam Louis. He had come into the room and his mother had proudly pushed him forward in an introduction, but keeping her hand on his wrist as though to restrain him too. Her fingers had been cold and trembly, her face bright pink. In Anais Boudreaux's mind there was no great lady in the world as great as this one. Aristide and she had lived at Des Roses for several years after their marriage, staying in his father's house even while 'Tide clerked in Bienville at the store he now owned. And Des Roses then had been the largest plantation on the bayou; few people knew that Louis Durel owed every acre of it to the banks in New Orleans. Madam Louis dressed always in satin, her crucifix was all gold, her daughters were the belles of the bayou. . . .

All this Peter had heard before he was three. Some of it his mother had seen herself, some had been handed down to her by Grandpere Boudreaux, who had witnessed the height of the Durel affluence before the Civil War. It was said that Louis had met and married his wife in Paris and that at first she had spoken of Des Roses as a "wilderness." And it was said that her very manner had shamed the Yankee looters quartered for a while at her home. Aristide used to laugh harshly at that, remarking that it was a pity no one had done the same to the Confederates, who had been worse thieves than the Northern troops, robbing the poor people. But Anais wouldn't listen to him. It was enough for her that Des Roses and its owners, when she first knew them, had long emerged intact from the horror of Reconstruction—a worse horror to her than to 'Tide, for her people, the "better class," had fought with the Confederacy. She, like many others in Bienville, still spoke of the plantation as "the Durel place" and regarded it as Madam Louis's domain.

Her son knew all that; he had learned all the legends, had even seen for himself, long ago, the satin and gold. Yet when Anais thrust him forward he had murmured a *bonjour* instead of the *à votre service* which the Durels expected from their inferiors, having taught them to say it in the first place. And he had looked directly at the great lady, with the calm inquisitiveness that he bestowed on any new acquaintance. There was nothing in her appearance to excite or startle him: neither the plain cotton of her gloves, since he knew that she had come in a cheap buggy, nor the costly looking old-lace fichu, since he could remember her when she drove out in her carriage behind four horses, with that strange, fixed yet dreamy look on her face that people naturally attributed to hauteur. No, the only thing that surprised him at all was his own impression that she looked happier now than she had in the carriage days. But probably he was mistaken. And at any rate, it didn't matter. It was not the great ladies, but their husbands, who mattered. He could remember Louis Durel much better. And the stories about *him!*

Peter treasured the stories, with a sharp, hating relish. It was the hatred he had for all planters, but Louis Durel had started it. There was the story told by his father, about the time Mr. Durel sent a Negro to revile him:

"I did not know, me, I was a big pighead—I did not know it was Mr. Louis Durel's nigger! I thought it was a Bagger nigger who seh to me *Saloperie!* Bot Louis Durel he had buyed that man; him it was who sant him to spit in my fess almost! And me, I did not find out till after Louis Durel was dead. A smot wan he was, that Mr. Durel—I could bost his nose when I think of it. To os he seh 'You ack like the nigger.' To nigger he seh 'You better than the *Cajin.*' And all the time he go at night to a black woman, the wan they call Crezzy Lize. He *med* her crezzy, you hear that? The things he donn to her at night, for his fon, they med her crezzy!"

Louis Durel on his big white mare, the white camellia in his buttonhole (*"pour la pureté"*). White hands on the reins, brass knuckles in his pocket. . . .

(1947)

AFTER YOU, MY DEAR ALPHONSE
by Shirley Jackson

Mrs. Wilson was just taking the gingerbread out of the oven when she heard Johnny outside talking to someone.

"Johnny," she called, "you're late. Come in and get your lunch."

"Just a minute, Mother," Johnny said. "After you, my dear Alphonse."

"After *you,* my dear Alphonse," another voice said.

"No, after *you,* my dear Alphonse," Johnny said.

Mrs. Wilson opened the door. "Johnny," she said, "you come in this minute and get your lunch. You can play after you've eaten."

Johnny came in after her, slowly. "Mother," he said, "I brought Boyd home for lunch with me."

"Boyd?" Mrs. Wilson thought for a moment. "I don't believe I've met Boyd. Bring him in, dear, since you've invited him. Lunch is ready."

"Boyd!" Johnny yelled. "Hey, Boyd, come on in!"

"I'm coming. Just got to unload this stuff."

"Well, hurry, or my mother'll be sore."

"Johnny, that's not very polite to either your friend or your mother," Mrs. Wilson said. "Come sit down, Boyd."

As she turned to show Boyd where to sit, she saw he was a Negro boy, smaller than Johnny but about the same age. His arms were loaded with split kindling wood. "Where'll I put this stuff, Johnny?" he asked.

Mrs. Wilson turned to Johnny. "Johnny," she said, "what did you make Boyd do? What is that wood?"

"Dead Japanese," Johnny said mildly. "We stand them in the ground and run over them with tanks."

"How do you do, Mrs. Wilson?" Boyd said.

"How do you do, Boyd? You shouldn't let Johnny make you carry all that wood. Sit down now and eat lunch, both of you."

"Why shouldn't he carry the wood, Mother? It's his wood. We got it at his place."

"Johnny," Mrs. Wilson said, "go on and eat your lunch."

"Sure," Johnny said. He held out the dish of scrambled eggs to Boyd. "After you, my dear Alphonse."

"After *you,* my dear Alphonse," Boyd said.

"After *you,* my dear Alphonse," Johnny said. They began to giggle.

"Are you hungry, Boyd?" Mrs. Wilson asked.

"Yes, Mrs. Wilson."

"Well, don't let Johnny stop you. He always fusses about eating, so you just see that you get a good lunch. There's plenty of food here for you to have all you want."

"Thank you, Mrs. Wilson."

"Come on, Alphonse," Johnny said. He pushed half the scrambled eggs on to Boyd's plate. Boyd watched while Mrs. Wilson put a dish of stewed tomatoes beside his plate.

"Boyd don't eat tomatoes, do you, Boyd?" Johnny said.

"Doesn't eat tomatoes, Johnny. And just because you don't like them, don't say that about Boyd. Boyd will eat *anything.*"

"Bet he won't," Johnny said, attacking his scrambled eggs.

"Boyd wants to grow up and be a big strong man so he can work hard," Mrs. Wilson said. "I'll bet Boyd's father eats stewed tomatoes."

"My father eats anything he wants to," Boyd said.

"So does mine," Johnny said. "Sometimes he doesn't eat hardly anything. He's a little guy, though. Wouldn't hurt a flea."

"Mine's a little guy, too," Boyd said.

"I'll bet he's strong, though," Mrs. Wilson said. She hesitated. "Does he . . . work?"

"Sure," Johnny said. "Boyd's father works in a factory."

"There, you see?" Mrs. Wilson said. "And he certainly has to be strong to do that—all that lifting and carrying at a factory."

"Boyd's father doesn't have to," Johnny said. "He's a foreman."

Mrs. Wilson felt defeated. "What does your mother do, Boyd?"

"My mother?" Boyd was surprised. "She takes care of us kids."

"Oh. She doesn't work, then?"

"Why should she?" Johnny said through a mouthful of eggs. "You don't work."

"You really don't want any stewed tomatoes, Boyd?"

"No, thank you, Mrs. Wilson," Boyd said.

"No, thank you, Mrs. Wilson, no, thank you, Mrs. Wilson, no, thank you, Mrs. Wilson," Johnny said. "Boyd's sister's going to work though. She's going to be a teacher."

"That's a very fine attitude for her to have, Boyd." Mrs. Wilson restrained an impulse to pat Boyd on the head. "I imagine you're all very proud of her?"

"I guess so," Boyd said.

"What about all your other brothers and sisters? I guess all of you want to make just as much of yourselves as you can."

"There's only me and Jean," Boyd said. "I don't know yet what I want to be when I grow up."

"We're going to be tank drivers, Boyd and me," Johnny said. "Zoom." Mrs. Wilson caught Boyd's glass of milk as Johnny's napkin ring, suddenly transformed into a tank, plowed heavily across the table.

"Look, Johnny," Boyd said. "Here's a foxhole. I'm shooting at you."

Mrs. Wilson, with the speed born of long experience, took the ginger-bread off the shelf and placed it carefully between the tank and the foxhole.

"Now eat as much as you want to, Boyd," she said. "I want to see you get filled up."

"Boyd eats a lot, but not as much as I do," Johnny said. "I'm bigger than he is."

"You're not much bigger," Boyd said. "I can beat you running."

Mrs. Wilson took a deep breath. "Boyd," she said. Both boys turned to her. "Boyd, Johnny has some suits that are a little too small for him, and a winter coat. It's not new, of course, but there's lots of wear in it still. And I have a few dresses that your mother or sister could probably use. Your mother can make them over into lots of things for all of you, and I'd be very happy to give them to you. Suppose before you leave I make up a big bundle and then you and Johnny can take it over to your mother right away . . ." Her voice trailed off as she saw Boyd's puzzled expression.

"But I have plenty of clothes, thank you," he said. "And I don't think my mother knows how to sew very well, and anyway I guess we buy about everything we need. Thank you very much, though."

"We don't have time to carry that old stuff around, Mother," Johnny said. "We got to play tanks with the kids today."

Mrs. Wilson lifted the plate of gingerbread off the table as Boyd was about to take another piece. "There are many little boys like you, Boyd, who would be very grateful for the clothes someone was kind enough to give them."

"Boyd will take them if you want him to, Mother," Johnny said.

"I didn't mean to make you mad, Mrs. Wilson," Boyd said.

"Don't think I'm angry, Boyd. I'm just disappointed in you, that's all. Now let's not say anything more about it."

She began clearing the plates off the table, and Johnny took Boyd's hand and pulled him to the door. "'Bye, Mother," Johnny said. Boyd stood for a minute, staring at Mrs. Wilson's back.

"After you, my dear Alphonse," Johnny said, holding the door open.

"Is your mother still mad?" Mrs. Wilson heard Boyd ask in a low voice.

"I don't know," Johnny said. "She's screwy sometimes."

"So's mine," Boyd said. He hesitated. "After *you*, my dear Alphonse."

(1948)

ETHNIC
ROUNDUP

. . . in this Continent, asylum of all nations, the energy of Irish, Germans, Swedes, Poles, & Cossacks, & all the European tribes, of the Africans, & of the Polynesians, will construct a new race, a new religion, a new State, a new literature. . . .
> Ralph Waldo Emerson
> *Journal*

The price of hating other human beings is loving oneself less.
> Eldridge Cleaver
> *Soul on Ice*

There is only one Maker in the world
and His children cover the earth
and they are named All God's Children.
> Carl Sandburg
> Timesweep

From

THE FANATICS
by Paul Laurence Dunbar

For a long time curiosity was rampant in a little country district not very far from Cincinnati. It was the proverbial rural locality where every one knows or wishes to know the business of every one else, and is offended if he doesn't. In this particular place, the object of interest was a white farmhouse set forward on the road, and fronting ample grounds both of field and garden. It was the home of John Metzinger, a prosperous German husbandman and his good wife, Gretchen. They were pleasant, easy-going people, warm-hearted and generous. Their neighbors had always looked upon them with favor, until one day—it was early in August, the eye of suspicion fell upon the house. Those who had lived near the Metzingers, and those who merely passed upon the road to and from town began to point questioning fingers at the place and to look askance at it. The gossips shook their heads and whispered together.

It all began with one woman who had unceremoniously "dropped in" on the couple; "dropping in" consisting of pushing open the door and entering unannounced by the formality of a knock. The easy-going neighbor had pursued this course only to find the door of an inner room hastily closed and the good wife profuse in embarrassed expostulations. Mrs. Metzinger was not good at dissimulation, and her explanation that the room was all torn up for she was housecleaning served but to arouse her visitor's suspicion. In her own words as she told it many times later, she said with fine indignation, "Think o' her sayin' to me that she was cleanin' house, an' she with as spick an' span a white apern on as ever you see. Says I to her, 'Ain't you pickin' out a funny time to clean, Mrs. Metzinger?' and she says with that Dutch brogue o' hers, 'Oh, I cleans anydimes de place gets dirty.' Then I says ca'm like, because I've allus liked that woman, 'I should think you'd get yer apern dirty,' an' all of a sudden she jerked it off an' stood there grinn' at me; but that was what give her away, for lo, an' behold, her dress was as clean as my bran' new calico. Then I says, 'Well, never min', I'll just come in an' help you,' an' would you believe it, that woman got right in my way an' wouldn't let me go in that room, all the time jabbering something about 'Nod troublin' me.' Right then an' there, thinks I, there's something wrong in that room."

355

She closed her remarks as one who says, "There's murder behind that door."

Her hearers were struck by her tragic presentation of the case, and they too, began to watch for signs of guilt in the Germans. These were soon plentiful. None was more convincing than that a room that had always been open to the light had now its blinds closed. Some one had said too, that they had seen the doctor's gig at the door one night, and had waited for him to come out. But on questioning him, as any man has a right to do, "Who's sick, doctor?" he had sprung into his vehicle, put whip to his horse and dashed away without answering. This in itself, looked dark. For why should a doctor of all men, refuse to be questioned about his patients? The little scattered community for three or four miles and even further up and down the road was awe-struck and properly indignant. Such communities have no respect for reticence.

Meanwhile the trouble went on, and the Metzingers grew in disfavor. What had been friendly greetings degenerated into stiff nods or grew into clumsily veiled inquiries. While their neighbors lost sleep asking each other what horror was going on behind those closed doors, the simple couple went on about their duty and kept their counsel. It was really not so much the horror that the community resented but that the particulars of it were being kept from them.

If the Metzingers could have told their story, it would have proved, after all, a very short and simple one. It would have been to the effect that late one night towards the end of July, they had been awakened by the tramping of feet and a knocking upon their door. Going thither, they had found four men unkempt and mudstained, who bore between them another, evidently wounded. They had brought him and laid him upon the sofa, and then with promises, that were half threats, had left him in their care. They came then to know who their visitors were; some of "Morgan's terrible men." Their promises to respect the farmer's stock had not been needed to secure attention for their wounded comrade, for the good wife's heart had gone out already to the young fellow who lay there so white and drabbled with blood.

John Metzinger would have told, though his good wife would never have mentioned it, how all that night and the next day, Gretchen had hovered over the wounded man, bandaging his arm, bathing it, and doing what she could to ease the pain, while the sufferer muttered strange things in his sleep and tossed like a restless child.

They could not get a doctor until the next night, for they knew that all must proceed with secrecy, and when the physician came, the fever had already set in and the chances for the man's recovery seemed very slight.

They could have told too, of the doctor's long fight with the fever, and what the gossips did not know, how one night two physicians came and amputated the wounded arm at the elbow. Then of the long fight for life through the hot August days, of the terrible nights when Death seemed crowding into the close room and the sufferer lay gasping for breath. But they told nothing. Silently they went their way, grieved by the distrust of those about them, but unfaltering in their course. And when Van Doren first looked up weakly enough into the German woman's face, his eyes full of the gratitude he could not speak, both she and her John were repaid for all that they had suffered.

The woman fell upon her knees by the bedside saying, "Dank Got, dank Got, he vill gid vell now, Shon," and "Shon" who was very big and very much a man, pressed his wife's hand and went behind the door to look for something that was not there.

With the cooler weather of autumn came more decided convalescence to the young trooper, but the earliest snows had fallen before he was able to creep to the door that looked out upon the road. He was only the shadow of his former self. Mrs. Metzinger looked at him, full of pity.

"I guess you petter led de toctor wride by your home now. Dey vill vant to hear from you."

"Not yet, not yet," he protested. "It would cause my father too much anxiety, and some others perhaps, too much joy to know how I am faring."

"Your poor fader, dough, he vill be vorried aboud you."

"Father knows the chances of war and he will not begin to worry yet. It would grieve him so much more to know that I am out of it all so soon."

"Mister Robert," said the woman impressively, "you don't know faders. Dey vas yoost like modders, pretty near, und modders, alvays vants to know; if he is vell, she is glad und she dank Got for dat. If he is det, she vants to gry und gry ofer dose leedle shoes dot he used to vear."

"He shall know, he shall know, Mrs. Metzinger, and very soon, for I am going home to him and his joy will make him forget how long he has waited."

"Yes, I guess maybe dot is so."

Robert had divined more by instinct than by any outward demonstration of his hosts that his secret stay in the house had aroused in their neighbors some sort of feeling against these people. He was perfectly sure that should he write to his father, he would come to him in spite of everything, and at any stir or unusual commotion about the house, what was only smouldering now might burst into flame. So, although it wrung his heart to do so, living within sixty miles of his father, he kept his lips closed and gave no sign. His heart had gone out to these people who had sacrificed so much for him, and he wanted to do something in return for them. At first, because of his very weakness, they had forborne to question him about his home and people, and when he was strong enough to act, he had unconsciously accepted this silence as his sacrifice, without divining that he was not the real sufferer, not the real bearer of the burden.

He had promised that he would go home soon, but the case had been a severe one, and it was December before he dared to venture out beyond the gate. Sometimes, when the days were warm and bright, he would sit wrapped up on the porch at the side, for the need of secrecy gone, the Metzingers were openly and humanly unhumble. They bowed proudly, even jauntily to their detractors, while the priest and the Levites passed by on the other side. There were no good Samaritans about save the Metzingers themselves, and their little devices might have gone unobserved, but that the priest and the Levites were curious people, and at last, came over to question.

"Who is the sick young man?" they questioned.

"He iss a friend of ours from de var," Mrs. Metzinger answered them.

"We'd like to talk to him," they volunteered.

"No, he must not talk to beoples, not yet," was the answer.

"Why don't he wear his uniform?" Robert wore a suit of "Shon's" jeans.

"It was yoost ruint and all spoilt mit blood."

But they looked at Robert askance, and the gossip which for awhile from inaction had faltered, sprang up anew. Who was he? Why so little about him? Why had they kept the secret so long?

The good people saw with dismay what they had done. They had only aroused the trouble which they had hoped to allay. Van Doren saw their trouble and determined immediately to relieve them.

"I am going home now," he told them one day.

"You are not yet so strong."

"Oh, yes I am. I'm quite a giant now."

"Vat you dinks Shon? Iss he strong enough?"

"I dinks he gan stay here so long as he vants."

"But I am going, my good friends, it's best for us all."

"Vy?"

"I have seen how the neighbors look at me and I have seen how they look at you. You shan't hurt yourselves any longer."

"Dat iss not right. We care nodings for de neighbors. Ve minds our own business."

Mrs. Metzinger's husband said something under his breath, only a word it was, but it made his wife gasp and cry, "Shon, for shame on you!"

"I'm going," Robert went on, "either with your consent or without. I don't know how I'm ever going to thank you. You've both been so good. It's nasty in a case like this to think of pay. I can't do it decently, but I'm going to do it. It's the nearest way a brute of a man can come to showing his appreciation."

"No pay," said John.

"Not vun cent," said his wife.

"Vee had some gompany," Gretchen put in.

Robert smiled on; they were so like big children.

"I am not going to let you two cheat me out of showing my gratitude by any such excuse."

Gretchen wept and John caused his wife to exclaim again, but it was of no use, and just at dusk, the old carryall took him away to the station, still in his host's suit, the empty sleeve turned up, and the stump of arm flapping at his side.

It was about an hour after John had gone with Robert to the station, that Mrs. Metzinger heard footsteps, and going to the door saw several men without.

"We want that man that's stayin' here," said the leader.

"He's yoost gone to his home in Dorbury."

"In Dorbury—why we thought—what side was he on?"

Mrs. Metzinger drew herself up in dignified anger and said, "I don'd dink Got has any sides, Deacon Callvell," then she slammed the door, and the deacon and his "Committee" went away feeling small, and glad that it was dark, while Mrs. Metzinger rocked out her pious anger until the floor cried again.

(1901)

From
THE SPLENDID IDLE FORTIES
by Gertrude Atherton

Thomas O. Larkin, United States Consul to California until the occupation left him without duties, had invited Monterey to meet the officers of the *Savannah, Cyane,* and *Levant,* and only Doña Modeste Castro had declined. At ten o'clock the sala of his large house on the rise of the hill was thronged with robed girls in every shade and device of white, sitting demurely behind the wide shoulders of coffee-coloured dowagers, also in white, and blazing with jewels. The young matrons were there, too, although they left the sala at intervals to visit the room set apart for the nurses and children; no Montereña ever left her little ones at home. The old men and the caballeros wore the black coats and white trousers which Monterey fashion dictated for evening wear; the hair of the younger men was braided with gay ribbons, and diamonds flashed in the lace of their ruffles.

The sala was on the second floor; the musicians sat on the corridor beyond the open windows and scraped their fiddles and twanged their guitars, awaiting the coming of the American officers. Before long the regular tramp of many feet turning from Alvarado Street up the little Primera del Este, facing Mr. Larkin's house, made dark eyes flash, lace and silken gowns flutter. Benicia and a group of girls were standing by Doña Eustaquia. They opened their large black fans as if to wave back the pink that had sprung to their cheeks. Only Benicia held her head saucily high, and her large brown eyes were full of defiant sparkles.

"Why art thou so excited, Blandina?" she asked of a girl who had grasped her arm. "I feel as if the war between the United States and Mexico began tonight."

"Ay, Benicia, thou hast so gay a spirit that nothing ever frightens thee! But, Mary! How many they are! They tramp as if they would go through the stair. Ay, the poor flag! No wonder—"

"Now, do not cry over the flag any more. Ah! there is not one to compare with General Castro!"

The character of the Californian sala had changed for ever; the blue and gold of the United States had invaded it.

The officers, young and old, looked with much interest at the faces, soft, piquant, tropical, which made the effect of pansies looking inquisitively over a snowdrift. The girls returned their glances with approval, for they were as fine and manly a set of men as ever had faced death or woman. Ten minutes later California and the United States were flirting outrageously.

Mr. Larkin presented a tall officer to Benicia. That the young man was very well-looking even Benicia admitted. True, his hair was golden, but it was cut short, and bore no resemblance to the coat of a bear; his mustache and brows were brown; his gray eyes were as laughing as her own.

"I suppose you do not speak any English, señorita," he said helplessly.

"No? I spik Eenglish like the Spanish. The Spanish people no have difficult at all to learn the other langues. But Señor Hartnell he say it no is easy at all for the Eenglish to spik the French and the Spanish, so I suppose you no spik one word our langue, no?"

He gallantly repressed a smile. "Thankfully I may say that I do not, else would I not have the pleasure of hearing you speak English. Never have I heard it so charmingly spoken before."

Benicia took her skirt between the tips of her fingers and swayed her graceful body forward, as a tule bends in the wind.

"You like dip the flag of the conqueror in honey, señor. Ay! We need have one compliment for every tear that fall since your eagle stab his beak in the neck de ours."

"Ah, the loyal women of Monterey! I have no words to express my admiration for them, señorita. A thousand compliments are not worth one tear."

Benicia turned swiftly to her mother, her eyes glittering with pleasure. "Mother, you hear! You hear!" she cried in Spanish. "These Americans are not so bad, after all."

Doña Eustaquia gave the young man one of her rare smiles; it flashed over her strong dark face until the light of youth was there once more.

"Very pretty speech," she said, with slow precision. "I thank you, Señor Russell, in the name of the women of Monterey."

"By Jove! Madam—señora—I assure you I never felt so cut up in my life as when I saw all those beautiful women crying down there by the Custom-house. I am a good American, but I would rather have thrown the flag under your feet than have seen you cry like that. And I assure you, dear señora, every man among us felt the same. As you have been good enough to thank me in the name of the women of Monterey, I, in behalf of the officers of the United States squadron, beg that you will forgive us."

Doña Eustaquia's cheek paled again, and she set her lips for a moment; then she held our her hand.

"Señor," she said, "we are conquered, but we are Californians; and although we do not bend the head, neither do we turn the back. We have invite you to our houses, and we cannot treat you like enemies. I will say with—how you say it—truth?—we did hate the thought that you come and take the country that was ours. But all is over and cannot be changed. So, it is better we are good friends than poor ones; and—and—my house is open to you, señor."

Russell was a young man of acute perceptions; moreover, he had heard of Doña Eustaquia; he divined in part the mighty effort by which good breeding and philosophy had conquered bitter resentment. He raised the little white hand to his lips.

"I would that I were twenty men, señora. Each would be your devoted servant."

"And then she have her necklace!" cried Benicia, delightedly.

"What is that?" asked Russell; but Doña Eustaquia shook her fan threateningly and turned away.

"I no tell you everything," said Benicia, "so no be too curiosa. You no dance the contradanza, no?"

"I regret to say that I do not. But this is a plain waltz; will you not give it to me?"

Benicia, disregarding the angry glances of approaching caballeros, laid her hand on the officer's shoulder, and he spun her down the room.

"Why, you no dance so bad!" she said with surprise. "I think always the Americanos dance so terreeblay."

"Who could not dance with a fairy in his arms?"

"What funny things you say. I never been called fairy before."

"You have never been interpreted." And then, in the whirl-waltz of that day, both lost their breath.

When the dance was over and they stood near Doña Eustaquia, he took the fan from Benicia's hand and waved it slowly before her. She laughed outright.

"You think I am so tired I no can fan myself?" she demanded. "How queer are these Americanos! Why, I have dance for three days and three nights and never estop."

"Señorita!"

"Si, señor. Oh, we estop sometimes, but no for long. It was at Sonoma two months ago. At the house de General Vallejo."

"You certainly are able to fan yourself; but it is no reflection upon your muscle. It is only a custom we have."

"Then I think much better you no have the custom. You no look like a man at all when you fan like a girl."

He handed her back the fan with some choler.

"Really, señorita, you are very frank. I suppose you would have a man lie in a hammock all day and roll cigaritos."

"Much better do that than take what no is yours."

"Which no American ever did!"

"Excep' when he pulled California out the pocket de Mexico."

"And what did Mexico do first? Did she not threaten the United States with hostilities for a year, and attack a small detachment of our troops with a force of seven thousand men—"

"No make any difference what she do. Si she do wrong, that no is excuse for you do wrong."

Two angry young people faced each other.

"You steal our country and insult our men. But they can fight, Madre de Dios! I like see General Castro take your little Commodore Sloat by the neck. He look like a little gray rat."

"Commodore Sloat is a brave and able man, Miss Ortega, and no officer in the United States navy will hear him insulted."

"Then much better you lock up the ears."

"My dear Captain Russell! Benicia! what is the matter?"

Mr. Larkin stood before them, an amused smile on his thin intellectual face. "Come, come, have we not met to-night to dance the waltz of peace? Benicia, your most humble admirer has a favour to crave of you. I would have my countrymen learn at once the utmost grace of the Californian. Dance El Jarabe, please, and with Don Fernando Altimira."

Benicia lifted her dainty white shoulders. She was not unwilling to avenge herself upon the American by dazzling him with her grace and beauty. Her eye's swift invitation brought Don Fernando, scowling, to her side. He led her to the middle of the room, and the musicians played the stately jig.

Benicia swept one glance of defiant coquetry at Russell from beneath her curling lashes, then fixed her eyes upon the floor, nor raised them again. She held her reed-like body very erect and took either side of her spangled skirt in the tips of her fingers, lifting it just enough to show the arched little feet in their embroidered stockings and satin slippers. Don Fernando crossed his hands behind him, and together they rattled their feet on the floor with dexterity and precision, whilst the girls sang the words of the dance. The officers gave genuine applause, delighted with this picturesque fragment of life on the edge of the Pacific. Don Fernando listened to their demonstrations with sombre contempt on his dark handsome face; Benicia indicated her pleasure by sundry archings of her narrow brows, or coquettish curves of her red lips. Suddenly she made a deep courtesy and ran to her mother, with a long sweeping movement, like the bending and lifting of grain in the wind. As she approached Russell he took a rose from his coat and threw it at her. She caught it, thrust it carelessly in one of her thick braids, and the next moment he was at her side again.

(1902)

From

TILLIE, A MENNONITE MAID
by Helen Reimensnyder Martin

Tillie was obliged, when about a half-mile from her father's farm, to hide her precious book. This she did by pinning her petticoat into a bag and concealing the book in it. It was in this way that she always carried home her "li-bries" from Sunday-school, for all story-book reading was prohibited by her father. It was uncomfortable walking along the highroad with the book knocking against her legs at every step, but that was not so painful as her father's punishment would be did he discover her bringing home a "novel"! She was not permitted to bring home even a school-book, and she had greatly astonished Miss Margaret, one day at the beginning of the term, by asking, "Please, will you leave me let my books in school? Pop says I darse n't bring 'em home."

"What you can't learn in school, you can do without," Tillie's father had said. "When you're home you'll work fur your wittles."

Tillie's father was a frugal, honest, hard-working, and very prosperous Pennsylvania Dutch farmer, who thought he religiously performed his parental duty in bringing up his many children in the fear of his heavy hand, in unceasing labor, and in almost total abstinence from all amusement and self-indulgence. Far from thinking himself cruel, he was convinced that the oftener and the more vigorously he applied "the strap," the more conscientious a parent was he.

His wife, Tillie's stepmother, was as submissive to his authority as were her five children and Tillie. Apathetic, anemic, overworked, she yet never dreamed of considering herself or her children abused, accepting her lot as the natural one of woman, who was created to be a child-bearer, and to keep man well fed and comfortable. The only variation from the deadly monotony of her mechanical and unceasing labor was found in her habit of irritability with her stepchild. She considered Tillie "a dopple" (a stupid, awkward person); for though usually a wonderful little household worker, Tillie, when very much tired out, was apt to drop dishes; and absent-mindedly she would put her sunbonnet instead of the bread into the oven, or pour molasses instead of batter on the griddle. Such misdemeanors were always plaintively reported by Mrs. Getz to Tillie's father, who, without fail, conscientiously applied what he considered the undoubted cure.

In practising the strenuous economy prescribed by her husband, Mrs. Getz had to manœuver very skilfully to keep her children decently clothed, and Tillie in this matter was a great help to her; for the little girl possessed a precocious skill in combining a pile of patches into a passably decent dress or coat for one of her little brothers or sisters. Nevertheless, it was invariably Tillie who was slighted in the small expenditures that were made each year for the family clothing. The child had always really preferred that the others should have "new things" rather than herself—until Miss Margaret came; and now, before Miss Margaret's daintiness, she felt ashamed of her own shabby appearance and longed unspeakably for fresh, pretty clothes. Tillie knew perfectly well that her father had plenty of money to buy them for her if he would. But she never thought of asking him or her stepmother for anything more than what they saw fit to give her.

The Getz family was a perfectly familiar type among the German farming class of southeastern Pennsylvania. Jacob Getz, though spoken of in the neighborhood as being "wonderful near," which means very penurious, and considered by the more gentle-minded Amish and Mennonites of the township to be "overly strict" with his family and "too ready with the strap still," was nevertheless highly respected as one who worked hard and was prosperous, lived economically, honestly, and in the fear of the Lord, and was "laying by."

The Getz farm was typical of the better sort to be found in that county. A neat walk, bordered by clam shells, led from a wooden gate to the porch of a rather large, and severely plain frame house, facing the road. Every shutter on the front and sides of the building was tightly closed, and there was no sign of life about the place. A stranger, ignorant of the Pennsylvania Dutch custom of living in the kitchen and shutting off the "best rooms,"—to be used in their mustiness and stiff unhomelikeness on Sunday only,—would have thought the house temporarily empty. It was forbiddingly and uncompromisingly spick-and-span.

A grass-plot, ornamented with a circular flower-bed, extended a short distance on either side of the house. But not too much land was put to such unproductive use; and the small lawn was closely bordered by a corn-field on the one side and on the other by an apple orchard. Beyond stretched the tobacco- and wheat-fields, and behind the house were the vegetable garden and the barn-yard.

Arrived at home by half-past three, Tillie hid her "Ivanhoe" under the pillow of her bed when she went up-stairs to change her faded calico school dress for the yet older garment she wore at her work.

If she had not been obliged to change her dress, she would have been puzzled to know how to hide her book, for she could not, without creating suspicion, have gone up-stairs in the daytime. In New Canaan one never went up-stairs during the day, except at the rare times when obliged to change one's clothes. Every one washed at the pump and used the one family roller-towel hanging on the porch. Miss Margaret, ever since her arrival in the neighborhood, had been the subject of wide-spread remark and even suspicion, because she "washed up-stairs" and even *sat* up-stairs!—in her bedroom! It was an unheard-of proceeding in New Canaan.

Tillie helped her father in the celery-beds until dark; then, weary, but excited at the prospect of her book, she went in from the fields and up-stairs to the little low-roofed bed-chamber which she shared with her two half-sisters. They were already in bed and asleep, as was their mother in the room across the hall, for every one went to bed at sundown in Canaan Township, and got up at sunrise.

Tillie was in bed in a few minutes, rejoicing in the feeling of the book under her pillow. Not yet dared she venture to light a candle and read it—not until she should hear her father's heavy snoring in the room across the hall.

The candles which she used for this surreptitious reading of Sunday-school "li-bries" and any other chance literature which fell in her way, were procured with money paid to her by Miss Margaret for helping her to clean the school-room on Friday afternoons after school. Tillie would have been happy to help her for the mere joy of being with her, but Miss Margaret insisted upon paying her ten cents for each such service.

The little girl was obliged to resort to a deep-laid plot in order to do this work for the teacher. It had been her father's custom—ever since, at the age of five, she had begun to go to school—to "time" her in coming home at noon and afternoon, and whenever she was not there on the minute, to mete out to her a dose of his ever-present strap.

"I ain't havin' no playin' on the way home, still! When school is done, you come right away home then, to help me or your mom, or I'll learn you once!"

But it happened that Miss Margaret, in her reign at "William Penn" school-house, had introduced the innovation of closing school on Friday afternoons at half-past three instead of four, and Tillie, with bribes of candy bought with part of her weekly wage of ten cents, secured secrecy as to this innovation from her little sister and brother who went to school with her—making them play in the school-grounds until she was ready to go home with them.

Before Miss Margaret had come to New Canaan, Tillie had done her midnight reading by the light of the kerosene lamp which, after every one was asleep, she would bring up from the kitchen to her bedside. But this was dangerous, as it often led to awkward inquiries as to the speedy consumption of the oil. Candles were safer. Tillie kept them and a box of matches hidden under the mattress.

It was eleven o'clock when at last the child, trembling with mingled delight and apprehension, rose from her bed, softly closed her bedroom door, and with extremely judicious carefulness lighted her candle, propped up her pillow, and settled down to read as long as she should be able to hold her eyes open. The little sister at her side and the one in the bed at the other side of the room slept too soundly to be disturbed by the faint flickering light of that one candle.

To-night her stolen pleasure proved more than usually engrossing. At first the book was interesting principally because of the fact, so vividly present with her, that Miss Margaret's eyes and mind had moved over every word and thought which she was now absorbing. But soon her intense interest in the story excluded every other idea—even the fear of discovery. Her young spirit was "out of the body" and following, as in a trance, this tale, the like of which she had never before read.

The clock down-stairs in the kitchen struck twelve—one—two, but Tillie never heard it. At half-past two o'clock in the morning, when the tallow candle was beginning to sputter to its end, she still was reading, her eyes bright as stars, her usually pale face flushed with excitement, her sensitive lips parted in breathless interest—when, suddenly, a stinging blow of "the strap" on her shoulders brought from her a cry of pain and fright.

"What you mean, doin' somepin like this yet!" sternly demanded her father. "What fur book's that there!"

He took the book from her hands and Tillie cowered beneath the covers, the wish flashing through her mind that the book could change into a Bible as he looked at it!—which miracle would surely temper the punishment that in a moment she knew would be meted out to her.

" 'Iwanhoe'—a novel! A *novel!*" he said in genuine horror. "Tillie, where d'you get this here?"

Tillie knew that if she told lies she would go to hell, but she preferred to burn in torment forever rather than betray Miss Margaret; for her father, like Absalom's, was a school director, and if he knew Miss Margaret read novels and lent them to the children, he would surely force her out of "William Penn."

"I lent it off of Elviny Dinkleberger!" she sobbed.

"You know I tole you a'ready you darse n't bring books home! And you know I don't uphold to novel-readin'! I'll have to learn you to mind better 'n this! Where d'you get that there candle?"

"I—bought it, pop."

"Bought? Where d'you get the money?"

Tillie did not like the lies she had to tell, but she knew she had already perjured her soul beyond redemption and one lie more or less could not make matters worse.

"I found it in the road."

"How much did you find?"

"Fi' cents."

"You had n't ought to spent it without astin' me dare you. Now I'm goin' to learn you once! Set up."

Tillie obeyed, and the strap fell across her shoulders. Her outcries awakened the household and started the youngest little sister, in her fright and sympathy with Tillie, to a high-pitched wailing. The rest of them took the incident phlegmatically, the only novelty about it being the strange hour of its happening.

But the hardest part of her punishment was to follow.

"Now this here book goes in the fire!" her father announced when at last his hand was stayed. "And any more that comes home goes after it in the stove. I'll see if you'll mind your pop or not!"

Left alone in her bed, her body quivering, her little soul hot with shame and hatred, the child stifled her sobs in her pillow, her whole heart one bleeding wound.

How could she ever tell Miss Margaret? Surely she would never like her any more!—never again lay her hand on her hair, or praise her compositions, or call her "honey," or, even, perhaps, allow her to help her on Fridays!—and what, then, would be the use of living? If only she could die and be dead like a cat or a bird and not go to hell, she would take the carving-knife and kill herself! But there was hell to be taken into consideration. And yet, could hell hold anything worse than the loss of Miss Margaret's kindness? *How* could she tell her of that burned-up book and endure to see her look at her with cold disapproval? Oh, to make such return for her kindness, when she so longed with all her soul to show her how much she loved her!

For the first time in all her school-days, Tillie went next morning with reluctance to school.

(1904)

OUR MOTHER POCAHONTAS
by Vachel Lindsay

I

Powhatan was conqueror.
Powhatan was emperor.
He was akin to wolf and bee,
Brother of the hickory tree.
Son of the red lightning stroke
And the lightning-shivered oak.
His panther-grace bloomed in the maid
Who laughed among the winds and played
In excellence of savage pride,
Wooing the forest, open-eyed,
In the springtime,
In Virginia,
Our Mother, Pocahontas.

Her skin was rosy copper-red.
And high she held her beauteous head.
Her step was like a rustling leaf;

Her heart a nest, untouched of grief.
She dreamed of sons like Powhatan,
And through her blood the lightning ran.
Love-cries with the birds she sung,
Birdlike
In the grape-vine swung.
The Forest, arching low and wide
Gloried in its Indian bride.
Rolfe, that dim adventurer,
Had not come a courtier.
John Rolfe is not our ancestor.
We rise from out the soul of her
Held in native wonderland,
While the sun's rays kissed her hand,
In the springtime,
In Virginia,
Our Mother, Pocahontas.

II

She heard the forest talking,
Across the sea came walking,
And traced the paths of Daniel Boone,
Then westward chased the painted moon.
She passed with wild young feet
On to Kansas wheat,
On to the miners' west,
The echoing cañons' guest,
Then the Pacific sand,
Walking,
Thrilling,
The midnight land. . . .

On Adams Street and Jefferson—
Flames coming up from the ground!
On Jackson Street and Washington—
Flames coming up from the ground!
And why, until the dawning sun
Are flames coming up from the ground?
Because, through drowsy Springfield sped
This redskin queen, with feathered head
With winds and stars, that pay her court
And leaping beasts, that make her sport;

Because, gray Europe's rags august
She tramples in the dust;
Because we are her fields of corn;
Because our fires are all reborn
From her bosom's deathless embers,
Flaming
As she remembers
The springtime
And Virginia,
Our Mother, Pocahontas.

III

We here renounce our Saxon blood.
Tomorrow's hopes, an April flood
Come roaring in. The newest race
Is born of her resilient grace.
We here renounce our Teuton pride:
Our Norse and Slavic boasts have died:
Italian dreams are swept away,
And Celtic feuds are lost today. . . .
She sings of lilacs, maples, wheat,
Her own soil sings beneath her feet,
Of springtime
And Virginia,
Our Mother, Pocahontas.

                                   (1917)

THE NEWLY-RICH GOLDSTEINS
by Konrad Bercovici

The Goldsteins were destined for light work and comfort. "Middle Class" was stamped on their faces and radiated from their speech and movements. Every stitch of clothing proclaimed that they belonged to the happy, contented-with-what-God-gives middle class.

"H. Goldstein & Co., Embroidery," occupied the first floor of a dilapidated building on St. Mark's Place near Third Avenue. The two daughters, Sophy and Leah, were the working force of the firm. H. Goldstein himself was the salesman, bookkeeper, deliverer, collector and buyer. Four sewing machines near the rear windows, a table, an assortment of cardboard boxes and a few shelves in a corner were all the machinery of the factory.

But the Goldsteins were a contented lot. They lived in a five-room apartment on Tenth Street, had good old soft chairs to sit on; Mrs. Goldstein prepared fine meals, and on Saturday as the factory was closed each one of the family had his own private joys. H. Goldstein went to the synagogue to meet his old friends and discuss the Talmud. Mrs. Goldstein visited all her relatives on the Sabbath. Sophy was out with her beau, Joseph Katz; and Leah strolled on Second Avenue on the arm of Maurice Feldman.

The factory just covered house expenses and a small dollar or two for a rainy day saved by Mrs. Goldstein from table money. But they were independent, in business for themselves, as befits the Goldsteins the whole world over, and not hired workers. At the synagogue, Hirsh Goldstein was respected for his learning and piety; and though his contributions were not very large, still they were never beggarly.

When America entered the war the embroidery business took a jump. The Goldsteins obtained orders for shoulder straps, epaulets, chevrons, hat bands and a lot of other paraphernalia absolutely necessary to soldiers and officers to go over the top. The Goldsteins added four more machines and hired half a dozen Italian girls for the work. Soon even this enlarged force could not cope with the orders. Another floor was hired, six more machines fixed up, and Joseph Katz, Sophy's beau, became the bookkeeper. Three months later the factory moved to a Bond Street loft and sixty machines, power driven and of the latest model, were installed. Little by little the Sabbath was neglected. The rush orders forced them to work seven days a week, seven days and seven nights. Maurice Feldman, Leah's beau, was engaged as assistant bookkeeper.

"Reb Goldstein, we missed you last Saturday," friends questioned him at the synagogue.

"The Talmud says, 'The welfare of the country you live in stands higher than your own rites.' " was all he answered.

Though people knew that his translation of the passage was a bit loose, they did not interfere.

After the factory had moved over to Bond Street, Sophy and Leah remained at home. Their presence in the factory was no longer needed.

Mother Goldstein argued that it ill-befitted the daughters of so big a manufacturer to be working. Goldstein was making money faster than he could count it. The girls were flattered and adulated wherever they went, and they began to think the Tenth Street apartment and the district they lived in entirely out of keeping with their new station in life. They had rich clothing now, and thought themselves too good for their former friends.

A large contribution to a charitable undertaking brought the young ladies an invitation to a party given by some wealthy people on Riverside Drive. It was the first time they had seen such living quarters. It sharpened their appetites to the pomps and vanities of the world. It made them feel the people living downtown were dust or dross.

Maurice Feldman and Joseph Katz were the first to feel the changed attitude. Sure enough! The young ladies were not going to marry their father's bookkeepers!

Riverside Drive became the ideal of the two sisters. At first the father refused even to hear of it. But when fortune had favored him and he made a lump sum in some side speculation, he half gave his consent.

At the synagogue he was seldom seen, and if he happened to come once in a while he was not as warmly greeted as formerly. He had offended several members of the congregation, had humbled them, by giving a donation of a hundred dollars when they had only given ten.

When the two sisters had won over their mother to the Riverside Drive plan the father could no longer resist. Soon an interior decorator was busy garnishing the nine-room two-bath apartment, with brand-new highly polished furniture. Gold-tinted hangings and gold-painted chairs, bookcases filled with deluxe sets in red and blue, an Oriental room, a Louis XV piano, and "real" oil paintings. Sophy and Leah were all the time buying new things. The visits to the great stores did not improve taste, but it pricked ambition. When the bustle ended, the Goldsteins had spent a young fortune on the Riverside apartment. The rooms were well filled with whatever could be bought, with all the Goldsteins could afford; and they could afford a good deal, because Hirsh Goldstein was making more money than he had ever dared to dream.

The war had to be won, and it could not be done without the assistance of "H. Goldstein & Co."

The first few days the Goldsteins enjoyed their acquisitions so much they had no time to think of anything else. Then they joined a fashionable temple. The daughters became members of charitable societies, the membership of which was composed of older parvenues. The downtown crowd and old associations were forgotten in the whirl. When some of the relatives came to visit the Goldsteins, they felt so outclassed and outdistanced that they never returned again.

But after the girls had wearied somewhat of their furniture and things, they began to notice that the new acquaintances made no friendly overtures. A feeling stole over them that their new friends laughed behind their backs. Whenever they happened to be in the company of the new aristocracy, the others spoke of things they knew nothing about. The others, college-bred most of them, mentioned names of authors and artists the Goldsteins had never heard of before. The others had tapering fine fingernails, slender wrists, thin ankles, and wore the simplest clothes with distinction.

Sophy and Leah felt that the young men of the new set avoided them. They were always courteous, but cold—cold to the invaders. But of course they could not think of marrying the firm's bookkeepers—twenty-five-dollar-a-week men! Yet they despaired ever to find mates from amongst those other people.

Once a collection was made to cover some minor expense of a children's party. Sophy gave a hundred dollars. She surprised the others laughing, and never knew whether she had given too much or too little. Hirsh Goldstein did not fare any better. The German Jews he met at the synagogue were nice and polite, but patronizing to an exasperating degree. Though they accepted his gifts for the synagogue and other charities, they looked down upon him. When he gave a small amount he was criticized as a miser, when he gave a big sum he was a parvenu. His missed his old cronies. He had no chance to exhibit learning to those "new people."

Mrs. Goldstein wandered about the rooms, as if in prison. It was seldom that anybody ever visited the family now. They were reputed to be so rich! Joseph and Maurice came once to Sophy's birthday party, but they found there other guests, and felt lonesome. The Goldsteins had not learned how to be idling busily.

The two sisters now lacked a certain freedom of movement, surety of action. Sophy began to long for the firm grasp of Maurice's hand. Leah longed to hear Joseph's simple songs. The house with all its new wealth was not their home. It was too cold, too new, too clean. The men and women they met were not of their kind. The Goldsteins felt daily that they were only tolerated by them.

This situation lasted six months.

Then Hirsh Goldstein returned to his old synagogue on Hester Street. He went there in his old coat. To make up with his old friends he gave only five dollars when he was called to read from the holy book.

"Hirsh is down from his high horse," they whispered, when he returned the next week bringing his wife also to the synagogue. She too came in her second-best wraps.

A few weeks later the news spread that the Goldsteins had lost most of their fortune or all of it. Sophy and Leah came downtown to a party to which former friends invited them, just to show that it mattered not. And it was so nice and friendly! Everybody was so familiar and intimate.

"If you want anyone to speak to you, leave all the junk here," Sophy told Leah, who had put on the greater part of her jewelry for the occasion.

The Goldsteins rented an apartment on Tenth Street, but this time the old people furnished it. They bought good soft chairs, the kind they had had before, and a multicolored carpet for the floor of the front room, and a red settee which did not look severe and stylish, but inviting. It was just one step ahead in point of comfort and luxury from the one they had had before the adventure on the Drive. It was home again.

The Drive apartment was sublet, all furnished. Maurice came back to Sophy, Joseph to Leah, and every time one of the family bought clothes or jewelry great care was taken not to overdo—not to scare away old friends, not to soar too high with the first wind. Every time some expensive dress was suggested by some friends they exclaimed in chorus.

"We can't afford it. Times are hard."

But they were happy again.

(1919)

MACDOUGAL STREET
by Edna St. Vincent Millay

As I went walking up and down to take the evening air,
    (Sweet to meet upon the street, why must I be so shy?)
I saw him lay his hand upon her torn black hair;
    ("Little dirty Latin child, let the lady by!")

The women squatting on the stoops were slovenly and fat,
    (Lay me out in organdie, lay me out in lawn!)
And everywhere I stepped there was a baby or a cat;
    (Lord God in Heaven, will it never be dawn?)

The fruit-carts and clam-carts were ribald as a fair,
    (Pink nets and wet shells trodden under heel)
She had haggled from the fruit-man of his rotting ware;
    (I shall never get to sleep, the way I feel!)

He walked like a king through the filth and the clutter,
    (Sweet to meet upon the street, why did you glance me by?)
But he caught the quaint Italian quip she flung him from the gutter;
    (What can there be to cry about that I should lie and cry?)

He laid his darling hand upon her little black head,
    (I wish I were a ragged child with ear-rings in my ears!)
And he said she was a baggage to have said what she had said;
    (Truly I shall be ill unless I stop these tears!)

(1920)

A NIGGER WHO WAS HANGED
by Ben Hecht

After I had talked to him awhile in his cell I realized that he owed his impending death to his sideburns and his van dyke. They had crystalized the fatal illusion of his greatness.

A nigger about to be hanged is as a rule less interesting than a white man in a similar predicament. Mystery and terror seem not to denude the black of his character, but merely to accentuate it. Under their influence he grows mystical and tuneful. Emotion does not twist his face into dramatic awkwardness. Awaiting death he becomes like a child, graceful, poignant and expectant.

With the white man, the character changes are more vivid. He is wrenched out of the materialistic surfaces within which he lives and plunged into a character foreign to him. Terror and death are things he forgot ages ago. He finds no subtle affinity with his fate. Until the moment he drops through the gallows trap he struggles pitifully in a nightmare.

When I left the black in his cell I wondered if he were insane. Yet to label illusion insanity is a wholesale evasion. The man had been educated in American schools. He had started out to be a physician. His soul had not kept pace with his intellect. In a curious way he had become awed of himself, of his learning and of the sideburns and van dyke that decorated his black face.

Gradually a duality had developed. He had begun referring to himself in the third person. He felt fearful and puzzled of this thing that was in his head—thought. His soul was like a naive face peering out of a dark and familiar wilderness. It watched this other thing striding authoritatively through a strange world. It watched men become respectful to this thing. It noted how there was a voice and a manner, a miraculous collection of words and ideas which the world deferentially greeted as Dr. Samuel Williams.

Nothing would have happened had it not been for this naive face peering out of the dark. But when Dr. Williams attired himself in a frock coat and a stiff white shirt and patent leather shoes, and when he turned his keen eyes and aristocratic beard to the mirror, the naive one in a transport of adulation began to whisper.

The adulation was too much for Dr. Williams. At first he was content to pose and preen before this awed and murmuring one. But slowly a curious thing happened. The soul of Dr. Williams tip-toed out of its exile and took possession of the frock coat, the van dyke and the strange thing in his head—thought. And there was no longer a separate Dr. Williams—a clever, shrewd and learned man. There was instead a gibbering and exultant noise behind an incongruous exterior. The noise proclaimed, "I am Prince Mulbo of Abyssinia, a man of royal blood. I will lead my people back to the dark and familiar place where I belong."

Things happened rapidly after this. Dr. Samuel Williams, who had been a convincing exterior, vanished rather swiftly. In his place walked an Abyssinian Prince, exuding opulent phrases and making regal gestures with the frock coat, the sideburns and the van dyke.

The doctor's friends were not unduly surprised. A few negro business and professional men shook their heads dubiously. But the others responded excitedly to the transformation. They pointed out that Dr. Williams was merely using his great learning and genius for leadership in a new way. And thousands of them exultantly enrolled under his banner—for he had a banner—a colored bit of bunting which he identified as the flag of Abyssinia.

It was while marching under this banner in South State street that the trouble happened. The Prince was riding on a horse and to the frock coat he had added other regalia—medals, ribbons and royal haberdashery. A group of U. S. marines appeared. The police had received instruction to break up the parade. Fanaticism was considered dangerous in the neighborhood.

It was the Prince who started the firing. Astride his horse and giving vent to mysterious and exultant war cries he blazed away at the uniforms of the enemy. There were several killed.

I watched the Prince of Abyssinia when they led him into the towering, slot-like chamber of the County Jail in which the scaffold is from time to time erected. He was dressed in his frock coat. His van dyke had been carefully trimmed. He wore no collar—a necessary physiological formality.

When he walked up the steps to the scaffold I noted that he seemed somewhat surprised. His eyes looked with a certain naive questioning at the scene. His manner was restrained and apologetic as if he were an interloper. He regarded the sheriff with polite curiosity and when anyone whispered near him he turned quickly and stared at the person.

It was obvious that there was no Dr. Williams, nor even an Abyssinian Prince. The soul of the man that had been masquerading under the awesome exterior of the frock coat and van dyke had fled back to its origin. And now it was again peering naively out of the dark and familiar place in which it lived. It was watching something happen, something with which it had no connection. They were doing something to the awesome one who used long words and made magnificent gestures. They were fixing a rope about his neck.

"Have you anything you wish to say?" inquired the sheriff.

The naive and bewildered one retreated still further. They were not addressing him. They were merely talking to the frock coat and the sideburns. And the frock coat and the sideburns grew somewhat puzzled. They turned around and seemed to be looking for someone—a familiar. But the familiar had fled. The sheriff was nervous.

"Anything you wish to say?" he repeated, stammering.

"No . . . not at this time," the frock coat answered. The puzzled, questioning eyes of Dr. Williams opened for an instant to an incomprehensible scene and then vanished behind a white hood.

(1926)

From

BORN TO BE
by Taylor Gordon

The Chinamen were having a big time in their wash-house on Main Street— lots of special dishes of food and drink were set on the floor and low tables for the occasion. Grover and I found lots of amusement with them, although most of their conversation we could not understand.

Once in a while, when one chink acted as if he were going mad in his debate with his fellow-men, we would ask Charley the Chinaman (the Boss of the laundry) what was the matter with him. We were surprised to learn that he was putting up all the fuss about some girl stealing his hop-pipe in Helena "long times ago," as Charley said, during a New Year's celebration, and every New Year since, when he got half drunk, he would argue the point that some day he would find her and kill her. His wrath impressed us that hop must be a grand thing, and a special pipe must have meant more than anything else in the world to a smoker.

From the Main Street festivities the chinks would visit down at Louie the Chinaman's place. He lived in a log cabin on the northwest corner of town. He owned a big truck-garden, kept plenty of hogs, and in his cabin he had ten hop-bunks. Grover and I would fall in line with the Chinamen as they strung out of the wash-house and wound their snakey trail down to Louie's, a mile away.

It was amazing how many people could get into Louie's cabin—one big room with small bunks all round the walls, two and three deep. Chinamen were playing dominoes, cards, and eating continually. A white woman here and there would be laying in a bunk—sound asleep or smoking a long hop-pipe. Her mouth seemed to be hardly big enough to gobble the big mouth piece. The stem of a hop-pipe is one inch in diameter. Every time I see a policeman's billy, I think of a hop-pipe.

White men sometimes gambled with the chinks, but most of them went to Louie's to smoke. It kept Louie very busy, getting up from his private bunk to get a paper of opium for a customer. He sold a little ladle-full from the small jars at a dollar a paper, as he called it—but it really should have been called tins. He had a hundred or more little round tins cut from tomato cans smoothed down, on which he put this opium. A dollar's worth would make three or four good pills. It's a funny thing about smoking hop. Most anyone can smoke, but few can cook it good, so that a nice round pill will stick to the pipe bowl without plugging up the little hole through which the smoke goes. Louie taught us to take care of the pipes and sell the opium.

Every night after dinner we were on the job until a married man of class came down too often and stayed too late. His wife put the Sheriff on Louie and he was run out of town; that necessarily cut our graft again. We used to steal the Yen Shee from the pipes and make a brown powder out of it and sell it to the cocaine fiends on the line. It gave them something of the same feeling as cocaine. Some snuffed it and a couple put it in whiskey and drank it. I would like to tell of other things that happened in Louie's den, but some fools reading about it might want to try them. If they didn't do it just right, they would wake up—maybe, and maybe not.

(1929)

From

THE GREEN PASTURES
by Marc Connelly

PART ONE

Scene I

A corner in a Negro church.
Ten children and an elderly preacher.

The costumes are those that might be seen in any lower Louisiana town at Sunday-School time. As the curtain rises, MR. DESHEE, *the preacher, is reading from a Bible. The* CHILDREN *are listening with varied degrees of interest. Three or four are wide-eyed in their attention. Two or three are obviously puzzled, but interested, and the smallest ones are engaged in more physical concerns. One is playing with a little doll, and another runs his finger on all the angles of his chair.*

DESHEE. "An' Adam lived a hundred and thirty years, an' begat a son in his own likeness, after his image; an' called his name Seth. An' de days of

Adam, after he had begotten Seth, were eight hundred years; an' he begat sons an' daughters; an' all de days dat Adam lived were nine hundred an' thirty years; an' he died. An' Seth lived a hundred an' five years an' begat Enos; an' Seth lived after he begat Enos eight hundred an' seven years and begat sons and daughters. An' all de days of Seth were nine hundred and twelve years; an' he died.'' An' it go on like dat till we come to Enoch an' de book say: "An' Enoch lived sixty an' five years and begat Methuselah.'' Den it say: "An' all de days of Methuselah were nine hund'ed an' sixty an' nine years an' he died.'' An' dat was de oldest man dat ever was. Dat's why we call ol' Mr. Gurney's mammy ol' Mrs. Methuselah, caize she's so ol'. Den a little later it tell about another member of de fam'ly. His name was Noah. Maybe some of you know about him already. I'm gonter tell you all about him next Sunday. Anyway dat's de meat an' substance of de first five chapters of Genesis. Now, how you think you gonter like de Bible?

MYRTLE. I think it's jest wonderful, Mr. Deshee. I cain't understand any of it.

FIRST BOY. Why did dey live so long, Mr. Deshee?

DESHEE. Why? Caize dat was de way God felt.

SECOND BOY. Dat made Adam a way back.

DESHEE. Yes, he certainly 'way back by de time Noah come along. Want to ask me any mo' questions?

SECOND BOY. What de worl' look like when de Lawd begin, Mr. Deshee?

DESHEE. How yo' mean what it look like?

MYRTLE. Carlisle mean who was in N'Orleans den.

DESHEE. Dey wasn't nobody in N'Orleans on 'count dey wasn't any N'Orleans. Dat's de whole idea I tol' you at de end of de first Chapter. Yo' got to git yo' minds fixed. Dey wasn't any Rampart Street. Dey wasn't any Canal Street. Dey wasn't any Louisiana. Dey wasn't nothin' on de earth at all caize fo' de reason dey wasn't any earth.

MYRTLE. Yes, but what Carlisle wanter know is—

DESHEE. *[Interrupting and addressing little boy who has been playing with his chair and paying no attention.]* Now Randolph, if you don't listen, how yo' gonter grow up and be a good man? Yo' wanter grow up an' be a transgressor?

LITTLE BOY. *[Frightened.]* No.

DESHEE. You tell yo' mammy yo' sister got to come wid you next time. She kin git de things done in time to bring you to de school. You content yo'self.

[The little boy straightens up in his chair.]

Now, what do Carlisle want to know?

CARLISLE. How he decide he want de worl' to be right yere and how he git de idea he wanted it?

MYRTLE. Caize de Book say, don't it, Mr. Deshee?

DESHEE. De Book say, but at de same time dat's a good question. I remember when I was a little boy de same thing recurred to me. An' ol' Mr. Dubois, he was a wonderful preacher at New Hope Chapel over in East Gretna, he said: "De answer is dat de Book ain't got time to go into all de details." And he was right. You know sometimes I think de Lawd expects us to figure out a few things for ourselves. We know that at one time dey wasn't anything except Heaven, we don't know jest where it was but we know it was dere. Maybe it was everywhere. Den one day de Lawd got the idea he'd like to make some places. He made de sun and de moon, de stars. An' he made de earth.

MYRTLE. Who was aroun' den, nothin' but angels?

DESHEE. I suppose so.

FIRST BOY. What was de angels doin' up dere?

DESHEE. I suppose dey jest flew aroun' and had a good time. Dey wasn't no sin, so dey musta had a good time.

FIRST BOY. Did dey have picnics?

DESHEE. Sho, dey had the nicest kind of picnics. Dey probably had fish frys, wid b'iled custard and ten cent seegars for de adults. God gives us humans lotsa ideas about havin' good times. Maybe dey were things he'd seen de angels do. Yes, sir, I bet dey had a fish fry every week.

MYRTLE. Did dey have Sunday School, too?

DESHEE. Yes, dey musta had Sunday School for de cherubs.

MYRTLE. What did God look like, Mr. Deshee?

DESHEE. Well, nobody knows exactly, what God looked like. But when I was a little boy I used to imagine dat he looked like de Reverend Dubois. He was de finest looking ol' man I ever knew. Yes, I used to bet de Lawd looked exactly like Mr. Dubois in de days when he walked de earth in de shape of a natchel man.

MYRTLE. When was dat, Mr. Deshee?

DESHEE. Why, when he was gettin' things started down heah. When He talked to Adam and Eve and Noah and Moses and all dem. He made mighty men in dem days. But aldo they was awful mighty dey always knew dat He was beyond dem all. Pretty near one o'clock, time fo' you chillun to go home to dinner, but before I let you go I wan' you to go over wid me de main facts of de first lesson. What's de name of de book?

CHILDREN. Genesis.

DESHEE. Dat's right. And what's de other name?

CHILDREN. First Book of Moses.

DESHEE. Dat's right. And dis yere's Chapter One.

[The lights begin to dim.] "In de beginnin' God created de heaven an' de earth. An' de earth was widout form an' void. An' de darkness was upon de face of de deep."

(1930)

From

ONE MORE SPRING
by Robert Nathan

The Sweenys lived in a tiny flat near the river, within sound of the tugs and river steamers, whose watery hootings, soft and mysterious, spoke to them at night with the voice of ocean. They seemed to say there are lands far away, there are countries beyond the sea. To Mary Sweeny they spoke of the hereafter. Gentle and ignorant, she expected to travel only when she was dead, and then to heaven.

During the day she ran an elevator in the office building owned by the Savings Bank. At first, when she was still green at her work, she had been unable to think of anything but the steep and narrow shaft in which her small square car rose with a gentle motion toward the sky, only to descend again before it got there. Straight up, above the clouds, above the busy offices, the bank, and real-estate companies, was heaven. If only her car might keep on going . . .

She knew she would be welcome there, for Father Duffy had told her so. And Mrs. Sweeny's God was kind and merciful to His own; He washed away the tears of His children in the blood of the Lamb and gave them life everlasting, and little wings, like a bird.

But would He do as much for Mr. Sweeny? Mrs. Sweeny had her doubts.

And when she heard that her husband was taking lessons on the fiddle, she couldn't get to Father Duffy fast enough. The good priest reassured her. "The Lord," he said, "enjoys His bit of music now and then, Mrs. Sweeny. Hasn't He had Saint Cecilia with Him these hundreds of years? Don't give it another thought, then. Still and all, a prayer to the saint would do no harm," said Father Duffy.

All day long Mrs. Sweeny sailed softly up in the direction of the sky and floated gently down again, wafted upon currents of electricity. As she grew more used to her work, she began to notice her passengers, some of whom were men of the greatest importance. Among them was Mr. Sheridan, the president of the bank. He came in every morning at ten, and left at four. He was small; his eyes were set too close together; and an expression of intense thought gave an abiding wrinkle to his forehead. "You'd never think he was the president of a bank," Mrs. Sweeny told her husband; "but he must be a smart man, God bless him, just the same."

For real beauty in a man, Mrs. Sweeny preferred the pictures of the archangels, by Michelangelo, copies of which hung on the walls of the Church of the Good Shepherd, where she went to mass and to confession. Nevertheless, she had deposited her savings in Mr. Sheridan's bank, because she liked to be near her money, and also because Mr. Sheridan had such a knowledgeable expression. He must think a great deal, she told herself, to look like that. And when he said good-morning to her in the elevator, she felt that her savings were safe and were sending her a greeting.

Alas, it was anxiety, not knowledge, that caused the frown upon Mr. Sheridan's forehead. But Mrs. Sweeny did not know that.

To experience bliss one must know either everything or nothing. Mrs. Sweeny knew very little; and for that reason she was happy. She went to her work in the morning and came home to her housework at night; she was never idle, and always a little tired; but early mass on Sundays and holidays served to keep her thoughts away from her body, and Satan could find no mischief for those worn and weary hands.

After supper, after the dishes and pots had been cleaned and put away, she sat down—for the first time, almost, that day—in the rocking-chair next to the table on which stood the lamp with the red and green shade, and a little pot with a rubber plant in it. Mr. Sweeny, in his stockinged feet, sat opposite, with the newspaper in his hand; he smoked his pipe, looked at the pictures, and read the headlines, while Mrs. Sweeny folded her hands and rocked.

"Mary," said Mr. Sweeny, removing his pipe.

"Yourself," she replied.

"Here's a piece in the paper says there's snow already in the west." He peered into the bowl of his pipe, to see how the ash was getting along. "It'll be time to get out my boots again," he said.

Mrs. Sweeny sighed. "I can hardly believe winter's coming," she declared. "It's so clear and quiet. You'll need some heavy woolens this year,

Michael; the old are all wore out. Maybe I could patch them so they'd stand you a little longer if I had the time. I tell you, I pity the poor, with the cold coming on. What more does it say?''

Mr. Sweeny read slowly: ''A cold winter is forecast by the weather authorities. Flights of geese have been seen moving south over the Carolinas. In Kansas . . .''

Mrs. Sweeny gave a shiver. ''Never mind,'' she said; ''read me something brighter.''

''There's naught brighter,'' said Mr. Sweeny.

''Read me the church news,'' said Mrs. Sweeny.

Mr. Sweeny turned to the religious section. ''It says here,'' he remarked after a pause, ''that the Methodist Board of Bishops has voted to raise fifty thousand dollars for Methodist missions in China.''

''May God forgive them for it,'' said Mrs. Sweeny. ''Is there nothing about the Catholics?''

''No,'' said Mr. Sweeny. His eye fell upon another item, farther down the page. ''But there's a bit about the Prince of Wales,'' he said. ''He's been made an admiral. 'Mellon congratulates the Prince,' it says. Mr. Mellon is our ambassador in England, Mary. An oldish man.''

''Go on,'' said Mary; ''read some more.''

''There's only murders left,'' said Mr. Sweeny.

Mr. Sweeny read the murders; he read the comic strips, a page on the theater, the department notices, and a recipe for cottage pudding. Then he returned to the Methodist Board of Missions. It seemed like a lot of money, for China.

Mrs. Sweeny agreed with him. ''And for what, may I ask?'' she exclaimed. ''To teach black ignorance to the heathen. Sometimes I think God doesn't know what's going on, Heaven forgive me for saying it.''

Mr. Sweeny closed his eyes. ''I could do with a bit of money myself,'' he said dreamily. ''I could buy something with money, Mary.''

And opening his eyes again, he gave his wife a wheedling look.

Mrs. Sweeny noticed the look with wonder. For her own part, she couldn't think of anything to buy—except a canary, she thought. ''You could buy a canary,'' she told him. And she gave a sigh, because she had always wanted a canary.

''I could buy a fiddle,'' said Mr. Sweeny boldly.

His wife sat up straight in her chair. ''A fiddle?'' she cried. ''Well, aren't you the grand one, Mr. Sweeny. And what, pray, would a fiddle cost you, while you're so bold and free?''

Mr. Sweeny gazed once more, and with embarrassment, into his pipe. ''I could buy a fiddle,'' he said, ''for thirty dollars. A sweet-toned fiddle, with a bow and all.

''And keep it here,'' he added, ''and play on it of an evening, for the practice.''

''But where,'' he concluded sadly, ''would I get thirty dollars?''

Mr. Sweeny had no savings. He gave his money each week to his wife, who paid the rent, and bought the food as they went along. One bank account—her own—was enough for them; and once money had been put into the bank, it rarely occurred to either of them to take it out again. As for a fiddle costing thirty dollars . . .

Mrs. Sweeny made no reply. For a good deal less than thirty dollars, she could buy a canary, with a cage, and a stone to sharpen his beak on. She'd often thought about it—what it would be like to have a singing bird to come home to of an evening. Then, when she was washing the dishes, she'd hear him trilling in the next room. Or maybe she'd even take him, cage and all, into the kitchen with her.

She'd never bought herself anything—never anything she wanted, like a canary. Good people, whom God cared for most, didn't go about buying themselves things; the blessed saints even gave away what they loved. Still and all, they had lived in the country; Saint Pachomius had a crocodile as his friend; and Saint Francis had the birds, they flew beside him while he walked the dusty roads, they sat down in front of him in the hedgerow's shade, they sang their loveliest songs for him.

That night Mr. Sweeny lay awake for a long while, listening to the river sounds, the misty tootings, the muffled noises of the street, cries and voices, the heavy rumble of trains on the elevated at Second Avenue. It seemed to him as though his whole life were in those sounds; as though his heart must make a sound too, or else spill over—a sound like the river steamers calling to each other on the free water; music, like Mr. Rosenberg, whose fiddle could be heard above the motors and the street-cars, whose scales and passages, rising above the noise of traffic, caused people to stop for a moment to listen, the rich and the poor together.

Oh, bright immeasurable dream . . .

And Mary, beside him, wakeful too, listened to the river voices, and thought of God, whose awful, loving presence, bearded and compassionate, moved through the night above her. Could she buy herself a bird while others were in want? Their poverty did not trouble her so much as her own extravagance. Thirty dollars for a fiddle to make Michael happy. . . . She felt a strange stir at her heart. It was a long time since she'd made anyone happy. Not since she'd been a girl, not since she'd said yes to him years before. The past came back to her, simple and fragrant: she had been young, and she had hoped for nothing. It was all she got; but life had been no worse than she had looked for. Her husband was a good man, for all he had so little to say for himself.

Christmas was coming; the smell of pine boughs would be in the air. She could borrow a little Christmas tree from the grocer and hang the fiddle on it, with the bow and all. Or the canary in his cage. . . .

Ah, what was Christmas for, getting or giving? Mary Mother of God, what would you do, if it was you?

Smiling, she fell asleep before Mary could answer.

(1933)

From

THE YOUNG MANHOOD OF STUDS LONIGAN
by James T. Farrell

Studs and Tommy Doyle leaned against the side of the drug store building, watching the punks. They were in old clothes and football outfits.

"Jesus, I'll bet they make a fine bunch of players," sneered Studs, wishing that he were in football togs.

"I'll bet they'll play that touch football so they don't get their hair mussed," said Tommy.

"If they get up against a good tough team, they'll be sweet," said Studs.

"Hello, Studs," said Phil who was in football regalia.

"What the hell do you play?" asked Tommy.

"I'm one of the halfbacks," said Phil.

"Sure, he's the All-American-Half-Ass," said Studs. Phil turned to say something to one of his teammates, acting as if he hadn't heard Studs' crack.

"OOPH!" Studs exclaimed, seeing Dapper Dan O'Doul in a football outfit.

"Jesus Christ, him too," said Tommy.

"You know they got their suits from Gorman. He's running for judge, and they're Gorman Boosters," said Studs.

"Well, he sure ought to make them lose the election," said Tommy.

"Here comes that kike pest," said Studs.

"Got a nickel or a butt, Studs?" Tommy mimicked.

"You got Father Abraham there down to a ''t'' that time," said Studs.

"Hello, boys," Davey Cohen said with ineffectual cheerfulness.

"Got a cigarette, Tommy?" said Studs. Tommy held out a pack and winked.

"Say, got another there, Tommy?" Davey asked.

Studs winked back. Davey took a cigarette.

"Boys, I saw Helen Shires," said Davey.

"How is she?" asked Tommy.

"Is she married?" asked Studs.

"I heard she's a Lesbian," said Davey, laughing sardonically.

"What the hell's that?" Studs asked.

"She's like a fairy only in love with women. I don't know if that's true, but that's what I heard," said Davey.

"Oh!" said Studs.

He remembered that show he'd seen at Burnham. He was disgusted. His disgust turned to a fierce but silent hatred of Davey. All his old liking and respect for Helen from the old days returned. It couldn't be true. It wasn't.

"Tell us the dope about her," said Studs.

"Well, I just heard it, that's all, that she was living with another girl, and that, well, a guy I know who knows her girl chum, he says he was up to their apartment, and that he saw plenty."

Davey bummed a cigarette off Studs and told Lesbian stories that he'd heard on the road. He was happy. And he hadn't been happy much since he'd returned. He had that cough. And the guys weren't the same. They didn't accept him as one of the boys. He knew it, and needn't kid himself. He was a little sick Jew now, a sick tormented Jew. He could see the way they looked at him, talked. And he was down, broke and sick. They weren't sick, and even the ones who hadn't any dough were able to raise more than he ever could. All he had was what he bummed. His kid brother had a good job, and once in a while gave him a half buck, but not often. Now, he was telling them stories that interested them, and he felt like it was the same as the old times when he was one of the boys, in with them, a battler who could go with the best of them; and goddamn it, he had been able to go with the best of them—once.

"That's queer, all right," said Studs.

"It ain't natural. They ought to take and shoot girls like that, they ain't natural, and they're a disgrace to the human race," Red Kelly said.

"I'll bet she must be awfully unhappy if that's true," Les said naively.

"That thing is against the natural law," said Red with unshakable self-conviction.

"Well, of course, I feel they can't help it. I think maybe they're born that way, or they are made that way because of something that happens in their life," Davey said, apologetically.

"B. S.," Red said.

"I suppose you'd like to kiss a girl like that," Tommy sneered.

"That's worse than having a nigger. Think of it, a girl comes from a self-respecting family, with a decent old man and old lady. She had a decent home, a chance for an education, an opportunity to meet decent fellows, and to become a fine, decent girl. And what does she do, but become worse than the hustler of a nigger pimp? And you try to say she can't help it! Why girls like that ought to be made to live with pigs," Red proclaimed.

"I wonder if much of that stuff goes on?" said Studs.

"Plenty, if you ask me. Only I said I just heard that," said Davey.

"She was always a tomboy as a kid," said Red.

"Yes, it wasn't natural for a girl to be like a boy," said Tommy.

"She was a swell pal as a kid," Studs said, nostalgically.

"Say what you want to, but the finest and most decent girls are Irish Catholic girls," said Red.

"No jane is decent if she meets the right guy," said Slug.

"Well, I don't know that I agree with you there, Slug," said Red.

"Say, it ain't a matter of what you call decency. It's all a matter of the right guy coming along at the right time," said Slug.

"No, sir, you get a good Catholic girl, who has a decent home, the right kind of parents, and fear of God in her, like Studs' sisters, and they're decent, they're fine, they're amongst the finest things you can find in life," said Red.

Studs felt proud of his sisters.

"And when girls don't, there's only two things to do. The old man to give her his razor strap, and the old man or brother or somebody to give the clouts to the guys that try and fool around with her," said Red.

"Well, boys, let's go to a show," said Studs.

"All right."

They walked off. Davey trailed after them, and asked if anyone had enough to lend him to come along. They didn't answer him.

"Studs, I can pay you back tomorrow," said Davey, half pleading.

"Sorry, Dave, all I got is enough for the show and coffee an' afterwards," Studs said.

Davey watched them straggle down towards Garfield Boulevard. He was sorry that he had returned. He had no pain in his chest, but he felt that he had. Only a poor sick Jew. He thought of Heine, whose poem he'd read in the Jamestown library.

"That Jew moocher," sneered Studs.

"Yeah," said Slug.

"Say, he's the kind, his kind, that sold out Wabash Avenue to the niggers. If it wasn't for the Jews, this would be a better neighborhood than it is. But anyway, with the new church, it will pick up," said Red.

"I know my old man is beginning to wonder if he ought to sell his building after all, and clear out," said Studs.

"Well, I tell you, once the kikes get in a neighborhood, it's all over," said Red with unanswerable argument.

(1934)

From

A COOL MILLION
by Nathanael West

Several chapters back I left our heroine, Betty Prail, lying naked under a bush. She was not quite so fortunate as Lem, and did not regain consciousness until after he had returned home.

When she recovered the full possession of her faculties, she found herself in what she thought was a large box that was being roughly shaken by some unknown agency. In a little while, however, she realized that she was in reality lying on the bottom of a wagon.

"Could it be that she was dead?" she asked herself. But no, she heard voices, and besides she was still naked. "No matter how poor a person is," she comforted herself, "they wrap him or her up in something before burial."

There were evidently two men on the driver's seat of the wagon. She tried to understand what they were saying, but could not because they spoke a foreign tongue. She was able to recognize their language as Italian, however, having had some few music lessons in the orphan asylum.

"*Gli diede uno scudo, il che lo rese subito gentile,*" said one of her captors to the other in a guttural voice.

"*Sì, sì,*" affirmed the other. "*Questa vita terrena è quasi un prato, che'l serpente tra fiori giace.*" After this bit of homely philosophy, they both lapsed into silence.

But I do not want to mystify my readers any longer. The truth was that the poor girl had been found by white slavers, and was being taken to a house of ill fame in New York City.

The trip was an exceedingly rough one for our heroine. The wagon in which she was conveyed had no springs to speak of, and her two captors made her serve a severe apprenticeship to the profession they planned for her to follow.

Late one night, the Italians halted their vehicle before the door of a Chinese laundry somewhere near Mott Street. After descending from their dilapidated conveyance, they scanned the street both up and down for a possible policeman. When they had made sure that it was deserted, they covered their captive with some old sacking and bundled her into the laundry.

There they were greeted by an ancient Chinaman, who was doing sums on an abacus. This son of the Celestial Empire was a graduate of the Yale University in Shanghai, and he spoke Italian perfectly.

"Qualche cosa de nuovo, signori?" he asked.

"Molto, molto," said the older and more villainous looking of the two foreigners. *"La vostra lettera l'abbiamo ricevuto, ma il denaro no,"* he added with a shrewd smile.

"Queste sette medaglie le troverò, compaesano," answered the Chinaman in the same language.

After this rather cryptic dialogue, the Chinaman led Betty through a secret door into a sort of reception room. This chamber was furnished in luxurious oriental splendour. The walls were sheathed in a pink satin that had been embroidered with herons in silver by some cunning workman. On the floor was a silk rug that must have cost more than a thousand dollars, the colours of which could well vie with the rainbow. Before a hideous idol, incense was burning, and its heady odour filled the air. It was evident that neither pains nor expense had been spared in the decoration of the room.

The old Chinaman struck a gong, and ere its musical note died away an oriental woman with bound feet came to lead Betty off.

When she had gone, Wu Fong, for that was the Chinaman's name, began to haggle with the two Italians over her purchase price. The bargaining was done in Italian, and rather than attempt to make a word-for-word report of the transaction I shall give only the result. Betty was knocked down to the Chinaman for six hundred dollars.

This was a big price, so far as prices went in the white slave market. But Wu Fong was set on having her. In fact it was he who had sent the two to scour the New England countryside for a real American girl. Betty suited him down to the ground.

The reader may be curious to know why he wanted an American girl so badly. Let me say now that Wu Fong's establishment was no ordinary house of ill fame. It was like that more famous one in the Rue Chabanis, Paris, France— a "House of All Nations." In his institution he already had a girl from every country in the known world except ours, and now Betty rounded out the collection.

Wu Fong was confident that he would soon have his six hundred dollars back with interest, for many of his clients were from non-Aryan countries, and would appreciate the services of a genuine American. Apropos of this, it is lamentable but a fact, nevertheless, that the inferior races greatly desire the women of their superiors. This is why the Negroes rape so many white women in our southern states.

Each one of the female inmates of Wu Fong's establishment had a tiny two-room suite for her own use, furnished and decorated in the style of the country from which she came. Thus, Marie, the French girl, had an apartment that was Directoire. Celeste's rooms (there were two French girls because of their traditional popularity) were Louis the Fourteenth; she being the fatter of the two.

In her suite, the girl from Spain, Conchita, had a grand piano with a fancy shawl gracefully draped over it. Her armchair was upholstered in horsehide fastened by large buttons, and it had enormous steer horns for arms. On one of her walls a tiny balcony had been painted by a poor but consummate artist.

There is little use in my listing the equipment of the remaining some fifty-odd apartments. Suffice it to say that the same idea was carried out with excellent taste and real historical knowledge in all of them.

Still wearing the sacking into which the Italians had bundled her, our heroine was led to the apartment that had been prepared against her arrival.

The proprietor of the house had hired Asa Goldstein to decorate this suite and it was a perfect colonial interior. Antimacassars, ships in bottles, carved whalebone, hooked rugs—all were there. It was Mr. Goldstein's boast that even Governor Windsor himself could not have found anything wrong with the design or furnishings.

Betty was exhausted, and immediately fell asleep on the poster bed with its candlewick spread. When she awoke, she was given a hot bath, which greatly refreshed her. She was then dressed by two skillful maids.

The costume that she was made to wear had been especially designed to go with her surroundings. While not exactly in period, it was very striking, and I will describe it as best I can for the benefit of my feminine readers.

The dress had a full waist made with a yoke and belt, a gored skirt, long, but not too long to afford a very distinct view of a well-turned ankle and a small, shapely foot encased in a snowy cotton stocking and a low-heeled black slipper. The material of the dress was chintz—white ground with a tiny brown figure—finished at the neck with a wide white ruffle. On her hands she was made to wear black silk mitts with half-fingers. Her hair was worn in a little knot on the top of her head, and one thick short curl was kept in place by a puff-comb at each side of her face.

Breakfast, for so much time had elapsed, was served her by an old Negro in livery. It consisted of buckwheat cakes with maple syrup, Rhode Island Johnny cakes, bacon biscuits, and a large slice of apple pie.

(Wu Fong was a great stickler for detail, and, like many another man, if he had expended as much energy and thought honestly he would have made even more money without having to carry the stigma of being a brothel-keeper. Alas!)

So resilient are the spirits of the young that Betty did the breakfast full justice. She even ordered a second helping of pie, which was brought to her at once by the darky.

After Betty had finished eating, she was given some embroidery to do. With the reader's kind permission we will leave her while she is still sewing, and before the arrival of her first client, a pockmarked Armenian rug merchant from Malta.

(1934)

From

BUTTERFIELD 8
by John O'Hara

"Well, I can see why you didn't want me to see the ending first. I never would have stayed in the theater if I'd seen that ending. And you wanted to see that again? God, I hope if you ever write anything it won't be like that."

"I hope if I ever write anything it affects somebody the way this affected you," said Jimmy.

"I suppose you think that's good. I mean good writing," said Isabel. "Where shall we go?"

"Are you hungry?"

"No, but I'd like a drink. One cocktail. Is that understood?"

"Always. Always one cocktail. That's always understood. I know a place I'd like to take you to, but I'm a little afraid to."

"Why, is it tough?"

"It isn't really tough. I mean it doesn't look tough, and the people— well, you don't think you're in the Racquet Club, but unless you know where you are, I mean unless you're tipped off about what the place has, what its distinction is, it's just another speakeasy, and right now if I told you what its distinguishing characteristic is, you wouldn't want to go there."

"Well, then let's not go there," she said. "What is peculiar about the place?"

"It's where the Chicago mob hangs out in New York."

"Oh, well, then by all means let's go there. That is, if it's safe."

"Of course it's safe. Either it's safe or it isn't. They tell me the local boys approve of this place, that is, they sanction it, allow it to exist and do business, because they figure there has to be one place as a sort of hangout for members of the Chicago mobs. There's only one real danger."

"What's that?"

"Well, if the Chicago mobs start shooting among themselves. So far that hasn't happened, and I don't imagine it will. You'll see why."

They walked down Broadway a few blocks and then turned and walked east. When they came to a highly polished brass sign which advertised a wig-maker, Jimmy steered Isabel into the narrow doorway, back a few steps and rang for the elevator. It grinded its way down, and a sick-eyed little Negro with a uniform cap opened the door. They got in and Jimmy said: "Sixth Avenue Club."

"Yessa," said the Negro. The elevator rose two stories and stopped. They got out and were standing then right in front of a steel door, painted red, and with a tiny door cut out in the middle. Jimmy rang the bell and a face appeared in the tiny door.

"Yes, sir," said the face. "What was the name again?"

"You're new or you'd know me," said Jimmy.

"Yes, sir, and what was the name again?"

"Malloy, for Christ's sake."

"And what was the address, Mr. Malloy?"

"Oh, nuts. Tell Luke Mr. Malloy is here."

There was a sound of chains and locks, and the door was opened. The waiter stood behind the door. "Have to be careful who we let in, sir. You know how it is."

It was a room with a high ceiling, a fairly long bar on one side, and in the corner on the other side was a food bar, filled with really good free lunch and with obviously expensive kitchen equipment behind the bar. Jimmy steered Isabel to the bar.

"Hello, Luke," he said.

"Howdy do, sir," said Luke, a huge man with a misleading pleasant face, not unlike Babe Ruth's.

"Have a whiskey sour, darling. Luke mixes the best whiskey sours you've ever had."

"I think I want a Planter's punch—all right, a whiskey sour."

"Yours, sir?"

"Scotch and soda, please."

Isabel looked around. The usual old rascal looking into a schooner of beer and the usual phony club license hung above the bar mirror. Many bottles, including a bottle of Rock and Rye, another specialty of Luke's, stood on the back bar. Except for the number and variety of the bottles, and the cleanliness of the bar, it was just like any number (up to 20,000) of speakeasies near to and far from Times Square. Then Isabel saw one little article that disturbed her: an "illuminated" calendar, with a pocket for letters or bills or something, with a picture of a voluptuous dame with nothing on above the waist. The calendar still had not only all the months intact, but also a top sheet with "1931" on it. And across the front of the pocket was the invitation. "When in Chicago Visit D'Agostino's Italian Cooking Steaks Chops At Your Service Private Dining Rooms," and the address and the telephone numbers, three of them.

By the time she had studied the calendar and understood the significance of it—what with Jimmy's advance description of the speakeasy—their drinks were served, and she began to lose the feeling that the people in the speakeasy were staring at her back. She looked around, and no one was staring at her. The place was less than half full. At one table there was a party of seven, four men and three women. One of the women was outstandingly pretty, was not a whore, was not the kind of blonde that is cast for gangster's moll in the movies, and was not anything but a very good-looking girl, with a very nice shy smile. Isabel could imagine knowing her, and then she suddenly realized why. "Jimmy," she said, "that girl looks like Caroline English."

He turned. "Yes, she does."

"But the other people, I've seen much worse at Coney Island, or even better places than that. You wouldn't invent a story just to make an ordinary little place seem attractive, would you?"

"In the first place, no, and in the second place, no. In the first place I couldn't be bothered. In the second place I wouldn't have to. People like you make me mad, I mean people like you, people whose families have money and send them to good schools and belong to country clubs and have good cars— the upper crust, the swells. You come to a place like this and you expect to see a Warner Brothers movie, one of those gangster pictures full of old worn-out comedians and heavies that haven't had a job since the two-reel Keystone Comedies. You expect to see shooting the minute you go slumming—"

"I beg your pardon, but why are you talking about you people, you people, your kind of people, people like you. *You* belong to a country club, you went to good schools and your family at least *had* money—"

"I want to tell you something about myself that will help to explain a lot of things about me. You might as well hear it now. First of all, I am a Mick. I wear Brooks clothes and I don't eat salad with a spoon and I probably could play five-goal polo in two years, but I am a Mick. Still a Mick. Now it's taken me a little time to find this out, but I have at last discovered that there are not two kinds of Irishmen. There's only one kind. I've studied enough pictures and known enough Irishmen personally to find that out."

"What do you mean, studied enough pictures?"

"I mean this, I've looked at dozens of pictures of the best Irish families at the Dublin Horse Show and places like that, and I've put my finger over their clothes and pretended I was looking at a Knights of Columbus picnic—and by God you can't tell the difference."

"Well, why should you? They're all Irish."

"Ah, that's exactly my point. Or at least we're getting to it. So, a while ago you say I look like James Cagney—"

"Not look like him. Remind me of him."

"Well, there's a faint resemblance, I happen to know, because I have a brother who looks enough like Cagney to be his brother. Well, Cagney is a Mick, without any pretense of being anything else, and he is America's ideal gangster. America, being a non-Irish, anti-Catholic country, has its own idea of what a real gangster looks like, and along comes a young Mick who looks like my brother, and he fills the bill. He is the typical gangster."

"Well, I don't see what you prove by that. I think—"

"I didn't prove anything yet. Here's the big point. You know about the Society of the Cincinnati? You've heard about them?"

"Certainly."

"Well, if I'm not mistaken I could be a member of that Society. Anyway I could be a Son of the Revolution. Which is nice to know sometimes, but for the present purpose I only mention it to show that I'm pretty God damn American, and therefore my brothers and sisters are, and yet we're not American. We're Micks, we're non-assimilable, we Micks. We've been here, at least some of my family, since before the Revolution—and we produce the perfect gangster type! At least it's you American Americans' idea of a perfect gangster type, and I suppose you're right. Yes, I guess you are. The first real gangsters in this country were Irish. The Mollie Maguires. Anyway, do you see what I mean by all this non-assimilable stuff?"

"Yes. I suppose I do."

"All right. Let me go on just a few sticks more. I show a sociological fact, I prove a sociological fact in one respect at least. I suppose I could walk through Grand Central at the same time President Hoover was arriving on a train, and the Secret Service boys wouldn't collar me on sight as a public enemy. That's because I dress the way I do, and I dress the way I do because I happen to prefer these clothes to Broadway clothes or Babbitt clothes. Also, I have nice manners because my mother was a lady and manners were important to her, also to my father in a curious way, but when I was learning manners I was at an age when my mother had greater influence on me than my father, so she gets whatever credit is due me for my manners. Sober.

"Well, I am often taken for a Yale man, by Yale men. That pleases me a little, because I like Yale best of all the colleges. There's another explanation for it, unfortunately. There was a football player at Yale in 1922 and around that time who looks like me and has a name something like mine. That's not important."

"No, except that it takes away from your point about producing public enemies, your family. You can't look like a gangster *and* a typical Yale man."

"That's true. I have an answer for that. Let me see. Oh, yes. The people who think I am a Yale man aren't very observing about people. I'm not making that up as a smart answer. It's true. In fact, I just thought of something funny."

"What?"

"Most men who think I'm a Yale man went to Princeton themselves."

"Oh, come on," she said. "You just said—"

"All right. I know. Well, that's not important and I'm only confusing the issue. What I want to say, what I started out to explain was why I said 'you people, you members of the upper crust,' and so on, implying that I am not a member of it. Well, I'm *not* a member of it, and now I never will be. If there was any chance of it it disappeared—let me see—two years ago."

"Why two years ago? You can't say that. What happened?"

"I starved. Two years ago I went for two days one time without a thing to eat or drink except water, and part of the time without a cigarette. I was living within two blocks of this place, and I didn't have a job, didn't have any prospect of one, I couldn't write to my family, because I'd written a bad check a while before that and I was in very bad at home. I couldn't borrow from anybody, because I owed everybody money. I'd borrowed from practically everybody I knew even slightly. A dollar here, ten dollars there. I stayed in for two days because I couldn't face the people on the street. Then the nigger woman that cleaned up and made the beds in this place where I lived, she knew what was happening, and the third morning she came to work she brought me a chicken sandwich. I'll never forget it. It was on rye bread, and home-cooked chicken, not flat and white, but chunky and more tan than white. It was wrapped in newspaper. She came in and said, 'Good morning, Mr. Malloy. I brought you a chicken sandwich if you like it.' That's all. She didn't say why she brought it, and then she went out and bought me a container of coffee and pinched a couple of cigarettes—Camels, and I smoke Luckies—from one of the other rooms. She was swell. She knew.''

"I should think she was swell enough for you to call her a colored woman instead of a nigger.''

"Oh, balls!''

"I'm leaving.''

"Go ahead.''

"Just a Mick.''

(1935)

MOTHER AND THE ARMENIAN
by Clarence Day

Mother used to take us boys to a summer resort in our vacations. In all such places there was usually an Armenian, prowling around the hotel piazza. Blue-black hair, dark skin, gleaming eyes, a hooked nose, perfect teeth. Mother said that there wasn't a lady on the piazza who didn't envy those teeth. The Armenian was always trying to catch the eye of one of them to see if he couldn't persuade her to look at his rugs or his silks. "Not buy, Madam! Just look!'' She would say no; but he would tell her they were "Oh, so beautiful,'' and offer to give her some perfume, till perhaps if it were a dull afternoon she would roll up her knitting, and saunter down to the end of the hall where his dark little room was.

Since Mother had both a kind heart and a weakness for rugs, she was occasionally snared in this fashion and shown some bargain, some rug that was intrinsically priceless and could never be duplicated, but which could be had for a few hundred dollars, as it happened, that morning. The crisis that made such a price possible would tomorrow be gone, but today it was here, and a wise and clever woman would seize it. Whoever did would be helping a most grateful young man get through college. He was no dealer; he was just a poor student with a few priceless rugs, and if the lady would only make him an offer she could buy at her own figure. She could make him an offer, surely, *some* offer; let it be what it might.

It began to seem unreasonable to Mother not to make him some offer, especially as he was trying to get through college, and it might be a bargain. So she silently tried to figure how much she'd have had to pay at places like Sloane's; and then she took a lot off; and then she felt a little ashamed at taking so much off—she didn't wish to cheat the young man. He seemed to mean well, poor creature. So she worked her price up a little, in her mind, and then got a bit frightened because, after all, it was a good deal of money—though it did seem perfectly safe to pay that much, since Lord & Taylor's or Arnold Constable's would have charged more. Still, you never could tell about a rug, because it might not be genuine, and she wished the young man had let her alone and could get through college without her, though he didn't much look as though he would manage it; he could hardly speak English—and how could the poor thing talk to the professors, or the professors to him, when even on the subject of rugs he had to use a sort of sign language which consisted of hunching his shoulders till she feared he would dislocate them, and picking out sums on his fingers in the most confusing manner. However, she had better make him an offer, she felt, and then perhaps he'd stop smiling, which no doubt he intended as pleasant, but his breath was so bad.

So she finally said, fingering the rug in a dissatisfied way, that she supposed she could give him a hundred for it. The Armenian's smile instantly disappeared. He walked off in gloom. Then he rushed back, excited and jerky, and began a long, rapid expostulation that threatened to deafen us. Mother reluctantly raised her bid to a hundred and twenty to stop him, whereupon it suddenly appeared that he had misunderstood her first offer. He had supposed it to be two hundred, not one. She meant *two* hundred and twenty? Mother said, No, one hundred and twenty was all she had offered. The Armenian then tottered around, sank into a chair, and sort of hissed through his teeth, with such a ghastly look that it made Mother fear he might be having a fit. It began to seem advisable to her to do anything she could to get out of it, and then never buy anything again for the rest of her life. So she miserably and angrily said she would make it one-fifty. She had to say it several times, however, before he seemed to hear her, and even then he received it only with low shrieks and groans in Armenian. He said that now he would have to give up college, because he could not bear such losses. All he had ever hoped of America, he said, was that he wouldn't lose too much money here, but he had found that no one cared how badly he ruined himself, nor did they understand rugs. Poor Mother, half dismayed, half indignant, said she did not want the rug; she had only made him an offer because he had asked her to, and she would now like to go. This brought on a frightful collapse, so full of despair it seemed mortal. He was heard, however, to murmur what she took to be a dying request that she would take the rug with her and split the difference and leave him alone in his agony. On the way out, she had to tell the hotel-clerk to pay him and have it charged on the bill.

At the end of the week, when Father came to visit us and stay over Sunday, Mother had to explain to him that he was now the owner of a rare Eastern rug. Her attempts to announce this to him as a triumph somehow fell very flat. He began by not believing his ears, no matter how many times she repeated it. "Rug? Rug? You say you've bought a *rug?* Nonsense! Pooh! Don't be ridiculous!" And when he found that the story seemed true, and that he couldn't thrust it away, his face turned a dark unhealthy red and he burst into roars of resentment. He shouted that he had only just arrived from hard toil in the city, in search of "a little damned peace," that was all that he asked, instead of which, before he had had time to smoke one cigar, he was harried and tortured and victimized by a pack of low swindlers, with whom his own family had leagued themselves, to render him penniless. He urgently demanded to see the rug so that he could throw it straight out of the window, and the Armenian after it. He swore he'd break every bone in his body. All reports as to the rarity and value of the rug he discredited, declaring he could buy better for fifty cents a barrel on Front Street. He then marched to the Armenian's parlor, with vague but violent intentions, only to find that that astute sufferer had closed his place up. The door was shut and locked and a sign was on it:

B A K
N E K S
W E K

"What's this gibberish?" Father demanded. "You said his name was Dourbabian."

Poor old fawning Dourbabian! His things were not good value at the time; but they at least have become so. That rug and the sofa-cushion covers and great squares of silk which Mother picked up in the eighties would cost a lot more today. She had to keep them out of Father's sight though, until he had forgotten their origin.

Years afterwards, one day, when the newspapers printed some clergyman's denunciations of Turkey for its cruel Armenian massacres, I thought of how Father had longed to massacre Dourbabian, and reminded him of it. Though older and calmer on some subjects he was still resentful on this. "That's just like a parson," he said, "to sympathize with those fellows, without even asking first what they have done to the Turks."

(1935)

From

THEIR EYES WERE WATCHING GOD
by Zora Neale Hurston

The season closed and people went away like they had come—in droves. Tea Cake and Janie decided to stay since they wanted to make another season on the muck. There was nothing to do, after they had gathered several bushels of dried beans to save over and sell to the planters in the fall. So Janie began to look around and see people and things she hadn't noticed during the season.

For instance during the summer when she heard the subtle but compelling rhythms of the Bahaman drummers, she'd walk over and watch the dances. She did not laugh the ''Saws'' to scorn as she had heard the people doing in the season. She got to like it a lot and she and Tea Cake were on hand every night till the others teased them about it.

Janie came to know Mrs. Turner now. She had seen her several times during the season, but neither ever spoke. Now they got to be visiting friends.

Mrs. Turner was a milky sort of a woman that belonged to child-bed. Her shoulders rounded a little, and she must have been conscious of her pelvis because she kept it stuck out in front of her so she could always see it. Tea Cake made a lot of fun about Mrs. Turner's shape behind her back. He claimed that she had been shaped up by a cow kicking her from behind. She was an ironing board with things throwed at it. Then that same cow took and stepped in her mouth when she was a baby and left it wide and flat with her chin and nose almost meeting.

But Mrs. Turner's shape and features were entirely approved by Mrs. Turner. Her nose was slightly pointed and she was proud. Her thin lips were an ever delight to her eyes. Even her buttocks in bas-relief were a source of pride. To her way of thinking all these things set her aside from Negroes. That was why she sought out Janie to friend with. Janie's coffee-and-cream complexion and her luxurious hair made Mrs. Turner forgive her for wearing overalls like the other women who worked in the fields. She didn't forgive her for marrying a man as dark as Tea Cake, but she felt that she could remedy that. That was what her brother was born for. She seldom stayed long when she found Tea Cake at home, but when she happened to drop in and catch Janie alone, she'd spend hours chatting away. Her disfavorite subject was Negroes.

''Mis' Woods, Ah have often said to mah husband, Ah don't see how uh lady like Mis' Woods can stand all them common niggers round her place all de time.''

"They don't worry me atall, Mis' Turner. Fact about de thing is, they tickles me wid they talk."

"You got mo' nerve than me. When somebody talked mah husband intuh comin' down heah tuh open up uh eatin' place Ah never dreamt so many different kins uh black folks could colleck in one place. Did Ah never woulda come. Ah ain't useter 'ssociatin' wid black folks. Mah son claims dey draws lightnin'." They laughed a little and after many of these talks Mrs. Turner said, "Yo' husband musta had plenty money when y'all got married."

"Whut make you think dat, Mis' Turner?"

"Tuh git hold of uh woman lak you. You got mo' nerve than me. Ah jus' couldn't see mahself married to no black man. It's too many black folks already. We oughta lighten up de race."

"Naw, mah husband didn't had nothin' but hisself. He's easy tuh love if you mess round 'im. Ah loves 'im."

"Why you, Mis' Woods! Ah don't b'lieve it. You'se jus' sorter hypnotized dat's all."

"Naw, it's real. Ah couldn't stand it if he wuz tuh quit me. Don't know whut Ah'd do. He kin take most any lil thing and make summertime out of it when times is dull. Then we lives offa dat happiness he made till some mo' happiness comes along."

"You'se different from me. Ah can't stand black niggers. Ah don't blame de white folks from hatin' 'em 'cause Ah can't stand 'em mahself. 'Nother thing, Ah hates tuh see folks lak me and you mixed up wid 'em. Us oughta class off."

"Us can't *do* it. We'se uh mingled people and all of us got black kinfolks as well as yaller kinfolks. How come you so against blacks?"

"And dey makes me tired. Always laughin'! Dey laughs too much and dey laughs too loud. Always singin' ol' nigger songs! Always cuttin' de monkey for white folks. If it wuzn't for so many black folks it wouldn't be no race problem. De white folks would take us in wid dem. De black ones is holdin' us back."

"You reckon? 'course Ah ain't never thought about it too much. But Ah don't figger dey even gointuh want us for comp'ny. We'se too poor."

" 'Tain't de poorness, it's de color and de features. Who want any lil ole black baby layin' up in de baby buggy lookin' lak uh fly in buttermilk? Who wants to be mixed up wid uh rusty black man, and uh black woman goin' down de street in all dem loud colors, and whoopin' and hollerin' and laughin' over nothin'? Ah don't know. Don't bring me no nigger doctor tuh hang over mah sick-bed. Ah done had six chillun—wuzn't lucky enough tuh raise but dat one—and ain't never had uh nigger tuh even feel mah pulse. White doctors always gits mah money. Ah don't go in no nigger store tuh buy nothin' neither. Colored folks don't know nothin' 'bout no business. Deliver me!"

Mrs. Turner was almost screaming in fanatical earnestness by now. Janie was dumb and bewildered before and she clucked sympathetically and wished she knew what to say. It was so evident that Mrs. Turner took black folk as a personal affront to herself.

"Look at me! Ah ain't got no flat nose and liver lips. Ah'm uh featured woman. Ah got white folks' features in mah face. Still and all Ah got tuh be lumped in wid all de rest. It ain't fair. Even if dey don't take us in wid de whites, dey oughta make us uh class tuh ourselves."

"It don't worry me atall, but Ah reckon Ah ain't got no real head fur thinkin'."

"You oughta meet mah brother. He's real smart. Got dead straight hair. Dey made him uh delegate tuh de Sunday School Convention and he read uh paper on Booker T. Washington and tore him tuh pieces!"

"Booker T.? He wuz a great big man, wusn't he?"

" 'Sposed tuh be. All he ever done was cut de monkey for white folks. So dey pomped him up. But you know whut de ole folks say 'de higher de monkey climbs de mo' he show his behind' so dat's de way it wuz wid Booker T. Mah brother hit 'im every time dey give 'im chance tuh speak."

"Ah was raised on de notion dat he wuz uh great big man," was all that Janie knew to say.

"He didn't do nothin' but hold us back—talkin' 'bout work when de race ain't never done nothin' else. He wuz uh enemy tuh us, dat's whut. He wuz uh white folks' nigger."

According to all Janie had been taught this was sacrilege so she sat without speaking at all. But Mrs. Turner went on.

"Ah done sent fuh mah brother tuh come down and spend uh while wid us. He's sorter outa work now. Ah wants yuh tuh meet him mo' special. You and him would make up uh swell couple if you wuzn't already married. He's uh fine carpenter, when he kin git anything tuh do."

"Yeah, maybe so. But Ah *is* married now, so 'tain't no use in considerin'."

Mrs. Turner finally rose to go after being very firm about several other view-points of either herself, her son or her brother. She begged Janie to drop in on her anytime, but never once mentioning Tea Cake. Finally she was gone and Janie hurried to her kitchen to put on supper and found Tea Cake sitting in there with his head between his hands.

"Tea Cake! Ah didn't know you wuz home."

"Ah know yuh didn't. Ah been heah uh long time listenin' to dat heifer run me down tuh de dawgs uh try tuh tole you off from me."

"So dat whut she wuz up to? Ah didn't know."

" 'Course she is. She got some no-count brother she wants yuh tuh hook up wid and take keer of Ah reckon."

"Shucks! If dat's her notion she's barkin' up de wrong tree. Mah hands is full already."

"Thanky Ma'am. Ah hates dat woman lak poison. Keep her from round dis house. Her look lak uh white woman! Wid dat meriny skin and hair jus' as close tuh her head as ninety-nine is tuh uh hundred! Since she hate black folks so, she don't need our money in her ol' eatin' place. Ah'll pass de word along. We kin go tuh dat white man's place and git good treatment. Her and dat whittled-down husband uh hers! And dat son! He's jus' uh dirty trick her womb played on her. Ah'm telling her husband tuh keep her home. Ah don't want her round dis house."

One day Tea Cake met Turner and his son on the street. He was a vanishing-looking kind of a man as if there used to be parts about him that stuck out individually but now he hadn't a thing about him that wasn't dwindled and blurred. Just like he had been sand-papered down to a long oval mass. Tea Cake felt sorry for him without knowing why. So he didn't blurt out the insults he had intended. But he couldn't hold in everything. They talked about the prospects for the coming season for a moment, then Tea Cake said, "Yo' wife don't seem tuh have nothin' much tuh do, so she kin visit uh lot. Mine got too much tuh do tuh go visitin' and too much tuh spend time talkin' tuh folks dat visit her."

"Mah wife takes time fuh whatever she wants tuh do. Real strong headed dat way. Yes indeed." He laughed a high lungless laugh. "De chillun don't keep her in no mo' so she visits when she chooses."

"De chillun?" Tea Cake asked him in surprise. "You got any smaller than him?" He indicated the son who seemed around twenty or so. "Ah ain't seen yo' others."

"Ah reckon you ain't 'cause dey all passed on befo' dis one wuz born. We ain't had no luck atall wid our chillun. We lucky to raise him. He's de last stroke of exhausted nature."

He gave his powerless laugh again and Tea Cake and the boy joined in with him. Then Tea Cake walked on off and went home to Janie.

"Her husband can't do nothin' wid dat butt-headed woman. All you can do is treat her cold whenever she come round here."

Janie tried that, but short of telling Mrs. Turner bluntly, there was nothing she could do to discourage her completely. She felt honored by Janie's acquaintance and she quickly forgave and forgot snubs in order to keep it. Anyone who looked more white folkish than herself was better than she was in her criteria, therefore it was right that they should be cruel to her at times, just as she was cruel to those more Negroid than herself in direct ratio to their Negroness. Like the pecking-order in a chicken yard. Insensate cruelty to those you can whip, and grovelling submission to those you can't. Once having set up her idols and built altars to them it was inevitable that she would worship there. It was inevitable that she should accept any inconsistency and cruelty from her deity as all good worshippers do from theirs. All gods who receive homage are cruel. All gods dispense suffering without reason. Otherwise they would not be worshipped. Through indiscriminate suffering men know fear and fear is the most divine emotion. It is the stones for altars and the beginning of wisdom. Half gods are worshipped in wine and flowers. Real gods require blood.

Mrs. Turner, like all other believers had built an altar to the unattainable—Caucasian characteristics for all. Her god would smite her, would hurl her from pinnacles and lose her in deserts. But she would not forsake his altars. Behind her crude words was a belief that somehow she and others through worship could attain her paradise—a heaven of straight-haired, thin-lipped, high-noseboned white seraphs. The physical impossibilities in no way injured faith. That was the mystery and mysteries are the chores of gods. Beyond her faith was a fanaticism to defend the altars of her god. It was distressing to emerge from her inner temple and find these black desecrators howling with laughter before the door. Oh, for an army, terrible with banners *and swords!*

So she didn't cling to Janie Woods the woman. She paid homage to Janie's Caucasian characteristics as such. And when she was with Janie she had a feeling of transmutation, as if she herself had become whiter and with straighter hair and she hated Tea Cake first for his defilement of divinity and next for his telling mockery of her. If she only knew something she could do about it! But she didn't. Once she was complaining about the carryings-on at the jook and Tea Cake snapped, "Aw, don't make God look so foolish—findin' fault wid everything He made."

So Mrs. Turner frowned most of the time. She had so much to disapprove of. It didn't affect Tea Cake and Janie too much. It just gave them something to talk about in the summertime when everything was dull on the muck. Otherwise they made little trips to Palm Beach, Fort Myers and Fort Lauderdale for their fun. Before they realized it the sun was cooler and the crowds came pouring onto the muck again.

(1937)

ARRANGEMENT IN BLACK AND WHITE
by Dorothy Parker

The woman with the pink velvet poppies turned round the assisted gold of her hair traversed the crowded room at an interesting gait combining a skip with a sidle, and clutched the lean arm of her host.

"Now I got you!" she said. "Now you can't get away!"

"Why, hello," said her host. "Well. How are you?"

"Oh, I'm finely," she said. "Just simply finely. Listen. I want you to do me the most terrible favor. Will you? Will you please? Pretty please?"

"What is it?" said her host.

"Listen," she said. "I want to meet Walter Williams. Honestly, I'm just simply crazy about that man. Oh, when he sings! When he sings those spirituals! Well, I said to Burton, 'It's a good thing for you Walter Williams is colored,' I said, 'or you'd have lots of reason to be jealous.' I'd really love to meet him. I'd like to tell him I've heard him sing. Will you be an angel and introduce me to him?''

"Why, certainly," said her host. "I thought you'd met him. The party's for him. Where is he, anyway?''

"He's over there by the bookcase," she said. "Let's wait till those people get through talking to him. Well, I think you're simply marvelous, giving this perfectly marvelous party for him, and having him meet all these white people, and all. Isn't he terribly grateful?''

"I hope not," said her host.

"I think it's really terribly nice," she said. "I do. I don't see why on earth it isn't perfectly all right to meet colored people. I haven't any feeling at all about it—not one single bit. Burton—oh, he's just the other way. Well, you know, he comes from Virginia, and you know how they are.''

"Did he come tonight?" said her host.

"No, he couldn't," she said. "I'm a regular grass widow tonight. I told him when I left, 'There's no telling what I'll do,' I said. He was just so tired out, he couldn't move. Isn't it a shame?''

"Ah," said her host.

"Wait till I tell him I met Walter Williams!" she said. "He'll just about die. Oh, we have more arguments about colored people. I talk to him like I don't know what, I get so excited. 'Oh, don't be so silly,' I say. But I must say for Burton, he's heaps broader-minded than lots of these Southerners. He's really awfully fond of colored people. Well, he says himself, he wouldn't have white servants. And you know, he had this old colored nurse, this regular old nigger mammy, and he just simply loves her. Why, every time he goes home, he goes out in the kitchen to see her. He does, really, to this day. All he says is, he says he hasn't got a word to say against colored people as long as they keep their place. He's always doing things for them—giving them clothes and I don't know what all. The only thing he says, he says he wouldn't sit down at the table with one for a million dollars. 'Oh,' I say to him, 'you make me sick, talking like that.' I'm just terrible to him. Aren't I terrible?''

"Oh, no, no, no," said her host. "No, no.''

"I am," she said. "I know I am. Poor Burton! Now, me, I don't feel that way at all. I haven't the slightest feeling about colored people. Why, I'm just crazy about some of them. They're just like children—just as easy going, and always singing and laughing and everything. Aren't they the happiest things you ever saw in your life? Honestly, it makes me laugh just to hear them. Oh, I like them. I really do. Well, now, listen, I have this colored laundress, I've had her for years, and I'm devoted to her. She's a real character. And I want to tell you, I think of her as my friend. That's the way I think of her. As I say to Burton, 'Well, for Heaven's sakes, we're all human beings!' Aren't we?''

"Yes," said her host. "Yes, indeed.''

"Now this Walter Williams," she said. "I think a man like that's a real artist. I do. I think he deserves an awful lot of credit. Goodness, I'm so crazy about music or anything, I don't care *what* color he is. I honestly think if a person's an artist, nobody ought to have any feeling at all about meeting them. That's absolutely what I say to Burton. Don't you think I'm right?''

"Yes," said her host. "Oh, yes."

"That's the way I feel," she said. "I just can't understand people being narrow-minded. Why, I absolutely think it's a privilege to meet a man like Walter Williams. Yes, I do. I haven't any feeling at all. Well, my goodness, the good Lord made him, just the same as He did any of us. Didn't He?''

"Surely," said her host. "Yes, indeed."

"That's what I say," she said. "Oh, I get so furious when people are narrow-minded about colored people. It's just all I can do not to say something. Of course, I do admit when you get a bad colored man, they're simply terrible. But as I say to Burton, there are some bad white people, too, in this world. Aren't there?''

"I guess there are," said her host.

"Why, I'd really be glad to have a man like Walter Williams come to my house and sing for us, some time," she said. "Of course, I couldn't ask him on account of Burton, but I wouldn't have any feeling about it at all. Oh, can't he sing! Isn't it marvelous, the way they all have music in them? It just seems to be right *in* them. Come on, let's us go on over and talk to him. Listen, what shall I do when I'm introduced? Ought I to shake hands? Or what?''

"Why, do whatever you want," said her host.

"I guess maybe I'd better," she said. "I wouldn't for the world have him think I had any feeling. I think I'd better shake hands, just the way I would with anybody else. That's just exactly what I'll do."

They reached the tall young Negro, standing by the bookcase. The host performed introductions; the Negro bowed.

"How do you do?" he said.

The woman with the pink velvet poppies extended her hand at the length of her arm and held it so for all the world to see, until the Negro took it, shook it, and gave it back to her.

"Oh, how do you do, Mr. Williams," she said. "Well, how do you do. I've just been saying, I've enjoyed your singing so awfully much. I've been to your concerts, and we have you on the phonograph and everything. Oh, I just enjoy it!''

She spoke with great distinctness, moving her lips meticulously, as if in parlance with the deaf.

"I'm so glad," he said.

"I'm just simply crazy about that 'Water Boy' thing you sing," she said. "Honestly, I can't get it out of my head. I have my husband nearly crazy, the way I go around humming it all the time. Oh, he looks just as black as the ace of—Well. Tell me, where on earth do you ever get all those songs of yours? How do you ever get hold of them?''

"Why," he said, "there are so many different——"

"I should think you'd love singing them," she said. "It must be more fun. All those darling old spirituals—oh, I just love them! Well, what are you doing, now? Are you still keeping up your singing? Why don't you have another concert, some time?"

"I'm having one the sixteenth of this month," he said.

"Well, I'll be there," she said. "I'll be there, if I possibly can. You can count on me. Goodness, here comes a whole raft of people to talk to you. You're just a regular guest of honor! Oh, who's that girl in white? I've seen her some place."

"That's Katherine Burke," said her host.

"Good Heavens," she said, "is that Katherine Burke? Why, she looks entirely different off the stage. I thought she was much better-looking. I had no idea she was so terribly dark. Why, she looks almost like—Oh, I think she's a wonderful actress! Don't you think she's a wonderful actress, Mr. Williams? Oh, I think she's marvelous. Don't you?"

"Yes, I do," he said.

"Oh, I do, too," she said. "Just wonderful. Well, goodness, we must give someone else a chance to talk to the guest of honor. Now, don't forget, Mr. Williams, I'm going to be at that concert if I possibly can. I'll be there applauding like everything. And if I can't come, I'm going to tell everybody I know to go, anyway. Don't you forget!"

"I won't," he said. "Thank you so much."

The host took her arm and piloted her into the next room.

"Oh, my dear," she said. "I nearly died! Honestly, I give you my word, I nearly passed away. Did you hear that terrible break I made? I was just going to say Katherine Burke looked almost like a nigger. I just caught myself in time. Oh, do you think he noticed?"

"I don't believe so," said her host.

"Well, thank goodness," she said, "because I wouldn't have embarrassed him for anything. Why, he's awfully nice. Just as nice as he can be. Nice manners, and everything. You know, so many colored people, you give them an inch, and they walk all over you. But he doesn't try any of that. Well, he's got more sense, I suppose. He's really nice. Don't you think so?"

"Yes," said her host.

"I liked him," she said. "I haven't any feeling at all because he's a colored man. I felt just as natural as I would with anybody. Talked to him just as naturally, and everything. But honestly, I could hardly keep a straight face. I kept thinking of Burton. Oh, wait till I tell Burton I called him 'Mister'!"

(1939)

TEN YEARS ON A DESERT ISLAND
by Edward Newhouse

When the Negro came into Jake's place on Third Avenue, there were four men drinking at the bar. They all looked at Jake to see what he would do.

The Negro ordered a beer and drank up as soon as Jake served him. Then Jake picked up the empty glass and deliberately broke it. He threw the fragments into a garbage can under the counter. The four men looked back at the Negro, who quickly ordered another beer. Two of the men were garage mechanics from Seventy-fifth Street. The third was an interne from Bellevue, and the fourth a tire salesman some years out of Georgia Tech.

"My boy came home with a queer one last night," said the mechanic named Birk. "His teacher gave him a composition to do about who the kid would choose to spend ten years with on a desert island. Wouldn't you say that was queer? In my day they used to make you write about George Washington or how to make a kite—things like that."

"Who'd he pick?" asked Tucker, the other mechanic.

"Johnny Weissmuller. I tried to argue him out of it, but nothing doing. It's these Tarzan pictures. I tried to tell him it's only a movie, but he says the way that guy can swim ain't no movie. So I tell him if it's an athlete you want, why don't you pick one that's all around and not just a swimmer, but he says when it comes to all-around athletes he'll string along with Weissmuller."

"I guess he's not old enough to know it's a woman he'll be wanting," said Tucker. "If I had a boy that age, I'd kind of expect him to pick me. When I was nine I thought my father was the greatest man ever lived. Well, he wasn't, but I'll be damned if he didn't have it all over Johnny Weissmuller. My father could grow mushrooms twice the size of your fist in a little old cellar when we lived down Raritan Bay. That's the sort of man who'd go good on a desert island."

"Not in my kid's book," Birk said. "Today a man would have to swing from trees and wrestle with alligators to rate with his own son. I say it's the teacher's fault for asking that kind of a question. I swear I myself wouldn't know who the hell to pick."

"I do."

"Who?"

"I'd take Benito Mussolini," said Tucker.

The Negro finished his second beer and waited. He gave no sign of ordering a third. Jake broke the glass again and threw the fragments away. The interne and the salesman stood at the far end of the bar, watching Jake and the Negro and listening to Birk and Tucker.

"Why?" asked Birk. "Why in hell take Benito Mussolini?"

"I don't like him, that's why. All you have to do is look at him to know the fellow has never done an honest day's work in his life. It'd be a big pleasure to make *him* toe the line. I'd work him from sunup to sundown."

"How do you know you could? How do you know he wouldn't make you do the dirty work? He looks pretty hefty to me."

"He wouldn't stand a Chinaman's chance," Tucker said. "I wasn't foreman on a construction gang for nothing. I know how to handle his kind. The dago never lived could monkey with me. I don't care if he's Primo Carnera."

"They're shifty though, don't kid yourself. Turn your back just once and there's the point of a stiletto sticking out of your chest."

"That's where my straw-boss experience comes in. I wouldn't *turn* my back. There's your answer. I'd just stand around and grin and make him work till he stood ankle-deep in his own sweat. No more speeches from balconies."

The tire salesman had been drinking beer, but now he switched to a double rye as ominously as he could manage. Jake had nothing to do. He wiped the bar in front of the mechanics. The Negro ordered again. This time he did not drink up, just nursed it. He was a slender, light Negro in a well-pressed suit, and he wore an American Legion button. The mechanics and the interne and Jake had all noticed the unmistakably threatening attitude of the man from Georgia Tech.

"On second thought," said Tucker, "I wouldn't take Mussolini, after all. Why the hell should *I* put in ten years of my life alone with a heel like that? Wouldn't be worth it."

"You see?" Birk said. "What did I tell you? That composition is not as simple as it sounds. Sweet Christ on a crutch, I could stand here all week and not figure out an answer! It's wrong for a teacher to make a boy rack his brains about something as useless as that. What do you say, Doc?"

The interne was not quite sober. He had a week of night duty ahead of him, and two months ago he had married a girl without the knowledge of his family. Now he was not certain he should have married at all.

"It's hard to tell," the interne said. "Conundrums like that are supposed to stimulate the imagination. There's a lot to be said for these new teaching methods. Don't the kids of today seem brighter to you than the ones you grew up with?"

"They do, that's a fact," Birk said. "But I'm not so sure it's a good thing."

"I'm all for it," the interne said. "If memory serves me right, half the time I didn't know what went on around me when I was a kid at school. It took twenty years before I could figure out what some of my nursery rhymes meant. Did you ever hear the one about the mouse that ran up the clock?"

"No."

"I did," said Tucker. "It went like this:

'Dickory, dickory, dock,
The mouse ran up the clock;
The clock struck one,
The mouse ran down,
Dickory, dickory, dock.' ''

"The way I remember it," the interne said, "it's '*Hick*ory, dickory, dock.'
Anyway, it means life is nothing. Do you get it? The clock struck one, the
mouse ran down, so what? So nothing. Life is nothing. You live and you work
and you work and you live and it all adds up to nothing. Of course, as a kid I
couldn't understand that. I probably don't understand it now."

Nobody said anything. The Negro finished his third beer and got ready to
go. Jake took his glass and broke it.

"You get my point, don't you?" the interne said. "The clock struck one,
the mouse ran down, so what? So nothing. Life is nothing."

"I get your point," the Negro said.

The salesman pushed his drink away. "Listen, you black son of a bitch,"
he said. "I've stood all I'm going to stand. First you come in and drink with
white folks, then you get up on your hind legs and start talking bigetty."

The Negro said, "I'm going because I was on my way anyhow. But this
ain't Arkansas. You meet me on the sidewalk and find out."

"I don't come from Arkansas," the salesman said. "I come from Georgia, where we don't soil our hands on apes. Only this time I'll make an exception. I know you bastards can run faster than human beings, so I don't aim to
chase you down any sidewalks. Nigger, you going to get it right in here."

He was within two steps of the Negro when Jake leaned over the bar and
hit him on the back of the head with a sawed-off baseball bat. He staggered
against the wall and sat down.

"I got to go," the Negro said. "I got things to do. You tell him my name
is Baxter and he can find me on the corner of a Hundred-and-thirty-first and
Lenox any time he feels like. I ain't scared of him." He left.

The salesman's eyes were open, but he seemed to have lost his power of
speech. Even after he staggered to his feet, he could only mumble. The interne
took his arm and led him out. Jake and the mechanics watched the man struggling to get his bearings on the seat of a taxi. The hackie finally got an address
out of him and drove off.

The interne came back. "You want to be careful where you hit these guys,"
he said.

"He'll be all right," Jake said. "I know just about how hard a one they'll
take. You pick those things up as you go along. I just made him try that one
on for size. I can't have no lush messing up my place."

"My own head isn't as clear as it ought to be," the interne said, "but it
seems to me you yourself were asking for trouble when you broke those glasses."

"That's different," said Jake. "That's policy. I make my living off these men from the garage. They wouldn't drink out of the same glass with a colored man. I got to destroy them glasses so's they know I don't use them again. I can't help it if the colored man gets his feelings hurt. He ought to have better sense than to come here in the first place.''

"Jake's right," Tucker said. "I wouldn't drink out of the same glass.''

"All right, I'm a little groggy," the interne said. "I still don't see why you can't refuse them service when they come in.''

"I just can't, that's all. He got a right to buy a drink in a public place, just like Tucker's got a right not to drink out of the same glass and I got a right to smash it. We all got to make a dollar and we all got a right to our own opinions. That's what they ought to teach them at school instead of making them worry about who to take on a desert island.''

"The thing that got me," said Birk, "was that this kid of mine didn't worry or hesitate a minute. He just picked Weissmuller right off the bat. What's the use of working and slaving away for your family when they'd rather live with a complete stranger? Like the Doc says, you live and you work and you work and you live and where are you?''

"Nowhere," the interne said. "That's what I was getting at a little while ago.''

"You guys sound like a funeral," said Jake. "I better turn on something cheerful.'' He tried several stations on the dial before deciding on a transcribed program of records by Kay Kyser and his College of Musical Knowledge.

(1940)

From

BLOOD BROTHER
by Elliott Arnold

Late in the night he saw distant fires of Apaches signaling to each other. He tried to line up the fires to ascertain how the Indians were dispersed, and he decided finally that his original plans to swing to the south of the Butterfield route, until Apache Pass, at least, were still sound.

He wondered if he would be able to keep up his rate of travel with the girl. He had to get unused to thinking of things in terms of Hank, and for the remainder of this journey to plan in terms of a fifteen-year-old girl. He wondered what he would do with her when they reached Tucson. What did you do with girls that age? Fifteen was not young out where they were now. Mexican and Indian girls that age were usually either married or close to it. If Tuscon were like the towns he had known in New Mexico she probably would not have much to worry about along that line.

Later he got up and eased his tired muscles. He looked at the animals. He walked around slowly until he had the veteran camper's feeling that dawn was not far off and then he knelt down and touched her gently. She stirred and then she opened her eyes. He saw bewilderment on her face and then brief fright and then she smiled. She sat up and yawned and asked, "Time for me to stand watch?"

"Time to move on."

She looked around. "Did you let me sleep all night?"

"Yes."

"That wasn't part of the bargain," she said. "You were going to treat me like another man."

"I know. But I started to think during the night and I enjoyed my thoughts so much the night was out before I knew it."

She looked at him angrily. "Tom Jeffords, I told you yesterday I was not to be treated like a child."

"Don't get redheaded so early in the morning," he said.

She shook her head furiously and stood up. She was stiff from lying on the ground and she would have fallen over if he had not reached out and caught her. "The mountains and the desert make funny country. You have to get used to them. Now bend up and down and loosen yourself."

"I will not," she said through her teeth.

"You have a lot of riding ahead of you today," he said. "I might have to leave you behind somewhere."

She tried to bend down and groaned. She put her hand on her back.

"Stiff?"

"It is," she admitted ruefully.

"Not used to riding steady like we did yesterday?"

"No."

"Lie down."

"What for?"

"I'll rub it loose." He dug the heels of his hands into the small of her back. She started to squirm and he held her there and worked her back. "Now try moving around."

"I feel as though I'm crippled," she said. She stood up and twisted her body. "It does feel better."

"Good. Now can you wait a little while before we eat?"

"Of course."

"Then let's get moving. Apaches usually attack at dawn."

"I know that," she said.

When they were on the trail again she said, "I don't know why the Army doesn't come out here and kill every one of them."

"I guess the Army has its hands full right now," he said.

"I wish this silly war would be over soon! All the soldiers ought to make up with each other and then come out here and wipe out these Indians."

"What are your sympathies in the war?"

"I haven't got any sympathies. My Daddy was against all war. He said of all wars civil wars were the cruelest. He didn't believe in slavery though and that was one of the reasons we started west. We started before the war started. When I think of all the boys back home out getting themselves killed I know Daddy was right. Killing each other while the Indians attack anybody they please. I'll never forget how my Daddy was lying there for more than three hours with a bullet in his side and still shooting at those Indians. He told me if he died before any help came to shoot myself quickly before they could capture me."

"What do you think the Indians would have done to you?"

"What do Indians usually do to women they capture?"

"Nowadays they kill them. Most of the time."

"That would be the most merciful thing. I wouldn't be as afraid of that as of some other things."

"Apaches seldom attack white women, Terry," he said. "You would either have been killed or else brought to the tribe as a servant. They would have worked you pretty hard and maybe after a while one of them would have wanted to take you as his wife. But I don't think that what you are most afraid of would have happened. And anyway it's nothing for a girl your age to be thinking of."

"I believe you are trying to defend them," she said.

"No," he said. "Perhaps to explain them a little."

"What is there to explain about them. They're wild animals."

"No, Terry, not quite."

"What do you mean?"

"It's a long argument, Terry," he said.

"We have a long ride. What do you mean?"

"They have something to be said for their side."

"For killing? For torturing travelers?"

"Well, we didn't exactly try to make friends with them."

"I don't know what you're talking about."

"It goes way back, Terry, before your time. Before my time. This was always Indian country. They considered that they belonged here."

"Belonged here? It's our country, isn't it?"

"Well, maybe as far as the rest of the world is concerned it's our country, all right. But the Indians always sort of figured that it was their country. They figured that living here for hundreds of years made it theirs. There was a great deal of double-crossing on both sides. Nobody can say now who started it. But there was plenty on both sides. For instance did you know that the Mexican government—not the people, but the government itself—will pay fifty dollars for every Apache scalp anybody brings in? Like a bounty on wild-cats?''

"I don't believe it.''

"And it is hard to tell from a scalp whether it came off an Apache head or off the head of another kind of Indian, say one of the friendly Indians like the Papagos or the Maricopas. Or even if it came from a Mexican or an American. A scalp is a scalp. There are Americans and Mexicans who make a living that way. They get Indians drunk and then kill them and scalp them for the bounty.''

"The Mexican government may do that but we don't,'' she said.

"No. We put the Indians on reservations.''

"What's wrong with that?''

"It depends how you look at it. From the American viewpoint there's nothing wrong with it. The Indian thinks different. What right have we to barge out here and tell people who've roamed around this country long before any white man ever heard of America that he has to stop roaming and stay put. Maybe it wouldn't be so bad at that, except that they always pick the worst sections of any country for reservations. Places with malaria, or where things won't grow, or where the wild animals have been scared off so the Indians can't hunt. They take these Indians who have lived pretty much as they please for as long as they can remember and overnight force them to live in a sort of outdoor jail. They become charity cases. If they behave they can live on government handouts. And some of the Indian Agents are no bargains. They're fools, some of them, and some of them are plain common crooks who steal from the Indians they're supposed to watch. Not all of them, but enough to make most Indians keep away from reservations to the point of going to war.''

"You sound as though you were a good friend of the Indians,'' she said.

"I kill hostile Indians when I see them,'' he replied. "My oldest friend was killed by them yesterday. That's the way it is out here now. You kill them or they kill you.''

"I hate them,'' she said passionately. "I'll always hate them. I'll never forget how they killed my Daddy.''

"No,'' he agreed. "You won't. And your father never harmed them. Only he and the other people in your party paid for what Americans did before them and those Americans were probably avenging something the Indians did before that. And that's how it goes.''

"You make it sound as though you think Indians are human like Americans and can be treated that way,'' she said.

(1950)

Index of Authors, Titles and Ethnic Groups

Page numbers for ethnic groups refer to selections in which there is some significant representation.

413